# Media, Power, and
# Politics in the Digital Age

# Media, Power, and Politics in the Digital Age

## The 2009 Presidential Election Uprising in Iran

Edited by
Yahya R. Kamalipour

ROWMAN & LITTLEFIELD PUBLISHERS, INC.
*Lanham • Boulder • New York • Toronto • Plymouth, UK*

Published by Rowman & Littlefield Publishers, Inc.
A wholly owned subsidiary of The Rowman & Littlefield Publishing Group, Inc.
4501 Forbes Boulevard, Suite 200, Lanham, Maryland 20706
http://www.rowmanlittlefield.com

Estover Road, Plymouth PL6 7PY, United Kingdom

British Library Cataloguing in Publication Information Available

**Library of Congress Cataloging-in-Publication Data**

Media, power, and politics in the digital age : the 2009 presidential election uprising in Iran / edited by Yahya R. Kamalipour.
    p. cm.
Includes bibliographical references and index.
ISBN 978-1-4422-0415-7 (cloth : alk. paper) — ISBN 978-1-4422-0417-1 (electronic)
  1. Presidents—Iran—Election—2009—Press coverage. 2. Mass media—Political aspects—Iran. 3. Iran—Politics and government—1997—Press coverage. I. Kamalipour, Yahya R.
    JQ1789.A5M43 2010
    324.955'061—dc22
                                                                        2010020804

∞ ᵀᴹ The paper used in this publication meets the minimum requirements of American National Standard for Information Sciences—Permanence of Paper for Printed Library Materials, ANSI/NISO Z39.48-1992.

Printed in the United States of America

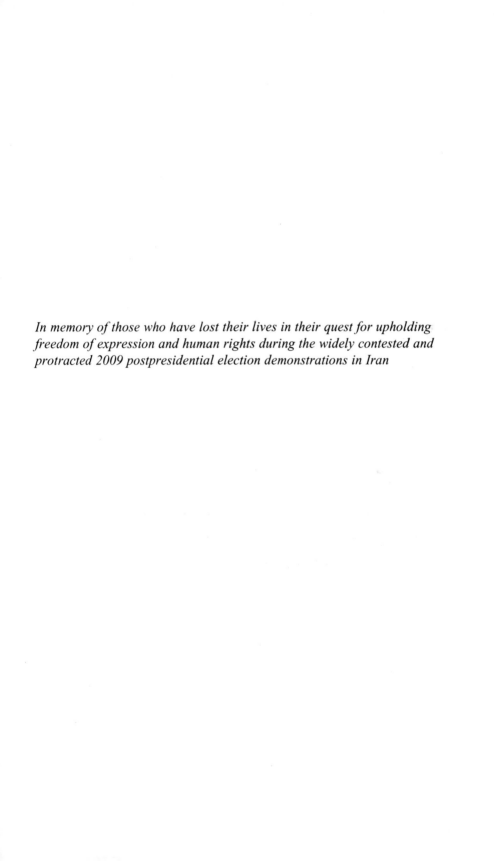

*In memory of those who have lost their lives in their quest for upholding freedom of expression and human rights during the widely contested and protracted 2009 postpresidential election demonstrations in Iran*

*Human beings are parts of a body, created from the same essence. When one part is hurt and in pain, the other parts remain restless. If the misery of others leaves you indifferent, you cannot be called a human being.*
—Sa'adi Shirazi, Persian poet-philosopher

*For to be free is not merely to cast off one's chains, but to live in a way that respects and enhances the freedom of others.*—Nelson Mandela

*Everything that is really great and inspiring is created by the individual who can labor in freedom.*—Albert Einstein

*Change does not roll in on the wheels of inevitability, but comes through continuous struggle. And so we must straighten our backs and work for our freedom. A man can't ride you unless your back is bent.*
—Martin Luther King Jr.

*If we don't believe in freedom of expression for people we despise, we don't believe in it at all.*—Noam Chomsky

*Nothing can be more abhorrent to democracy than to imprison a person or keep him in prison because he is unpopular. This is really the test of civilization.*—Winston Churchill

*When I despair, I remember that all through history the way of truth and love has always won. There have been tyrants, and murderers, and for a time they can seem invincible, but in the end they always fall, always.*
—Mahatma Gandhi

*I have estimated the influence of Reason upon Love and found that it is like that of a raindrop upon the ocean, which makes one little mark upon the water's face and disappears.*—Hafez Shirazi, Persian poet

*Out beyond our ideas of right-doing and wrong-doing, there is a field. I'll meet you there.*—Mowlana Jalaluddin Rumi, Persian poet

# Contents

# Acknowledgments

This book project could not have come to fruition without the support and cooperation of many friends and colleagues from throughout the world. I offer my sincere gratitude to the thirty contributors from fifteen countries throughout the world and Cees Hamelink for his thoughtful foreword to this book.

I thank Dr. Sandra Littleton-Uetz for her careful and professional reviewing and editing of this volume. Her continued support and expertise are appreciated.

At Rowman & Littlefield, I am grateful to Niels Aaboe, executive editor of political science, American history, and communication, for his enthusiasm and interest in this project. Also, Janice Braunstein, Michelle Cassidy, Elisa Weeks, and the marketing and publicity teams deserve my sincere gratitude. Their collective contribution and involvement during the various stages of this publication have been quite valuable and necessary in the success of this volume.

I am, of course, indebted to my family members for their unconditional love, emotional support, and understanding throughout this project.

*YRK*
*March 2010*

# Foreword

## Cees J. Hamelink

The book you are about to read combines arguably the most essential variables for an understanding of the contemporary context. That context is largely shaped by processes in which the key resource in today's world—"information"—is generated, distributed, consulted, and exchanged in digital formats. At the center stage of these informational developments, media—both conventional and new—are the crucial intermediaries between the governed and the governors. This mediascape has important implications for the management and the perception of political realities. It creates both unprecedented forms of access to information and massive overloads of data. It both hampers and facilitates social communication and reshapes power configurations, in both empowering and disempowering ways.

All of this implies sufficient complexity for the contents of one volume. The editor and the authors, however, ventured even further and focused their investigations and reflections on one of the most challenging and puzzling events of 2009: all that happened in connection with the presidential elections in Iran.

This intellectual courage brought us a fascinating book. It is common knowledge that the topic of global media coverage of national news events has received over past decades much attention. Although there is quite a library of valuable studies on news coverage, the present book not only adds a collection of original contributions from a variety of countries, it also helps to further our still somewhat limited theoretical understanding of the manufacturing of news and the resultant shaping of worldviews.

The world has been largely exposed to what happened in Iran in 2009 through new social networking formats of information provision. Several chapters of the book address the rise of new communication tools, discuss their role in citizen journalism, and assess their (limited) effects. It is particularly helpful that the authors in the part on New Media and Social Networking Dimensions did resist the temptation to declare that the new tools brought the world a social revolution. There is a sound dose of skepticism and a useful reminder that the role of the conventional or traditional media is not fundamentally diminished.

An interesting issue—not directly addressed in the book—is the relationship between new mobile technologies and their application in the political power struggle. Western firms—such as the Finnish Nokia—have provided Iran with communication technologies that both supported governmental surveillance tactics and made pictures available to global audiences that otherwise would not have been seen. Evidently, technology always is double-faced, and in the Iran case, this has raised perplexing questions for "green" banks (for example, in the Netherlands) regarding the social responsibility of their investments in companies that (possibly inevitably) facilitate suppressive and liberating uses of modern technologies.

The coverage of the 2009 presidential elections in Iran became a theme of particular importance in my home country, the Netherlands. This was due to a new radio station that was established in Amsterdam. Radio Zamaneh ("The Times" in Farsi) began broadcasts through the Internet in 2006 followed by transmissions via satellite and shortwave radio. Radio Zamaneh became an important forum for a large number of very popular Iranian webloggers. Financial support came from the Dutch government and from independent foundations such as Press Now. Press Now supports independent news sources that play important roles in the political developments of their country of origin.

The Iranian government has intimidated the station from its inception and has—particularly at the time of the elections uprising—expressed its discontent over Dutch funding. The Iranian representative in the Netherlands complained in June 2009 to the Dutch minister of foreign affairs about the "terrorist" and propagandistic activities of Radio Zamaneh.

The book—and this is touched upon in one of the chapters—offers implicitly a strong and convincing argument for the need of media literacy. In complex historical processes—such as the Iranian presidential elections and the related protest movements (and countermovements)—the larger volume of news stories that is now available through many different vehicles makes the issue of what to believe and what not to believe and how to distinguish propaganda from journalism for media audiences a tall order. Therefore, unless there is a global effort to empower audiences to meet information flows with critical, alert, and discerning minds, the greater availability and greater diversity of information provision could be a massive exercise in futility. We need—as recipients—to find ways to deal with a rapidly expanding supply of multiple perspectives. The information multiplicity can make us into detached nonparticipants who want to remain at safe distances from disturbing realities; it can also render us utterly confused and clueless observers, but it can also trigger our sociopolitical activism.

Actually, the present volume suggests the urgent need for a follow-up: Yet another book—to be edited by the indefatigable and prolific Yahya Kamalipour. This time its focus and title should be *Making Sense of a Chaotic World: Guidelines for Survival in Modern Complexities.*

I wish you enjoyable, instructive, and reflexive times with the collection in front of you.

# Introduction

## Yahya R. Kamalipour

*It is a terrible thing to see and have no vision.*

—Helen Keller

As a successful author, lecturer, and activist of her time, the legendary Helen Keller was both blind and deaf. Apropos her above comment, how true it is of our shortsighted politicians and self-centered world leaders who refuse to change in spite of monumental challenges taking place before their very eyes, including globalization, technological advancements, information flow, global interconnectedness, increased public awareness, and enhanced education.

For over a century, Iranians have relentlessly pursued—sadly, without much success—their quest for the institutionalization of freedom, human rights, and the rule of law in Iran. Since the 1906 Constitutional Revolution, which was derailed by Russia and, again, the 1953 revolution that was de-railed by a CIA-British coup, their historical quest has remained a lofty aspiration and continues to reemerge in various historical contexts, including the 1979 Islamic Revolution and the 2009 contested presidential elections, which resulted in sustained and often bloody public protestations. After the release of the June 12 election results in favor of the incumbent candidate, Mahmoud Ahmadinejad, and public endorsement of the Supreme Leader Ayatollah Ali Khamenei, supporters of Mir Hossein Mousavi believe that the elections were rigged. The officially declared election results were viewed as inconclusive and unfair; hence a huge number of unsatisfied Iranians took to the streets of Tehran and other major cities en masse, proclaiming "Where is my vote?" Their initially peaceful and sustained demonstrations turned bloody after the

Iranian government forces attempted to crush them by force, which resulted in killings, beatings, and arrests and jailings of hundreds of protestors. The unfolding events quickly captured people's attention everywhere and remained, for at least two weeks, the top media news story around the world. As of this writing, and seven months after the elections, the "Green Movement" or "Green Wave" continues to gather momentum within and without Iran.

In retrospect and in view of Western countries' historical miscalculations and repeated mistakes, such as the derailment of the 1953 democratic movement headed by Dr. Mohammad Mossadegh and their continued meddling in the internal affairs of Iran, let's hope this time they will have the fortitude and foresight to allow Iranians to determine the political destiny of their own nation.

## MEDIA AS AGENTS OF CHANGE

Media experts, foreign policy experts, commentators, and academicians have often outlined the benefits of new media technology for consumers and confidently predicted that the global information revolution will result in political, economic, and social democratization in the developing and underdeveloped countries around the world. This hopeful outlook, however, requires certain prerequisites including education, infrastructures, cultural basis, access to technology, and adherence to the time-tested and successful political, economic, social structures, and diverse media outlets, as evidenced in the developed nations.

In his chapter, Ibrahim Al-Marashi quite keenly observes that "the crisis in Iran was not merely a domestic conflict between reformists and a conservative establishment but represented another greater battle for information." The reality is that most people make decisions, vis-à-vis political candidates and even consumer products, based on what they hear, read, and see in the media. In today's digital age, it is clearly evident that we now possess an array of highly sophisticated communication and telecommunication technologies that span the entire globe and, indeed, can be used to engender such basic and vital human values as human rights, freedom of expression, mutual respect, peaceful coexistence, and the rule of law. Alternatively, with the concentration of global media in the hands of autocratic governments and a few self-serving global corporations, it is possible to use the media to brainwash, agitate, fuel conflict, and create a divisive and polarized political and cultural environment within and without nations.

During the post–Iranian election demonstrations in June 2009, the video footage of the death of Neda Agha-Soltan, which was captured by cell phones and distributed widely via the Internet and subsequently published in the global media, drew international attention and rallied public opinion and sentiments toward the liberal movement, commonly known as the "Green Movement." In fact, several chapters in this book focus on this particular phenomenon and the power of the new digital technologies to bypass altogether the physical-geographical boundaries and governmental restrictions and censorships. Indeed, the heart-wrenching postelection events in Iran illustrate that the new digital media have empowered the traditionally voiceless and marginalized people.

In his Noble Prize speech (Obama 2009), the president of the United States, Barack Obama, referred to Neda indirectly by saying "that's why this award must be shared with everyone who strives for justice and dignity; for the young woman who marches silently in the streets on behalf of her right to be heard, even in the face of beatings and bullets."

All political and religious leaders around the world have the responsibility to adhere to the Universal Declaration of Human Rights, including emphasis on "faith in fundamental human rights, in the dignity and worth of the human person and in the equal rights of men and women" (United Nations).

## OBJECTIVES OF THIS BOOK

Given the significance, prominence, and unique utilization of new digital technologies, and the continuing debate vis-à-vis the recent controversial Iranian presidential elections, this timely volume provides a multifaceted and diverse perspective and analysis of the global media coverage of the postelection uprisings.

Focusing on the pre– and post–Iranian presidential elections and the ensuing demonstrations in major cities across Iran and the world, this book is intended to provide an intellectual, multifaceted, and balanced discussion of the role and impact of modern communication technologies, particularly the novel utilization of "small digital media" vis-à-vis the elections and global media coverage. Further goals are to explore the interplay between various national and global forces, which tend to stifle free expression and restrict reporters from covering certain events such as the postelection uprisings in Iran. Given the global scope, timeliness, and significance of the Iranian election and its prominence in the global media and public discourse, this book should shed some light on the interplay of media, power, and politics. At the invitation of the editor, prominent scholars, media professionals, and researchers from throughout the world have contributed original chapters to this timely volume.

In terms of content and representation, this book is comprehensive and inclusive and, to the extent possible, the editor has tried to avoid promoting a specific worldview, political faction, or ideology. Hence, attempts have been made to ensure objective, reasoned, and balanced perspectives. A cornerstone of this truly global and multifaceted volume is to inform, educate, enlighten, and contribute to the existing literature in media, power, and politics. Another aim is to illustrate the complexity of the Iranian social-political-religious structure and help readers to understand and appreciate the continued struggle of Iranians toward achieving freedom and democracy.

As globalization continues to spread at a dizzying pace throughout the world, the role and functions of new digital technologies in politics, commerce, culture, human relations, international communication, and international relations become more apparent. Focusing on the various aspects of the 2009 contested presidential elections in Iran, this book is intended to:

- provide a multifaceted analysis of the role of global media in reporting the 2009 controversial and widely contested elections in Iran;
- provide a multifaceted global analysis of the postelection uprisings and media coverage around the globe;
- discuss the impact of government-imposed restrictions on foreign reporters in Iran;
- analyze the reliance of major global media on documented and personalized but yet difficult-to-confirm sources of blogs, video footage, photos, and reports;
- provide an analysis and critique of the role and impact of new social networking channels and technologies (e.g., Facebook, YouTube, Twitter, cell phones) in the dissemination of news and information about the uprisings;
- discuss the international and Iranian media coverage of the elections;
- discuss the social-political-ideological dimensions of the elections;
- discuss the cultural and communication dimensions of the elections;
- analyze the role and impact of "e-journalism" and "e-diplomacy" and social messaging tools on the modern international communication processes;
- trace and describe similar historical instances in which communication media played a crucial role; and
- discuss the global interface between new media, politics, and religion and its consequences for nation-states.

## CONTRIBUTORS TO THIS BOOK

This volume brings together a collection of twenty-four original chapters by thirty-one contributors from fifteen countries throughout the world. Each original chapter (not previously published) is written by a leading media scholar, media professional, author, and researcher familiar and in tune with the events in Iran and elsewhere. The contributors' areas of expertise include the Middle East, international communication, new technologies, mass media, journalism, religion, history, sociopolitical studies, and cultural studies.

## INTENDED AUDIENCE OF THIS BOOK

In view of the rapid and evolutionary changes in communication modes and human interactions, this book provides media professionals, scholars, researchers, and students a wealth of information regarding novel uses, efficacy, and consequences of the new digital communication technologies.

Written in a nontechnical, easy-to-read, and accessible manner, this book has appeal for:

- mass media, international, intercultural and political communication scholars, researchers, and students—graduate and undergraduate—including members of professional associations, and others;
- courses in journalism, international communication, media and politics, persuasion and propaganda, international news, and others;
- policy makers and stakeholders concerned with media, democracy, globalization, international news, and intercultural communication;
- broadcast and print media professionals, educators, and students;
- universities in Europe, Asia, Latin America, Africa, the Middle East, and the United States;
- internationally concerned independent writers, critics, researchers, and readers;
- members of cultural groups, organizations, and those interested in international, cross-cultural communication, especially mediated communication.

## STRUCTURE OF THIS BOOK

To provide a global overview of media coverage and diverse perspectives on the controversial 2009 presidential election, this book consists of twenty-four original chapters plus a foreword and introduction. The authors have written their chapters in a nontechnical and easy-to-read style. The book is divided into the following segments:

1. Global Media Dimensions
2. New Media and Social Networking Dimensions

3. Ideological-Political Dimensions
4. Cultural and Communication Dimensions

It should be noted that the chapters do not neatly fit into these general themes and, in some cases, overlap. Nonetheless, readers should find the categorizations helpful, especially when the book is used as either a required or a recommended text in university courses.

## A FEW FINAL WORDS

Although I have tried to organize the chapters in a cohesive manner, the writing styles and presentation remain varied yet rich and informative in terms of content. Unlike single-authored or coauthored books, edited volumes tend to be diverse in every respect, including writing style, tone, choice of words, and approach.

Nonetheless, I trust you will find the contents of this book engaging, provocative, and informative. Clearly, all governments have the necessary resources and military apparatus to suppress any uprising, dissent, and demonstration by force. But they must not abuse their power to stifle the legitimate arguments of opposing factions, restrain peaceful demonstrations, inhibit free expression, censor the media, and violate human rights. My hope is that readers of this book will come to the realization that, in any national and international conflict, peaceful means are always the best strategies to settle disputed claims and issues. In order to achieve a relatively peaceful and harmonious global environment, we must collectively reject violence and killings—anywhere and in any form or context—in favor of promoting peaceful assembly, peaceful dialogue, freedom of expression, and human rights. As Dr. Martin Luther King Jr. once commented, "violence never brings permanent peace. It solves no social problem: it merely creates new and more complicated ones."

Finally, it should be noted that the views expressed in this book are of the contributing authors and are not necessarily endorsed by either the editor or publisher.

## REFERENCES

Obama, Barack. 2009. Obama's Nobel Remarks (transcript). *New York Times*, December 10. http://www.nytimes.com/2009/12/11/world/europe/11prexy.text .html?ref=europe.
United Nations. The Universal Declaration of Human Rights. http://www.un.org/en/ documents/udhr/index.shtml#atop.

# About Iran

Official name: Islamic Republic of Iran

Former names: Persia or Pars, prior to 1935

Population: About 73 million (World Bank 2009)

Capital: Tehran

Major cities: Isfahan, Shiraz, Mashhad, Tabriz

Languages: The national language is Persian or Farsi. Other languages include Azeri, Turkish, Kurdish, Balochi, and Arabic.

Religions: Islam (includes Shiite and Sunni) 98 percent, 2 percent Christian, Jewish, Zoroastrians, and Assyrians.

Ethnic groups: Important ethnic groups include the Persians (51 percent), Azeris (24 percent), Mazandarani and Gilaki (8 percent), Kurds (7 percent), Iraqi Arabs (3 percent), and Lurs, Balochis, and Turkmens (2 percent each).

Supreme Leader: Seyyed Ali Khamenei

President: Mahmoud Ahmadinejad

Area: Slightly larger than the U.S. state of Alaska, Iran covers 1.6 million square kilometers (636,295 square miles).

Currency: Rial (2009 exchange rate: $1.00 = 10,000 Rials)

Main exports: Petroleum, carpets, agricultural products

GNI per capita: U.S. $3,540 (World Bank 2008)

Climate: Four seasons with varying climate and temperature ranging from very cold in the north (the Caspian Sea area) to very hot in the south (the Persian Gulf area).

Ancient Persia: The earliest archaeological findings from Iran date to the Paleolithic era, 100,000 years ago. By 5000 BC, Iran hosted sophisticated agriculture and early cities.

## REFERENCES

World Bank. http://web.worldbank.org/WBSITE/EXTERNAL/COUNTRIES/MENAEXT/IRANEXTN/0,,menuPK:312962~pagePK:141159~piPK:141110~the SitePK:312943,00.html.

About.com. http://asianhistory.about.com/od/iran/p/iranprofile.htm.

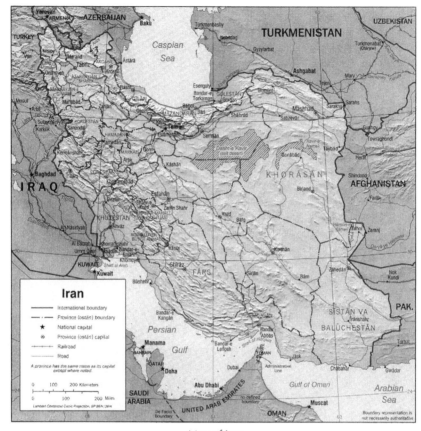

*Map of Iran*

*Part One*

# GLOBAL MEDIA DIMENSIONS

*Chapter One*

# The 2009 Iranian Presidential Election in the Coverage of CNN and Al-Jazeera English Websites

Mohammed el-Nawawy

Iran's presidential election, which took place on June 12, 2009, resulting in the disputed victory of Mahmoud Ahmadinejad and the violent demonstrations that ensued, attracted the attention of Western and Middle Eastern media. The news media, particularly the Internet, webcams, blogs, and Twitter, played a critical role in the coverage of this election and its aftermath. "Thanks to the Internet, dedicated news watchers knew what they were missing" in this election (Twitter 2009). This chapter utilizes a qualitative textual analysis of the stories that appeared on the CNN and Al-Jazeera English websites during the month following Iran's election to investigate how it and the postelection protests were covered on both websites.

## BACKGROUND OF THE ELECTION AND ITS AFTERMATH

The official results of Iran's election that took place on June 12, 2009, showed that the incumbent candidate Ahmadinejad, who has been Iran's president since 2005, was reelected with 62.6 percent of the vote. Ahmadinejad was "the first non-cleric to be elected president since 1981 when he won a run-off vote against former president Ali Akbar Hashemi Rafsanjani in election in June 2005. Much of [Ahmadinejad's] support comes from poorer and more religious sections of Iran's rapidly growing population particularly outside Tehran" (Who's Who 2009). Three other candidates ran against Ahmadinejad in the latest election: Mir Hossein Mousavi, Ahmadinejad's main challenger, who received 33.8 percent of the vote; Mohsen Rezai, who received 1.7 percent; and Mehdi Karroubi, who received 0.9 percent.

These results were controversial, and many Iranians called for an election rerun on grounds of possible election fraud on the part of the authorities. This led to demonstrations on the streets of the Iranian capital Tehran, which drew "the largest crowds since the Iranian Revolution in 1979" (Muir 2009). These demonstrations, which took place despite the government's ban on public protests, resulted in violent clashes with the police and led to several fatalities and the arrest of hundreds of protesters. These protests reflected a growing gap between what observers referred to as Iran's "hardliners" headed by the current Iranian government and the "reformists" led by Mousavi (Muir 2009). The antigovernment demonstrators were supportive of Mousavi, who served as Iran's prime minister from 1981 to 1989, and "was given high ratings from running the country through almost all of the eight years of war with neighboring Iraq" (Muir 2009).

The violent protests, in which the Iranian police forces used tear gas, water cannons, and batons to break up the demonstrators, led to several serious repercussions, such as the following:

> Foreign ambassadors . . . [were] called in . . . and given a dressing down for even daring to criticize the shooting of demonstrators. . . . Student dormitories [were] ransacked. Protestors [were] picked off on the edge of demonstrations. Apartment blocks where Iranians [were] chanting on the roof [were] broken into, and cars trashed. (Leyne 2009)

Moreover, many red lines were crossed by the demonstrators, "with unprecedented public condemnation of [Iran's] supreme leader, Ayatollah Ali Khamanei" (Iran Confirms 2009). During these protests, the Iranian government placed strict reporting restrictions on most foreign media. This meant that "protest reports [could] not be verified independently as correspondents [were] unable to move around . . . [Tehran] freely or cover unauthorized gatherings" (Protests 2009).

## BACKGROUND ON CNN AND AL-JAZEERA ENGLISH

Cable News Network (CNN) was launched by Ted Turner in 1980 as a pioneer in twenty-four-hour global television news coverage. Currently owned by Time Warner, CNN has a number of bureaus as well as foreign-language networks scattered around the globe. CNN's coverage of the 1991 Gulf War, which was the first war in which coverage of the conflict was instantaneously broadcast into millions of homes, highlighted the enhanced role played by news networks in today's networked society and led many scholars and media analysts to coin the phrase *CNN effect.* "Since then the phrase has become the generic term" (Robinson 2002) that refers to the tremendous power of the news media, particularly satellite channels, in shaping the audiences' opinions about current events and even accelerating the political and diplomatic processes by providing a platform through which political leaders can communicate with each other via television.

There has been a fierce debate in the academic literature around the term *CNN effect* and its implications on foreign policy formulation and world politics in general. Within the perimeters of this debate, some communication scholars such as Volkmer (1999) have gone as far as arguing that Cable News Network International (CNNI), by setting new journalistic standards and affecting the domestic and international political processes, has contributed to the formulation of a "global public sphere" in a way that has given "a homogeneous global shape to diverse news events." According to Volkmer,

> *CNNI* has inaugurated a market-force-oriented process which shifts global communication onto a new level by mixing the conventional reference-system of national news presentation, with its "home" and "foreign" news . . . with a global juxtaposition of the "internal" and the "external," a substantial new interrelationship which can shape political action. (1999)

On the other side of the debate, scholars such as Piers Robinson (2002) and Eytan Gilboa (2005) are more cautious and conservative in attributing power to the global news networks, particularly CNN, whose influence on the political scene, they argued, has been overstated and exaggerated. It can be argued that such a cautious approach to CNN, and media power in general, started in the early years of the twenty-first century, which has witnessed a complication in the global political environment coupled with a proliferation of media technologies, particularly satellite television. "Despite the radical claims of some, new communication technologies have not transformed world politics and media-state relations" (Robinson 2002). Robinson did not totally rule out the influence of networks such as CNN on politics, but he argued that the media ought to be perceived as one of several factors that affect political decisions rather than a main cause for such decisions. In other words, the politicians, according to Robinson, base their final political decisions on several considerations, one of which is the media coverage (2002). "But in no way [can] media coverage drive or compel policymakers into taking action where they would have otherwise not" (Robinson 2002).

Kai Hafez (2007) has taken an even more conservative approach, compared to Robinson, in his criticism of the global impact of news channels such as CNN. He described the global media system as a "utopia" and argued that the CNN effect is a "myth":

There are many "*CNNs*," but no complete global programme. Through the pro-liferation of satellite programmes in the last decade, *CNN* has lost its elevated position and is now merely a decentralized variant of an American television programme, whose country of origin remains easily recognizable in its agenda and framing. *CNN* tends to be a mixture of characteristics of the American system and the target system of the specific window; it is thus at best a multina-tional but not a global programme. (Hafez 2007)

According to Hafez, "the media *follow* rather than *lead*. The true strength of the media consists not in its capacity to influence politics, as evoked in the '*CNN* effect,' but in the affirmation and legitimation of national politics" (Hafez 2007). Hafez argued that the news content provided by satellite chan-nels such as CNN is often "domesticated" to serve the interests and address the concerns of particular culturally and politically aligned audience members rather than the general interests of the global audience at large (2007).

Al-Jazeera English (AJE) is a subsidiary of Qatar's Al-Jazeera Arabic net-work. AJE was launched on November 15, 2006, as the world's first global English-language news channel to be headquartered in the Middle East. AJE is available in over 110 million households spread across forty countries and has agreed to provide distribution (often free of charge) via multiple video-sharing websites, making it accessible to anyone with a connection to the World Wide Web.

AJE represents a new form of transnational media that has the declared purpose of revolutionizing the global mediascape. With over twenty-five bureaus worldwide, AJE is hyped as "the voice of the South." In this context, Ibrahim Helal, AJE's deputy manager for news and programs, suggests: "The 'South' here is not meant to be geographical. It is symbolic. It is a lifestyle be-cause in the West, you have a lot of South as well. In Britain, you have South. In Europe, you have South. The South denotes to the voiceless in general" (personal communication, April 2008). The network promises that it contains the technological capacity and the ideological wherewithal to provide new and productive fora for cross-cultural communications.

Importantly, AJE is trying to bridge the gap between old and new media paradigms, covering global issues but always from a local perspective. AJE is considered by many an anomaly when it comes to its journalistic mission and identity. It stands out from its competitors in that it presents a challenge to the existing paradigms guiding international news broadcasters. It is neither dominated by geopolitical nor commercial interests and is the first of its kind to have the resources, mandate, and journalistic capacity to reach out to typi-cally isolated and ignored audiences throughout the world.

According to its proponents, AJE presents a tremendous opportunity for a new direction in the discourse of global news flow. With its avowed promise of giving a "voice to the voiceless," AJE's launch and growing popularity represent a new style of media structure and content that provide an important test case for existing research regarding the influence of transnational media organizations in today's highly particularized and saturated media environment.

Serving as a "voice to the voiceless," AJE represents a phenomenon that has not been familiar among many Western news media networks. With a huge budget, mostly coming from the emir of Qatar, AJE has opened up four broadcasting centers (in Qatar, the UK, Malaysia, and the United States) and twenty-one supporting bureaus in Africa, Latin America, and Asia—parts of the world that have often been marginalized or altogether neglected by the mainstream Western media. Thanks to its sizable and remarkably market-independent resources, AJE is not subject to the economic pressures that control and have resulted in a decline in the quality of the many Western media (McChesney 2000).

Thus, AJE represents an interesting test case for media scholars. While encompassing many of the traditional journalistic strengths of traditional broadcast news media, its identity, mission, and brand are cloaked in a message that personifies its message to a global South. Compared to CNNI, which is largely considered to have a Western agenda, AJE's agenda is not associated with any particular region or politics but rather a global audience of the historically and currently disenfranchised.

According to AJE's code of ethics, "the channel aims to give voice to untold stories, promote debate, and challenge established perceptions" (About Us 2006). Originating from the "global South," AJE demonstrates what Naomi Sakr (2007) described as a contra-flow action. Sakr cited the Sinclair et al. (1996) definition of contra-flow as a situation where "countries [that were] once considered clients of media imperialism have successfully exported their output into the metropolis." According to Sakr, "Contra-flow in its full sense would seem to imply not just reversed or alternative media flows, but a flow that is also counter-hegemonic" (Sakr 2007).

AJE is not just a global network, but it is part of a whole trend that symbolizes a "new, media-centric world" that was referred to by Seib (2008) as the *Al-Jazeera effect*. Just as the CNN effect was used as a paradigm for media influence in general, the "'*Al-Jazeera* effect' [concept reflects] much more than the Qatar-based media company. . . . [It] encompasses the use of new media as tools in every aspect of global affairs, ranging from democratization to terrorism and including the concept of 'virtual states'" (Seib 2008). According to Seib, Al-Jazeera "is just the most visible player in a huge universe of new communications and information providers that are changing the relationship between those who govern and those who are governed. It is also assisting those with previously unachievable political agendas" (2008).

## TEXTUAL ANALYSIS OF CNN AND AJE WEBSITES' COVERAGE OF THE IRANIAN ELECTION

Textual analysis entails "seeing texts in terms of the different discourses, genres and styles they draw upon and articulate together" (Fairclough 2003). Conducting textual analysis requires studying the actual text and interpreting the meaning(s) constructed through that text. In this study, the textual analysis of the stories on the Iranian election that appeared on both CNN and AJE websites stretched over a period of one month from June 12 to July 12, 2009. The researcher used the search term *the election in Iran* to find stories on both websites. This search term identified fifty-eight articles on the CNN website and forty-nine articles on the AJE website during the one-month period referred to above.

Major differences were found between CNN and AJE websites with regard to how they covered the election and the immediate aftermath. To start with, CNN relied more on secondhand information because it did not have any reporters in the area, and that put it at a disadvantage to AJE. AJE had two permanent reporters (Alireza Ronaghi and Teymoor Nabil) on the ground in Tehran and Isfahan. Those two reporters covered events at the voting centers, Iran's Interior Ministry, and the protest scenes. This helped AJE provide a close, firsthand glimpse into the day-to-day developments and interview more eyewitnesses on the ground.

Differences were also noticed in the sources used by both networks' websites. CNN did interview Iranian officials, but it leaned more toward a Euro-American source-base, such as American and European officials, London-based Mideast analysts, researchers at U.S. think tanks (e.g., Carnegie Endowment for International Peace), research fellows at New America Foundation, and professors at major American universities, such as Columbia and Harvard. The CNN website also interviewed Iranian Americans, including the former Iranian shah's son, who currently resides in the United States—something that the AJE website did not cover. On the AJE website, there were more sources based in Iran, such as IRNA (Iran's official news agency), spokespersons for Iran's Guardian Council, professors at Tehran University, leaders of Iran's banned Freedom Movement, Iran's deputy national police commander and police chief, and reporters and editors from various Iranian newspapers.

Both websites also differed in the angles and points of interest that they decided to focus on and the slant that they adopted in covering them. Over the one-month period that was covered in this study, the CNN website included eight commentaries in which the network's reporters and political experts expressed their views on the election. The AJE website, however, included only two commentaries.

Stories on the CNN website focused on the race or the contention between two camps by framing the conflict as a "divide within the Islamic Republic [that] has pitted the reformists against the conservatives" (Ansari 2009). This divide was framed in CNN terms as a "tug-of-war between the [Iranian] people and their hardline government" and between "conservative incumbent President Mahmoud Ahmadinejad and reformist challenger Mir Hossein Mousavi" (Ansari 2009). In the website's focus on contention, only two CNN stories referred briefly to pro-Ahmadinejad crowds, but eighteen stories on the CNN website tended to side with Mousavi's supporters by shedding more light on him and focusing on the antigovernment protests and the possibility that the election's results were fraudulent. Several of these stories framed Mousavi as a "reformist" whose motivating message calling for more political freedoms was able to gain the support of Iran's youth. One CNN story even shed light on Mousavi's Facebook page in which he called on the Iranian authorities to hold new elections.

During the time frame under study, several stories and commentaries on CNN's website (nine to be specific) had an anti-Ahmadinejad slant that was reflected in the terms used to describe his election rallies and victory. For example, one CNN commentary described his supporters' rallies as "well-orchestrated and carefully staged events" (Dabashi 2009). Another CNN commentary referred to Ahmadinejad's election victory as "alleged reelection" (Rollins 2009). In addition, these CNN stories included sources that blamed Ahmadinejad for Iran's economic problems, for his anti-Israeli rhetoric, and for "stealing" the election. For example, one CNN article stated that Ahmadinejad is "blamed by many Iranians for the nation's four-year economic turmoil and [is] known in the West for his vehement rhetoric regarding Iran's nuclear program and condemnation of Israel" (Zakaria 2009). A CNN commentary argued that "the consensus in Iran, particularly among young voters, is that the election was stolen from reformist candidate . . . Mousavi, and that the outcome did not reflect the electorate's genuine will" (Gerges 2009).

Stories on the AJE website during the one-month period under study also covered the pro-Mousavi demonstrations (seventeen stories referred to the protests opposing the election results). However, the AJE website was more balanced than the CNN website by refraining from taking sides in the race and by shedding more light on the progovernment demonstrations as well. For example, one article stated:

> Tens of thousands of pro- and anti-government demonstrators held rival rallies in the capital, Tehran. . . . *Al-Jazeera*'s Teymoor Nabil, reporting from Tehran, said the pro-Ahmadinejad rally in the south was a much more organized affair than the smaller anti-government rally that took place just a few kilometers away. (Iran Protesters 2009)

Several other AJE articles referred to "pro" and "anti" government rallies. One AJE article included an extensive interview with a progovernment Twitter user to show that "not all those who are part of the information uprising in Iran are against the government" (McCaul 2009).

AJE stories referred to the opposition's allegations of a fraudulent election as "alleged fraud" or "perceived fraud" (LeVine 2009). In the election's aftermath, they referred to Mousavi as "defeated presidential candidate" (Khamenei 2009) and to Ahmadinejad as "the declared winner [of the election]" (U.S. and Iran 2009).

AJE's balanced approach was best exemplified in a story covering the speech by Iran's supreme leader, Ali Khamenei, in which he defended the election's results. Sources used in the AJE story represented various perspectives: a senior reporter from the British *Independent* newspaper, an Iran analyst based in Tehran, a Middle East analyst from Washington, D.C., and a professor of Iranian studies at Columbia University. CNN's story on Khamenei's speech included one feedback from Britain's Foreign Office.

Both CNN and AJE websites shed some light on the Iranian Guardian Council's decision to recount the votes. But several stories on the AJE website (five to be specific) devoted more space and delved more deeply into the details of the concessions announced by the Iranian authorities to address the concerns voiced by the opposition. Some of these concessions included meeting with the candidates to discuss complaints over the election, "investigating allegations of election irregularities" (Calm 2009), and having partial counts of the votes.

The research showed that both websites failed to provide the readers with enough background and contextual information that would help them understand the postelection developments; however, AJE's website provided more context. The CNN website included only four articles that provided contextual information on issues such as Khamenei's rise to power and America's history in Iran. On the other hand, over a one-month period, the AJE website included twelve stories that explained background aspects, such as the history of the Islamic revolution in Iran, the Iranian constitution, the functioning of Iran's Assembly of Experts, and the *Basij* militia. The research also showed that CNN's website had fifteen stories devoted to the U.S. role in Iran compared to nine stories on the AJE website.

The research found that CNN's website coverage leaned more toward humanizing the victims of the postelection protests compared to coverage on the AJE website. A case in point was the fatal shooting of a young Iranian female protester whose name was Neda Agha-Soltan. Four stories on the CNN website referred to Soltan's case compared to one story on the AJE website. The CNN stories humanized Soltan's killing, and one story included a detailed and dramatic description of the video that was widely circulated about her bleeding to death, as follows:

> It looks as though she is shot in the chest and drops to the ground. Blood runs from the side of her mouth as a few people . . . press on her chest and shout her name. One pleads, "Do not be afraid." . . . The camera closes in on her face as her eyes roll back and are still. She appears to die on camera. (From Iranian Rooftops 2009)

The one story on the AJE website that had a brief mention of Soltan's death presented the facts that surrounded her shooting, a statement from the doctor who tried to save her life, and Ahmadinejad's order to the authorities to investigate her killing. AJE's coverage of Soltan's story reflects a general trend that was noticed in the AJE stories included in this study, which is to present the hard facts on the ground and provide feedback from the relevant sources.

Both websites included articles referring to the Iranian government's restrictions on foreign reporters' coverage of the street protests. However, the CNN website, unlike the AJE website, included stories that focused on the Iranian officials' criticism of Western media, particularly their accusation against CNN of hacking government websites. One CNN article included a response to this accusation as follows:

> The accusations are completely false. *CNN* stands by its comprehensive coverage of the Iranian election and the protests that followed. *CNN* has been and will remain committed to continuing its efforts to bring news from Iran to the world in whatever way it can. (CNN Responds 2009)

## DISCUSSION AND CONCLUSION

It is clear from this brief analysis of the CNN and AJE websites' coverage of the Iranian election over a one-month period that CNN coverage was more slanted to the antigovernment protests than AJE, which appeared to be more balanced. The CNN coverage portrayed the tension as a "rivalry . . . between Good (Mousavi) vs. Evil (Ahmadinejad)" (Hamedani 2009). CNN's coverage might have been affected by the strained relationship between the United States and Iran, particularly when it comes to the issue of Iran's attempts to become a nuclear power. CNN's negative coverage of Ahmadinejad might also have been a result of the Iranian government's accusation of CNN trying to hack the Iranian officials' websites, as mentioned above. This incident might have put CNN in a direct confrontation with the Iranian regime—an issue that was then reflected in CNN's coverage of the election. In the context of the Iranian election, it seemed that CNN was part of the clashes rather than a neutral media observer.

As the research showed, not enough context was provided by either website, but it was particularly lacking from the CNN website. A possible explanation for this phenomenon is

> the historically tense relationship between Washington and Tehran [which] left the U.S. out of the loop well before the post-election media blackout [set by the Iranian government]. The U.S. has no interests section, consulate, or embassy in Iran. As a result, American media and diplomats are absent from the situation on the ground, raising the question of how much they really understand about what is happening in Iran, and why. (Hamedani 2009)

The situation might have been different with regard to AJE, which, as mentioned above, had two permanent reporters on the ground in Iran and through them was able to provide a more in-depth and nuanced insight into what took place in the immediate aftermath of the election. Still, even the AJE website did not provide enough contextual background information that would have helped its readers better understand what was happening during and after the election. This circumstance might have been the result of the stringent restrictions that have been set by the Iranian government over the functioning of foreign media in general.

Findings of this study seem to provide only partial evidence for Hafez's argument that the media networks follow the political agenda rather than set it and that they appeal to their particular constituencies rather than to a universal audience. According to Hafez (2007),

> When all is said and done, the mass media are not in the least oriented towards a "world system," but in fact concentrate upon national markets, whose interests and stereotypes they largely reproduce. Moreover, the influence of the media on politics is negligible, particularly in relation to international conflicts that touch upon vital national interests.

In the context of this study's findings, AJE's website—given its cross-regional and global focus and its more balanced coverage of the Iranian election—presents a challenge to Hafez's suggestion that today's news media concentrate on national markets. AJE's coverage of the election did reflect its philosophy of "giving a voice to the voiceless" by shedding light on the antigovernment demonstrations, but this did not prevent it from providing equal coverage to the progovernment protests that tended to reinforce the political status quo in Tehran. However, the Iranian election's coverage on the CNN website, which seemed to be anti-Ahmadinejad and pro-Mousavi in a way that reflected the current U.S. political agenda toward Iran, does support the argument that the news media may become more likely to reinforce existing agendas of current events rather than challenge them.

The fact that this study focused on the CNN and AJE websites' coverage of the Iranian election may have implications with regard to the role of the new media, particularly through the Internet, in covering politics and shaping global public opinion. The tension that accompanied the Iranian election was widely circulated, disseminated, and discussed across various circles of the global public sphere, thanks to the Internet coverage.

To varying degrees throughout the world, the connectivity of new media is superseding the traditional political connections that have brought identity and structure to global politics. This rewiring of the world's neural system is proceeding at remarkable speed, and its reach keeps extending ever farther (Seib 2008).

The question remains: How will the satellite television power embodied in the "CNN effect" and the news media power embodied in the "Al-Jazeera effect" continue to make their marks in covering critical events of the magnitude and scale of the Iranian election and its aftermath?

## REFERENCES

About us. http://english.aljazeera.net/aboutus/2006/11/2008525185555444449.html.

Ansari, A. (2009, June 16). Iranian-Americans say history is at hand. CNN.com.

Calm in Tehran after day of unrest. (2009, June 21). Al-Jazeera.net.

CNN responds to Iranian hacking accusation. (2009, June 22). CNN.com.

Dabashi, H. (2009, June 17). Commentary: Rigged or not, vote fractures Iran. CNN.com.

Fairclough, N. (2003). *Analysing discourse: Textual analysis for social research.* London: Routledge.

From Iranian rooftops, a view of protest and violence. (2009, June 22). CNN.com.

Gerges, F. (2009, June 15). Commentary: Iran's hardliners are the real losers. CNN.com.

Gilboa, E. (2005). The CNN effect: The search for a communication theory of international relations. *Political Communication, 22,* 27–44.

Hafez, K. (2007). *The myth of media globalization.* London: Polity.

Hamedani, N. (2009, August). "The world is watching" . . . A blurry picture in Iran. *Washington Report on Middle East Affairs, 28*(6), 11–16.

Iran confirms Ahmadinejad victory. (2009, June 29). http://news.bbc.co.uk/2/hi/8125284.stm.

Iran protesters to keep up pressure. (2009, June 17). Al-Jazeera.net.

Khamenei: Vote protests must end. (2009, June 20). Al-Jazeera.net.

LeVine, M. (2009, June 17). Iran on the brink? Al-Jazeera.net.

Leyne, J. (2009, June 18). Analysis: Titanic clash for Iran's future. http://news.bbc.co.uk/2/hi/middle_east/8108065.stm.

McCaul, K. (2009, June 20). Q&A: Tweeting from Tehran. Al-Jazeera.net.

McChesney, R. W. (2000). *Rich media, poor democracy: Communication politics in dubious times.* Champaign, IL: University of Illinois Press.

Muir, J. (2009, June 22). Q&A: Iran election aftermath. http://news.bbc.co.uk/2/hi/middle_east/8101621.stm.

Protests in Iran capital "halted." (2009, June 22). http://news.bbc.co.uk/2/hi/8116025.stm.

Robinson, P. (2002). *The CNN effect: The myth of news, foreign policy and intervention.* London: Routledge.

Rollins, E. (2009, June 18). Commentary: Salute the "bravehearts" of Iran. CNN.com.

Sakr, N. (2007). Challenger or lackey? The politics of news on Al-Jazeera. In D. K. Thussu (Ed.), *Media on the move: Global flow and contra-flow* (pp. 116–132). London: Routledge.

Seib, P. (2008). *The Al-Jazeera effect: How the new global media are reshaping world politics.* Washington, DC: Potomac Books.

Sinclair, J., Elizabeth Jacka, and Stuart Cunningham, ed. (1996). *New patterns in global television: Peripheral vision.* Oxford, UK: Oxford University Press.

Twitter 1, CNN 0. (2009, June 18). http://www.financialexpress.com/news/twitter-1-cnn-0/482474.

U.S. and Iran escalate war of words. (2009, June 26). Al-Jazeera.net.

Volkmer, I. (1999). *News in the global sphere: A study of CNN and its impact on global communication.* Luton, UK: University of Luton Press.

Who's who in Iran. (2009, June 19). BBC News. http://news.bbc.co.uk/2/hi/8102406.stm.

Zakaria: Iran election could make history. (2009, June 12). CNN.com.

*Chapter Two*

# The Canadian Media-Framing of the 2009 Iranian Presidential Election

## Mahmoud Eid and Aliaa Dakroury

Mahmoud Ahmadinejad's victory in the 2009 Iranian presidential election has witnessed a flood of global news media coverage coupled with some doubts of the legitimacy of his win and accusations of election fraud and rigging. News stories of civil unrest in the form of riots, protests, and demonstrations emerged not too long after the announced win of Ahmadinejad, and censorship reports of his government keeping opposition at a bay were also making headlines. Increased civil unrest in Iran certainly was a rising concern not merely for the Iranian citizens, but also around the world. While the election itself was not an international event, its very coverage by international news media agencies before, during, and especially after is a testament to its global significance. Much of the media in the Western world viewed the election with the anticipation that a new president holding views more politically consonant with their own values would emerge. Needless to recall, tensions already present due to Iran's nuclear ambitions contributed to antagonism between Iran and much of the world.

Traditional and new media are relied on heavily for information about international affairs. With such a significant role, the media can shape mass perceptions of events and nations. In his *The Press and Foreign Policy* (1963), Bernard Cohen pinpoints the important role of the media not only in setting their audiences' news agenda, but rather in their abilities to "frame" the news in certain ways, arguing that the press "may not be successful much of the time in telling people what to think, but it is stunningly successful in telling its readers what to think about."

Framing is a term used in media studies to refer to the social construction of a phenomenon or an event by mass media sources. Erving Goffman (1922–1982) was a Canadian sociologist whose work has formed the basis for the media studies' concept of framing. Goffman's 1974 *Frame Analysis: An Essay on the Organization of Experience* provides the explanation of how conceptual frames structure the individual's perception of society. Frame analysis is a multidisciplinary research method used to analyze how people understand events. In communication studies, framing is "the process by which a communication source, such as a news organization, defines and constructs a political issue or public controversy" (Nelson, Oxley, and Clawson 1997). As Robert Entman explains, to frame is to "select some aspects of a perceived reality and make them more salient in a communication text" (1993).

The news media tend to frame issues in various ways; hence, media scholars have found the concept of framing useful in examining media coverage of news. Research has shown that media-framing can have an effect on the way audience members end up interpreting an issue or event (Severin and Tankard 2001). A media-constructed frame is "a central organizing idea for news content that supplies a context and suggests what the issue is through the use of selection, emphasis, exclusion, and elaboration" (Severin and Tankard 2001). As Claes Vreese explains, news media frames "affect attitudes by stressing specific values, facts, or other considerations and endowing them with greater relevance to an issue than under an alternative frame" (2004). With application to unique media events such as political elections, Kent Asp (1983) argues that news media are of significant mediated power as "agenda setters for the voters" than for the parties.

Looking at the various controversies during and after the 2009 Iranian presidential election, this chapter critically analyzes the Canadian media coverage vis-à-vis a framing theory lens. With a primary focus on the official Canadian media (news agency, newspapers, television, radio, and online), this chapter thematically investigates the framing of news about the event in the Canadian Press, the *National Post*, the *Globe and Mail*, CBC Television, CBC Radio, and CBC.ca. A total of 229 news stories from the six media—sixty (Canadian Press), thirty-seven (*National Post*), thirty-two (*Globe and Mail*), thirty-two (CBC Television), thirty-one (CBC Radio), and thirty-seven (CBC.ca)—within the period of June 1 to 30, 2009, have been qualitatively analyzed.

## CANADIAN FRAME SET

The Canadian media coverage of the 2009 Iranian presidential election has concentrated on eight major themes or frames: election procedure; corruption; demonstrations; human rights; democracy; media censorship; technology and cyberspace; and international politics.

## Frame 1: Election Procedure

Discussion of the June 12, 2009, Iranian election procedure in the Canadian Press, the *National Post*, CBC.ca, and CBC Radio concentrated on the reported deception and questionable nature of the election process leading to the victory of Mahmoud Ahmadinejad as Iran's president. Various reasons were discussed extensively that reportedly contributed to the allegations of fraud and corruption that resulted in Ahmadinejad's win. Issues such as the lack of procedural transparency needed to facilitate a sound election, the rapid ballot tallying, and Ahmadinejad's large victory margin (62.6 percent for Ahmadinejad and 33.75 percent for Mousavi) sparked concerns over the authenticity of election results. Following the announcement of Ahmadinejad's presidential victory, opposition leader Hossein Mousavi made accusations of fraud, stated that the vote was tainted, and lodged an official appeal of the results while urging the Iranian people to fight the outcome without committing acts of violence.

Concerns regarding Ahmadinejad's win in relation to the election process were focused on the history of Iranian politics and their tendency to exhibit corruption. It was also revealed that international monitors were barred from observing Iranian elections and that there were no clear mechanisms in place to accredit domestic observers. The preponderance of media released on this subject emphasized the concerns and suspicion of the international community and the Iranian people regarding the election process. A high frequency of articles utilized quotes or stated opinions of individuals working outside of Iran, acclaimed mostly for their knowledge or experience in identifying irregularities or corruption (Akbar Dareini and Keyser 2009; Smith 2009). Reported flaws in the election process stemmed from various critiques discussing the conditions of ballot casting and tallying systems. As such, many articles discussed reports of missing national identification numbers, making ballots and the timeline in which final tallies were made and announced untraceable (Hosseinian and Jascb 2009; Keyser 2009). Accounts based on this idea suggest that it is impossible for all of the ballots to have been counted in the election time frame, leading to conclusions of possible fraud and corruption in the polling process. Other reports concerning the voting process have speculated that polling stations were shut down early, robbing citizens of the right to vote. Following massive protests in the streets of Iran, fueled by rumors about the election's lack of authenticity, the Iranian Supreme Leader announced that a recount of 10 percent of the votes would be conducted in response to public outcry and pressure from the opposition leader, Hossein Mousavi. Following violent protests and passionate efforts both nationally and internationally, Iran's Supreme Leader ruled out a revote, stating no major fraud was found, despite the Guardian Council's acknowledgment of irregularities in the votes (Iranian Cleric 2009; Iranian Police 2009).

CBC Television dedicated a large amount of its coverage to dissecting the electoral procedure in depth. This included reports on the opinions of voters about their expectations of the outcome prior to election day. Coverage also included other factors influencing the election, such as the past history of Iranian presidents and incidences of fraud and irregularity that had occurred during their time (Solomon and MacNeil 2009). Regardless of apprehension among many Iranians fearful of corruption in the political system, they hoped for change, and in turn, voting participation was high. CBC Television broadcast various interview clips of Iranian voters speaking out about their aspirations for an improved Iranian governmental system (Nichols 2009, June 13). All of these interviews voiced the opinions of people against Ahmadinejad and their discontentment with his previous leadership performance (many accused him of mishandling the economy and blamed him for inflation and unemployment).

In describing the election candidates, the *Globe and Mail* depicted Mousavi as being soft-spoken and dignified, drawing a comparison to Barack Obama as a figure for change. In discussing the varying policies of these candidates, the *Globe and Mail* noted on several occasions that despite their different views and perspectives, all candidates shared similar views on Iran's nuclear technology development, resisting criticism from other countries in this regard (Koring 2009, June 27; Leeder 2009; Simpson 2009).

**Frame 2: Corruption**

CBC.ca's coverage of the 2009 Iranian presidential election illustrated corruption in the Iranian political system. These reports vaguely portrayed problems in the governmental system, often alluding to suspicious discrepancies and practices that had sparked accusations of corruption. Interviews with Iranian citizens in Tehran revealed the negative attitude projected toward the political system and the heightened desire for change, culminating from the most recent presidency of Ahmadinejad. These reports drew on many Iranians' lack of trust in the government, stemming from past corrupted electoral procedures. As such, "Mousavi has indicated he does not expect the review to be successful. He alleges the Guardian Council is not neutral and has already indicated it supports Ahmadinejad. He wants an independent investigation" (Iran's Supreme Leader 2009). More allegations of corruption in the government were evident in many news stories detailing the electoral procedures. Suspicion in the ballot tallying and the government's harsh reaction to the spread of information, to protests, or to accusations of malpractice in the election depicted a system possibly constituted on a fraudulent basis. Similarly, CBC Radio reported that some elements of the Iranian government generated critique because of corruption qualms. The bulk of the discussion was found in interviews of pro-Mousavi Iranians, speaking of their dissatisfaction with the state of their political system. In a broadcast segment entitled "Presidential Election in Iran on Friday," aired on June 9, 2009, an interviewed Mousavi supporter said that Ahmadinejad has been lying to his own people for years (Fitzgerald 2009, June 9). Further commentary in this segment discussed government misconduct in the past as a contributing factor to many citizens' growing lack of faith in their government.

The *National Post* coverage of this event included repeated references of the leading governmental regime as anti-Western, nuclear-proud, Holocaust-denying (mainly because of Ahmadinejad's claims contradicting the validity of the Holocaust), and supporters of terrorism. "People are tired of dictatorship. People are tired of not having freedom of expression, of high inflation and 'adventurism' in foreign relations. That is why they wanted to change Ahmadinejad" (Freeman and Blair 2009). Claims were also made on the corruption in Iran by focusing on policies and traditions enforced by state authorities that leave religious minorities in fear of control by the judiciary, military, and police; a state broadcasting system; and mosques and religious charities that dominate the economy. Furthermore, the language used to describe practices and political leadership in Iran was often harsh, indicating that Iran was a "dislocated" place, experiencing a great divide among its people (Clarfield 2009; Cohen 2009, June 16; Goodspeed 2009, June 13). Parallel to the coverage found in the *National Post*, the *Globe and Mail* included several statements and quotes to support this view. In Patrick Martin's article, "A Theocratic Sermon Thick with Threats" (2009, June 20), the Supreme Leader of Iran, Ayatollah Ali Khamenei, admits to problems of corruption, but not in a large capacity. In his article, "Man in the News: Iran's Supreme Leader," Sebastian Abbot says:

> Ayatollah Khamenei is a hard-liner who has battled reformists in the past, and whose support helped Mr. Ahmadinejad first get elected in 2005. But analysts say he is also a political realist, and in the past he has made concessions to ensure his main goals—his own survival and that of Iran's cleric-run system. (2009, June 16)

### Frame 3: Demonstrations

Word of the election fraud and dangerous protests influenced demonstrations and public outcry globally. CBC Radio highlighted these demonstrations and protests as often organized by Iranians in other countries (Lamb 2009). Such reports depict rallies occurring in Australia, Britain, France, and Spain in an effort to raise awareness on the dangerous potential of political turmoil in order to pressure government leaders to speak out against the situation in Tehran. Accordingly, CBC.ca featured many news stories on the rallies and protests that occurred on Canadian soil in response to the 2009 Iranian presidential election. Stories of people in Calgary, Montreal, Toronto, Ottawa, Vancouver, and Edmonton discussed the numerous Canadians, mostly of Iranian heritage, who spoke out against these events in Iran (Calgarians 2009; Protestors Gather 2009). Some rallies were also organized to mourn the deaths of the Iranians killed in the protests in Tehran. In addition, numerous articles in the Canadian Press and the *National Post* reported on the number and intensity of these protests occurring in Canada, France, Belgium, Germany, and Britain (Hewitt 2009).

With regard to the demonstrations and protests in Iran, the *National Post* presented a comprehensive depiction of the violence and bloodshed occurring specifically in the country's capital, Tehran. Reports discussed the outbreak from a variety of angles, most notably the severity of the state authority crackdown, the number of injuries and deaths, as well as detailed descriptions of the clash, using quotes and statements from bystanders and protestors (Cohen 2009, June 16; Goodspeed 2009, June 13, June 24). Coverage of the public outcry that occurred in Tehran utilized harsh language to indicate the intensity of the situation in Iran, particularly when describing the actions of police and military crackdown—noted as savage, vicious, and ruthless. To elaborate on the severity of the conflict that occurred during protests, there were recurring references to weapons used by state authorities on protesters, such as tear gas, batons, firearms, and truncheons. Despite the violence in Tehran caused by the protests, the *National Post* framed demonstrators opposing Ahmadinejad's win as people fighting for democratic rights. Beyond the implications of symbolism attached to their title as protestors, the *National Post* glorified their actions by depicting them as soldiers against corruption and brave innovators for a new Iran.

In the Canadian Press, the protests were described as the "Green Wave movement." The movement claimed that Ahmadinejad's victory was based on lies, fraud, and corruption. Protests were reportedly to have broken out in places throughout Iran. They were quite large and eventful in Tehran and generated the most media attention. Demonstrations against the new president sparked a harsh response from police and militia loyal to Ahmadinejad's regime, resulting in brutal violence, injuries, and death of both protestors and bystanders. Descriptions of such occurrences in the Canadian Press included graphic accounts of the mistreatment and harm inflicted on protestors by state-run authorities (Akbar Dareini and Heintz 2009; Akbar Dareini and Karimi 2009; Kole 2009, June 26). Most descriptions of the protests discussed the general brutality and severity of the state's response, noting the tragic death of protestor Neda Agha-Soltan. This event was captured on film just after Agha-Soltan was shot in the chest by the military, and then it was uploaded to the Internet. Soon after the footage was shared online, it was uploaded to various sites and viewed by people around the world. This type of coverage focused media attention on this woman and her strong beliefs against Ahmadinejad's regime. The *Globe and Mail* stated that banners mourning her death outside of her house and posters of her face placed all over Tehran were torn down by police and militia. The *Globe and Mail* revealed the power of her image as a weapon in the protests, often alluding to her as a revered figure (Garton Ash 2009; Hafezi 2009; Leeder 2009).

CBC.ca provided detailed descriptions of the protesters who flooded the streets of Iran in reaction to the election results as being brave, passionate, and also violent. CBC.ca reported on some of the protests, noting that rally participants in support of the reformist candidate, Mousavi, exhibited destructive behavior in response to the brutality of state police and militia. CBC.ca highlighted the profound impact that students had in the organization of protests. In addition, CBC.ca also reported on the sensation generated when the Iranian soccer team sported green headbands and wristbands during a match (green representing presidential candidate Mousavi), representing their support for the defeated opposition (Iran's Soccer 2009). Interestingly, CBC.ca also reported on participants in rallies supporting Ahmadinejad's presidential victory by covering their celebratory gatherings occurring in Tehran in which they used posters and chants that glorified the Ahmadinejad regime while putting shame on Mousavi supporters.

CBC Television's coverage began prior to the announcement of the results, noting that even before the polls were closed, state authorities began to occupy the streets of Tehran. Reports that covered the violent protests often included details of the situation occurring in the Tehran rallies, such as descriptions of the progovernment militia that was speculated to have been composed of more than one million paid volunteers, conservatives who were loyal to Ahmadinejad's regime. Further information was provided, noting that this group was designed to be able to move among the people and gain intelligence on protest planning as well as to attack and suppress the demonstrators opposing Ahmadinejad's win. Many of these reports came directly from journalists stationed in Tehran, detailing the gruesome scene and brutality of the events (Kelley 2009, June 23a, June 24a). CBC Radio reported on the massive rallies of Iranians who opposed the results (Fitzgerald 2009, June 15). Although CBC Radio noted that there were reports of people protesting in various Iranian towns and cities, the coverage concentrated on events taking place in Tehran. Protests were said to have been extremely large, full of people chanting and marching, many of whom were dressed in green. Protests in opposition of Ahmadinejad's victory were deemed illegal by state authorities, triggering a violent crackdown of police and militia on many people involved in the rallies.

## Frame 4: Human Rights

Human rights issues were discussed in relation to the 2009 Iranian presidential election from a variety of angles, specifically the extreme violence and brutal attacks launched on protesters by state authorities. Segments covered footage and comments of different political leaders voicing their concern for the Iranian people experiencing police and militia brutality. CBC Television and CBC Radio coverage included statements issued by Human Rights Watch, which expressed deep concern about the state of human rights in Iran (Kelley 2009, June 24a). Reports of protestors in Canada speaking out against violations of human rights in Iran worked toward raising awareness of the turbulence occurring as well as pressuring Canadian officials to respond firmly (Kelley 2009, June 23a). According to CBC.ca, "Western-based human rights organizations have said at least 500 people have been arrested, detained, or disappeared since the election, including many prominent activists and politicians" (Iran's Supreme Leader 2009).

The topic of human rights was also discussed in the *Globe and Mail*, the *National Post*, and the Canadian Press. Statements and opinions from several Western political leaders were conveyed, specifically with regard to human rights violation concerns in Iran. Western politicians such as President Barack Obama spoke sternly about the violent acts of state authorities against protesters, urging them to stop such acts and resort to peaceful methods of conflict resolution. Efforts by human right activists such as Amnesty International were covered briefly in some articles, noting that statements had been released from them urging the Iranian government to stop all violent acts and to respect the rights of their citizens (Koring 2009, June 27). In response, Iranian government officials issued combative statements that were covered in Patrick Martin's article, "A Theocratic Sermon Thick with Threats" (2009); for example, the statement that was made by the Supreme Leader of Iran, Ayatollah Ali Khamenei, "We do not need any advice in human rights."

Furthermore, the role of women in the 2009 Iranian election received high attention by the Canadian media. Women who participated in activism and protests against the elected political forces generated attention in the *Globe and Mail* coverage because of the strong role they played in the growth and development of equality and human rights. Contrary to traditional Iranian social standards, Iranian women worked to share their desires to gain equal rights and freedoms, pressuring presidential candidates to support their aspirations in political policies. Several articles illustrated the uprising by Iranian women, including Patrick Martin's article, "Women Emerge as Major Political Force in Iran" (2009, June 13), highlighted this specific phenomena through a comprehensive scan of the influence of Iranian women in the presidential debate. Ahmadinejad's allegedly fraudulent win was a minor setback to the Iranian women's movement because his political regime worked to continue the oppression of women through policies such as the enforcement of mandatory headscarves and reinforcing their domestic roles at home as mothers and wives. Despite this, Martin (2009, June 13) discussed the tremendous advancement of Iranian women, noting that because of increasing literacy, education, and affluence, women are gaining the power needed to facilitate change. As a groundbreaking example, Martin's article described the actions of Zahra Rahnavard (the wife of defeated presidential candidate, Mousavi) who had actively participated in her husband's political campaign and was featured in a photograph with her husband on his promotional posters.

The story of Neda Agha-Soltan was also covered in CBC Radio and CBC.ca, describing her tragic death and her brave role as a female protester: "Since her death, vigils in her honour have been held around the world, and her image has become a global symbol for the Iranian opposition movement" (Neda Shot 2009). CBC.ca paid significant attention to her involvement in the protests as being important for the development of women's rights in Iran as well as the symbolism of the struggle endured by those protesting against the hard-line Iranian government regime. CBC.ca had also featured coverage of brief interviews with women who took great pride in their roles, emphasizing their important positions as wives, mothers, and homemakers.

Furthermore, CBC Television noted the obstacles women in Iran face, mainly concerning the forces of the laws that are stacked strongly against them. Women in Iran with strong convictions against the oppressive social climate in their country played a significant role in the election and the protests because of their desire to promote change in political policies. Although Iran's ruling clerics blocked all potential women candidates from running for the presidency, CBC Television diverted attention to the stories of the various Iranian women who had an impact on the events and development of this election (Mansbridge 2009, June 10). CBC Television also reported on the subordination of Iranian women, noting that laws still mitigate women's jobs, travel, marriages, and dress codes, often devaluing them as subsidiary citizens in comparison to their male counterparts. Nevertheless, the rising number of educated women has also been reported, indicating the potential and crucial role that they may play in the workplace.

The population makeup of Iran attracted the *Globe and Mail* because of the large number of young citizens. As stated by Timothy Garton Ash in his article, "Tweeting for Freedom" (2009), two out of every three Iranians is under thirty, and the number of individuals obtaining higher education levels has expanded immensely, with women representing approximately half of all university graduates. Along with many other articles, he compared the political crisis in Iran and violent public protests to the 1979 Islamic Revolution, stating that the youth involved in this movement have the ability to withstand the unrest and political injustices committed by the strict Ahmadinejad leadership. Reports often noted the suffering and violence inflicted by state police and militia occurring on Iranian university campuses and in dorms because of the large role that this demographic played in the opposition against Ahmadinejad's win, as well as their ability to create, access, and harness innovative communication- and information-sharing techniques (McLeod 2009).

Moreover, the youth of Iran played a large role in their protests against the win of Mahmoud Ahmadinejad. CBC.ca reported on their crucial involvement in various aspects of the election as well as their efforts to facilitate and participate in the protests (Ayed 2009). Coverage emphasized the large presence of youthful activists working to endorse a new face of leadership and to encourage change in political policies that were viewed as oppressive to the growth and development of Iran. The young generation was also reported to play a large role in the activism against Ahmadinejad's regime because of their knowledge and understanding of new technological tools that aided in the spread of information during the election. In response to the amount of activism occurring, universities including Tehran University experienced severe attacks from state authorities (Seven Die 2009). Reports aired stories of the ransacking of dormitories, noting that numerous students were beaten and arrested. A mass confiscation of computers, laptops, and memory cards was also suspected. At CBC Radio, Iranian youth described their interest in encouraging political change, and many who were interviewed commented on their discontent with Ahmadinejad as Iran's president (Fitzgerald 2009, June 17a). Reporters articulated the great energy and excitement among students, commenting on their strong motivation to support the defeated Mousavi. Although not all students rallied behind him, they spoke out of their discontent with the political system and utilized new communication tools and information-sharing devices to spread knowledge regarding their perspectives.

**Frame 5: Democracy**

The topic of democracy has often appeared in the Canadian media coverage of the 2009 Iranian presidential election. Both CBC Radio and CBC.ca have similarly framed this topic, raising questions and discussion of the role (or lack) of democracy in Iran's political system. Many articles featured statements by Iranians commenting on their expectations of the election as well as their opinion on the status of their governmental system. The correspondents almost always mentioned the role of democracy in the Iranian political system, often noting that presidential candidate Mousavi represented hope for an increasingly democratic system. The opinions of Iranians being quoted in the articles usually expressed discontent with the Iranian political regime, describing it as oppressive and detrimental to the growth and development of Iran as a country and as a participant in the global community (Stewart 2009). A special article featured on CBC.ca reported on the Iranian Canadian band, Blurred Vision, who wrote and produced songs that included connotations of the political struggles in Iran (Iranian-Canadian Band 2009).

Prior to the political crisis that followed the announcement of the presidential results, CBC Television covered debates on democracy in Iranian politics, specifically through interview clips of Iranian Canadians. The segment "Iran Election Day: Reflections from Canada's Iranian Community" (Hiscox 2009) featured opinions of Iranian Canadians expressing their perspectives on the election as well as the political status in Iran. Many of those featured in the segment made mention of their faith in the election, hoping that change would occur with a new government. One person who was interviewed stated, "We're here to show that Iran is actually democratic, and we're here to vote for it and just demonstrate democracy here" (Hiscox 2009). However, in the coverage following the announcement of the election results and as protests intensified, CBC Television reports of democracy within the Iranian political system took a less optimistic tone (Mansbridge 2009, June 16a). Coverage featured narratives that spoke of Ahmadinejad's win as a defeat of any aspirations toward a new democratic system. The state authority clampdown made in response to allegations of vote rigging was seen by some to demonstrate an oppressive government.

Some stories in the Canadian Press issued statements of protestors and others, critiquing Iran's political situation as failing to offer any democratic value and instead exhibiting a dictatorship (Hundreds Gather 2009). In the *Globe and Mail*, references to democracy were teamed with many aspects of the election, for instance in describing or critiquing the Iranian political system and when discussing the election procedure. Most frequently, the *Globe and Mail* discussed the topic of democracy in relation to the protests and the dialogue of those against Ahmadinejad's presidential win. Many of the protests were pictured as rallies fighting for democratic rights, with such prevalent ideas seen in quotes and descriptions of many protestors speaking of their desire for a democratic government. A twenty-four-year-old student was quoted in Parisa Hafezi's article entitled "Protests Continue as Iran's Supreme Leader Prepares to Address Nation," stating that "[Iranian citizens] want a modern government in Iran—[they] want freedom. The government is trying to make small concessions, but [citizens] want real change" (2009). Many articles in the *Globe and Mail* were also dedicated to analyzing the Iranian political system, and therefore touching on perspectives of the functioning (or lack) of democracy in Iran. Some offered hopeful perspectives, such as Jeffrey Simpson's article, "In Tehran, Theocracy Has Morphed into Thugocracy" (2009), noting that there are important aspects of democracy in Iran's political bureaucracy, but much of it is tainted or eroded because of the great corruption that occurs among politicians. Other perspectives described Iran's political system as failing to demonstrate little or no democratic traits, using examples such as the rules in place that allow only certain people to run for the presidency and the large role of religion in government policies that can suppress the operation of democracy (Luttwak 2009; Martin 2009, June 12, June 15; McLeod 2009).

In the *National Post*, democracy coincided with freedom. Discussion of the protests was often accompanied by mention that Iranians were unhappy with the election results and fighting for freedom fueled demonstrations in the streets. Iran's struggle with democracy historically and currently was blamed on the large role of religion in their governing style and corrupt involvement of mullahs (often referred to as "mullah millionaires" because of their great wealth, assumed to be a result of repeated crime and control of Iran's wealth). Despite less positive discussions on perspectives of Iran's political makeup, the *National Post* covered many stories of young people speaking out and working to gain attention for their discontent with their political system. Described as being a tide of youth interested in democratic rights in Iran, the coverage also illuminated the desires of many Iranians interested in a new era of freedom and prosperity (Akhavan 2009).

**Frame 6: Media Censorship**

Media censorship was discussed frequently throughout the Canadian media coverage of the 2009 Iranian presidential election. The Canadian Press reported heavily on the Iranian government authorities' numerous attempts to impede the spread of information. Authorities worked to inhibit media coverage of the mass protests and violence that occurred following the election in both the Iranian and international media. Tight restrictions were put on journalists in an effort to reduce attention on the violence and great disruption occurring in Iran. Authorities said foreign media and Iranians involved in the media could only work from their offices, conduct interviews via telephone, and rely on official sources such as state television (Akbar Dareini and Keyser 2009). The state television, however, is said to only have portrayed opinions and views in support of the winning party and failed to cover depictions of the extreme violence and conflicting perspectives regarding the election outcome. Media outlets were banned from sending videos or photographs that captured street rallies and protests. This media crackdown also involved the expulsion of various journalists, suspensions of media networks, and the detainment of many journalists working for both Iranian and international outlets (Laub 2009; Tayefe Mohajer 2009). Statements released by the Foreign Ministry in Iran have been also reported, due to their discontent with Western media depictions of their situation. In these reports, the West was accused of framing falsified and racist portrayals of the Iranian government and people. Although such reports included general statements about the West, many speculations surrounding these comments were thought to have been intended for Europe. European governments, as such, were less conservative in expressing their opinions regarding events taking place in Iran, while North American leaders, particularly President Barack Obama, initially worked toward a more neutral stance. Media coverage analysis of Obama's reluctant attitude on the Iranian situation was linked to his recent talks with Iran in the hope of developing better relations between the two countries. Despite this, as reports of violence continued to flood the international media in response to the crackdown by Iranian militia and police, Obama was reported as urging Iran to find resolution that avoided extreme measures.

Voices in the *National Post* and the *Globe and Mail* offered information on the dangerous climate journalists were subjected to in Iran as well as a critique of the Iranian political system that disallows reporters, media outlets, and online journalistic entities the ability to share their perspectives free of fear, prosecution, or punishment. Descriptions included the estimated number of jailed journalists as well as comments on the large number of those suspected to have gone into hiding following the Iranian government's harsh clampdown on those working to share stories, videos, and photographs of the political and public turmoil that occurred in Iran (Clarfield 2009). Although the era of instant communication and its great power in the world today was discussed extensively, framed with encouraging views of the Iranian people in search of an alternate political makeup, coverage also focused on the ability of Ahmadinejad's regime to censor a large amount of information in the media. The *National Post* discussed the tendency for crippling bias in the state-run media coverage of the election, which was seen to be full of misconstrued statements and fabrications. Other media outlets working to refute the statements of the state-run establishments were said to be shut down due to authorities' claims that such messages were causing the protests and public uproar. Additionally, other online media sources, such as blogs in support of the defeated Hossein Mousavi, were said to have been shutdown and blocked. This includes Mousavi's official website that was shutdown immediately following an update documenting the alleged fraud and manipulation that occurred in the vote tallying. CBC.ca reported on the many journalists arrested and punished, featuring a story of a Canadian journalist, George McLeod, who was detained by Iranian authorities before being released. Coverage of a similar story reported a case of Maziar Bahari, an Iranian Canadian journalist working in Iran for *Newsweek* who was taken from his mother's home and later featured in a government-affiliated news agency broadcast reporting he admitted that his election coverage was biased and in favor of the opposition—Mousavi. Reports of his confessions went on to state that along with the media outlet he was working for, other Western sources such as CNN and the *New York Times* had fueled attempts trying to devalue the legitimacy of the election. This arrest immediately triggered action by the Canadian government, which began working to have him released by Iranian authorities (Canada 2009). CBC Radio also covered stories reporting on the numerous journalists who had been arrested, including specific narratives of Canadian reporters who had been detained. Bloggers, photographers, and even people caught taking photos on mobile phones in the streets were also at risk of serious punishment. As such, many were arrested or subject to violence if caught partaking in these activities. CBC Radio reported on the contrasting viewpoints of Western media and Iranian media, stating that Western coverage was full of reports on the violence and alleged election fraud while Iranian coverage showed very little of the political unrest, usually downplaying the severity because of the state control initiatives (Fitzgerald 2009, June 17a).

In a CBC Television segment entitled *"Newsweek* Demands Release of Canadian Journalist Detained in Iran"* (2009, June 22a), host Mark Kelley commented on the immense state control of information, reporting that working conditions for journalists were worsening, and approximately one hundred had been kidnapped or murdered. CBC Television coverage of the state of media censorship also discussed the shutdown of countless Iranian media outlets that published material opposing Ahmadinejad's election, as well as the mysterious shutdown of online blogs and websites working to circulate material regarding the status of Iran (Kelley 2009, June 24b; Mansbridge 2009, June 16a). With the elevation of protests, journalists were banned from reporting on the rallies. Foreign journalists who avoided arrest were also forced to leave the country in fear of punishment. However, broadcasting from the state-controlled media outlets depicted a very different perspective of the events occurring in Iran. Footage of the protests was minimal and worked to frame activists and protestors as criminals inflicting torment and harm to the country. CBC Television expanded on the immense censorship occurring in the Iranian media, urging the importance of digital devices and online tools during the crisis to spread information and alternative perspectives to both those inside and outside the country.

## Frame 7: Technology and Cyberspace

The Canadian media have reported on the various impacts and incidences of technological tools being used during the period of the 2009 Iranian presidential election. Beyond discussion of the role of technology and cyberspace in the spread of information prior to and after the June 12 election, the *Globe and Mail* reported on a novel grassroots movement that occurred at the University of Toronto, one that worked to help Iranian activists gain access to Internet sites blocked by state authorities. "Psiphon," an online censorship avoidance tool created in 2006 at the University of Toronto, was designed primarily to help victims of censorship in repressive regimes bypass walls working to limit the flow of information online. In his article, "Iran's Cyber-Revolution Gets a Hand from Canada," El Akkad illuminated the great power of the advent of new online devices, stating, "Iran's biggest mass protest since the 1979 Islamic Revolution has become a full-fledged global movement, fought on and fuelled by the World Wide Web" (2009). With the help of global initiatives, such as the efforts of researchers at the University of Toronto, Iranians were able to access strategies against Ahmadinejad's regime that took the form of information, enabling them to facilitate communication and to organize protests. Contrary to the advantages researchers at the University of Toronto shared with Iranian activists, the *Globe and Mail* also reported on technology created in the Western world suspected to be behind the mass restrictions of information sharing in Iran prior to and after the June 12 election (Santana 2009). In an article entitled "Iran Can Monitor Calls with Our Technology: Nokia" (2009), the *Globe and Mail* unveiled a dark side of the technological involvement in Iran's political turmoil, stating that Nokia (the Finnish-German telecom maker) said they had sold technology to Iran in 2008 that could be used for call monitoring. Further accusations arose upon the release of this information, as Nokia was then linked to suspicions of e-mail and text-message filtering that occurred during protests. With discussion on the profound impact of the World Wide Web and equal banter of democracy found in coverage of the 2009 Iranian presidential election, the

*Globe and Mail* also published an article that offered a refreshing perspective in relation to the West's participation in this crisis. In Garton Ash's article, "Tweeting for Freedom" (2009), the importance of aiding those in need was discussed, stating: "One thing democratic governments can and should do: maintain and enhance the 21st-century global information infrastructure, which allows Iranians to keep in touch with each other and to find out what is really happening in their own country." He went on to discuss the importance of "people power" in political crises and the value of unity and support among people on a global scale, which can now be attained with the help of new technological tools, online communities, and the blogosphere.

Reports by the Canadian Press on the role of technology and cyberspace focused on the innovative ways in which citizens communicated around election time, specifically their usage of social networking sites, microblogging sites, and text messaging on mobile personal communication devices. Not only were these media used leading up to and during the election to communicate messages concerning the process and the presidential candidates, they were most notably used to communicate after the results were announced to share opinions and information protesting Ahmadinejad's presidential victory. Twitter, the widely popular microblogging site, attracted a large amount of attention during the aftermath of the election because of its ability to act as a user-run media outlet. Iranian citizens were able to share messages questioning the validity and transparency of the election while avoiding state censorship or punishment. It was reported that many Iranians experienced interference on mobile devices when attempting to send text messages through networks regarding discontent of the election results or organizing rallies to protest the results (suspected to be linked to government censorship). Twitter gained international attention because of its unique communication abilities among the Iranian people working to object to Ahmadinejad's win and to raise awareness of the suspicions and allegations of corruption in the electoral process (Lee 2009). In response to its success, Twitter executives were asked by U.S. government officials to postpone a ninety-minute shutdown of the site due to maintenance scheduled to fall just days after the election (June 15) because of its value in Iran as a crucial communication tool. Footage of the death of Neda Agha-Soltan, the young female Iranian protestor shot by the militia in the streets of Tehran during protests, captured digitally and uploaded to the Internet, spread rapidly through social networking sites and microblogging sites, showing people around the world a snapshot of the clashes occurring in the streets of Tehran. User-run sites allowed for information and digital materials (photos, videos) to spread quickly with minimal interference by a state-governed body.

The *National Post* expanded on the discussion of the online world by covering the help given by cyberspace members around the world who worked to aid Iranians in the spread of information, despite mysterious Internet and cell phone network shutdowns. "Cybersympathizers" reportedly acted internationally, battling online to help Iranians dodge censorship and avoid real-world capture and punishment (Protestors Have Allies 2009). An example of this is seen through the coverage of Twitter users in other countries described as having changed the time and location settings of their accounts in order to make it appear that they were messaging from within Tehran. In so doing, they succeeded in making it hard for authorities to locate those actually tweeting within the country.

CBC.ca reported on the usage of Twitter and Facebook as methods of sharing information as well as the usage of digital technology such as cell phone photographs and video recordings that allowed Iranians to capture and share images of the situation in their country (Iran Blames U.S. 2009; Twitter Emerges 2009). CBC.ca featured an article that discussed the incidence of online hacking in the Iranian election, noting that this form of online crime has increased in sophistication and popularity. According to this CBC .ca report, the Oregon University system website was hacked, redirecting all visitors to the site to a political message that criticized the protests in Iran for approximately ninety minutes. CBC.ca expanded on this occurrence, noting that the online world holds new opportunity for crime, especially during crisis or influential world events. The article "Iran Turmoil Fuels 'Hacktivist' Attacks on Websites" (2009) went on to further discuss the implications and dangers of online warfare and how it has been used in similar circumstances. CBC Television and CBC Radio's coverage followed the many functions of the Internet during the political crisis as well as the impact of digital technology on the spread of information. Many Iranians were unable to rely on cell phone access as there were many reports of call and text message interceptions. State authorities were blamed for this, along with the blocking of several websites in support of opposition candidates. In response to the government's attempt to lockdown communication and information, many activists worked to broadcast information via nontraditional methods, such as the usage of Twitter, Facebook, Flickr, and YouTube (Fitzgerald 2009, June 17b; Kelley 2009, June 22a, June 22b; Mansbridge 2009, June 16b; Nichols 2009, June 20).

## Frame 8: International Politics

A large amount of the Canadian media coverage of the 2009 Iranian presidential election was oriented toward sharing the opinions and statements of

international political leaders working toward pressuring the Iranian government to properly evaluate the validity of the election results while also reducing or eliminating police and military crackdown on protestors. The reports
in the Canadian Press ranged from discussing opinions of leaders in Europe
(France, Italy, Belgium, Britain, Germany) and those in North America
(Canada and the United States), complimented with quotes and statements to
back up the coverage. The European Union generated a great media stir, urging that violence be stopped and the concerns of a lack of authenticity in the
election be thoroughly investigated. Doing so would ensure the results were
fair and truthful (Barchfield 2009; Brand 2009). Interestingly, U.S. president
Barack Obama received more media attention than Canadian governmental
leaders did, as more articles focused on Obama's reaction to the events in
Iran as opposed to Canadian feedback (Akbar Dareini and Keyser 2009).
Discussion among politicians in the United States, such as Republican views
on Obama's reaction, captured the attention of the Canadian Press, reporting
that Obama's opposition felt he was being too submissive about expressing
discontent with the election results in Iran (Feller 2009; Kole 2009, June 29;
Laub 2009; Max 2009). Little coverage surfaced describing views of Canadian politicians, although some material discussed the conflicting views between the Conservative and Liberal parties. Liberal leader Michael Ignatieff
wanted the Canadian embassy in Tehran to help injured protestors in the Iranian government crackdown, while Foreign Affairs refuted this, claiming that
it could only offer refuge to people in exceptional circumstances (Ignatieff
Says 2009). As media releases continued to flood international news regarding opinions of leaders worldwide, the Iranian government issued responses
stating that the United States was encouraging violence among protestors
in Iran and endorsing and encouraging falsified opinions of the election.
Contrary to the opinions of Western leaders, Russian and Syrian government
officials reportedly supported the Iranian election results and opted to avoid
any disputes in this regard.

Amid all of the discussion on the alleged fraud and protests that occurred
in the streets of Tehran, the *National Post* directed a significant amount of
attention to the opinions and statements released by other political leaders,
particularly those of the Western world. As politicians and activists around
the world responded to the political crisis in Iran, the *National Post* worked
to follow the evolving opinions and dialogue that arose from the elections.
Although articles of this nature grew in volume following the announcement of the results and the ensuing violence, attention to statements issued
by Western political leaders prior to the election also generated momentum.
Articles that spoke of such were framed to illuminate the different opinions of
Western leaders, such as politicians in Britain, France, Germany, the United

States, and Canada (Deshmukh 2009). Most opinions were based around these countries' concerns about the violence and outbreak of protests in Iran. Some statements focused on coercing the leaders of Iran to cease violence against demonstrators and work to calm the election proceedings in a nonviolent manner while other politicians, such as those in France, chose to directly blame Ahmadinejad's regime of election fraud. A high volume of articles discussed internal squabbles occurring between the U.S. political parties, specifically the Republicans' performance appraisal of Obama. Seemingly, his words and opinions were of great value to the Canadian people, while very little information was shared on the Canadian government's stance or role in this issue. Contrary to the previous Bush administration, Obama was framed as being less assertive and failing to apply his global credibility in a time of crisis (Gerson 2009). Beyond coverage of internal critique within the United States of his behavior, many articles in the *National Post* were dedicated to dissecting Obama's perceived faults in this situation, such as his unrealistic and vague comments on the alleged election fraud and his unwillingness to speak boldly of the dangerous nature of the political problems in Iran. However, his timid response to this situation morphed as Ahmadinejad began issuing statements wherein the United States was accused of fueling the violence in Iran and meddling in their politics. As the state of protests elevated and bloodshed continued, Obama's stance was reported to toughen, as his invitations to reach out to Iran were quickly retracted and his statements offered an increasingly stern tone.

The *Globe and Mail* discussed Obama's reactions to the alleged fraud of the election results and violent protests and also included discussion on the history of the relations between the United States and Iran. In Paul Koring's article "Obama's Caution on Iran Uprising Treads Fine Line" (2009, June 18), some light was shed on Obama's perceived deference of the issue, highlighting that Obama's sideline approach contradicted his created persona of change whereby a continued timid response to a potential uprising of authoritarianism in Iran would be a huge setback to his presidency, having so much riding on his image. Other Western countries such as Germany, France, and Britain also landed coverage in the *Globe and Mail*, with reports on their comments of strong disagreement with the election outcome and violence. Some articles were dedicated to discussing the attacks made by Ahmadinejad's regime on Britain's response to the election results and the violence inflicted by police and militia on citizens, stating that Britain was blamed for initiating and encouraging the public demonstrations and protests (Leeder 2009). Arrests of British embassy employees were also covered, as it was suspected that these incidences were in direct relation to the blame Iran assigned to Britain for the problems in Tehran.

CBC.ca expanded on the comments of Canadian governmental opinions, providing a large span of coverage on the statements and reactions of Canadian politicians. An article entitled "Seven Die after Gunfire Breaks Out at Tehran Protest" (2009) reported on the alleged election fraud and the protests that occurred in Tehran in opposition to Ahmadinejad's win. It included a quote of Foreign Affairs Minister Lawrence Cannon, stating that Canada was deeply troubled by the situation in Iran and called for a fully transparent investigation into electoral discrepancies. Many reports similar in nature featured the various opinions of Canadian leaders speaking out against the violence and misconduct of the Iranian government. CBC Radio coverage included reports on Barack Obama's comments and the controversy that ensued because of his apprehension to comment directly on fraud allegations (Fitzgerald 2009, June 16; Obama Condemns Iran 2009). Canadian prime minister Stephen Harper was also featured in reports, specifically his stance on the Iranian political situation, urging Iran's government to respect democracy and human rights. What is worth noting here is that CBC Radio broadcast a segment that featured commentary from a Middle Eastern political analyst who noted that other Middle Eastern countries such as Saudi Arabia, Jordan, and Egypt had chosen to remain silent about Ahmadinejad's win. In a CBC Television segment entitled "Ottawa Calls for Investigation into Election Result in Iran" (Mansbridge 2009, June 15), comments from Canadian politicians were aired that reflected Canada's discontent with the election process and concern about how the protestors in Iran were treated. Canada's opinions on the situation were thoroughly reported, featuring discussion of Canada's alarm toward protestors and journalists unjustly detained, the shutdown of Iranian communication systems (cell phone networks, text messaging, Internet sites, etc.), and the bloodshed that occurred in protests as a result of a clampdown by state authorities. Statements issued by various Canadian political leaders were featured, such as Jack Layton (leader of the New Democratic Party) who was pressuring the Canadian government to speak out very strongly against the violence in Iran (Kelley 2009, June 22b, June 23b; MacNeil 2009).

## OCTAGONAL PORTRAIT

To conclude, the Canadian media have framed the developments and discussions of the 2009 Iranian presidential election within eight major dimensions—election procedure; corruption; demonstrations; human rights; democracy; media censorship; technology and cyberspace; and international politics—hence, the octagonal portrait metaphor. Through this portrayal, the

Canadian media provided their audiences with information, depicting the event according to specific themes. The rationalization of reasons behind such media-framing is beyond the scope of this chapter. However, the frame analysis provides substantial descriptions of themes or frames that can be further linked, in future studies, to the political, social, and cultural interests and directions of the Canadian media.

The 2009 Iranian presidential election procedure has been framed in the Canadian media, dissecting the Iranian election system and the flaws perceived to have contributed to the development of a political environment in which corruption occurred. Following the announcement of the election results, the Canadian media reported on the fraud allegations and accusations of misconduct of Ahmadinejad's regime that triggered the massive protests. The historical background of Iranian politics generated great attention as well as various perspectives on the corruption of governmental practices in Iran. The Canadian media coverage of the politics in Iran (past and present) presented perspectives on corruption, dishonesty, and inequality. These problems were illuminated through narratives of past conflict in Iran and descriptions of policies and traditions that were framed as oppressive.

The Canadian media presented quotes and stories of particular people involved in the protests and victims of the clashes, humanizing the situation in Iran for Canadian audiences. The protestors were represented as very active in demonstrating their discontent with Ahmadinejad's win, despite statements issued by government officials warning that the rallies were deemed as illegal and those participating or instigating them would be severely punished. Following the announcement of the election results, journalists reported on the violence that ensued, comparing the severity of the protests to a natural disaster. The Canadian media reported on the conflict that occurred in the streets of Iran, specifically the injuries and deaths that occurred. Concerns of human rights violations occurring in Iran were reported in the Canadian media. Coverage of women in Iran and their involvement in the presidential election focused mainly on the women working to change long-standing traditional political views and policies that preach strict guidelines for the role of females in society. Coverage also highlighted their pivotal role in activism against the oppression imposed on them by the Ahmadinejad regime. Women activists followed the brave actions of Mousavi's wife, participating in protest and campaigning for equal rights and democracy in Iran's political system. The role of the youth in Iran's political history was also discussed, noting their growing momentum as political activists working for change. Democracy was a common theme in the majority of stories in the Canadian media, particularly from the perspective that Iranian government officials associated with, and in support of Ahmadinejad's win, had robbed the Iranian citizens' of the right to have a fair election. Many reports were on protests communicating messages of discontent with Iran's lack of democracy and encouraging Iranians to fight for democracy. Iran's struggle with democracy was discussed, alluding to their political struggles in the past and often describing their political methods as a dictatorship or theocracy. The Canadian media described the Iranian government's firm hold on communication- and information-sharing devices, specifically the interception of cell phone networks and Internet sites. The reports revealed that state authorities banned journalists from reporting firsthand on the streets in order to block images and eyewitness accounts of the rallies. Additionally, reports highlighted the dangerous working conditions for journalists in Iran, noting that those affiliated with international media organizations had been ordered to stay in their offices and were banned from covering rallies.

Although the online world was disrupted during the election and protests, it allowed for the development of online support systems through activists spreading messages that would not have been safe or possible via other media. Twitter was reported to be an important communication tool to Iranians due to unreliable mobile networks that had suppressed information sharing due to network interference of text messages and calls. The Canadian media reports regarding how the Internet and new technologies impacted communication during the election linked the value of the advancement in digital media technologies and their importance as journalistic tools and informal user-run media outlets.

The Canadian media coverage also focused on comments of political leaders in Britain, France, the United States, and Canada, stating their reactions to the election fraud allegations, Ahmadinejad's presidential victory, and the violence that occurred during protests. Increased focus was directed toward the actions and reactions of the U.S. president Barack Obama—a subject of critique and scrutiny because of his initial reluctance to speak sternly of the Iranian political turmoil. Furthermore, some coverage was dedicated to the opinions of the Canadian government and Canadian political leaders as well as to international opinions of those who were not in support of the Iranian election results or actions of the police and military against Iranian protestors.

## REFERENCES

Abbot, S. (2009, June 16). Man in the news: Iran's supreme leader. *Globe and Mail*, p. A17.
Akbar Dareini, A., and Heintz, J. (2009, June 22). Iran's opposition calls for continued protests, but strategy for avoiding violence unclear. Canadian Press.

Akbar Dareini, A., and Karimi, N. (2009, June 21). Iran's top leader addresses nation after mass opposition protests challenge ruling clerics. Canadian Press.

Akbar Dareini, A., and Keyser, J. (2009, June 17). Rival demonstrations held in Iranian capital; government offers to recount some ballots. Canadian Press.

Akhavan, P. (2009, June 16). Revolution in the air. *National Post*, p. A18.

Asp, K. (1983). The struggle for the agenda: Party agenda, media agenda, and voter agenda in the 1979 Swedish election campaign. *Communication Research, 10*(3), 333–355.

Ayed, N. (2009, June 10). Inside Iran election blog: A vitality that wasn't expected. CBC.ca. http://www.cbc.ca/world/story/2009/06/08/f-iran-blog.html.

Barchfield, J. (2009, June 14). EU concerned over Iranian vote results; France condemns police response. Canadian Press.

Brand, C. (2009, June 15). EU calls for full probe into allegation of election fraud in Iran. Canadian Press.

Calgarians hold lunchtime demonstrations for democracy in Iran. (2009, June 23). CBC.ca. http://www.cbc.ca/canada/calgary/story/2009/06/23/calgary-iran-rally-stephen-ave.html.

Canada will not "stay out" of Iranian politics: Cannon. (2009, June 18). CBC.ca. http://www.cbc.ca/world/story/2009/06/18/iran-canada-foreign-affairs-meeting847.html.

Clarfield, G. (2009, June 24). Theocracy of thugs. *National Post*, p. A18.

Cohen, B. (1963). *The press and foreign policy*. Princeton, NJ: Princeton University Press.

Cohen, R. (2009, June 16). Dark days for Iran. *National Post*, p. A18.

———. (2009, June 29). A tale of two Irans at war. *National Post*, p. A6.

Deshmukh, J. (2009, June 23). Protestors defy elite guard threat; travel warnings issued; Obama urges Tehran to avoid "violent and unjust" response. *National Post*, p. A14.

El Akkad, O. (2009, June 17). Iran's cyber-revolution gets a hand from Canada; Psiphon, a censorship avoidance tool created at U of T, has been "pushing" government-blocked Internet content to Iranian activists. *Globe and Mail*, p. A14.

Entman, R. M. (1993). Framing: Toward clarification of a fractured paradigm. *Journal of Communication, 43*(4), 51–58.

Feller, B. (2009, June 20). Obama: Iran's leaders must stop all "violent and unjust actions" amid postelection crackdown. Canadian Press.

Fitzgerald, M. (2009, June 9). Presidential election in Iran on Friday. *World Report* [Radio transcript]. CBC Radio.

———. (2009, June 15). Reactions to election results in Iran. *World Report* [Radio transcript]. CBC Radio.

———. (2009, June 16). Barack Obama comments on the outcome of Iran's election. *World Report* [Radio transcript]. CBC Radio.

———. (2009, June 17a). Day five of Iran's political crisis. *World Report* [Radio transcript]. CBC Radio.

———. (2009, June 17b). Mir Hossein Mousavi has called for a mass rally. *World Report* [Radio transcript]. CBC Radio.

Freeman, C., and Blair, D. (2009, June 15). Ahmadinejad rival seeks to overturn results; Iranian Election. *National Post*, p. A1.

Garton Ash, T. (2009, June 19). Tweeting for freedom. *Globe and Mail*, p. A21.

Gerson, M. (2009, June 18). For Iran: Freedom now. *National Post*, p. A23.

Goodspeed, P. (2009, June 13). Election leaves Iran polarized; Generational divide may mean violent stalemate. *National Post*, p. A21.

———. (2009, June 24). Tehran settles in for the long marathon; Backlash against protestors shows every sign of intensifying. *National Post*, p. A11.

Goffman, E. (1974). *Frame analysis: An essay on the organization of experience.* New York: Harper and Row.

Hafezi, P. (2009, June 19). Protests continue as Iran's supreme leader prepares to address nation. *Globe and Mail*, p. A17.

Hewitt, P. (2009, June 14). Hundreds rally across Canada to protest Iran's election results. Canadian Press.

Hiscox, H. (2009, June 12). Iran election day: Reflections from Canada's Iranian community. *The National* [Television transcript]. CBC Television.

Hosseinian, Z., and Jaseb, H. (2009, June 25). Ayatollah declares election results will stand. *Globe and Mail*, p. A14.

Hundreds gather in Toronto to protest Iran's election results. (2009, June 14). Canadian Press.

Ignatieff says embassy in Tehran should help injured. (2009, June 21). Canadian Press.

Iran blames U.S. for bitter post-election dispute. (2009, June 17). CBC.ca. http://www.cbc.ca/technology/story/2009/06/17/iran-election-protests-tehran821.html.

Iran can monitor calls with our technology: Nokia. (2009, June 30). *Globe and Mail*, p. B7.

Iran turmoil fuels "hacktivist" attacks on websites. (2009, June 26). CBC.ca. http://www.cbc.ca/technology/story/2009/06/25/tech-hacktivist-iran-protest.html.

Iran's soccer team shows Mousavi support. (2009, June 17). CBC.ca. http://www.cbc.ca/news/story/2009/06/17/sp-world-cup-qualify.html.

Iran's supreme leader hints at crackdown on protestors. (2009, June 19). CBC.ca .http://www.cbc.ca/world/story/2009/06/19/iran-tehran-election-protests-khamenei821.html.

Iranian-Canadian band Blurred Vision focuses attention on Iranian youth. (2009, June 22). CBC.ca. http://www.cbc.ca/arts/music/story/2009/06/22/iran-blurred-vision.html.

Iranian cleric calls for harsh punishment for protest leaders. (2009, June 26). CBC.ca .http://www.cbc.ca/world/story/2009/06/26/iran-mousavi-election-protest453.html.

Iranian police break up fresh Tehran protest. (2009, June 22). CBC.ca. http://www.cbc.ca/world/story/2009/06/22/iran-election-results-protest452.html.

Kelley, M. (2009, June 22a). *Newsweek* demands release of Canadian journalist detained in Iran. *The National* [Television transcript]. CBC Television.

———. (2009, June 22b). A shocking video from Iran becomes a powerful symbol. *The National* [Television transcript]. CBC Television.

———. (2009, June 23a). Fear in the streets: Iran tightens its grip. *The National* [Television transcript]. CBC Television.

———. (2009, June 23b). Obama sends tougher message to Iran. *The National* [Television transcript]. CBC Television.

———. (2009, June 24a). Glimpse of violence in Iran. *The National* [Television transcript]. CBC Television.

———. (2009, June 24b). Iranian government blames foreigners for protests. *The National* [Television transcript]. CBC Television.

Keyser, J. (2009, June 15). The speed of Iran's presidential vote count and lack of detailed data fuel fraud suspicions. Canadian Press.

Kole, W. J. (2009, June 26). Cleric's call for executing some protestors signals harsh new turn in Iran. Canadian Press.

———. (2009, June 29). Iran rules out downgrading ties with Britain despite soaring tensions over embassy arrest. Canadian Press.

Koring, P. (2009, June 18). Obama's caution on Iran uprising treads fine line. *Globe and Mail*, p. A20.

———. (2009, June 27). Protest leaders worthy "worthy of execution." *Globe and Mail*, p. A21.

Lamb, D. M. (2009, June 14). Possible reformist demonstrations in Iran today. *World Report* [Radio transcript]. CBC Radio.

Laub, K. (2009, June 23). Iran's top electoral body rules out vote annulment, says found no "major fraud" in election. Canadian Press.

Lee, M. (2009, June 16). Officials: U.S. State Department intervenes to keep Twitter online during Iran election crisis. Canadian Press.

Leeder, J. (2009, June 29). Iran's battle with Britain escalates as EU embassy arrests. *Globe and Mail*, p. A1.

Luttwak, E. (2009, June 23). End times for Iran's theocracy. *Globe and Mail*, p. A19.

MacNeil, C. (2009, June 21). Canadian protestors condemn actions of Iranian government. *Sunday Night* [Television transcript]. CBC Television.

Mansbridge, P. (2009, June 10). Women voters in Iran hoping for new freedoms. *The National* [Television transcript]. CBC Television.

———. (2009, June 15). Ottawa calls for investigation into election result in Iran. *The National* [Television transcript]. CBC Television.

———. (2009, June 16a). Iran orders partial vote recount amid continued protests. *The National* [Television transcript]. CBC Television.

———. (2009, June 16b). Iran's emerging "netwar": Canadians help keep Iranians connected. *The National* [Television transcript]. CBC Television.

Martin, P. (2009, June 12). A vote controlled by those who rule. *Globe and Mail*, p. A17.

———. (2009, June 13). Women emerge as major political force in Iran. *Globe and Mail*, p. A19.

———. (2009, June 15). Simmering culture war erupts in Iran. *Globe and Mail*, p. A10.

———. (2009, June 20). A theocratic sermon thick with threats. *Globe and Mail*, p. A20.

Max, A. (2009, June 22). Europe protests Iranian crackdown, taking the heat from Tehran instead of Obama. Canadian Press.

McLeod, G. (2009, June 12). Not so much a campaign, as a cry of protest. *Globe and Mail*, p. A17.

Neda shot by Iranian militiaman, doctor tells BBC. (2009, June 26). CBC.ca. http:// www.cbc.ca/canada/story/2009/06/25/iran-neda-doctor-bbc-062509.html.

Nelson, T. E., Oxley, Z. M., and Clawson, R. A. (1997). Toward a psychology of framing effects. *Political Behavior, 19*(3), 221–246.

Nichols, A. (2009, June 13). Turmoil in Tehran. *Saturday Report* [Television transcript]. CBC Television.

———. (2009, June 20). Thousands protest in Iran despite warnings of a crackdown. *Saturday Report* [Television transcript]. CBC Television.

Obama condemns Iran violence as "outrageous." (2009, June 26). CBC.ca. http:// www.cbc.ca/world/story/2009/06/26/g8-iran-violence062609.html.

Protestors gather at Iranian embassy. (2009, June 26). CBC.ca. http://www.cbc.ca/ canada/ottawa/story/2009/06/26/ottawa-iran-protest.html.

Protestors have allies around cyberworld; "Proxy servers" help divert Twitter traffic. (2009, June 18). *National Post*, p. A17.

Santana, R. (2009, June 16). Iran's twitter users. *Globe and Mail*, p. A17.

Seven die after gunfire breaks out at Tehran protest. (2009, June 15). CBC.ca. http:// www.cbc.ca/world/story/2009/06/15/iran-tehran-election856.html.

Severin, W. J., and Tankard, J. W. (2001). *Communication theories: Origins, methods, and uses in the mass media*. New York: Longman.

Simpson, J. (2009, June 19). In Tehran, theocracy has morphed into thugocracy. *Globe and Mail*, p. A21.

Smith, D. (2009, June 13). Controversy over Ahmadinejad's reported election victory. *World Report* [Radio transcript]. CBC Radio.

Solomon, E., and MacNeil, C. (2009, June 14). Allegations of election fraud in Iran. *Sunday Night* [Television transcript]. CBC Television.

Stewart, B. (2009, June 18). From Iran to Bangladesh, the rise of the ballot box. CBC .ca. http://www.cbc.ca/world/story/2009/06/18/f-vp-stewart.html.

Tayefe Mohajer, S. (2009, June 28). "Hacktivists" attack sites for Iranian government and media as clashes in streets quiet. Canadian Press.

Twitter emerges as news source during Iran media crackdown. (2009, June 16). CBC .ca. http://www.cbc.ca/technology/story/2009/06/15/iran-twitter-election-protest .html.

Vreese, C. H. (2004). The effects of frames in political television news on issue interpretation and frame salience. *Journalism and Mass Communication Quarterly, 81*(1), 36–52.

*Chapter Three*

# The 2009 Iranian Presidential Election in the Polish Media

Tomasz Płudowski

Despite Poland's last twenty prosperous years during which the country shed Communism, removed Soviet troops from its soil, joined the European Union (EU) and North Atlantic Treaty Organization (NATO), largely increased its Gross Domestic Product (GDP), and became a liberal democracy with a free market economy and free media, many Poles tend to see their country as a victim of the games of world powers in general and specifically of the country's mighty and often unfriendly neighbors and even its former allies, which is largely attributable to the country's recent history. Yet, the year 1989 stands out in the country's last three hundred years as a bright point, when Poland was not only making history and influencing world politics but also being victorious. In early 1989 Poland initiated roundtable talks between the Communist government and the opposition and held the first free (at least partly free) parliamentary elections in the region, and even had the first non-Communist government, all of which happened months before the fall of the Berlin Wall. Yet, it is the latter occurrence that has received the most attention and is remembered worldwide as the symbol of the fall of Communism. Arguably, the fall of the Berlin Wall was a major television event, a memorable and symbolic scene that captured the hearts and minds of global citizens. Even the peaceful events in Prague's Wenceslas Square made for better television viewing than the Polish roundtable talks that started in February 1989 and ended two months later, leading to the first free elections in all of Eastern Europe. However, it is those Polish roundtable talks between an authoritarian government and its opposition that epitomize what is known as the Velvet Revolution.

What is a Velvet Revolution? A recognized British historian familiar with the region of East and Central Europe and fluent in Polish, Timothy Garton Ash, who, not unlike Norman Davies, skillfully combines the traditional Western perspective with the more rare, in-depth knowledge of Eastern European sources, events, and sensibilities, juxtaposes the generic Velvet Revolution, rampant in the region and elsewhere (Poland, Czech Republic, Estonia, Latvia, Lithuania, South Africa, Chile, Slovakia, Croatia, Georgia, etc.) with an ideal, traditional type of 1789-style revolution (e.g., the Russian Revolution of 1917 and Mao's Chinese Revolution). What is the difference? While the traditional revolution is "violent, utopian, professedly class-based, and characterized by a progressive radicalization, culminating in terror," the Velvet Revolution [is] nonviolent, antiutopian, based not on a single class but on broad social coalitions, and characterized by the application of mass social pressure—"people power"—to bring the current power holders to negotiate. It culminates not in terror, but in compromise. If the totem of 1789-type revolution is the guillotine, that of 1989 is the round table (Garton Ash 2009).

Ironically, even though the term *Velvet Revolution* has positive connotations in the West, as it highlights democratic change through nonviolence, its reception in other regions can be different. In fact, when the Islamic Republic of Iran tried political leaders during a show trial in the summer of 2009, exactly twenty years after the Velvet Revolution of 1989, it accused them of *enghelab-e makhmali*, in other words, precisely a Velvet Revolution, reminds Garton Ash.

Poland's most prominent newspaper, *Gazeta Wyborcza* [*Electoral Gazette*], which was established as a result of the roundtable talks by the Polish Solidarity activists directly prior to the first free elections of 1989 as a mass, independent voice of the non-Communist opposition, has devoted a significant amount of space and attention to the 2009 Iranian election. Illustrated stories on the subject have appeared numerous times since the election day of June 12, 2009, including as front-page news on June 13 and 14 "*Płonne nadzieje na zmianę w Iranie*" ["Vain Hopes for Change in Iran"]; on June 15, "*Iran zadrżał*" ["Iran Is Shaken"]; on June 16, "*Iran się burzy*" ["Iran Rebels"]; on June 17, "*Teherańczycy znów na ulicach*" ["Tehranians Take to the Streets Again"]; on June 20 and 21, "*Ajatollah grozi rozlewem krwi*" ["Ayatollah Threatens with Bloodshed"]; on June 22, "*Irański reżim strzela do ludzi*" ["Iran's Regime Shoots at People"]; and on June 23 "*Siła bierze górę w Iranie*" ["Violence Takes Over in Iran"].

The first postelection story reports the initial pro-Ahmadinejad election results as surprising to all those who saw the great pro-Mousavi rallies in Tehran and concludes that "all seems to indicate that the anti-western Mahmoud

Ahmadinejad, who negates the Holocaust and promises the end of Israel, will keep the post" (*Płonne* 2009, June 13 and 14). After the postelectoral weekend of demonstrations, the Iranian election story took central stage on the front page with a large photo captioned, "Tehran, Sunday. Civilian-dressed police are beating with their truncheons opponents of President Ahmadinejad, who think the election has been a fraud" (*Iran zadrżał* 2009, June 16). The story focuses on the demonstrations and the violence, while the president is introduced later in the story as "the old, well-known Ahmadinejad" who at a press conference threatens: "Everyone who attacks Iran will sorely regret it," and assures that the elections were free and fair.

An article entitled *"Perskie cuda nad urną"* ["Persian Miracles over the Voting Urn"] explains how Ahmadinejad paints himself as one of the people:

> takes pride in being a smith's son . . . , lives humbly, . . . tells people what they want to hear: that people in power steal . . . and that Israel will disappear from the map. The conclusion is that the President, after four years in power, has managed to convince the people that he is rebelling against the government is this election's first miracle. Were there other miracles over the voting urn? We might never know. One way or another, the election, which still has a big question mark hanging over its head, is a defeat for the ayatollahs. Instead of defusing the tensions, . . . it has led to unrests and arrests. Ahmadinejad's speech looked surrealistic when, armed with a smile, he announced the victory of the Iranian people and was unfolding the vision of a bright future, built together with the youth. At the very moment he was uttering these words, the police were battering young people in the streets of Tehran. (Zawadzki 2009, June 15)

Another article from the same issue explains that:

> At the same time, many Iranians, those poorer and less educated ones, are indeed happy about Ahmadinejad's victory. Yesterday, thousands of people celebrated his reelection. To them, he is the embodiment of the just ruler who attacks the rich officials of the regime. Ahmadinejad looks like one of them; he is evidence that in Iran even such a simple man can get that far. The gulf between the protesters from the streets of Teheran and Ahmadinejad's supporters is enormous. It cannot be bridged by Iranian intellectuals, who live in north Iran, in their own world, outside the regime, outside the rest of the society, like strangers from a far-away country. (Włodek-Biernat 2009, June 15)

At the same time, Mousavi is pictured as much more complicated and sinister than as an idealistic freedom fighter. In a June 16 article, entitled *"Ulubieniec Chomeiniego"* ["Chomeini's Darling"], the subtitle explains: "There are two Mir Hossein Mousavis. The first one, hostile to the West, was created by the Islamic Revolution. The other, liberal and open to the world,

appeared 30 years later as the main opponent to Mahmoud Ahmadinejad."
The story concludes:

> The new Mousavi ultimately radicalized when he was announced to have lost the
> election, which he had expected to win easily. Calling on his supporters to rebel
> and protest in the streets, suddenly he, one of the revolution's pioneers, became
> the system's main dissident and radical reformer. (Zawadzki 2009, June 16)

However, the paper's reporting and commentary is sympathetic to Mousavi's supporters, particularly when the government resorts to violence against
the opponents. Ten days after election day, front-page articles got smaller,
but the headlines more dramatic: "*Irański reżim strzela do ludzi*" ["Iran's Regime Shoots at People"] on June 22; "*Siła bierze górę w Iranie*" ["Violence
Takes Over in Iran"] on June 23. Inside the paper, the coverage continues
with troubling illustrations of protesters covered in blood. The focus seems
to change from a more or less objective coverage of two conflicting visions
of the country that clash on election day, visions less different than many
observers expect (and certainly not that different in terms of foreign policy
since the Iranian president does not control that area of government), to the
familiar story of freedom-seeking people versus totalitarian authority and an
illegitimate government resorting to violence ("*Początek końca*" ["The Beginning of the End"] 2009, June 22). Interviewed in this article, Ali Pahlavan,
an Iraqi who reports for the BBC in Tehran, claims that the anti-Ahmadinejad
movement has been growing strong for four years, ever since the president
was first elected, and explains that in contrast to Iraqi or Afghani people,
the Iranians are not used to violence and can therefore change the means of
protest when faced with the government's brutality. That is why, instead of
open confrontation, people can choose passive resistance: strikes, which have
already been announced, or sabotage ("*Początek końca*" ["The Beginning of
the End"] 2009, June 22).

Strangely enough, during the initial period of reporting or commentary, par-
allels were not drawn between the Iranian election and the events of 1989 in
East and Central Europe. It was only later, both in Polish and Western media,
that the similarities (and differences) became apparent. What became particularly clear was that the Iranian situation was more akin to Tiananmen Square
on June 4, 1989, where protesters were brutally clamped down on, than to what
occurred that very same day in Poland, but with fewer cameras and much less
international coverage—the first free elections in East and Central Europe.
Why did the events happen the way they did in Eastern Europe, in China, and
more recently in Iran? Why were some movements successful, while in other
countries, change did not prevail and was actually impeded? There is no single
explanation: in 1989 it was not the Polish pope, Ronald Reagan, or Gorbachev
alone, but rather it was the interplay of powerful forces, both internal and ex-

ternal factors, that led to success. Furthermore, as Roger Cohen rightly points out, it was a matter of the right individuals at the right time (2009, November 3). Also in this *New York Times* column, he remembers the now-retired East German official who opened the gates between East and West Berlin. The Iranian protests of the summer of 2009 constitute events that the country had not seen in over thirty years. They mark the rebirth of civil society in that country. And while the protesters might not constitute a majority, while they might not all want the same thing, particularly a Western-style state and democracy, they definitely want their voices to be heard, or as Cohen put it, they want the second word in the phrase, Islamic Republic, to really mean something. Twenty years after the wave of Velvet Revolutions that swept Central and Eastern Europe, this new type of social change is spreading elsewhere. The fate of its Iranian variety will be primarily decided by the Iranian people themselves in the years to come.

## REFERENCES

*Ajatollah grozi rozlewem krwi* [Ayatollah threatens with a bloodshed]. (2009, June 20 and 21). *Gazeta Wyborcza* [*Electoral Gazette*], p. 1.

Cohen, R. (2009, November 3). The hinge of history. *New York Times*. http://www.nytimes.com/2009/11/03/opinion/03iht-edcohen.html.

Garton Ash, T. (2009, December 3). Velvet revolution: The prospects. *New York Review of Books*. http://www.nybooks.com/articles/23437.

*Iran się burzy* [Iran rebels]. (2009, June 16). *Gazeta Wyborcza* [*Electoral Gazette*], p. 1.

*Iran zadrżał* [Iran Is shaken]. (2009, June 15). *Gazeta Wyborcza* [*Electoral Gazette*], p. 1.

*Irański reżim strzela do ludzi* [Iran's regime shoots at people]. (2009, June 22). *Gazeta Wyborcza* [*Electoral Gazette*], p. 1.

*Płonne nadzieje na zmianę w Iranie* [Vain hopes for change in Iran]. (2009, June 13 and 14). *Gazeta Wyborcza* [*Electoral Gazette*], p. 1.

*Początek końca reżimu Ahmadineżada* [The beginning of the end of Ahmadinejad's regime]. (2009, June 22). *Gazeta Wyborcza* [*Electoral Gazette*], p. 2.

*Siła bierze górę w Iranie* [Violence takes over in Iran]. (2009, June 23). *Gazeta Wyborcza* [*Electoral Gazette*], p. 1.

*Teherańczycy znów na ulicach* [Tehranians take to the streets again]. (2009, June 17). *Gazeta Wyborcza* [*Electoral Gazette*], p. 1.

Włodek-Biernat, L. (2009, June 15). *Teheran nie pogodził się z porażką* [Teheran has not accepted defeat]. *Gazeta Wyborcza* [*Electoral Gazette*], p. 11.

Zawadzki, M. (2009, June 15). *Perskie cuda nad urną* [Persian miracles over the voting urn]. *Gazeta Wyborcza* [*Electoral Gazette*], p. 2.

———. (2009, June 16). *Ulubieniec Chomeiniego* [Chomeini's darling]. *Gazeta Wyborcza* [*Electoral Gazette*], p. 2.

*Chapter Four*

# The Portrait of Iran

## *How the Turkish Press Covered the 2009 Presidential Election*

Banu Akdenizli

In June of 2009, Iran, a country that usually registers minimally on the international media screen, despite its political rhetoric as the key player in Islamic fundamentalism, found itself as the major international story when the presidential election in the country exploded into what so many in the media described as a violent unrest. Globally, the narrative that drove the coverage of Iran's election news seemed to be evolving around three main elements: (1) Dramatic scenes of unrest which involved clear protagonists and antagonists (protesters demanding reform versus forces allied with the president); (2) world reaction to the election; and (3) a surprising subtext which involved the role of social media outlets in organizing the uprisings nationally and documenting it internationally for the rest of the world to see (Pew Research Center [PEJ] 2009). In Turkey, the coverage was not that much different than in the rest of the world.

The purpose of this study is to see to what extent the Iranian presidential election has been a part of the Turkish online newspaper agenda, which aspects of the election received the most coverage in Turkey, which newspapers in Turkey offered the most coverage of the election, and if there was a difference of coverage among these Turkish newspapers in terms of tone.

Analysis of the 2009 presidential election in Iran coverage in Turkey comes from the in-depth analysis of news coverage of 630 stories from six online newspaper in Turkey between June 12, 2009, election day, and June 29, 2009, when the partial recount of the election was completed. This study employs the coding scheme devised by PEJ (2009).

Some of the general findings are:


- The storyline that received the most coverage overall within Iran election stories were not the protests that fascinated so many internationally, but stories devoted to postelection analysis. Of the overall newshole (the space available in an outlet for news content), 22.2 percent were devoted to stories that focused on what the election results meant and if there was any wrongdoing involved. Comparison to the 1979 revolution in Iran, discussions on whether a Velvet Revolution was possible, and some comparison of Iran and Turkey to each other were some of the issues covered.
- Not all newspapers devoted the same amount of coverage to the Iran election. Of the newspapers' newshole on Iran stories, 24.3 percent were stories published in *Hürriyet*, one of the most populist and popular newspapers in Turkey. In contrast, *Cumhuriyet* and *Radikal*, two of the newspapers that fall on the left of the political spectrum, devoted the fewest amount of stories to the election in Iran.
- The focus of stories or press narratives about the Iranian presidential election featured considerably much more attention to tactics and strategy. Almost half of the stories overall, 48 percent, were cast in a highly tactical and strategic context. These numbers suggest the tendency of the press to frame coverage of national elections as running narratives about the relative position of the candidates in polls and internal tactical maneuvering to alter those positions.
- While it was expected to see the two candidates, Iranian president Mahmoud Ahmadinejad and opposition presidential candidate Mir Hossein Mousavi, emerge as the two top lead newsmakers (meaning at least 50 percent of a story was about them), a surprise figure, President Barack Obama, emerged as the fourth central figure of the Iranian election.
- Media coverage of the social media component of the Iran election did not find much coverage within Turkish print media. As many mainstream journalists were prohibited from covering the story, much of the Western coverage of the Iran election seemed to be focused on the Twitter revolution narrative. This was not the case in Turkey. Among all the storylines, media coverage of the Iran election ranked as eighth, with a 5.5 percent newshole. And even among those stories, there were only a handful that focused on the role of social outlets in organizing and documenting the uprising. Most of the focus was on foreign journalists who were asked to leave the country.

## THE IRANIAN ELECTION AS A MAJOR STORY

The universe of this study includes six newspapers: *Hürriyet, Sabah, Cumhuriyet, Radikal, Zaman,* and *Yeni Şafak.* These newspapers were chosen according to the following criteria: circulation, industry power, and political stance. The average circulation figures of Turkish newspapers for the month of June 2009 was about 4.7 million (Medyatava 2009). Within this time frame, we see that *Zaman,* with an average of 800,000 circulation rate, ranks at the top; *Hürriyet* at third with 460,000, *Sabah* as fourth with about 352,000. These numbers, of course, do not include the pass-along rate of newspapers, which, depending on the paper, could be estimated to be approximately twice the circulation rate. The same pattern holds true for the online versions of these newspapers. Figures show that the most read newspapers online are *Hürriyet* (number one), *Sabah* (number two), and *Zaman* (number five) (XGazete 2009). In this study due to archival restrictions, online versions of these specific newspapers were considered.

In Turkey, much like in many other countries, specific newspapers, such as *Hürriyet, Sabah,* and *Cumhuriyet,* have an even greater influence because they serve as sources of news that many other outlets look to in making their own programming and editorial decisions. So while it holds true that the overall audience of newspapers has declined over recent years, newspapers still play an important and consequential role in setting the overall news agenda.

The *Zaman* newspaper falls on the right of the political spectrum with its Islamist moderate stance. It is regarded as a voice for Fetullah Gülen (a reformist Islamic scholar and *Nurcu* sect leader in exile in the United States), who through Feza Publishing—which not only hosts *Zaman* but also is home to twenty-five radio stations, a TV channel, and magazines—is able to reach his audience. Besides its high circulation rate, it is also of importance that *Zaman* was the first newspaper to go online in Turkey.

*Hürriyet,* founded in 1948 by Sedat Semavi, is now owned and operated by Doğan Media Group, Turkey's leading media and entertainment conglomerate. Considered as one of the most popular and populist newspapers, *Hürriyet* also has considerable power in setting the news agenda in Turkey, mostly through op-eds written by well-known and established columnists, and it is widely considered to be a nationalistic, prostate, and prosecular newspaper.

*Cumhuriyet,* the oldest newspaper in this sample, was established in 1924. Despite its lower circulation figures today, *Cumhuriyet,* with its reputable and tenured columnists and its center-left political stance, is a newspaper most widely followed by the members of the military, diplomacy, and academia. Despite the trend of media concentration by ownership, this individual newspaper with its oppositional and secular stance has been able to carve out a special position within the Turkish print media landscape.

*Radikal*, owned by Doğan Media Group, was launched in 1996 as an alternative to the existing newspapers at the time. With its liberal left political stance and its name that translates as *Radical*, this Turkish newspaper in comparison to others in print media includes more coverage of news of high culture. Despite its lower circulation rates, *Radikal* is considered to be a newspaper largely for the niche, educated, and urban populations of Turkey.

The *Sabah* newspaper was established in 1985 by Dinç Bilgin. Since 2008, it is owned and operated by Turkuaz Media Holding, part of the Çalık Group. *Sabah* is considered a nationalistic paper, supportive of the ruling Adalet Ve Kalkinma Partisi (AKP) [Justice and Development Party] government in Turkey, mostly due to Çalık's holding owner's affiliation with the Turkish prime minister Tayyip Erdoğan.

*Yeni Şafak* started publication in 1994 as one of the media companies of the Albayrak family, a long-time supporter of Prime Minister Erdoğan. The paper holds a pro-AKP government line and is considered to be a moderately Islamic newspaper.

## THE GENERAL TIMELINE OF THE IRAN
## ELECTION COVERAGE

The time frame under study for the coverage of the Iranian presidential election was between June 12 (the day of the election) and June 29 (the day Mahmoud Ahmadinejad's presidency was confirmed). A look into the coverage timeline (see figure 4.1) revealed that the coverage was somewhat continuous with episodic spikes. The dates that received the highest amount of stories within this time frame were June 23 (with sixty stories, which was 9.8 percent of the Iran election stories newshole), June 22 (with fifty-two stories overall, 7.4 percent of the newshole of Iran election stories), and June 16 (with fifty stories, but with a higher newshole of 7.7 percent due to mainly the length of the stories written).

A closer look at data shows that on June 16 most of the stories centered around the protests. Of the newshole for that day, 33.5 percent consisted of detailed reports on the protests in Tehran. *Sabah* newspaper spotlighted the thousands who flooded the streets in Iran in an article titled *"Yüz binler sel oldu"* ["Thousands Turned into Floods"]. A similar story in *Yeni Şafak* drew attention to civilian loss with *"Iran'da seçim bilançosu: 7 ölü"* ["The Election Balance Sheet in Iran: 7 Deaths"].

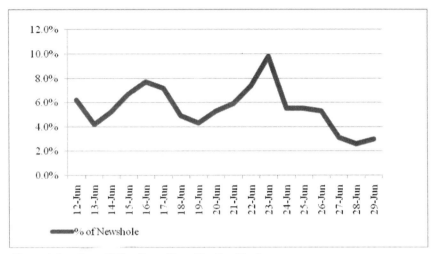

**Figure 4.1. Overall Timeline of Iran Election Stories**

June 22 was the day that a cell phone video of a young woman bleeding to death after she was shot during a protest appeared online. Neda Agha-Soltan instantly became the face of the protest movement. The video of her dying became a staple on YouTube, and her image appeared repeatedly across media outlets. Turkish print media, however, chose to emphasize more the general protests that day (15.2 percent of the Iran election stories for that day), and world reaction to the election (18.3 percent). The death of Neda ranked as the third biggest story at 8.4 percent of the newshole. "*Devrimin Nida'sı sustu*" ["The Revolution's Nida Is Silent"] appeared in *Hürriyet*. It is important here to note that the name *Neda* in Turkish translates into *Nida*, which means "cry, voice" in Turkish. "*Nida Iran'da isyanın simgesi oldu*" ["Nida Became the Face of the Riots"] in *Radikal* was another of the typical headlines that focused on Neda.

A close look at June 23 revealed that more than one-third (34.6 percent) of that day's newshole was devoted to postelection campaign analysis stories in which mostly columnists across all the newspapers devoted their attention to making sense of the complex political turmoil in Iran. In fact, for the period under study, data showed that June 23 was the day with the most op-ed and editorial stories. Lengthy stories that analyzed what a democratic Islamic society means in *Yeni Şafak*, how the mullahs are nervous over the possibility of a Velvet Revolution in *Cumhuriyet*, and drawing out lessons for Turkey from the Iran election drama in *Hürriyet* were some of the examples of analysis stories for June 23. It is also important to note that though shorter in length, June 23 also was home to most of the world reaction stories for the period under study. The increasing diplomatic rift between England and Iran, which resulted in the reciprocal release of diplomatic staff, the European Union countries' negative responses to the political crackdown in Iran, and President Barack Obama's sharpest criticism of Iran's election and protest, saying that he was appalled and outraged, were among the top international stories that were covered across all newspapers in this sample.

## THE MAJOR STORYLINES OF THE ELECTION

As Iran fascinated most of the international media during June 2009, what was the portrait from Turkey? A study of the major storylines of the Iran election coverage in the Turkish press (see figure 4.2) shows that most of the attention was devoted to postelection campaign analysis—22.1 percent of the newspaper newshole.

A June 24 article in *Cumhuriyet* titled *"Cinden mucize beklememeli"* ["Shouldn't Expect a Miracle from the Genie"], focused on how Middle Eastern scholars argued that events in Iran would not result in a regime change due to the fact that Mir Hossein Mousavi himself was part of the old established system. A *Zaman* article on June 22, *"Iran'daki seçimler ve sonuçları"* ["The Iranian Election and Its Results"], argued this point further, saying that the difference between the two candidates was not the main principles of

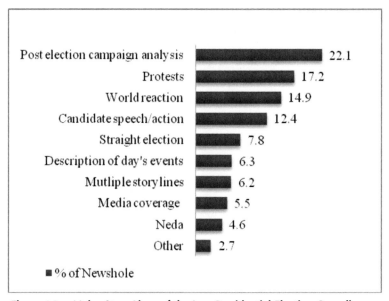

**Figure 4.2.  Major Story Lines of the Iran Presidential Election Overall**

politics but rather their different styles of execution of thought. *"Iran'a bir de buradan bakın"* ["Let's Look at Iran from This Side"], an article in *Hürriyet* on June 15, tried to make sense of how Turkey should approach and respond to the election drama unfolding in Iran.

Coverage of the protests centered around themes of confusion about a controversial and contested Ahmadinejad victory, charges of vote fraud, and Mousavi supporters taking to the streets. Stories in this category focused on the massive outpouring in the streets, clashes between police and the reformist Iranians, how the protests were not confined to Tehran anymore, and the occasional death and damage toll. Some of the typical headlines were *"Iran durulmuyor"* ["Iran Not Settling Down"] June 15 in *Zaman*; *"Muhalefet yasak dinlemedi"* ["The Opposition Did Not Obey the Orders"] June 16 in *Cumhuriyet*; *"Tahran savaş alanı gibi"* ["Tehran Is Like a War Zone"] June 18 in *Hürriyet*; and *"Protestolarda 7 kişi öldü"* ["7 Dead in Protests"] June 16 in *Radikal*.

Since many mainstream journalists were prohibited from covering the story, much of the Western coverage of the Iran election seemed to be focused on the Twitter revolution narrative. This was not the case in Turkey. Among all the story lines, media coverage of the Iran election ranked as eighth, with a 5.5 percent newshole. And even among those stories, there were only a handful that focused on the role of social outlets in organizing and documenting the uprising. Most of the focus was on foreign journalists who were asked to leave the country. Most of the attention to the role of social media seemed to be lost in multiple narrative stories that focused more on the complexities of political maneuvering and turmoil. BBC reporter Jon Leyne, *Newsweek*'s Maziar Bahari, and *Washington Times* reporter Iason Athanasiadis-Fowden were some of the reporters who became part of the story line that focused on the major restrictions on reporting from Iran.

## FRAME

In addition to the topics of the Iran election news coverage, another question is how these stories were framed. A story involving a presidential election could focus on what the candidates said, their strategy, or more. To get at this, the study also looked into how the story line was developed, what the story really was informing the readers about this topic, and what point(s) it was making.

Data show that Iran election stories coverage in the Turkish press were predominantly framed as involving tactics and strategy (see figure 4.3). A close look within the story line level shows that 79.5 percent of the straight election stories were framed as tactics and strategy. Voting-day stories high-lighting the fact that the battle was clearly between the incumbent President Ahmadinejad and his more moderate challenger, Mir Hossein Mousavi, pro-jections of results, and both sides claiming victory were some of the stories in this category.

Also, 61.7 percent of all candidate speech/action stories in the sample such as stories focusing on Mousavi declaring the elections as fraud, Ahmadinejad stat-ing that the Iranians have made their choice, Khamenei's speeches calling for an end to protests, and warnings frequently issued by Ahmadinejad to the West to stop interfering in Iran's internal affairs were framed as tactics and strategy. This scenario was also the case for world reaction stories. More than half (53 percent) of the stories focusing on other countries' response to the Iran election drama were framed as tactics and strategy. Hugo Chavez, Hamid Kharzai, Turkey's president Abdullah Gül, and Prime Minister Tayyip Erdoğan were highlighted as the first officials to congratulate Ahmadinejad for his victory. Concerns voiced by mainly Israel, Germany, England, France, and the United States over the violence against protesters were framed in diplomatic policy and strategy. *"Seçim dünyanın gündeminde"* ["The Election Is on the World's Agenda"] in *Cumhuriyet*; *"Ahmadinejad sevindi batı üzüldü"* ["Ahmadinejad Happy, the West Sad"] in *Yeni Şafak*; *"Ahmadinejad ile yaşamayı öğrenmeliyiz"* ["We Need to Learn to Live with Ahmadinejad"] in *Hürriyet* on June 14, all highlight the cautious approach of the West to the Iran presidential election.

As the protests continued and the death toll began to rise, the frame of world reaction stories also changed. In total, 26 percent of Iran election

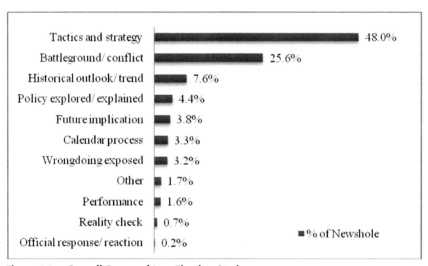

**Figure 4.3. Overall Frame of Iran Election Stories**

stories' newsholes were framed as conflict stories. But within this category, when looked at by story line, we see that 41 percent of the world reaction stories were framed as battleground/conflict stories. The more direct rhetoric, where one group was pitted against another, was coded under this category. A June 22 story in *Zaman* explained how Shimon Perez hoped for the poor Iranian government to disappear. The diplomatic crisis between Iran and England was covered on June 23 in *Hürriyet, Sabah,* and *Cumhuriyet* respectively. President Obama's change of tone, condemnation of Iran's crackdown on protesters, and accusation of Iran's leaders as having fabricated charges against the United States made headlines in *Hürriyet, Yeni Şafak,* and *Sabah* on June 23.

The dramatic scenes of unrest within Iran also changed the portrait of the protest coverage. Specifically, 55 percent of the protest stories in this sample were framed as conflict. Headlines such as *"Tahran'da meydan savaşı"* ["War in Tehran"] (*Cumhuriyet*, June 17); *"Iran'da kan döküldü"* ["Bloodshed in Iran"] (*Hürriyet*, June 17); and articles about followers of Mousavi versus Ahmadinejad followers, as well as protesters demanding reform versus the *Basij* forces, were stories of groups positioned against each other and clearly labeled as protagonists and antagonists. These were predominant in the news.

Historical outlook and trend stories and stories that were framed as policy explanation only made up 12 percent of the newshole. Most of the articles that were framed as such were stories offering a postelection campaign analysis. In fact, 74 percent of the stories that offered a historical context and trend analysis were op-ed pieces that mainly tried to decipher the meaning of the Iran election drama through the lens of the 1979 Islamic Revolution, as well as religious, geopolitical, and cultural underpinnings.

## DATELINE AND FORMAT

During the first day of the election, June 12, 2009, there were a couple of reports with a Tehran dateline. *Hürriyet, Radikal,* and *Yeni Şafak* were the main newspapers in Turkey that had reporters in Iran covering the election firsthand. *"Coşku, nezaket ve hoşgörüyle sandığa"* ["Enthusiasm, Kindness, and Tolerance Mark the Polls"] in an article dated June 12 in *Radikal* describes election day with these words, "Today in Tehran street corners are filled with people from 5 to 65 displaying their support either for Ahmadinejad or Mousavi. People from opposite ends of the sidewalks are displaying their slogans, but without a scuffle or a rumble." As the story with an evident enthusiasm for a real race in Iran gave way to the confusion and contested

Ahmadinejad victory, Mousavi supporters took to the streets, triggering fierce encounters with authorities. Effectively, many mainstream journalists were prohibited from covering the story. Many foreign journalists were unable to renew their expired visas; thus, the world was deprived to a certain extent of firsthand information on the Iran election drama. With this turn of events, much of the firsthand coverage started to come from social media sources such as Twitter and YouTube (PEJ 2009).

Data shows that the overwhelming majority of the Iran election stories in Turkey were filed from Istanbul (see figure 4.4). A close look reveals that more than 80 percent of the newshole were stories with datelines of Turkish national origin. Only about 13 percent of the stories were from Tehran.

This situation also influenced the format of the stories. We see that more than half of the stories were written by staff (see figure 4.5). And, more than one-third were wire stories. Yet, this number can be a bit misleading. It is important to note that, within internal staff stories, 35.8 percent of the newshole were stories that had no bylines. Reports from different sources were compiled and presented by the Dış Haberler Servisi, the Foreign News Bureau, which in Turkish media implies a foreign desk rather than a foreign bureau located in a foreign country and refers mainly to editorial functions within the news organization's home office.

It is also important to note that 24.7 percent of the newshole was devoted to opinion columns written by internal staff reflecting on the Iranian revolution

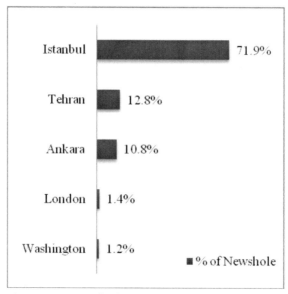

Figure 4.4.   Iran Election Stories Dateline

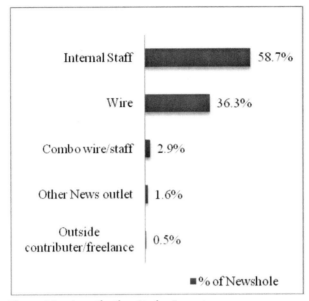

Internal Staff 58.7%

Wire 36.3%

Combo wire/staff 2.9%

Other News outlet 1.6%

Outside contributer/freelance 0.5%

■ % of Newshole

**Figure 4.5. Iran Election Stories Format**

both in an international and national context. "*Iran devrimi yeniden*" ["The Iranian Revolution Again"] in *Cumhuriyet* on June 22 and "*Komsuya uzaktan bakmak*" ["Looking at the Neighbor from Afar"] in *Yeni Şafak* on June 14 were two of the seventy-one opinion pieces in our sample.

## THE MAIN ACTORS OF THE IRAN ELECTION COVERAGE

As a narrative began to emerge with a clear protagonist (Mir Hossein Mousavi who contested the election and demanded a vote recount) and a clear antagonist (Mahmoud Ahmadinejad who declared victory with a solid majority amid charges of vote fraud), Mousavi and Ahmadinejad naturally became the lead newsmakers of the Iran election coverage in Turkey (see figure 4.6).

Three of the leading newsmakers were major players in Iran. With 18.9 percent of the stories, Ahmadinejad emerged as the main newsmaker of the period between June 12 to June 29—meaning at least 50 percent of a story was about him—(about 44 percent of the stories did not have a lead newsmaker). Mousavi, the candidate whose defeat triggered the protests, was the second-leading newsmaker, registering at 13.3 percent. Ayatollah Ali Khamenei, Iran's Supreme Leader, who backed the result and Ahmadinejad's victory, was number three at 8.3 percent.

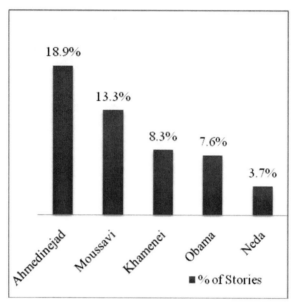

**Figure 4.6.** Lead Newsmakers of the Iran Election Coverage

What is interesting is that President Barack Obama, a central figure in world politics and a respondent to events in Iran, became the fourth lead newsmaker at 7.6 percent. This suggests that the U.S. policy aspect of the election drama became a significant theme within Turkish media as well.

There have been a number of conflicting reports about the death of Neda Agha-Soltan in the world media. Some have indicated that she was part of the Iranian protest movement. Others suggested she was passing by the protests and got out of her car to see the events and to get some fresh air (PEJ 2009). Whatever the case, the image of her dying—caught on amateur video and spread throughout the world via sites like YouTube and Facebook—made her death the symbol of protest. Neda Agha-Soltan, who by many was made into the face, the angel, of the revolution, managed to become the fifth lead newsmaker of the Iran election stories, but with only 3.7 percent of the coverage within the Turkish press.

Tone is an elusive yet unavoidable question when examining the role of news media, particularly during the coverage of an election. The media coverage of the race for president in Iran, which was heavily framed as tactics and strategy, in the end portrayed both candidates in a neutral tone. The tone of 44 percent of stories that had Ahmadinejad as lead newsmaker and 61 percent of the ones about Mousavi were primarily neutral (see table 4.1).

Table 4.1. Tone for Lead Newsmakers, Percent of Stories

| Tone | Ahmadinejad | Mousavi |
|------|-------------|---------|
| Neutral | 43.7 | 60.9 |
| Positive | 34.5 | 32.2 |
| Negative | 21.8 | 6.9 |

To examine tone, this study employed PEJ's cautious and conservative approach. The study examined not just whether assertions in stories were positive or negative, but also if they were inherently neutral. Coverage was measured by story, and for a story to be deemed as having a negative or positive tone, the negative assertions in a story had to outweigh positive assertions by a margin of at least 1.5 to 1 in order for that story to be deemed negative.

The findings of this study suggest that the Turkish press, in their treatment of Ahmadinejad and Mousavi, overall were fairly balanced. An even closer look shows that for both candidates their positive outweighed their negative assertions. While 34.5 percent of Ahmadinejad lead newsmaker stories were positive, 21.8 percent were negative. The same pattern was true for Mousavi, but what is important to notice here is that his positive outnumbered his negative stories by a bigger margin. While there were only 6.9 percent of stories that were negative, 32.2 percent of stories with Mousavi as the lead newsmaker were positive.

## HOW IRAN ELECTION COVERAGE VARIED BY OUTLETS

Another important element in considering tone coverage is the source of the news. The evidence in this study suggests that while overall the coverage of the government and the opposition forces in Iran were mostly neutral across all newspapers, there were differences when it came to individual outlets in comparing the ratio of positive stories to negative ones.

To further assess tone in coverage in this study besides considering tone for stories with distinct lead newsmakers, we also considered tone for stories which had no apparent lead newsmaker. All comments that have either a negative or positive tone in the reporting for each of the two variables, government (such as stories on Ahmadinejad and Khamenei) and opposition (such as stories on Mousavi and the protesters), were tallied. Direct and indirect quotes were counted along with assertions made by the journalists themselves.

A general assessment of tone both for government and opposition within our sample showed that 76.8 percent of stories were neutral in tone for the government, and 91.4 were neutral for the opposition. Yet, by and large, the negatives for the government at 14.4 percent outweighed the negative tones for the opposition by a wider margin. Only 1.9 percent of the total stories were negative in tone for the opposition.

The tone of *Hürriyet*'s coverage, one of the more populist nationalistic pro-state newspapers, who also provided the most Iran election coverage within our sample (see figure 4.7), was more negative when it came to evaluating tone for the ones in power. Of election stories, 19.1 percent were negative in tone for the government forces. Only 3.8 percent of Iran election stories reflected the protesters in a negative way. The same tendency held true for the *Sabah* newspaper. In its coverage of the election stories, 13.9 percent was unfavorable toward the government. Strikingly, *Sabah* had no negative coverage of the protesters.

*Cumhuriyet*, with its oppositional secular stance on issues, had mostly neutral stories both for the government and the opposition. While it had no stories that portrayed the government forces in a positive way, the amount of positive and negative coverage of the opposition was equal at 2.0 percent.

*Radikal*, another newspaper that falls more on the left side of the political spectrum, had more negative stories for the government at 16.3 percent. Of the stories in *Radikal*, 14 percent had a positive tone for the opposition, and only 2.3 percent of the stories portrayed Mousavi and his followers in a negative way.

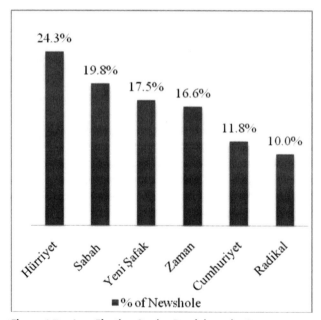

**Figure 4.7.   Iran Election Stories Breakdown by Source**

The Iranian government fared best in *Zaman* and *Yeni Şafak*, the two newspapers considered to be the two Islamic newspapers within this sample. In both of these newspapers, the tone of coverage for government forces was more positive than negative. While 13.1 percent of the election stories had a positive portrayal of the government forces in *Zaman*, only 3.8 percent of the stories were positive for the opposition. The margin was even bigger in *Yeni Şafak* stories. In this newspaper, 10.7 percent of election stories had positive assertions in regards to the government. Only 1.8 percent of stories had a positive tone for the opposition.

The newspapers exhibited minor differences when it came to the story line of the election. Out of the six newspapers in our sample, four of them had the same top four stories: *Hürriyet*, *Zaman*, *Sabah*, and *Yeni Şafak* put postcampaign analysis, protests, world reaction to the election, and candidate speeches or actions at the top of their agenda. Three of these four, *Hürriyet*, *Sabah*, and *Yeni Şafak*, all devoted the most coverage to the postelection analysis (21.9 percent, 28.0 percent, and 28.4 percent respectively). While protests were second in number of story lines in *Hürriyet* (20.5 percent), *Zaman* (17.3 percent), and *Sabah* (19.3 percent), *Yeni Şafak* gave the least amount of coverage to the protests among all six newspapers with 11.0 percent of its newshole as the fourth biggest story.

*Cumhuriyet* and *Radikal* were the two newspapers that offered multiple story lines in their coverage. A roundup of various events and overlapping story lines differentiated the coverage here. Of the two, *Cumhuriyet* showed more resemblance to the newspapers mentioned above. Just like the others, it also devoted the most coverage to postelection analysis, with 21.9 percent of its newshole. *Radikal*, in contrast, chose to highlight candidate speeches or actions at number one with 19.4 percent. It was the only newspaper to have straight election result stories as the second biggest story line at 14.5 percent. In all other newspapers' stories, though dominant the first day of the election, straight election results did not register in the top five of their respective newsholes.

## DISCUSSION AND CONCLUSION

As neighboring non-Arab Islamic countries, Turkey and Iran's relationship is marked by ups and downs in history (Gunter 1998). Secularism versus Islamism, Turkey's cooperation with Israel, Northern Iraq, and the Kurdish problem are some of the ongoing issues that have from time to time put pressure on the rapport of these two countries (Olson 2004). In recent years, especially with the AKP in power, Turkey and Iran appear to be getting closer, exhibiting intent to improve bilateral relationships. Turkish president Abdullah Gül in November 2009, during a meeting in Ankara, said "that his country is keen to bolster relations with neighboring Iran," and Turkish prime minister Tayyip Erdoğan's exhibiting what some regard as a "conciliatory view toward Iran's nuclear program" (Jones 2009) are some of the examples of this approach cited in the media. Add to this circumstance Turkey's geopolitical importance for the Western world as a longtime NATO member and ally and Turkey's approach to Iran and related news becomes a politically charged issue.

A more qualitative assessment of the overall coverage of the 2009 presidential election in Iran suggests how significant the election was for not only Turkey but also other countries such as the United States, the European Union, Israel, and the Middle East in general. Volatile Middle East politics, a nuclear program in the making, coupled with images of protesters flooding the streets of Iran's major cities cheering for the opposition made the events in Iran headline news throughout the world.

The story of the Iranian election in the Turkish press was a political one. The coverage mostly centered around analyzing what the results meant for both Iran and Turkey, and once again on a larger scale seemed to concentrate on issues such as the compatibility between Islam and the Western conception of democracy.

## REFERENCES

Gunter, M. M. (1998). Turkey and Iran face off in Kurdistan. *Middle East Quarterly,* *5*(1), 32–40.

Jones, D. (2009). Turkey–Iran ties continue to worry West. *Voice of America.* http://www.voa.com.

Medyatava. (2009). Circulation data for newspapers. http://www.medyatava.com/tiraj.asp.

Olson, R. (2004). *Turkey-Iran relations, 1979–2004: Revolution, ideology, war, coups and geopolitics.* Costa Mesa, CA: Mazda Publishers.

Pew Research Center's Project for Excellence in Journalism (PEJ). (2009). *News coverage index reports.* Washington, D.C. http://www.journalism.org.

XGazete. (2009). İnternette en çok okunan gazeteler. http://www.xgazete.com/net-tiraj.php.

*Chapter Five*

# A Comparative Analysis of the Egyptian and Iranian Presidential Elections Media Coverage

Rasha Allam

Fair and independent election is an integral component in the democratic life of any country. The media are considered one of the main players whose role is to inform citizens about different choices through professional reporting. In this glasnost era and with the rapid technological developmental trends, the way of media coverage has started to take new shapes; presidential elections coverage becomes one of the media's top agenda topics for the inclusion of complicated values and variables that affect the way of coverage. The appearance of the new media and its widespread usage has placed the state-owned media in jeopardy as suppression of opinion becomes quite difficult.

The political environment affects the kind of media coverage within all outlets: state-owned, oppositional, and independent. The Egyptian presidential election in 2005 and the Iranian election in 2009, although not identical, have some features in common. Both countries' traditional media coverage show bias and were not objective toward all the candidates. Both countries have media laws which are powerful tools to suppress media freedoms.

The Egyptian presidential election in 2005 has urged the analysis of different media outlets and the degree of abidance by the news values. In Iran, the social media networks have showed the powerful impact of the new media in threatening government control over the media, questioning its credibility.

In both countries, media ownership plays an influential role in the kind of news depicted. News in particular is largely affected by the kind of ownership; therefore, a government or state-owned media propagates merely for the government, and the programs are designed to be conventional with the owners' (government) perspectives (Tehranian 2001).

## CHANGING ENVIRONMENT

In Egypt, the constitutional change has marked a significant change in the Egyptian political sphere. The media were trying to reflect this change in the media sector in order to exhibit a more democratic type of coverage when Egyptian television tried to provide a forum for the multicandidate presidential election as a credible source of information for the Egyptian citizens.

In Iran, the new media have played a tremendous role as carrier for news feeds and organizers for specific movements promoting freedom of expression (Center for International Media Assistance 2009). This trend calls into question the concept that only allows the media system to be a reflection of the political system. New trends in media are challenging the current authoritarian systems (Hafez 2009).

## LEGAL OBLIGATIONS

Authoritarian media systems always encompass media laws that stifle freedom of expression and enable the government to indirectly suppress opinions and oppositional voices. Both Egypt, an authoritarian/transitional country, and Iran, an authoritarian one, have ratified the International Covenant on Civil and Political Rights, in which Article 19 states:

> Everyone shall have the right to freedom of expression; this right shall include freedom to seek, receive and impart information and ideas of all kinds, regardless of frontiers, either orally, in writing or in print, in the form of art, or through any other media of his choice.

However, this article is violated in practice through different laws that suppress freedom of expression.

For example, in Egypt, within the Constitution, there are many articles that have double meanings, guaranteeing freedom of expression on one side, and on the other side, demanding restrictions that hold back this freedom. In Article 47 of the Egyptian Constitution, freedom of expression is guaranteed: "Freedom of opinion shall be guaranteed. Every individual shall have the right to express his opinion and to publicize it verbally or in writing or by photography or by other means within the limits of the law" (Egyptian Constitution). Moreover, Article 48 also reads that "Freedom of the press, printing, publication and mass media shall be guaranteed. Censorship on newspapers is forbidden as well as notifying, suspending or canceling them by administrative methods" (International Foundation for Electoral Systems 2005).

Yet, that article is followed by a statement that reads: "In a state of emergency or in time of war a limited censorship may be imposed on the newspapers, publications and mass media in matters related to public safety or purposes of national security in accordance with the law." This mirrors the vagueness of the Iranian emergency law where there is no definition of the term *emergency*, nor an explanation of what might be considered a threat to the national security. In return, journalists must practice self-censorship since the contradicting laws are in themselves restrictive tools that inhibit freedom of expression.

As for Iran, Article 500 of Iran's Penal Code states that "anyone who undertakes any form of propaganda against the state . . . will be sentenced to between three months and one year in prison." Yet, the existence of vague terms such as *propaganda*, without a well-defined subcode, leaves enough room for the government to interfere and to suppress opinions. Moreover, Article 4 states: "no government or non-government official should resort to coercive measures against the press . . . or attempt to censure and control the press"; and Article 25 states that those who "instigate and encourage people to commit crimes against the domestic security or foreign policies of the state, should those actions bear adverse consequences," and adds, "if no evidence is found of such consequences, [writers] shall be subject to a decision of the religious judge according to Islamic penal code." Again, no definition is stated for the phrase *crimes against the domestic security* or how inappropriateness is to be measured (False Freedom 2007).

## PRESIDENTIAL ELECTIONS MEDIA COVERAGE

The presidential election in Egypt that took place in 2005 included several candidates who were running, yet the focus was on three main players: the National Democratic candidate, Mohamed Hosni Mubarak; the Ghad oppositional party candidate, Ayman Nour; and El Wafd oppositional party candidate No'man Gomaa. Similarly, in Iran, although Mahmoud Ahmadinejad was running against three other candidates, the focus was on Ahmadinejad and Mir Hossein Mousavi.

For the first time in both countries, media monitoring was adapted for elections. In Egypt, because media monitoring was experienced for the first time, and due to the lack of media monitoring poll centers, several entities have conducted independent studies on their own with their own methodologies and criteria for determining the main variables to measure the efficacy of the media outlets in the presidential election coverage. First, the Egyptian Radio and Television Union (ERTU) organized a committee under the Egyptian

Minister of Information to establish the guideline principles for presidential election coverage in radio and television. Moreover, a media-monitoring committee was established to observe the coverage of the different channels to the presidential election and their abidance by these principles (Egyptian State Information System 2005).

Among the main principles are equal coverage for all candidates, clear differentiation between personal opinions and facts, prevention of any liable information or the intrusion of the candidates' private lives, differentiation between candidates' coverage and paid advertising, ensuring equal access for all candidates in their paid advertising (Egyptian State Information System 2005). Yet, some vague principles were included as well, such as to preserve the national unity of the Egyptian society without setting subcodes that defines the term *national unity*, which led journalists to practice self-censorship to avoid being exposed to penalties.

The state-owned media were mainly aiming toward three goals: generate public awareness about the importance of participating in the election, reflect the activities of the candidates through news coverage, and present all candidates to the audience, stating each one's program. Law 174 regulates the election campaigning and states the following:

> Providing full disclosure, when broadcasting public opinion polls, of the parties who conducted and financed the poll, the questions that were included in the poll, the size and location of the sample, the method by which the poll was conducted, the means by which the data was collected, the date on which it was conducted, and the margin of error of the results. (Egyptian State Information System 2005)

A committee was established to monitor the campaigns conducted by all candidates and to evaluate their abidance by the above-mentioned standards of Law 174.

Although the national Egyptian television networks were trying to give equal time for candidates to broadcast their programs and interviews were held with all candidates with almost equal timing, the national newspapers showed a bias toward the president. One media-monitoring organization found that Egypt's largest daily newspaper, *Al Ahram*, devoted more space to Mubarak than to all other candidates combined. The Egyptian Organization for Human Rights released a report on August 29 detailing the media's progovernment bias. "The ruling newspapers have been conscripted for daily propaganda for the candidate of the ruling National Democratic Party," it concluded (Assaf 2007). Private satellite television exercised more freedom than the national television channels as in-depth interviews, in terms of sensitive issues tackled and equal time given to the candidates, were conducted more often in these private channels.

Another media-monitoring organization, the Cairo Institute for Human Rights (CIHR), conducted a comprehensive study in order to monitor the coverage of the different media outlets for the multicandidate presidential campaigns. The CIHR conducted a content analysis study for six television channels: Channel 1, Channel 2, and Channel 3, which are the three main terrestrial channels; and Nile News, which is a specialized news channel. These channels operate under the ERTU. The second set includes Dream TV2 and Al Mehwer TV, which are the first two Egyptian private satellite channels. As for the print media, a set of seventeen newspapers and magazines were chosen, ranging from daily, weekly, national, partisan, and independent. The CIHR measured the amount dedicated for each candidate in the different television channels that started daily from 6 p.m. until 1 a.m. It also measured the space given for each candidate in the different print outlets. Additionally, the CIHR studied the amount of positive and negative coverage presented about each candidate.

The study's results were similar to the ERTU's where the broadcast media were more balanced in their coverage toward different candidates when compared to the print media. Yet, the print media were able to tackle more sensitive issues, more than the broadcast media, which focused mainly on reports about candidates. The study found that although the national newspapers have shown great bias toward the National Democratic Party (NDP) candidate, the independent newspapers maintained balanced coverage between the presidential candidates. And although the national television channels were balanced, the private satellite channels showed a bias toward the NDP presidential candidate (Media and Presidential Elections 2005).

This situation is similar to Iran, where the term *equitability* was not professionally practiced. President Ahmadinejad was given ten times the amount of time on national radio and TV, more than other candidates running against him (No Independent Coverage 2009). Moreover, it was reported that the press freedom organization stated: "There are many state-owned newspapers but their reporting is all the same. The radio and TV stations are used by the government while the so-called opposition newspapers are used above all for factional infighting. They do not unfortunately serve as forums where opinions can be expressed freely" (Center for International Media Assistance 2009). In addition, the government practiced some form of suppression over nongovernmental newspapers. For example, the proreform newspaper *Yas-e No* [*New Jasmine*] was banned on June 11, 2009, one day before the election. The *Yas-e No* was banned previously for criticizing the government (Ridley 2009).

Reporters without Borders reported that independency of coverage was not practiced as about fifteen journalists were threatened or sent to be questioned since the Iranian election campaigns started in May 21, 2009. These journalists were questioned for writing political opinions against President Mahmoud Ahmadinejad (No Independent Coverage 2009).

For Iran, the BBC had published its monitoring report of Iran's presidential election and stated that the state-owned media had supported the "principle-ists"; nevertheless, the Internet, with its new social networks, have played a role in influencing the public (Iran's Presidential Election Guide 2009, June 12). The Western media have heavily criticized the Iranian presidential election results, claiming abnormalities in the results since there was very little difference between the percentages of votes for each candidate. These small differences mean that Mahmoud Ahmadinejad got lots of votes in both rural and urban areas, and his opponents got few votes even in their home regions and provinces (Iran's Presidential Election 2009, July).

## SOCIAL MEDIA IN EGYPT AND IRAN

For Egypt's 2005 presidential election, the social media was still in its infant stage, and because usage was very poor, not much was accomplished. Although these websites have a remarkable impact today and have promoted public movements, such as the April 6 strike initiated by a girl using Facebook, they were not on the scene during the 2005 election.

However, the social media in Iran, including bloggers, Facebook, and Twitter, have played a powerful role in Iran's 2009 presidential election. This new media altered the way Iranian citizens communicate, as they proved their efficacy in organizing social movements. Through the Twitter feeds that captured scenes and videos, citizens were able to organize protests and show their outraged feelings. Social media also played a role in informing people all over the world about the events taking place in Iran.

Although the social media had a powerful effect in the communication process, the Iranian government blocked several websites for the oppositional parties, especially Facebook, Twitter, and YouTube. This highly regulated environment is a reflection of the authoritarian regime operating in the country and the legal environment that disables freedom of expression (Heacock 2009).

## TRANSNATIONAL MEDIA

In Egypt, there is only one transitional channel, the Nile TV International in English. It operates with the ERTU, which is governmentally controlled.

So, not only did the social media in Iran have a great influence and played a role in influencing the public, transnational media was also a main player in the

Iranian sphere. Press TV was established in 2007 to provide political commentary and news in English targeted toward the Western countries with something similar to the content broadcast on CNN, BBC, and other Western news services. Moreover, Al Alam satellite station addressed the Arab countries in their language. Both channels have played a role in the Iranian presidential election through their coverage, especially Press TV, where the foreign journalists were banned from covering any of the election process or the protests.

## DISCUSSION AND CONCLUSION

- In Egypt, there are several challenges to the media in the election coverage. First, the presidential election presents a new model for citizens where they have to choose from multiple candidates. In this transitional stage, the media have a developmental role in educating people about how to make choices between candidates and why it is important to vote.
- As for Iran, although the traditional media face heavy restrictions from the government due to its full control and due to the authoritarian system that the Iranian media operate under, the social media have marked their influence on citizens' mobilization and the implications of the new technologies in pushing democratic movements forward.

Both countries should ensure the following:

- News values such as accuracy, fairness, and balance must be ensured through a set code of conduct.
- Equitability measures in all types of media should be provided: governmental, oppositional, and independent.
- A well-defined media-monitoring criteria still needs to develop.
- Regulations for media election coverage must be adapted to ensure efficacy of coverage for all media outlets: governmental, oppositional, and independent.

## REFERENCES

Assaf, S. (2007, May). Comparative report of the state of the media in Egypt, Jordan, Lebanon, and Morocco. *Promoting the rule of law and integrity in Arab countries project*. UNDP.

Center for International Media Assistance National Endowment for Democracy. (2009, July). *The role of new media in 2009 Iranian elections*. http://cima.ned.org.

70 *Rasha Allam*

The Egyptian Constitution. The Electoral Knowledge Network. http://aceproject.org/ero-en/regions/mideast/EG/Egyptian%20Constitution%20-%20english.pdf/view.

Egyptian State Information System. (2005). *Presidential election 2005: Principles and standards.* http://www.sis.gov.eg/En/Politics/PElection/election/Standards/040202050000000001.htm.

False freedom: Online censorship in the Middle East and North Africa. (2007). Press Freedom Index.

Hafez, K. (2009, July). Communicative trends: Arab media and the culture of democracy. Paper presented at the meeting of The Arab-U.S. Association for Communication Educators (AUSCE). Cairo, Egypt.

Heacock, R. (2009, June). Cracking down on digital communication and political organizing in Iran. OpenNet Initiative.

International Foundation for Electoral Systems (IFES). (2005). A regional strategy for promoting a free media and freedom of expression in the Middle East and North Africa: Decriminalizing defamation and insult laws against journalists and the media through legislative reforms, executive decrees and prioritized law enforcement policy statements. Rule of Law White Paper Series.

Iran's presidential election 2009. (2009, July). Wikipedia. http://en.wikipedia.org/wiki/Iranian_presidential_election_2009.

Iran's presidential election guide. (2009, June 12). BBC Monitoring.

Media and presidential elections. (2005, May). Cairo Institute for Human Rights (CIHR).

No independent coverage of presidential election campaign in Iranian media. (2009, June 10). Reporters without Borders. http://www.rsf.org/No-independent-coverage-of.html.

Ridley, Y. (2009). Media coverage of the Iranian elections. Media Monitors Network—Mobile Edition.

Tehranian, M. (2001, April 18). Diverse ownership, diverse media. You own it, you control it. *The Iranian.* http://www.iranian.com/MajidTehranian/2001/April/Media/index.html.

*Chapter Six*

# The Presidential Election in Iran in 2009

## Pre- and Postelection News Coverage in the German Press

Christine Horz

The presidential election of the Islamic Republic of Iran (IRI) in June 2009 and the coverage in selected German newspapers are the subject of this chapter. The conflict over the presidential election in Iran began after the final count between the four approved presidential candidates, Mousavi, Karubi, Rezai, and the incumbent Ahmadinejad. Triggered by the possible manipulation to the benefit of Ahmadinejad, the voters started demonstrating peacefully in the streets and demanded a new election, which had been rejected by the Guardian Council. The decision of the Supreme Leader Khamenei to declare the election completed and the confirmation of Ahmadinejad as the president for four more years led to protests in Iran, where demonstrating people also died. The demonstrations continued for days.

The topic of Iran in general attracts a lot of interest in the German media, especially since the Islamic Revolution of 1979. Whereas most of the press coverage formerly confined the news about the IRI to the nuclear program and to the anti-Western rhetoric of its president Ahmadinejad, the events after the presidential election made the necessity of a completely different perception of Iran obvious (Steinbach 2009, June 6). Journalists, as well as the audience, realized the paradox that Iran is at the same time a theocratic regime, rejecting foreign journalists, and a dynamic, young, cosmopolitan society that informed the world about their situation via modern and up-to-date Internet media. This new flow of information raises questions about the coverage of the election and the protests in the German press. Due to the briefness of this survey, only three nationwide newspapers have been selected, and a choice of their articles on the subject will be analyzed: the *Frankfurter Allgemeine*

*Zeitung (FAZ)*, which reflects the conservative and neoliberal milieu; the *Frankfurter Rundschau (FR)*, with a liberal attitude; and the *Junge Welt (jw)*, which stands for leftist tendencies. All three can be acquired in Germany at the local newspaper kiosk. In each paper, two dominant authors and their selected articles for the time frame of June 2009 will be described in order to contribute to a better understanding of the spectrum of opinions about the presidential election in Iran found in German newspapers.

## FRANKFURTER ALLGEMEINE ZEITUNG

The *Frankfurter Allgemeine Zeitung (FAZ)* was founded shortly after WWII. The first issue was released on November 1, 1949, in the city of Frankfurt am Main in Western Germany. The *FAZ* has a print run of 479,541 in the third quarter of 2009 and is one of the biggest and the most influential nationwide newspapers in Germany. The editorial policy is established by the five publishers, not by the editor in charge, and is focused on in-depth reporting and background analysis. With this policy and its factual style, the *FAZ* reflects conservative milieus and elites, politicians, and—because of its extensive economy section—the financial sector. The broadsheet-formatted newspaper started to insert a few photographs only after a makeover in 2007. Before, it was made exclusively of written text. In addition to the daily paper *FAZ*, the publishers serve the audience with a weekend edition, the *Frankfurter Allgemeine Sonntagszeitung (FAS)*. It follows a different concept and style and is not the subject of this study. The daily *FAZ* traditionally uses a text medium, rather than photographs, and thus does not aim to provoke emotions. The selected authors and therefore the actors of the editorial strategy refer to their own experience in Iran. Four rather well-known journalists occupy the position of Middle Eastern correspondents in the *FAZ* and are currently involved in news reporting about this country: Rainer Hermann, Christiane Hoffmann, Ahmad Taheri, and Wolfgang Günther Lerch. The two first journalists and their articles will be described in the following paragraph.

Rainer Hermann is fifty-four years old, is an Islamic studies scholar, and has worked as a foreign news correspondent for the *FAZ* since 1998. Hermann reported in situ from Tehran with the beginning protests. He wrote, "Mousavi Demands for Annulment of the Election in Iran" (2009, June 15a). The article can be seen as an example for the author's matter-of-fact reports. It is focused on the particular election results per candidate, the second term of Ahmadinejad, and on the mass protests in the streets of Tehran. His commentary in the article "The Power of the Armed Forces" predicts a new era when the theocrats will be replaced by a militia which recruits in the underprivileged classes (2009, June 15b). The author uses the term *the mullahs* to express a rejection of the theocrats in Iran. Hermann speaks of the unlikelihood of a new election and links Ahmadinejad's victory with European and U.S. political relations with the IRI. The correspondent thus establishes a frame that the incumbent Ahmadinejad will undoubtedly be the new president and that Western countries will not see major changes in Iran in the near future. Hermann underlines his perspective with a report about the yet silent *Bazaris*, the powerful traders in Tehran's major marketplace, who played a historic role in the Islamic Revolution in 1979 (2009, June 18). A further characteristic of Hermann's reporting is his distance from the Iranian protesters for which the following subheading can serve as an example: "The People Enjoy the Protests." He continues in the article: "Possibly, some will stay at home during the summer and make demonstrating their most important holiday-activity. Obviously, a lot of them enjoy the demonstrations; they consider demonstrating as their only 'weapon'" (2009, June 17).

The second journalist for the *FAZ*, Christiane Hoffmann, is forty-two years old and has studied Slavic and Eastern European History. She joined the *FAZ* in 1994. Only after she followed her husband, the former Swiss ambassador in Iran, did she start reporting for five years from Tehran. Returning to Germany, she covers Iranian topics in the *FAZ* and in public events like the International Bookfair in Frankfurt, or in television interviews. One of her articles in June 2009 can be translated: "With Obama's Means: Mousavi's Election Campaign against Ahmadinejad" (2009, June 6). She compares the modern means of campaigning via Facebook and YouTube used by the reformist candidate with those of U.S. president Obama's. In contrast to Hermann's articles, she goes into detail about the Green Movement in Iran, but in following articles, she points out that "the reformers are not against the system" and that a regime change is "mere wishful thinking" (2009, June 17). She depicts the presidential candidate Mir Hossein Mousavi as a weak political figure who "neither has the charisma nor the authority to make him a revolution leader" (2009, June 22).

## FRANKFURTER RUNDSCHAU

The liberal *Frankfurter Rundschau (FR)* was licensed on August 1, 1945, by the U.S.-Allied Forces in the west sector of postwar Germany. At present, it has a scope of 192,297 daily copies and has a clear affiliation to the Social-Democratic Party and the Green Party—a connection that is unique in the German press landscape. The *FR* cannot refer to in situ correspondents in Iran. During the coverage of the presidential election and the protests in the aftermath, the *FR* clearly committed itself by text, image, color, and political symbols to the Green Movement in Iran. To make this position visible, headlines and articles were provided with large-sized photographs or computer-generated pictures. On June 17, 2009, the Islamic and now politically symbolic color green was adopted to cover the front page of the *FR* together with the Persian words *Iran-o azad kon!* (Free Iran!) with a German translation in the footnote.

Currently, Middle Eastern correspondents Inge Günther, Birgit Cerha, Martin Gehlen, and Karl Grobe are reporting for the *FR*. The articles of two authors are described here: the political journalists Martin Gehlen and Karl Grobe. Gehlen is part of the editorial staff for international politics for the *FR* and is not reporting from Iran. He studied social science. In his interview with the former foreign minister and unofficial party leader of the *mehzat-e azadi* (freedom movement) in Iran, Ebrahim Yazdi (Gehlen 2009, June 12), Gehlen asks Yazdi about the chance of a regime change in Iran and the possible harmonization between Iran and the West. This focus has been cemented in his future articles; in fact, Gehlen depicted a positive image of the protesters in the *FR*. This can be underlined by his crucial contribution entitled, "We Are the People" (2009, June 16). This headline is well known to German readers since it was this slogan that was shouted by Eastern German citizens against the former German Democratic Republic (GDR) regime at "Monday demonstrations" before the Berlin Wall was torn down in 1989. Through this rhetoric, Gehlen linked the protests in Iran with the demonstrations of Eastern German citizens against the oppression of an unjust regime. At the same time, he thus legitimizes the strategy of his advocacy for the Green Movement in the IRI as utter solidarity with the Iranian people.

The second journalist, Karl Grobe, worked for the *FR* for over thirty-three years before his retirement in 2001, but he still contributes as a freelance journalist for this newspaper. Grobe describes Mousavi as "a mere symbol of the people demonstrating. They would like to block the dogmatism of the Iranian society out" (2009, June 17). He discusses a "cultural revolution" and the wish of the young urban citizens who "long for freedom of literature and of music, for equal rights for women, but without becoming a clone of the western capitalist culture." He thus tries to analyze the motivations of the Green Movement and considers background information. In his article, "Waiting for the Twelfth Imam" (Grobe 2009, June 20), as an experienced correspondent Grobe describes the theocratical system in the IRI and the conflicting ideas. He argues that Islam can be harmonized with "modern reasons of state" that make it unnecessary to overthrow the whole Iranian system. In contrast to Martin Gehlen, he stresses ways to transform Iran from within and thus promotes a rather evolutionary process in the country.

## *JUNGE WELT*

The *Junge Welt (jw)* was founded on January 12, 1947, in East Germany. The newspaper has been the official organ of the Free German Youth (FDJ) affiliated to the socialist politburo in the former GDR. After the reunification of both German states in 1989, the *jw* was relaunched with a new editorial board. Since 1995, the newspaper is organized as a cooperative, and that is what makes it independent from advertisement. Its status as a cooperative explains why the intertrade organization IVW provides no information about the print run. By its own account, *jw* puts out about 20,000 printed copies a day. Pictures and images are used, but not extensively. This newspaper incorporates factions, typical for the younger German history: *jw* maintained a reservoir for leftist ideologies. The editorial strategy is focused on an anti-imperialistic battle. The presidential election in Iran has been covered from an Ahmadinejad-friendly perspective. The *jw* is observed by the German secret service.

Correspondents Karin Leukefeld, Rainer Rupp, Jürgen Cain Külbel, and Werner Pirker cover Middle Eastern topics. Two journalists were selected from this list who delivered major contributions—Jürgen Cain Külbel, as correspondent reporting from Tehran, and Werner Pirker.

Külbel worked as a criminologist in East Germany before being expelled. After the reunification in 1989, he became a journalist and book author. He works for the Syrian newspaper *Al Watan* and has written a book about the homicide of the Lebanese prime minister Hariri. After the protests in Iran began, Külbel described the protesters in his article "Loser Wants to Win" as hooligans, rioting and burning across the city (2009, June 16). He depicts Ahmadinejad as the clear winner of the elections and thus links the editorial strategy with the supposed struggle of Ahmadinejad against imperialistic pressure from the United States and Europe. Mousavi's demand for annulment of the vote is in Külbel's view the reason for the riots and the proof that the candidate is a bad loser (2009, June 17).

The second reporter for *jw*, Werner Pirker, is a long-term member of the editorial board. He worked between 1975 to early 1990 as a journalist for the Austrian Communist Party, and between 1997 and 2000, he occupied the position of the vice-editor in charge in the *Junge Welt*. Pirker criticized the Green Movement in Iran as an "antisocial revolution as it stands against the anti-imperialist aspect of the Islamic Revolution" and only serves the consumerist elites (2009, June 20). He criticized the news coverage of the *FAZ* and their wishful thinking of a possible change in Iran. Finally, Pirker saw the risk of this change in making this "Obama's first success in foreign affairs, without having paid for it." The sovereignty of the Iranian leadership and the Iranian state as it is should be maintained, for Pirker saw it as a precondition for democracy (2009, June 22).

## IRANIAN EXILES IN THE GERMAN PUBLIC SPHERE

Next to German journalists and correspondents, diasporic Iranian experts contributed their own newspaper articles about the election and the protests in Iran. Whereas the press coverage from German journalists is mostly based on information from news agencies or second- or thirdhand information, the Iranian authors deliver important contributions to the public discourse as correspondents. While a foreign news correspondent in general is perceived to fulfill the position of a translator of different cultural orientation systems and codes (Hafez 2001), it means he needs in-depth knowledge about the culture and language he will translate. Major parts of the German press do not want to or are not able to pay a correspondent. Moreover, German journalists and their families find it hard to live in Islamic countries. Ideally, a correspondent reporting about or from a different country has a similar cultural background. Despite the existing heterogeneous, multicultural German society, journalists or media professionals with non-German backgrounds in general are rare or have marginal positions in the editorial departments (Ouaj 1999). It was not until the presidential election in Iran that co-workers of Iranian origin were asked their opinions and taken seriously as experts in the media.

There are currently four authors of Iranian origin. The first two are the experienced correspondent Ahmad Taheri and the publicist Bahman Nirumand. Both belong to the generation of Iranian exiles after the Islamic Revolution. Nirumand is still not allowed to reenter the IRI. Katajun Amirpur and Navid Kermani, a married couple who are both well-known Islamic studies scholars, are intellectuals who grew up in Germany. Kermani has been the only Iranian author who flew to Iran during the protests and took part in a demonstration.

Next to these experts, translators like Shahram Najafi worked for the newspapers and published translations of Iranian blogs, tweets, and websites in June 2009. A characteristic economic strategy of the press is to get firsthand reporting or at least additional information on demand from these freelance journalists or experts. Furthermore, the particular translations of Iranian protests online in June 2009 reflects editorial strategies because it allows the reader an intuitive impression about the struggle of the Green Movement and can thus provoke positive emotions toward the Iranian demonstrators.

## DISCUSSION AND CONCLUSION

This brief chapter can only draw an exemplary sketch of the news coverage about the presidential election in Iran in the German press. For now, it can be concluded that each newspaper reflects a specific approach toward the pre- and postelection events in Iran. If a reciprocity between journalists and the public is assumed, it could be said that the audiences of each newspaper live in different worlds. In reference to the presidential elections in Iran and the protests in the aftermath, the conservative or neoliberal milieu of the *FAZ* is confronted with an unemotional image of that election. The matter-of-fact style of this newspaper makes clear that its readers are not about to witness a power-shift in Iran.

In comparison, the liberal recipients of the *FR* agree to the solidarity with the Green Movement, which is reflected in this newspaper. The *FR* linked its reporting about the protests with the green color of the Internet Blogs, distributed by the activists in Iran. Through this intermedial visualization of the protests the *FR* itself appeared to be part of or at least seemed to be very closely linked to the Green Movement. The *jw* reflected again a third attitude toward the protests, for it saw things from the perspective of anti-imperialist ideologies. Each of the surveyed newspapers in this study has thus a specific preferred reading of the events in June 2009 in Iran. As such, they also have a major impact on the formation of opinion in their respective social milieus.

## REFERENCES

Gehlen, M. (2009, June 12). More and more Iranians want change. *Frankfurter Rundschau*, p. 3.
———. (2009, June 16). We are the people. *Frankfurter Rundschau*, p. 2.
Grobe, K. (2009, June 17). Iran's cultural revolution. *Frankfurter Rundschau*, p. 11.
———. (2009, June 20). Waiting for the twelfth Imam. *Frankfurter Rundschau*, p. 4.
Hafez, K. (2001). *Die politische Dimension der Auslandsberichterstattung*. Baden-Baden: Nomos.
Hermann, R. (2009, June 15a). Mousavi demands for annulment of the election in Iran. *Frankfurter Allgemeine Zeitung*, p. 1.
———. (2009, June 15b). The power of the armed forces. *Frankfurter Allgemeine Zeitung*, p. 1.
———. (2009, June 17). It could be a hot summer. *Frankfurter Allgemeine Zeitung*, p. 3.
———. (2009, June 18). Ominous silence. *Frankfurter Allgemeine Zeitung*, p. 3.
Hoffmann, C. (2009, June 6). With Obama's means: Mousavi's election campaign against Ahmadinejad. *Frankfurter Allgemeine Zeitung*, p. 3.

———. (2009, June 17). Unified by a common enemy. *Frankfurter Allgemeine Zeitung*, p. 3.

———. (2009, June 22). Days of destiny in Iran. *Frankfurter Allgemeine Zeitung*, p. 3.

Külbel, J. C. (2009, June 16). Loser wants to win. *Junge Welt*, p. 3.

———. (2009, June 17). Moderation and protest. *Junge Welt*, p. 6.

Ouaj, J. (1999). *More colour in the media*. European Institute for the Media: Utrecht, NL.

Pirker, W. (2009, June 20). The black channel: Antisocial revolution. *Junge Welt*, p. 3.

———. (2009, June 22). Revolutionary crisis. *Junge Welt*, p. 8.

Steinbach, U. (2009, June 29). For the short term the movement failed. *Readers Edition*. http://www.readers-edition.de/2009/06/29/kurzfristig-ist-die-bewegung-gescheitert-iran-experte-udo-steinbach-im-interview.

*Chapter Seven*

# How the Mass Media Defined Iran's Destiny

## *A General Overview of the Role of Media Outlets in Iran's June 2009 Presidential Election*

### Kourosh Ziabari

By structurally reviewing and exploring the course of events leading to Iran's June 2009 presidential election and its controversial aftermath that immersed the country in a month-long political crisis, one can justifiably conclude that mass media played a prominent role in the formation of political equations and directing the public response to the whole episode. Several unique features of this election, which contemporary Iran had never witnessed before, stressed the significance of media impact and intensified the political enthusiasm among the people during the preelection season and also contributed to the fomentation of postelection turmoil.

In the special coverage of Iran's presidential race and its turbulent aftermath, both national and international media outlets resorted to certain tactics which kept them from providing an impartial and objective investigation into the crisis. This created a wide gap, not only between politicians, state officials, and high-ranking clerics inside Iran, but amid international observers and analysts as well. This study will probe the impact of mass media on the results and aftermath of Iran's 2009 presidential election and the way it drew reactions from both the state-linked and opposition figures.

On March 16, only a few days after announcing his bid for a third-term presidency, Iran's former president Seyed Mohammad Khatami dropped his candidacy for the 2009 presidential election. Subsequently, Iran's popular former prime minister Mir Hossein Mousavi declared that he would run, a statement which quickly altered the assumptions and speculations among the majority of politically active Iranians. This appeared to be an unexpected and surprising occurrence to both the reformists and conservatives, who could hardly foresee the reappearance of a sixty-seven-year-old Mousavi following some twenty years of self-imposed political seclusion.

For several years, reformists had made collective attempts to bring Mir Hossein Mousavi back to the stage of political contest and nominate him for the presidency; however, the staunch refusals by the veteran politician due to equivocal reasons which primarily remained unexplained to the public until now had left no doubts that the reformers would again fail to find their ideal option to put forward for the defining contest.

Mousavi's unanticipated admittance and his declaration of candidacy accelerated the emergence of a widening gap between the different factions of conservatives as a number of them gradually dared to cast doubts over the reendorsement of incumbent President Mahmoud Ahmadinejad, who had proved to be the unconditional candidate of conservatives for so long.

As a pragmatist manager and theoretician, whom the American and British newspapers of 1980s explicitly accused of being a fanatic radical (Jockeying 1986), Mousavi was both a moderate reformist with excellent academic qualifications—which would make him a popular yet uncharismatic leader among the youth—and a practicing, devout Muslim as well, whose revolutionary credits as a close ally of the late Ayatollah Khomeini had long made him an admirable figure among the religious-revolutionary families of Iran. He had served as the last prime minister of Iran from October 31, 1981, to August 3, 1989, when the young Seyed Ali Khamenei was still president and had not yet risen to supreme leadership. When Khamenei showed reluctance in endorsing his second term as a prime minister in 1985, Ayatollah Khomeini sent a message to him, stating that "I announce as a citizen that endorsing anyone except him (Mousavi) is a betrayal to Islam" (Nateq-Nouri 2005).

Some political analysts compare the foreign policy and confrontational stance of ex-premier Mousavi in the 1980s with the stance of President Ahmadinejad in 2009. However, the long passage of time and his perpetual alignment to centrist parties progressively eroded the fervent sentiments of the young Mousavi. And he became a tolerant, old-hand politician who could competently direct the country in the wake of the growing international tensions of the twenty-first century.

Contrary to their professional responsibilities, state-sponsored media began to unilaterally set out attacks against the reformists' campaign and to embark upon a project to discredit their main nominee, Mir Hossein Mousavi, shortly after he entered the presidential race.

The first step was taken subsequent to Mousavi's first appearance in public, where he attended a press conference on April 6, 2009. Certain parts of Mousavi's statements were excessively used by extremist media outlets to portray him as a deviant, liberal, and apostate politician—a matter which would unquestionably provoke the sentiments of Iran's religious majority. In his press conference, the last prime minister of Iran had promised governmental policies different from his predecessor (Sotoudeh 2009). He vowed to abolish the Guidance Patrol (religious police), repair the "fanatic image of Iran in public opinions" (Sotoudeh 2009), pursue a foreign policy of détente and reconciliation with the world, and to constitutionally expand social freedom, freedom of the press, and freedom of expression.

A large group of the numerous state-linked news agencies, websites, newspapers, and magazines staged a multilateral maneuver after this press conference to exaggerate the conjecture that Mousavi displayed tendencies to liberalize the country by wiping religion off the societal map and incorporating the instances of Western civilization instead. Several conservative MPs, pundits, and scholars were interviewed by these media outlets to express their concern over the perceived threat that Mousavi's intention to abolish the Guidance Patrol would pose to the society's religious foundations and to warn the public of such dangers.

A few weeks later, the second phase started—this time more vehemently. By astutely identifying the religious and moral concerns of Iran's traditional public, prominent state-linked websites and news agencies began to publish frequent pictorial reports of the gatherings of Mousavi's female fans and supporters. These were women whom the society might consider as not properly clad in the Islamic modest dressing code, or commonly referred to as mal-*hijabs* or bad-*hijabs*. These reports were widely syndicated by the governmental media outlets and soon circulated all over the country and the world.

They began writing commentaries on the feeble religiousness of Mousavi's fans, who by adopting Western dressing styles purportedly intended to eradicate the religious values of the society and replace a moral anarchy as a substitute. The young fans of Mousavi were deliberately called impious and secular by those state-linked media outlets who attempted to progressively build up the assumption that whoever votes for Mousavi is a nonbelieving traitor to religion. In a country where 98 percent of the 70 million people of the population are Muslim, such a libel against a politician who wants to run for the most high-ranking executive office is nothing less than a lethal blow.

They warned the religious, conservative, and moderate families that the moral decline of the Islamic society would unmistakably follow, and the *hijab* would gradually disappear if Mousavi were to win the contest. State-run news agencies also applied similar methods in regards to Mahdi Karroubi, the other reformist candidate. They published reports that Karroubi's fans staged dancing carnivals at the attendance of their beloved candidate—a cause for shame in Islamic society.

The state-linked media outlets were insistent in their charges against Mousavi in order to denigrate him and the reform campaign ideologically. At the same time, they ignored several controversial decisions made during President Ahmadinejad's administration: decisions which high-ranking clerics and theologians had unanimously considered as non-Islamic and contrary to religious fundamentals and that the conservative MPs had critically spoken out against. In April 2006, Ahmadinejad came under fire from Iran's senior clerics after he ordered the head of Iran's Physical Education Organization to "properly lay the groundwork" (Stadium 2006) for allowing women to attend national soccer matches taking place in stadiums. Such an unprecedented decision—which not even the reformist president Mohammad Khatami had dared to take in the wake of growing demands by women's rights activists— drew harsh criticism from the clerics, conservative politicians, and opponents of Ahmadinejad, despite being lauded by the Iranian women who had long sought an equal opportunity with men to watch national soccer matches unrestrictedly.

Instigations against Mousavi's young fans persisted among conservative media outlets until he inexorably gave an interview to the Persian daily *Jomhouri-Eslami* on May 30 and criticized the appearance of his female fans: "I respect Islamic values and believe such moves are aimed at damaging [my] reputation" (Mousavi 2009). This was, however, an indisputable exercise of double standards by the state-funded media since the same appearance and non-Islamic dressing style could be rampantly found among the "principalist" president's young fans. The news websites linked to Mousavi, despite their unwillingness to do so, published reports which alluded to this sameness as a customary routine in the society which should not be used as an instrument to denounce a political competitor. Mousavi and his proponents strongly believed the youth to be a powerful and dynamic majority within the Iranian society who should not be demonized or reprimanded because of their appearance, which may differ slightly from the religious standards or the social agreements which are supposed to be adhered to. However, the seeds of uncertainty had been sown and scattered effectively: the devout former prime minister, who because of his bright revolutionary credits had counted largely on the votes of religious and conservative families, lost many of them overnight.

As days went by, reformists learned that the charges that the state-run media had used to conspicuously level against Mousavi and his supporters would hardly come to an end. Just a few weeks prior to the elections, some state-allied news websites orchestrated a new set of efforts to dispute and call into question the reputation of Zahra Rahnavard, a renowned academician and the first female university chancellor after the Iranian Revolution. Rahnavard played a considerable role in the political restoration of her husband, Mousavi, and appeared in campaign meetings and provincial trips alongside him. The right-wing media outlets doubted the religious legitimacy of Zahra Rahnavard's public accompaniment of Mousavi during the campaign season and leveled personal accusations against her overtly; at the same time, the public relations department of Iran's Ministry of Science, Research, and Technology raised serious doubts over the authenticity of her doctorate degree (There Is No Documentation 2009). This was one of the numerous instances of the government's direct involvement in the preelection rivalry that favored the incumbent president and which was later protested with intensity by the reformists.

The traditionally erosive confrontation between the two rival camps—conservatives and reformists—however, transpired to become an acrimonious and unexpectedly aggressive clash following a hard-hitting June 3 televised debate between Ahmadinejad and Mousavi. The debate, which was broadcast live by Iran's Channel 3 TV, set the groundwork for a long-running quarrel between the two wings and spanned the unfriendly dissension throughout the postelection turmoil. Some political critics expressed their disapproval of President Ahmadinejad's debating style, among them the moderate conservative MP Ali Motahari, who gave an interview a few weeks after the election and demanded an apology to the Iranian nation by the state-run Islamic Republic of Iran Broadcasting (IRIB), and from Mousavi and Ahmadinejad, who he claimed had equally endangered national security with their behavior. He stressed that the surprising approach of President Ahmadinejad in his debate with Mousavi played into the hands of the government's dissidents and partially was responsible for the postelection unrest (Motahari 2009).

In the historic June 3 debate, Ahmadinejad, who had been randomly selected as the starter, made some initial remarks and then abruptly brought up the names of Mousavi, ex-president Khatami, and former president Hashemi Rafsanjani, whom he accused of collectively "allying" to fight against and bring down his government. Ahmadinejad spoke of Rafsanjani's "secret meeting with an Arab leader in the Persian Gulf," which the incumbent president alleged had been held to discuss the obliteration of his government just a few months after he took office in 2005. He called Rafsanjani, the implicit supporter of Mousavi and reformists, a "founder of feudalism in Iran" and accused his family members, along with Tehran's former mayor Gholamhossein Karbaschi and the former chairman of Iran's Football Federation, Mohsen Safaei Farahani, of being financially corrupt (Debate 2009).

Although Mousavi generally responded to some parts of the criticism from his prevailing rival, the stringent and impressive tone of Ahmadinejad and his fluent articulateness made a remarkable impact on many Iranians. This was especially true of those who had not been much in favor of Rafsanjani's family aristocracy over the years following Iran's 1979 revolution. Many undecided Iranians who had left their final voting decision to the outcome of the debates categorically acclaimed the president's courage to quake the foundations of feudalism and unveil the corruption. It is believed that the president's uncompromising stance in this interview won him a large number of votes throughout the country.

Following the conclusion of all the unprecedented six live television debates between the candidates, IRIB allocated an extra twenty-two minutes to Ahmadinejad to defend himself against the criticism which the other three candidates had directed against him while he was absent, for example, in the debate between Mousavi and Karroubi. Upon the announcement of the decision to give Ahmadinejad such an additional chance, IRIB officials cited a preliminary regulation of debates that would give the candidates who were criticized in the debates for which they were not present a proper opportunity to respond to the criticisms. IRIB announced that it measured the total duration of other candidates' critical remarks about the president, which surpassed twenty-two minutes.

The state-run TV, however, refused to dedicate a proportionate chance to Ayatollah Hashemi Rafsanjani, the chairman of Iran's Expediency Council, to defend himself and his family members against the accusations made by President Ahmadinejad. The head of IRIB surprisingly left unanswered a letter by the senior cleric who had requested an opportunity to clarify the ambiguities of Ahmadinejad's claims against him and to defend his reputation.

IRIB also refused to offer the same opportunity to the rest of the people who had been labeled as corrupt so that they could provide explanations to the public. IRIB, furthermore, had been long pursuing a policy of tacitly supporting President Ahmadinejad by broadcasting news and reports on his international popularity. They also reported his attendance at the inaugural ceremonies, speeches, governmental meetings, and so forth; this was something that did not take place during the campaign season in past elections, hence it invoked many arguments.

This lopsided stance, which was largely perceived by the reformists as explicitly taking the side of the incumbent president, drew harsh criticism domestically. The Association of Combatant Clerics on April 27, about five weeks before the controversial debate, issued a condemnatory statement and accused IRIB of "expressively violating the principle of neutrality" and unjustly serving as the "electoral campaign of a certain candidate" (Association 2009).

Nevertheless, reformists took similar steps and campaigned vigorously. Mousavi traveled to nearly all of the country's thirty provinces and delivered speeches to the public, students, and youths. A number of websites associated with Mousavi started working several months prior to the election and set forth the agenda of severely criticizing Ahmadinejad's government. Ghalamnews, the main website of Mousavi's office, conducted hundreds of interviews with university professors, politicians, journalists, students, and former state officials to underline the alleged mismanagement of President Ahmadinejad's cabinet and to magnify the shortages the country had suffered under his administration. Prominent artists and celebrities released artworks and issued statements in solidarity with Mousavi and his Green Wave. Thousands of brochures, catalogues, booklets, and pamphlets were published to highlight the necessity of taking new steps and voting for a major transformation.

However, reformists ultimately failed to triumph the destiny of the election in spite of their spirited efforts and lost another competition to the authoritative camp of conservatives in a highly dramatic challenge. Putting the allegations of vote-rigging aside, Mousavi and his reform-minded slogans did not predominantly appeal to Iran's lower-income, below-average, and rural community which has generally determined the eventual outcome of elections in Iran—a meaningful reality. Mousavi noticeably lost much of the strong backing which he could have potentially received from the religious and conservative Iranians as a result of the indoctrinatory messages which he fell subject to. Some other undecided Iranians also preferred not to vote for him once President Ahmadinejad wisely drew public attention to Mousavi's alignment with former President Hashemi Rafsanjani, who had dramatically lost much of his popularity over the past years due to the growing public sentiments against his family fortune and opulence.

Some analysts also believe that a remarkable number of Mousavi's apolitical fans whose criteria for supporting the former prime minister was something other than their observations on Iran's domestic developments and international position. They finally lost interest in him for what they deemed to be the excess of criticism against Ahmadinejad's government on behalf of the reformists, their associated media, and Mousavi himself. Verifiably, Iran's average public typically dislikes uncompromising and straightforward criticism against the government by the opposition as this generates a sense of instability and volatility within habitual daily lifestyles and rings the alarm for a plausible drastic change. This antigovernment criticism is something which many Iranians, even the dissident and unhappy citizens, find objectionable, especially those who prefer a deficient steadiness to a turbulent improvement. The Iranians who enjoyed the increased freedoms and improved social privileges in conjunction with growing tensions and conflicts with the government establishment under President Khatami are quite familiar with this harsh conclusion.

At any rate, reformists lost the elections startlingly and are now simply at the verge of being politically expunged, rather than isolated, as a result of the inflexible measures the government has taken against them. Should we raise the possibility of fraud and vote-rigging, the story would be entirely different, but from a media-oriented viewpoint, reformists lost the elections due to the unequal media coverage and opportunities resulting from the state's dominance over IRIB; the lack of appeal to and interaction with the country's lower-income and rural majority; the cleverly devised news stories by the opponent's media which successfully undermined the religious credits of Mousavi and his supporters; and finally, the unprompted dislike for pragmatist cleric Hashemi Rafsanjani, whom today's conservative critics had enthusiastically campaigned for in the 1993 presidential election.

## REFERENCES

The Association of Combatant Clerics. (2009, April 7). http://www.rouhanioon.com/news/2/index.php?NewsID=513.

Debate between Mahmoud Ahmadinejad and Mir Hossein Mousavi (in Persian). (2009, June 3). http://www.irna.ir/View/FullStory/?NewsId=526001.

Jockeying for position. (1986, November 17). http://www.time.com/time/magazine/article/0917196285700.html.

Motahari: Ahmadinejad should also respond. (2009, August 2). http://www.jamejamonline.ir/newstext.aspx?newsnum=100915993515.

Mousavi slams female fans' choice of dress. (2009, May 31). http://www.presstv.ir/detail.aspx?id=96596&sectionid=351020101.

Nateq-Nouri. (2005, January 21). The re-endorsement of Mir-Hossein Mousavi to prime ministry and the story of 99 people. http://www.irdc.ir/fa/content/4913/default.aspx.

Sotoudeh, M. (2009, April 24). I will abolish the Guidance Patrol. *Etemaad Daily.*

Stadium doors opened to women. (2006, April 24). http://www.farsnews.com/newstext.php?nn=8502040153.

There is no documentation in the Ministry of Science to prove Zahra Rahnavard's doctorate degree. (2009, June 7). http://www.farsnews.com/newstext.php?nn=8803170433.

## Chapter Eight

# Televised Presidential Election Debates

## A Brief Comparative Analysis of the American and Iranian Debates

### Negin Hosseini

The U.S. presidential elections provide relevant background information on the history of televised presidential election debates. In 1960, the Democratic and Republican candidates, John F. Kennedy and Richard Nixon, appeared on TV to engage in a live political discussion which was reportedly viewed by over 66 million of the then 179-million population in the United States, hence making it one of the most watched broadcast programs in American television history (Museum of Broadcast Communication).

The four Kennedy-Nixon debates, commonly known as "The Great Debates," marked television's grand entrance into presidential politics (Museum of Broadcast Communication). They afforded the first real opportunity for voters to see their candidates in competition, and the visual contrast was dramatic. While there were no presidential debates between the years 1960 and 1976, televised debates has been the main part of every U.S. presidential election campaign following that period.

According to Larry Diamond et al.,

> Democracy denotes . . . a system of government that meets three essential conditions: meaningful and extensive *competition* among individuals and groups (especially political parties) for all effective positions of government power, at regular intervals and excluding the use of force; a highly inclusive level of political *participation* in the selection of leaders and policies, at least through regular, free and fair elections, such that no major (adult) social group is excluded; and a level of *civil and political liberties*—freedom of expression, freedom of the press, freedom to form and join organizations—sufficient to ensure the integrity of political competition and participation. (1988, xvi)

Applying the three essential conditions noted above to the 2009 Iranian presidential elections, to some extent the four candidates were able to compete with one another but the lack of political parties posed a void. Although the nomination process in Iran allows anyone to nominate himself/herself as a candidate, the elimination of candidates and confirmation of a finalist seems to be exclusive, not inclusive. Also, lack of private media in Iran, especially broadcast media, is a major hindrance to free flow of information and expression. Freedom of the press is certainly a key factor in any democratic system.

## TELEVISED DEBATES IN IRAN

Forty-eight years after the United States first televised presidential debate in 1960, a similar event took place in Iran: In June 2009, the very first live television political debates took place between Iran's four presidential candidates, Mahmoud Ahmadinejad, Mir Hossein Mousavi, Mehdi Karoubi, and Mohsen Rezai. Their often heated, highly controversial, and lively debates marked a new era in the history of television and politics in Iran.

In previous Iranian presidential debates, routine discussions were held involving mainly the candidates' representatives, and candidates themselves had only one opportunity to appear in a single televised debate in which all candidates participated. Furthermore, for a short period immediately after the 1979 Islamic Revolution, Iranian TV broadcast a series of heated talks involving members of revolutionary parties, but those discussions were eventually abandoned.

The tenth presidential election of June 12, 2009, marked a new era in the history of live television debates and the political landscape in Iran. In addition to the presidential candidates' debates, a few Iranian politicians and party members participated in several postelection televised discussions, in which they focused on analyzing the contested results and the ensuing demonstrations. It is not, however, clear whether these live televised political debates will continue in the future or not.

## A REVIEW OF IRAN'S 2009 PRESIDENTIAL ELECTION DEBATES

According to the Research Center of Islamic Republic of Iran Broadcasting, the tenth presidential debates were declared to be the most-watched programs in Iran's history of broadcasting. Drawing some 200 million viewers, the debate between Mahmoud Ahmadinejad and Mir Hossein Mousavi (June 3) gained the largest audience, 50 million of which were inside Iran while the other 150 million lived outside its borders. Mehdi Karoubi and Mahmoud Ahmadinejad's debate also attracted 40 million viewers inside the country (Research Center of the Islamic Republic of Iran's Broadcasting 2009). Allocating 540 minutes to presidential election discussions, Channel 3 of the Islamic Republic of Iran Broadcasting (IRIB) devoted a substantial amount of time to election debates and attracted the highest viewership as well. The debates took place on the following dates:

June 2: Karoubi–Rezai
June 3: Ahmadinejad–Mousavi
June 4: Mousavi–Rezai
June 6: Ahmadinejad–Karoubi
June 7: Karoubi–Mousavi
June 8: Ahmadinejad–Rezai

## THE EFFECTS OF THE TELEVISED DEBATES

Although most voters were anticipating hot discussions during Iran's first-ever presidential debates, the reality exceeded expectations. None of the commentators could have ever foreseen that red lines would be crossed, the taboos of Islamic rules broken, and the names of high-ranking officials mentioned in discussions.

These controversial debates left the Iranian society in a complete state of shock, possibly because they hadn't expected the candidates to slam each other's credibility so harshly. While some commentators argue that the heated discussions led to the maximized percentage of voter turnout, others say the debates created a profound gap in Iran's society, and in some cases, even among members of the same family. Diversity of political opinions that sounded pretty natural before televised debates turned into vengeance and divided the societal body into two oppositional factions after the debates.

In the process, a big gap appeared within the political structure and the Supreme Leader Ayattollah Ali Khamenei, who publically endorsed the incumbent candidate, Mahmoud Ahmadinejad. In this milieu, most politicians and statesmen opposed and contradicted each other and, at the same time, the upraised opposition took to the streets, claiming "cheating" and fraud in voting tabulations. This opposition intensified day by day, especially after the official declaration of Ahmadinejad's victory.

It seems that the taboo-breaking events and the crossing of official red lines, which unfolded in front of the television cameras, culminated in an unprecedented series of events and public discontent and demonstrations. One can safely argue that the single most significant reason behind public unrest was the televised debates and the IRIB's imbalanced pre- and postelection coverage.

## A COMPARISON: USA AND IRAN

The televised presidential debates in Iran were very different from that of the American presidential television debates. Some of these differences are outlined below.

### 1. Commission for Debate:

In the United States, the nonpartisan Commission on Presidential Debates (CPD) was established in 1987 to sponsor and conduct the debates, while no such independent organization existed to undertake the responsibility of holding Iran's presidential debates. In the June 2009 presidential election, IRIB suggested broadcasting televised debates to the Interior Ministry and after its approval, live debates were held. Owned and operated by the government and siding with the conservative political faction, both explicitly and implicitly, IRIB could not be viewed as an independent and impartial organization to hold the presidential debates.

### 2. The Number of Candidates/Debate Sessions

The U.S. election process eventually keeps only two candidates, each representing the two major parties, who get involved in the final televised debates, while in Iran not only are there no formal political parties but the number of approved finalist candidates often exceeds four. Therefore, the number of debate sessions increases accordingly.

### 3. Ethics of Debate

According to Zelinsky (2008), prior to their debates, the presidential candidates John McCain and Barack Obama negotiated and signed a thirty-one-page memorandum of understanding. This document was intended to govern every aspect of the presidential debates, from speaking times to follow-up questions.

Iran's televised presidential debates, however, lacked a mutually-agreed-upon set of rules and agreement, especially in terms of ethics. Consequently, the debating candidates crossed the implicit and explicit red lines, brought up very private and family matters, accused each other of unsubstantiated conduct, and made references to high-ranking statesmen and questioned their records.

American viewers usually observe two candidates shaking hands before and after the debates. On the contrary, Iran's presidential candidates not only did not shake hands but offered no sign relieving tensions between them. In a largely hospitable and polite nation, their overall conduct and abrupt endings left the viewers in a state of shock.

## 4. Debate Performance/Moderator

According to CPD (2007), each debate had a single moderator and lasted for ninety minutes. For instance, it was specified that in the first and third presidential debates and the vice presidential debate, the candidates should be seated, with the moderator at a table. Furthermore, the debates were not moderated by one person; each of the 2008 U.S. presidential debates were moderated by different media professionals:

- First presidential debate (Friday, September 26, University of Mississippi, Oxford, Mississippi): Jim Lehrer, Executive Editor and Anchor, *The News Hour*, PBS.
- Vice presidential debate (Thursday, October 2, Washington University in St. Louis, Missouri): Gwen Ifill, Senior Correspondent, *The News Hour*, and Moderator and Managing Editor, *Washington Week*, PBS.
- Second presidential debate (town meeting), (Tuesday, October 7, Belmont University, Nashville, Tennessee): Tom Brokaw, Special Correspondent, *NBC News*.
- Third presidential debate (Wednesday, October 15, Hofstra University, Hempstead, New York): Bob Schieffer, *CBS News* Chief Washington Correspondent, and Host, *Face the Nation* (The Swamp).

Furthermore, a comparison between the U.S. and Iran debates demonstrate that the American debate sessions were held at universities while the presidential Iranian debates took place inside of the IRIB's television studios, without any live audience. The participants, including journalists, were permitted to take part in sessions either as silent observers or as question-posing individuals.

It is obvious that a successful and productive debate needs a very professional moderator who is knowledgeable about national and international affairs, has experience in conducting live talk shows, and has the ability to control the flow of discussion, especially in the rough-and-tumble situation of political debates.

All of Iran's presidential debates were held in a TV studio devoid of any audience and, hence, without any question-and-answer period. Also, the moderator of all six debates was one person, Reza Pourhossein, who is a faculty member at the University of Tehran and holds a PhD in psychology. He is also the manager of the IRIB's Channel 4. He was assigned as the moderator of the 2009 debates without having any professional experience in hosting, moderating, debating, or even journalism.

Many viewers, expert or not, argued that Pourhossein was unable to moderate and lead the debates. Since discussions lacked a specified frame, he was unable to provide the candidates with questions and, consequently, they initiated the topics of the debates themselves, which led to controversies. He merely performed as a chronometer, although it was said that he even failed to succeed in time keeping.

## 5. Debates' Subjects

According to the CPD format for the debates, announced on November 21, 2007, one presidential debate will focus primarily on domestic policy and one will focus primarily on foreign policy. The vice presidential debate will cover both foreign and domestic topics. During the first and third presidential debates, and the vice presidential debate, the time will be divided into eight ten-minute segments. The moderator will introduce each segment with an issue on which each candidate will comment, after which the moderator will facilitate further discussion of the issue, including direct exchange between the candidates for the balance of that segment. During the town meeting, the moderator has discretion to use questions submitted by the Internet. Also, at the end of the final presidential debate, time will be reserved for closing statements (The Swamp).

Since Iran's televised presidential debates lacked fixed themes and rules, a number of domestic and foreign, private and public, political and economic issues were raised during the debates. In other words, the debates were disorganized and unplanned; hence the candidates determined the issues in a spontaneous and free-flow manner.

## DISCUSSION AND CONCLUSION

Although the 2009 presidential debates were a major step toward the possibility of establishing an open political forum in Iran, clearly much thinking and planning has to take place in conducting any future political debates. The results of my brief case study on Ahmadinejad and Mousavi's debate indicates that during their controversial discussion:

- The two candidates put forward thirty-six and thirty-four different topics, respectively;
- In almost every paragraph, a new subject was raised;
- A couple of topics were either personal in nature or accusatory of the absent candidate;
- Candidates shifted drastically in their discussion of various subjects;
- The discussion lacked logical flow and topical coherence.

According to CPD, the questions of debate should be posed by both the moderator and the participants, who will pose their questions to the candidates after reviewing their questions with the moderator for the sole purpose of avoiding duplication. Journalists were also permitted to ask questions.

While the format of the U.S. presidential debates forbids participants to ask each other questions and restricts discussion of particular topics to short time frames, the Iranian presidential debates looked like a controversial dispute, or argument, between the two challengers.

There was a serious lack of questioning format in Iran's televised presidential debates. The moderator was not able to put forward any questions, and no viewers were present to pose any challenges to the candidates.

The differences seem to be quite great at first glance, but these differences can be justified by looking at the determining factors such as lack of precedence for debates in Iran, a political system different from that of the United States, and distinct media frameworks and controls in the two countries.

Iran's future televised presidential debates need to adhere to the tested and proven standards and practices employed in other countries, including the United States. The first step in doing so is to form an independent organization or commission, followed by the compilation of a set of rules and regulations for conducting formal televised debates.

## REFERENCES

Commission on the Presidential Debates (CPD) (2007). http://www.debates.org.
———. Our Mission. http://www.debates.org/index.php?page=about-cpd.
Diamond, Larry, et al. (1988). *Democracy in Developing Countries, Vol. 2, Africa* (Boulder, Colo.: Lynne Rienner).
Museum of Broadcast Communication (n.d.). "The Kennedy-Nixon presidential debates, 1960." http://www.museum.tv/eotvsection.php?entrycode=kennedy-nixon.
Research Center of the Islamic Republic of Iran's Broadcasting (2009). http://www.irib.ir/English.
The Swamp Politics. (n.d.). http://www.swamppolitics.com/cgi-bin/mt4/mtsearch.cgi?search=2008+U.S.+presidential+debates&IncludeBlogs=79.

———. Presidential debate moderators named. http://www.swamppolitics.com/news/
politics/blog/2008/08/presidential_debate_moderators.html.

Zelinksy, Aaron (2008, October 14). A secret memo controls the rules of the
presidential debates—should it? http://articles.sfgate.com/2008-10/14/opinion/
17136993_1_presidential-debate-presidential-candidates-follow-up-questions.

*Part Two*

# NEW MEDIA AND SOCIAL NETWORKING DIMENSIONS

*Chapter Nine*

# What's That Chirping I Hear?

## *From the CNN Effect to the Twitter Effect*

Nancy Snow

In June 1980, a broadcast television network was born in Atlanta, Georgia, that would change the face of public opinion and foreign policy. Entrepreneur Ted Turner, CEO of Turner Broadcasting Systems, launched Cable News Network (CNN) on that date as the first twenty-four-hour all-news network. The Turner Broadcast Company would add *Headline News* in January 1982 to CNN's growing brand and CNN International in 1985. CNN was initially mocked as the "Chicken Noodle Network," not expected to have any lasting impact, and was bleeding revenue at the rate of $2 million per month. It did not turn a profit until 1985. But in August 1990, CNN sent its correspondents to cover the Iraqi invasion of Kuwait, and Desert Storm in January 1991, making the network and many of its reporters, like Peter Arnett, Bernard Shaw, and Christiane Amanpour, household names. The Museum of Broadcast Communications (Gomery 2009) explains CNN's global impact on politics:

> In 1991, as the only TV network in the world operating live from the very beginning of Operation Desert Storm, CNN reported everything the military permitted—from the first bombing of Baghdad to the tank blitz that ended the conflict. Indeed at a press conference after the initial air bombing runs by the U.S. Air Force, Defense Secretary Richard B. Cheney and General Colin L. Powell, Chairman of the Joint Chiefs of Staff, admitted that they were getting much of their war information from CNN.

In the last three decades since CNN's founding, major global events have been brought into the living room of cable subscribers' homes, including the Persian Gulf War of 1990–1991 and the Iraq War (2003). CNN broadcast the tragedy of Tiananmen Square live to the world in June 1989, followed by the fall of the Berlin Wall six months later on November 9, 1989. Iconic images of a young man facing a tank in Beijing and young people cheering atop the Berlin Wall flash across the memory bank of a global viewing audience whose perceptions about politics have been affected by around-the-clock television. For the millennial generation born between 1980 and 1995, there has never been a waking moment without CNN. Without question, CNN is the godfather of global television news (McPhail 2006). The seminal condition for its kingpin status is the global satellite. Without the rise of telecommunications and global satellites, television news would remain largely in the hands of nation-states and under tight government control.

CNN was not the first broadcaster to cover global news. The British Broadcasting Corporation (BBC) preceded CNN's founding as a world news broadcaster by nearly six decades (1922). The BBC website reports that experimental television service began in 1932, followed by the establishment of the BBC Television Service in 1936. The "Beeb," along with other foreign broadcasters like Germany's Deutsche Welle, maintains a traditional delivery format of thirty- to sixty-minute prime time newscasts while CNN blazed a trail, driven by breaking news in a dramatic and conflict-driven context. The all-news, all-the-time format can go on for hours, days, and even weeks as witnessed by CNN's blanket coverage of the December 2004 Asian tsunami or the 2000 Florida presidential election recount.

CNN's success has spawned competition from Rupert Murdoch's BSkyB and the BBC, but the CNN logo and brand remain the most powerful symbols for international broadcast news. Even with Time Warner's acquisition of Turner Broadcasting Systems in 1996, nothing has stopped the worldwide recognition that CNN represents to the global viewer. If a story is covered by CNN, it is certain that the whole world is watching.

CNN's impact on global news and foreign policy led to a theory among political communication scholars called the *CNN effect*. George Washington University scholar Steven Livingston (1997) describes the CNN effect as "1) a policy agenda-setting agent, 2) an impediment to the achievement of desired policy goals, and 3) an accelerant to policy decision making." The instantaneous aspect of global media today can light a fire of public outrage at government, as it did following Hurricane Katrina in 2005, or extinguish policy options, as happened after the broadcast footage of insurgents dragging the bodies of American soldiers through the streets of Mogadishu in 1993. CNN's Anderson Cooper, who reported from the ground in New Orleans, exhibited the type of emotional news coverage that kept viewers tuned in for hours. The *New York Observer* quickly dubbed him the "emo-anchor." Cooper's reporting directly and angrily challenged government officials like

FEMA director Michael Brown and Democratic senator Mary Landrieu of Louisiana about the poor public relief response. He was quickly promoted up the ranks at CNN as one of the main news anchors with his own two-hour prime time program, *Anderson Cooper 360.* Cooper said of his Katrina reporting, "Yeah, I would prefer not to be emotional and I would prefer not to get upset, but it's hard not to when you're surrounded by brave people who are suffering and in need" (Van Meter 2005).

In today's global media environment, government officials are more likely to react to public opinion manufactured by media celebrities like Cooper. In contrast, President John F. Kennedy had the first six days of the Cuban Missile Crisis to consider policy options before his administration alerted the national media and, in turn, a public who naturally would respond with fear and hysteria. As presidential historian Michael Beschloss (1993) notes, "Kennedy had the luxury of operating in what they would probably consider to be the halcyon age before modern television news coverage."

Similarly, CNN once had the luxury of serving as the main global source for news and information. In 2009, CNN made its own headline news when its journalistic credibility was undermined by an upstart technology known as Twitter. The Iranian presidential election of June 2009 was monitored by what was quickly labeled the Twitter Revolution—mass protesters tweeting messages of hope, inspiration, and alarm to the rest of the world. Twitter users were able to circumvent government censors who restricted access to mobile text messaging by utilizing the microblogging website Twitter, famous for its self-contained 140-character tweets.

Twitter's pitch is to answer the simple question, "What's happening?" Its pitch is "share and discover what's happening right now, anywhere in the world." A person can do that from a computer, cell phone, or handheld device. This is exactly what happened last June 2009 in Iran. As the unrest and protests grew against the reelection win of Mahmoud Ahmadinejad, another protest popped up in the "Twitterverse." Tweets from Iran marked with the hashtag #cnnfail (CNNfail 2009) began attacking the global news brand for being an early absentee in reporting the protests. It was Saturday, June 13, 2009, and thousands of Iranians were on the streets of Tehran. The "Twitterverse" was alive with eyewitness accounts, but CNN was silent about the disputed election and those coming out to support the Iranian presidential challenger Mir Hossein Mousavi. A global news network that had cut its journalistic teeth on Mideast reporting had missed the biggest political protest of the year (Terdiman 2009, June 14). It wasn't until Sunday, June 14, that CNN.com posted its first news story (Tehran Tense 2009), one that emphasized the perspectives of President Mahmoud Ahmadinejad and Supreme Leader Ayatollah Ali Khamenei in the first three paragraphs:

Iran's supreme leader gave his blessing to the outcome of the country's presidential election Sunday despite widespread allegations of fraud, calling the results "a divine miracle," the official Islamic Republic News Agency [IRNA] reported. Ayatollah Ali Khamenei said the record voter turnout in Friday's election showed Iranians value "resistance against oppressors," the agency reported. Pointing to enemies' massive propaganda campaign to discourage people from taking part in the elections, Ayatollah Khamenei also said there was really a divine miracle behind this election, given its results that were 10 million higher than any of the previous ones in the 30-year history of elections in Iran, IRNA reported.

By late Sunday, CNN was reporting that Twitter had "out-CNNed" CNN: "At the height of the protests and disorder in Tehran on Saturday and Sunday, Twitter was used to give graphic accounts to a worldwide audience—even if they were a maximum of 140 characters" (Nasr 2009). Though mobile services and text messaging were officially blocked by the Iranian government protest weekend, Iranians were still able to access the Internet to send out tweets. Their messages, like this one from "Change for Iran," reflected voices challenging the power of state-sponsored media messages: "my friend saying more than 100 students arrested, I can't confirm this but the numbers are high. bastards just attacked us for no reason, I lost count of how much tear gas they launched at us! we have now some students with urgent need of medical attention I'm calling out to all ppl who can come here don't leave us" (Nasr 2009).

The "Twitterverse" faulted CNN for not only being slow with its coverage but also for not pursuing a skeptical line with its initial coverage. Despite CNN's media status, it had restrictions to field polling and research in Iran that would have revealed a gap between Ahmadinejad's professed majority voter support and actual support. Twitter revealed public frustration in real time, like a street-level focus group. Twitter comments reflected a population of Iranians who were pro-West, social-media savvy, and global-media conscious. Tweets skewed overwhelmingly toward Ahmadinejad's main challenger, Mousavi, who was not just a real challenger but also a symbolic representation of a new Iran. Twitter in Iran showed itself to be a legitimate media watchdog platform and real-time media critic of mainstream media outlets (Poniewozik 2009). CNN initially towed the official line, relying on the state media and government's interpretation of the presidential election. The news organization also seemed to have dropped the ball on its own Twitter feed. Had it better monitored the news via Twitter from the start of the election results, it would have been ahead and not behind the global news media wave.

On June 17, 2009, several social-media savvy U.S. media journalists, including CNN's Rick Sanchez and NBC's Ann Curry, spoke at the timely 140 Characters Conference in New York City. Its theme, exploring the state of "NOW," was not in reference to the National Organization for Women, but rather the state of now media like Twitter. As Brian Solis (2009) reported triumphantly for TechCrunch:

> This past weekend the Twitterverse spoke out in exasperation and opposition against traditional media networks (CNN specifically) and the absence of instantaneous coverage of the Iranian election and the resulting fallout. "We the people" wanted real-time information regarding the violent protests that erupted on the streets of Iran and the stories probing potential foul play in the results. We took to Twitter to express discontent and to also uncover the real story as it was unfolding live through citizen journalism.

The world was watching . . . and it did so on Twitter, not on CNN or any other news network. Jeff Pulver (2009, June 16), Internet entrepreneur and organizer of the inaugural New York City conference, said that now media is user-driven. People expect information as it happens and is developing, even if it is not fully accurate or complete. The immediacy trumps the accuracy. Conference speaker David Saranga (2009, June 16), then Consul for Media and Public Affairs at the Israeli Consulate, said that Twitter has the power to transform government and media relations. Saranga received some notoriety for organizing the first Twitter news conference December 30, 2008, during the war in Gaza. Not all were impressed by the effort. MSNBC anchor Rachel Maddow said that "the Israeli government is trying to explain a conflict that people write books about, a conflict that newspaper writers struggle to explain in 2,000 words, in 140 characters at a time" (N. Cohen 2009). As *New York Times* reporter Noam Cohen (2009) noted, the Israeli Defense Forces recognize that good public relations is as important a challenge as a military success. But does text-messaging dialect hold the key? Some typical questions and answers from the news conference were as follows:

peoplesworld: 40 years of military confrontation hasn't brought security to Israel, why is this different?

israelconsulate: We hav 2 prtct R ctzens 2, only way fwd through negotiations, & left Gaza in 05. y Hamas launch missiles not peace?

shahidkamal: Your nation has been disgraced on Twitter. This inverted Nuremberg Trial will not rescue your image.

israelconsulate: the point of this was to hear what ppl say and to share our POV with fellow twitters.

Saranga defends not only the use of social media in government but also the text-messaging abbreviations style that is a long way from sit-down negotiations around the table. He says that traditional media concentrate on the conflict domain of what constitutes the state of Israel, notably an image of a young Palestinian child before an Israeli army tank. The use of Twitter during Gaza changed the definition of public diplomacy. In the past, in order to convey a message to the public, government officials had to appeal to third parties like the media to get out their stories. Now the Israeli government, just like an individual, can bring its message directly to the public. Saranga says:

> This is a revolution when it comes to the government. For the first time we can have a dialogue with the public opinion. All of a sudden we can also hear what people are thinking. For us, for the Israeli government, this is something very, very important. We want to know what people think about us. (2009)

So what can Twitter bring to news and information distribution that traditional media like CNN cannot? Twitter creator and cofounder Jack Dorsey has said, "Twitter is about approach, transparency, and immediacy" (Pulver 2009). Twitter is the medium of the moment, according to culture watcher *Time* magazine, a corporate media partner of CNN. "It's free, highly mobile, very personal, and very quick. It's also built to spread, and fast" (Grossman 2009). CNN may have recognizable personalities like Larry King and Anderson Cooper, but it cannot compete with Twitter time. That is, unless its users embrace the integration of traditional media with now media. Rick Sanchez is a CNN reporter who fully embraces and uses Twitter. He is frustrated with the fixed deadlines of cable news networks and values the contributions citizen journalists bring to CNN. Citizens using now media are reliable sources and should be recognized as such, according to Sanchez. "Is news judgment changing? Yes!" He continued, "This is the first time we can connect directly with citizens who could be a reliable source aside from the talking heads and pretty faces that serve as news anchors" (Grossman 2009).

The CNNfail social media movement is recognition that despite the rise of new media like Twitter, Facebook, and YouTube, the world still expects the old global media like CNN and the BBC to put news in a landscape context (Cashmore 2009). Old media, like elder statesmen, lend credibility that new media "youth" cannot compete with, at least not at this time. Further, traditional media still shape public opinion and impact public policy direction to a much larger degree than social media. In tandem, old and new media challenge the status quo power of closed societies like Iran and China. But social media's effect is still nascent to that of old media (television and radio), where most of the audience remains tuned in. New media are reliable tools for spotlight coverage and in-the-moment reflection, but they are no substitute for trained reporters who can provide the relevant Ws (who, what, when, where, why) beyond the confines of character space.

Any communications tool, be it cable news in the 1990s or social networking media Twitter in the 2000s, has limited effects. The now media are not panaceas against ignorance, censorship, or deception. *Time* magazine writer Lev Grossman (2009) notes that while Twitter is the darling of today's new media, communication strengths are also communication weaknesses. Twitter is fast, which means it is chaotic. It is instantaneous, which also means it is subjective. It is pop-up information from every source, which means that it is "totally unverifiable." Twitter, like CNN, like direct mail before it, is not a magic bullet in communication theory. Grossman describes the Iranian protest use of Iran against the government as "an arms race crossed with whack-a-mole." It cannot take down a dictator or government since it is not just a pure tool of the masses engaged in human rights action. As the David Saranga–arranged Israeli news conference example shows, government is becoming just as savvy with new media as the rest of us. Nevertheless, the Twitter effect made its world debut in Iran as a major tool of protest and media criticism. Roger Cohen (2009) reports that recognition of Twitter's impact in Iran was told in the following anecdote by Iranian American scholar Mahasti Afshar at the University of Southern California: "Two mullahs gaze out on a crowd of protesters in Tehran. The one says, 'Arrest the correspondents.' To which the despondent reply is: But they're all correspondents!'"

Cohen says that while Iranian citizen-journalists "tweet-transformed" the image of their country to the rest of the world, the mainstream media that got kicked out of Iran were missed. A Twitter user in the moment cannot replace a trained on-the-ground and fully present journalist who can reveal a landscape theme and deliver coherence. The level of professionalism that experienced journalists bring can guard against the new media advantage of reporting an account as it is happening, even if all the facts may not yet be in place. All of us who use communications tools at our fingertips must heed the words of Noam Cohen and remember to be vigilant about not only their best use and inspiration, but just as important, their limitations, abuse, and misuse as weapons of social change.

## REFERENCES

BBC. The BBC Story. (2009). http://www.bbc.co.uk/historyofthebbc.

Beschloss, M. R. (1993). Presidents, television, and foreign crises. http://www.annenberg.northwestern.edu/pubs/pres.

Cashmore, P. (2009, June 14). #CNNfail: Twitter blasts CNN over Iran election. http://mashable.com/2009/06/14/cnnfail.

CNNfail & the social media revolution. (2009). http://cnn.fail.com.

Cohen, N. (2009, January 3). The toughest q's answered in the briefest tweets. http://www.nytimes.com/2009/01/04/weekinreview/04cohen.html.

Cohen, R. (2009, September 10). New tweets, old needs. http://www.nytimes.com/2009/09/10/opinion/10iht-edcohen.html.

Gomery, D. (2009). Cable news network. http://www.museum.tv/eotvsection.php?entrycode=cablenewsne.

Grossman, L. (2009, June 17). Iran protests: Twitter, the medium of the moment. http://www.time.com/time/printout/0,8816,1905125,00.html.

Livingston, S. (1997). Clarifying the CNN effect: An examination of media effects according to type of military intervention. Research Paper R-18, 2. Joan Shorenstein Center for Press and Politics, Harvard University.

McPhail. T. L. (2006). CNN international: Role, impact, and global competitors. In T. L. McPhail (Ed.). *Global communication: Theories, stakeholders, and trends* (3rd ed.), (pp. 243–273). Malden, MA: Blackwell.

Nasr, O. (2009, June 14). Tear gas and Twitter: Iranians take their protests online. http://www.cnn.com/2009/WORLD/meast/06/14/iran.protests.twitter/index.html.

Poniewozik, J. (2009, June 15). Iranians protest election, tweeps protest CNN. http://tunedin.blogs.time.com/2009/06/15/iranians-protest-election-tweeps-protest-cnn.

Pulver, J. (2009, June 16). Morning keynote. http://nyc.140conf.com.

Saranga, D. (2009, June 16). Morning speech. http://www.youtube.com/watch?v=zjQfgaqy3K4.

Solis, B. (2009, June 17). Is Twitter the CNN of the new media generation? http://www.techcrunch.com/2009/06/17/is-twitter-the-cnn-of-the-new-media-generation.

Tehran tense as Iran's supreme leader endorses votes outcome. (2009, June 14). CNN Tehran, Iran. http://www.cnn.com/2009/WORLD/meast/06/14/iran.election/index.html.

Terdiman, D. (2009, June 14). "#CNNFail": Twitterverse slams network's Iran absence. http://news.cnet.com/8301-17939_109-10264398-2.html.

Van Meter, J. (2005, September 11). Anderson Cooper's Hurricane Katrina coverage: A breakthrough for TV news. http://nymag.com/nymetro/news/features/14301.

*Chapter Ten*

# Bullets with Butterfly Wings

*Tweets, Protest Networks,*
*and the Iranian Election*

Ali Fisher

The student protests in Iran during July 1999 came a few months before the street battles outside the World Trade Organization (WTO) Ministerial Conference held in Seattle. The notorious and violent encounters between protesters and police became known as N30 or the Battle in Seattle. Despite the use of tear gas and pepper spray, followed later by concussion grenades and rubber bullets, the protestors managed to defy the police and block streets, thereby limiting access to the WTO conference for three days. This resistance relied on a variety of communication devices which allowed the protesters to coordinate at street level and communicate with a national and even international audience. In 1999, the N30 protesters were more successful than their Iranian contemporaries in using digital communications for these purposes. Paul de Armond (2001) recalled that at N30, "floating above the tear gas was a pulsing infosphere of enormous bandwidth, reaching around the planet via the internet."

While the context following the election in Iran is not fully analogous to 1999, protesters in 2009 have been much more successful in engaging with the infosphere, metaphorically floating above the streets. Twitter provided a relatively easy yet powerful means of passing information while maintaining degrees of anonymity. The ability to combine credibility and anonymity was important as this struggle played out over months rather than three days.

## DISPERSED RESPONSE TO THE
## IRANIAN ELECTION THROUGH TWITTER

Since last June's election in Iran, updates of developments, whether news, rumor, or speculation along with detailed analysis, have appeared via Twitter from a large number of citizen journalists. This appeared alongside attempts to coordinate protests and messages of support. As Neri Zilber (2009) reported, "With the inevitable regime crackdown on the international press, the place of traditional print and television reporting has shifted overwhelmingly to new media platforms such as YouTube, Twitter, Facebook and other similar peer-to-peer social networking sites."

Social media played an important role as Western news media were struggling to keep pace with events or were criticized for the slow speed with which, in particular, cable news began to cover the protests. As Brian Stelter (2009) reported, "Untold thousands used the label '#CNNfail' on Twitter to vent their frustrations" about CNN's failure to cover events as some viewers had expected. Ultimately, as Neri Zilber (2009) wrote, "While some restraint is warranted before proclaiming this the 'Twitter revolution,' what should be obvious is that the only reason we're able to see, hear, read—and yes, argue—about what's been unfolding in Iran is due almost entirely to new media technologies."

Highlighting this perspective, the Web Ecology Project produced *The Iranian Election on Twitter: The First Eighteen Days* (2009), which studied the over two million tweets about Iran. Smaller analysis was offered by Nicholas Thompson (2009) in his article, "Iran: Before You Have That Twitter-gasm," which focused on the languages and location details of individuals using Twitter. Further complexity comes from those outside Iran changing the location on their Twitter profiles to Tehran or time zone to +3:30 in an attempt to create cover for those tweeting in Iran. Whatever the relative merits of flooding the infosphere to make it harder for state representatives to tell who was actually in the region, those who only changed location were largely transparent as their time zone that was shown in any download of user details pretty much gave the game away. Ironically, however successful these individuals were at providing cover, they were equally successful at making it harder for those taking their first steps in seeking to interact with protesters to locate them.

## MAPPING THE IRANIAN CONTEXT

Recent studies published in *First Monday* (Huberman, Romero, and Fang 2009) or conducted at Harvard Business School (Heil and Piskorski 2009)

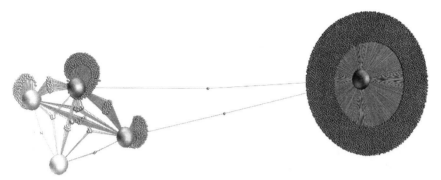

**Figure 10.1.   Network of Users Tweeting to Five #tags up to July 2009**

have demonstrated the power of network mapping. In the context of the Iranian election, mapping can be applied to show the interaction between groups of protesters, observers, analysts, and supporters. Producing network mapping based on the #tags adopted by Twitter users highlights the groups with which that user chose to identify. This approach focuses on the behavior of users rather than by sampling the data or by a researcher categorizing tweets after the fact.

This image shows that in the weeks after the election two separate conversations existed in almost total isolation; the conversation between users of the four #tags represented by the spheres on the right, and the second interaction

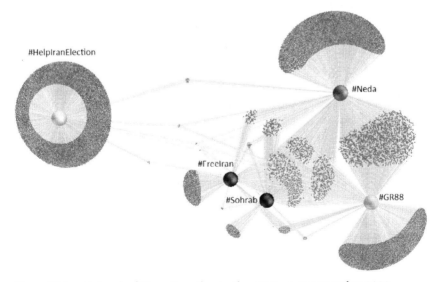

**Figure 10.2.   Network of Users Tweeting to Five #tags up to November 2009**

between users of the single #tag on the left. The interlinked set of four spheres on the right represent the tags #GR88, #FreeIran, #Neda, and #Sohrab. The large sphere on the left represents #HelpIranElection. #Neda took the name of Neda Agha-Soltan/Neda Soltani who was shot and killed on June 20 (Stoltz 2009). Likewise, #Sohrab took the name of Sohrab Arabi, who went missing after joining the protests; his body was returned to his family weeks later. These tags were often used as symbols of solidarity and resistance. #GR88 was abbreviated from Green Revolution 1388 and often functioned as a coordination point for networks of activists. The left-hand conversation focused on, for example, coordinating forthcoming protests, including suggesting using cars to block streets as a way of protecting the protesters and using shortened URLs to share stories or video. The users of these tags can be thought of, broadly, as insiders. This insider group is a diverse combination of individuals who may be protesters physically located in Iran, physically outside Iran but with strong links to individuals in Iran, Iranian Diaspora, analysts, and commentators.

A common thread in the early tweets from this insider group was the desire to get stories then on niche local websites or uploaded onto YouTube to the attention of international broadcasters or a loosely defined Western audience. This was particularly successful when the video of Neda Agha-Soltan/Neda Soltani was uploaded to the Internet, where it was distributed widely through Facebook, YouTube, and Twitter and then run by major news organizations (Tait and Weaver 2009). Other examples of using Twitter to share media included Revolutionary Road, Iran Network Now, Tehran Bureau, Anonymous Iran, United4Iran, and Iranallday.

The right-hand cluster appeared to have large numbers engaging in the days immediately after the election but with the greater emphasis on "showing your support for democracy" than discussion, coordination, or media sharing. Instead of long-term interaction, many users applied a green overlay on their avatar. As a result, this #tag is heavily linked to helpiranelection.com, created by a software developer in Israel (Arik 2009). In the weeks after the election, only two small groups of users had contributed to both groups, identified on the two lines linking the larger clusters. Through November 2009, this situation has barely changed.

The difference between the content of the tweets can also be seen through word clouds of the most common words in the tweets. The larger the word in the cloud, the more often, comparatively, that word has appeared.

Among the observations which can be made are, first, there are significantly fewer words visible in the #HelpIranElection cloud. This is because the #tag was used almost entirely to retweet the same message. Almost 78 percent of #HelpIranElection tweets were identical: #helpiranelection—show

Figure 10.3.   Word Cloud of Common Words Used in #FreeIran

Figure 10.4.   Word Cloud of Common Words Used in #Sohrab

# Iran
## avatar                            support
### Twitter        democracy
## http://helpiranelection.com add
### overlayhelpiranelection
## green     1-click
### show

**Figure 10.5.    Word Cloud of Common Words Used in #HelpIranElection**

support for democracy in Iran add green overlay to your Twitter avatar with
1-click—http://helpiranelection.com.

In contrast, the other clouds have many more words, as the tweets were
more often individual messages rather than repetition. RT appeared in 37
percent of tweets using #FreeIran during the four weeks after the election.

Similarly, the characteristics of the activity are significantly different. For
example, the #HelpIranElection had a massive surge of activity in the days
following the election. Use of the tag dropped off rapidly to only a couple of
tweets a day before falling into disuse. This is indicative of short-term viral
spread. In combination with the network mapping, this also demonstrates that
users of #HelpIranElection were largely isolated outsiders. For most users,
this was the extent of their involvement on Twitter, the majority having never
used the #tags used by activists or insiders.

This is in sharp contrast to the use of #FreeIran. Analysis of this #tag shows
a much slower uptake, but a much longer usage.

#Sohrab also demonstrated longer usage, up to November, but declined as
time passed from the event which led to its creation.

The differing levels of tweets per user also highlight the distinction between insiders and outsiders. In the case of #FreeIran, the average tweets per
user was 15.4, for #Sohrab it was 11.99, while #HelpIranElection was used
on average 1.09 times, demonstrating the difference between genuine engagement and the ephemeral click to show support of the #HelpIranElection users.

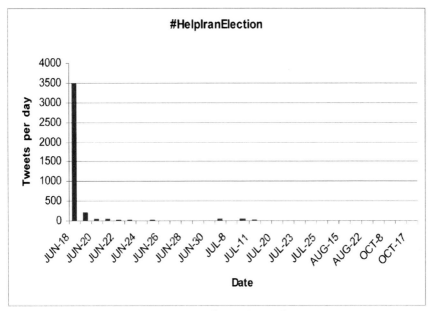

Figure 10.6.   Number of Tweets per Day for #HelpIranElection

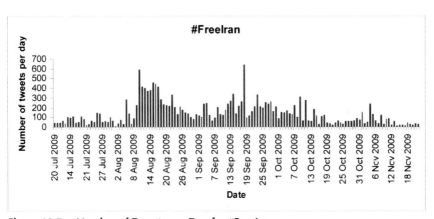

Figure 10.7.   Number of Tweets per Day for #FreeIran

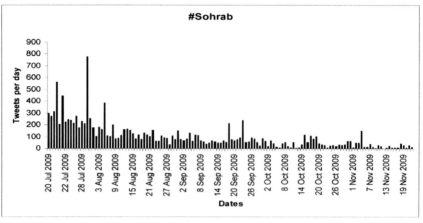

**Figure 10.8.	Number of Tweets per Day for #Sohrab**

The example of these #tags aligns with the research from the Web Ecology Project (2009) of tweets on Iran during the eighteen days surrounding the election: "59.3% of users tweet just once, and these users contribute 14.1% of the total number" (p. 1). Equally, "The top 10% of users in our study account for 65.5% of total tweets" (Web Ecology Project 2009). Both numbers challenge the idea of a global discussion or the conclusions drawn from highlighting the huge numbers of users involved, and they demonstrate the importance of differentiating between the levels of interaction by Twitter users.

## INFORMATION OVERLOAD

In addition to those #tags mapped, there was another vastly more popular tag, #IranElection, which may have provided a source of overlap between some of the conversations. However, analysis of this tag has to consider the practical ability of a user to read or interact with the volume of data. #IranElection had so much data that on average a user would have had to scan 1,000 tweets every hour to keep up; however, at times the reality was actually even harder to monitor.

Ben Parr (2009), writing on Mashable.com, highlighted the massive surge in tweets mentioning Iran on June 16 when users produced 221,744 tweets in one hour. Tweets using #IranElection were regularly above 10,000 per hour during June, with over 22,500 tweets in an hour on June 16 (Parr 2009). At these volumes, readers would have needed to read 3,695 tweets a minute or sixty-one tweets a second to read all of the Iran content and 375 tweets a minute to keep up with #IranElection. The result was that other #tags became the coordination points for particular groups online as shown by the mapping of interaction between #Neda, #GR88, #Sohrab, and #FreeIran.

Users were not only being sent a tweet, but also Twitter was being used as a means to transfer links to stories or video, so a single tweet could occupy a reader for significantly longer than the time it took to read 140 characters. The information overload also included 2,250,000 blog posts and 3,000 videos posted about Iran in twenty-four hours around June 16. As Ben Parr (2009) observed, "Even if every video were just two minutes, that would be over 6,000 minutes of video related to the Iran situation," which would take just over four days to watch if it were possible to view video for that long without a break. While numbers may well be inflated by RT and many people reposting the same video, along with regional or linguistic factors influencing access to particular videos, Twitter became a means of coordination for media sharing as well as coordination on the streets. While the quantity of material produced is an interesting aspect of the analysis covered in depth by the Web Ecology Project (2009), analysis of the behavior of Twitter users must consider the practical ability to engage with that volume of data and the subsequent coordination games which influenced the decision to adopt alternative focal points (Castronova 2005).

The coordination was in two forms; the first was the tagging used within social media as shown by the example of Twitter. Despite the image of the Internet providing the potential to reach any information, human behavior leads to local clusters of individuals huddling around certain points. The development of local coordination points by different groups in turn influenced the information which each group accessed.

The second aspect of coordination is an expansion of coordination on Twitter to the wider social media. Specifically, bloggers were attempting to identify major developments for readers. These efforts included words by Trita Parsi (National Iranian American Council), Nico Pitney (Huffington Post), Andrew Sullivan (Daily Dish, *The Atlantic*), and sites such as Enduring America. The differing choices of tags and individuals to follow led these bloggers to different sources of information and influenced their interpretations. In addition, these coordination points can be read in English; further coordination points existed in other languages, for example http://balatarin.com. This, despite the passable Google translation, meant that many would have still coordinated around information in the language they were able to read.

Differentiating between the volume of tweets and interaction or coordination around specific points provides a means to begin to understand the use of social media in protest. Twitter is important in this process as it functioned as a filter through which content from many other forms of social media was shared. The result was not a story of a genuine mass engagement around a single issue but a mass of smaller pockets of interaction.

These pockets of local interaction and different levels of interaction resulted in one loosely engaged outsider group seeking to show support, while other more deeply involved insider groups were seeking to get their story heard by a wider audience. Unfortunately, each group was telling themselves rather than each other, with very few exceptions.

## PERSPECTIVES ON PROTEST

The 2009 protests had much more in common with the use of social media by the N30 protesters than did the 1999 student protests in Iran. Iran 2009 and N30 demonstrate activity by a number of groups as a means to achieve the dual goals of coordinating activity on the streets while publicizing their efforts to a wider audience. Both used dispersed communications systems similar to that conceived by Paul Baran (1964), which provided great strength to the networks. In both cases, the networks were able to quickly adapt to changing circumstance and continue to interact despite state attempts to curtail access to communications and to remove important nodes from the network.

While writing about the Battle in Seattle, Paul de Armond (2001) noted that the new factor which led to success of protesters at N30 was "the richer informational environment, which makes the organization of civil (and uncivil) society into networks easier, less costly, and more efficient." Ten years on from N30, the information environment had become even richer, with services such as Twitter providing a means to share links to further sources of information. There is little doubt that in the face of state pressure the technology made organization easier and less costly (whether in terms of financial cost or level of risk). However, the case of Iran 2009 calls into question whether this level of information actually made the network more efficient.

The data shows messages spread via Twitter to promote particular gatherings or events demonstrate a degree of coordination at street level as effectively insider-to-insider communication. However, the second goal of engagement with the infosphere is more problematic. Twitter was certainly an efficient means to transmit information and links to material into the infosphere, as shown by the volume of tweets. However, it is less clear whether it was an efficient form of interaction between groups of insiders and outsiders. For example, the choice of tags such as #GR88, #Neda, and #Sohrab by insiders demonstrated an introspective tendency that required a degree of knowledge before the reader would understand the link to the election.

The surge in interest in the days following the election provided protesters with an opportunity for engagement with a group within the wider infosphere, but those insiders trying to get the message out predominantly engaged with each other rather than proactively with outsiders. The difficulty outsiders may have had recognizing those points required proactive outreach if insider groups wanted to engage outsiders. This might have been possible through RT to #HelpIranElection of tweets from key tags such as #Neda or #GR88. However, this happened very little in the month after the election, and nearly all the RT which appear in #HelpIranElection were merely repeating the dominant message.

These insights from the Iranian protests suggest three interrelated points which have wider implications for the conducting, reporting, and analyzing of future large-scale protest movements when they produce a massive volume of information. First, a key factor which hampered wider understanding of events by outsiders, perhaps counterintuitively, was the sheer volume of material. It was not finding information which was the problem; it was making sense of it, whether in terms of recognizing tags or filtering information.

The attempt to restrict access to communications in Iran also appears to have had perhaps unforeseen impacts on engagement in the infosphere. The restrictions led those individuals looking for external interaction, rather than internal coordination, to focus on getting the message out; for example, 25 percent of Tweets studied by the Web Ecology Project (2009) were RT. While understandable, the focus was on sending the message rather than engaging outsiders.

Strangely, if the restrictions had been more successful, it may have simplified the situation for outsiders by reducing the volume of information and making it easier to identify those with which they needed to interact. This is most likely the opposite impact from that which was intended. In future, states facing dispersed networks of protesters might seek to respond by flooding channels of communication rather than restricting access, mimicking the swarm tactics (Arquilla and Ronfeldt 2000) of protesters at N30 and COP 15 along with the thinking behind outsiders changing their location to Tehran or time zone to +3.30.

Second, the volume of material and the lack of highly visible but independent news coordination points limited the ease with which loosely interested outsiders could engage and through which stories could reach journalists. The rise of Indymedia, since the inception of IMC Seattle to cover the WTO in 1999, with over forty nodes subsequently established, has provided a stable platform through which dispersed information could be accessed. This maintained the flexibility of noncentralized communications while creating a rallying point for individuals seeking to show support and access information which was distinct from the traditional and commercial news sources.

The website created to cover N30 received almost 1.5 million hits during the WTO protests, and today the IMC sites globally are estimated to receive between 500,000 and two million page views daily (IndyMedia 2007). In contrast, the Iranian protest movement lacked a coordination point for resources, information, and support which was obvious to outsiders. Facing limitations on the use of traditional media whether due to state control or linked to #CNNfail, with a few exceptions, material discovery largely relied on viral pathways or an active interest in the subject by the reader. Those blogs offering commentary, such as the Daily Dish or Enduring America, that did attempt to provide some sort of coordinated coverage, were themselves having to pick up what they could from around the web or via Twitter.

The success of viral sharing of certain videos did not result in Twitter outsiders who showed support in the days after the election subsequently engaging with discussions such as #GR88 in the following months. Equally, individuals with a few thousand followers repeatedly required outsiders to be proactive in identifying individuals to follow if they were to gain the range of information which they could get through certain #tags. It also lost the resilience of the dispersed network, shown when @PerisanKiwi, who had 32,000 followers, stopped tweeting on June 24 shortly after sending the message, "we must go—dont know when we can get internet—they take 1 of us, they will torture and get names—now we must move fast" (PersianKiwi 2009).

Third, as a result of the difficulty of interacting in such a rich environment, the Iranian protesters may well have been less successful at engaging the wider audience than the N30 protesters ten years earlier. While not ignoring the events which were as iconic as they were tragic, this did not result in large-scale interaction with outsiders who were previously disengaged from Iranian politics, as shown by the content of tweets and the mapping of the resulting network.


## FUTURE PROTEST


Ultimately the struggle for power between those behind protest movements and those who seek to resist them will continue to rely on how effectively interlocutors are able to utilize the networks of resources available to them. Protest movements will continually have to find ways to identify coordination points which outsiders can recognize without losing the strength and flexibility of a dispersed communications system. As they do so, it will be increasingly important that protesters remember the observation made by John

Arquilla and David Ronfeldt (2000); "Swarming is seemingly amorphous, but it is a deliberately structured, coordinated, strategic way to strike from all directions" (p. vii). If the protest appears amorphous to sympathetic outsiders, then protesters will struggle to gain support but become too structured, and authorities may find it easier to disrupt the channels used for coordination. In effect, protest movements will have to tread a line somewhere between viral transmission and establishing centralized followers.

However, as analysis has shown, the ability for protesters to coordinate and get the message from the streets to the infosphere may not be their greatest challenge; it may be getting their message through the infosphere to recipients seeking to interact with them. In which case, future struggles might not be won or lost on the ability to transmit. They will be influenced by which side can most effectively:

- identify coordination points outsiders can easily recognize, while weakening or flooding those of the opposition;
- allow filtering of their information while hampering the other side's attempts;
- engage and interact with the wider groups while preventing the protagonists' attempts at communication from leaving the infosphere.

Academic study of protest movements will be increasingly able to track digital communications between different groups and identify the points around which they coordinate. The ability to identify these points within the chosen means of communication may provide a further opportunity to map not just the coordination points within one means of communication, but also to map the other forms of digital material spread through tools such as Twitter.

## REFERENCES

Arik. (2009). About. http://www.arikfr.com/blog/about.

Arquilla, J., and Ronfeldt, D. (2000). *Swarming and the future of conflict.* Santa Monica, CA: RAND

Baran, P. (1964). *On distributed communications: Introduction to distributed communications networks.* Santa Monica, CA: RAND.

Castronova, E. (2005, December). *On the research value of large games: Natural experiments in Norrath and Camelot.* CESifo Working Paper Series No. 1621. http://ssrn.com/abstract=875571.

de Armond, P. (2001). Netwar in the Emerald City: WTO protest strategy and tactics. In J. A. Ronfeldt (Ed.). *Networks and netwar: The future of crime terror and militancy* (pp. 201–235). Santa Monica, CA: RAND.

Grossman, L. (2009, June 17). *Iran protests: Twitter, the medium of the movement.* http://www.time.com/time/world/article/0,8599,1905125,00.html.

Heil, B., and Piskorski, M. (2009, June 1). New Twitter research: Men follow men and nobody tweets. http://blogs.harvardbusiness.org/cs/2009/06/new_twitter_research_men_follo.html.

Huberman, B. A., Romero, D. M., and Fang, W. (2009, January 5). Social networks that matter: Twitter under the microscope. First Monday.org.

IndyMedia. (2007, July 25). Indymedia's frequently asked questions. http://docs.indymedia.org/view/Global/FrequentlyAskedQuestions.

Parr, B. (2009, June 17). Mindblowing #IranElection stats: 221,744 tweets per hour at peak. http://mashable.com/2009/06/17/iranelection-crisis-numbers.

PersianKiwi. (2009, June 24). PersianKiwi. http://twitter.com/persiankiwi.

Stelter, B. (2009, June 15). Real-time criticism of CNN's Iran coverage. *New York Times*, p. B5.

Stoltz, C. (2009, June 22). #Neda the power of the viral image. http://www.huffingtonpost.com/craig-stoltz/neda-and-the-power-of-the_b_218594.html.

Tait, R., and Weaver, M. (2009, June 22). How Neda Soltani became the face of Iran's struggle. http://www.guardian.co.uk/world/2009/jun/22/neda-soltani-death-iran.

Thompson, N. (2009, June 17). Iran: Before you have that Twitter-gasm . . . http://www.wired.com/dangerroom/2009/06/iran-before-you-have-that-twitter-gasm.

Web Ecology Project. (2009). The Iranian election on Twitter: The first eighteen days.

Zilber, N. (2009, June 25). Twitter against the ayatollahs: The upheaval in Iran is a milestone in the influence of new media technology on global politics. http://www.guardian .co.uk/commentisfree/2009/jun/25/iran-new-media-upheaval.

*Chapter Eleven*

# Graphic Content

## *The Semiotics of a YouTube Uprising*

### Setareh Sabety

The chance of the Iranian elections being rigged was so great and palpable that it became the subject of a chant for the supporters of presidential candidates Mir Hossein Mousavi and Mehdi Karoubi long before the election day on June 12, 2009. For a nation that has never really experienced free elections, the allegation of rigging came as no surprise. Yet no one expected that the government would conduct itself so blatantly, so audaciously. This conduct is why so many were offended, hurt, and angry. The incumbent candidate President Mahmoud Ahmadinejad, with the backing of the Supreme Leader Ayatollah Ali Khamenei and the Revolutionary Guards, or the coup d'état government as they were called by the opposition, seemed to be oblivious to the wishes of a goodly percentage of the nation, once again reminding them that they did not care for public or international opinion. In fact, defying the opinion of the whole world has become the defining characteristic of the hardliners since the very beginning of the Islamic Republic. From the time when they stabbed women who protested the enforcement of the *hejab* some thirty years ago, the Islamic regime has demonstrated repeatedly that it takes pride in its almost ascetic indifference to keeping a good image in the world. Nevertheless, the possibility of a popular uprising was so imminent after Ahmadinejad was announced as the landslide winner with over 60 percent of the vote that a media blackout was imposed by the regime within hours of that announcement on June 12, 2009.

Since the media crackdown, video clips posted on YouTube have been the most common and widespread means of getting information out of Iran. Nothing other than these short videos, usually taken by the protesters themselves with cell phones, has conveyed more abundantly to the outside world what is happening on the streets of Tehran. Within hours, sometimes minutes of a demonstration, a clash, or an atrocity, viewers saw clips disseminated all over the Internet via YouTube and social networking sites such as Twitter and Facebook and Iranian Diaspora websites such as Iranian.com, Tehran Bureau, Gooya, and the Persian blogger's site Balatarin.com. These visual records of a people struggling for their rights have managed to capture the sympathy of the world for the cause of democracy in Iran. Taken by amateurs and often hard to verify, they are not as significant as sources of information as they are as narratives that show the world from the street level the struggle of a people fighting for justice.

Despite the ban on foreign journalists, the election protest movement was soon a global cause célèbre largely due to the fact that raw amateur images made most people feel like eyewitnesses to the crimes committed by the regime. In the first few weeks, the Internet was flooded with video clips, and viewers felt overwhelmed. Bloggers started collecting them, and websites were dedicated to these short films. Music was put to the images, and tearful and revolutionary songs were composed by Iranian and Western artists as tributes to the victims of the uprising (YouTube, A Persian Girl). Soon almost everyone knew that whenever an event or demonstration was scheduled in Iran, before journalists could report or mainstream media could air the news, ordinary people on the Internet, especially Twitter and Facebook, saw video clips of it. CNN and Western mainstream networks started using Twitter, YouTube, and Facebook to spruce up their reports on Iran. They, too, started airing the video clips. The news became an amateur's story line captured on a cell phone. For an audience jaded by polished twenty-four-hour news on cable networks, this raw footage coming out of Iran was captivating. This was a form, if you will, of extreme reality TV. The Iran election protests became the uprising that made citizen journalism a household term. It made those guilty about spending too much time on social networking sites feel like they were not wasting time. Many non-Iranians and Iranians of the Diaspora joined the struggle, promoting it via their personal computers, drawing up petitions, organizing hunger strikes and solidarity rallies in major cities of the world.

Those first hours after the media blackout were troubled. News was slow in coming out of Iran. As the election results unfolded and showed an increasingly sobering face, those of us who were on Twitter realized that the best and most up-to-date news was coming first to us. We soon became news gatherers and disseminators eagerly trying to decipher between what was rumor and what was true. I found myself passing on information on the use of proxies and first-aid for gun wounds. Suddenly, our cybervoyeurism turned into activism as we were encouraged by the international media and the protesters' use of our information. We thought the revolution would be "Twitterized," in the words of one Twitterer.

Much of what came through was hard to watch, yet it was morosely addictive. I remember watching the now famous video of Neda on June 20, the day she was shot (YouTube, Girl Shot Dead). It came on my Twitter page a good many hours before the first network, CNN, aired it. I was accustomed to graphic clips and pictures since there had been many clashes and many had already died, but nothing could prepare me for that less-than-a-minute video of a young woman dying from a gunshot wound right in front of the camera. The way we saw the life go out of her, the speed of it, the meaningless and random cruelty of it shocked the world.

Why did the Neda video clip have such a dramatic impact? The timing, nature, and content of the video clip all contributed to making it iconic. June 20 was the Saturday after the now infamous Friday prayer given by the Supreme Leader, Ayatollah Khamenei, when he warned protesters that they would face grave consequences if they continued their demonstrations. Everyone knew that the following Saturday was a dangerous day to go out. In a blog that I wrote, in the early morning that day, I expressed my own misgivings:

It is Saturday morning June 20th: my daughter's birthday. Fifteen years ago I gave birth to her hoping that someday she would live in a free Iran. Today there is a protest march planned in Tehran despite the warnings of crackdown by Ayatollah Khamenei. The events of the past week, the YouTubed courage that we have witnessed, has awakened us again this time more than ever. Images cross my mind like a slide show of video stills to the sound of screaming mothers. I see a young man shot in the face, another being beaten to a pulp by basiji thugs, a group of young Kurds hanging from nooses in the middle of a main street. I see a girl kicking a security policeman, kids throwing rocks at gunmen, a perfectly manicured hand of a young woman holding a rock ready to throw. I see a sea of people who share my hopes and fears for Iran in their silence on the wide avenues and squares of my beloved, polluted, and overpopulated Tehran. I see old women in chadors and young women with newfound courage chanting the wishes of my heart even when to do so may mean arrest, beating and death. I pray that today, this all important day, courage and justice is triumphant and that there will be no bloodshed. I pray that no mother has to hear bad news, no woman is martyred and no young man beaten or arrested. I pray that these people, whom I love, who are risking their lives with incredible courage are not harmed and that their silent, persistent message of the basic need for freedom and democracy wins the day. (Sabety)

By that afternoon, sitting in front of my computer, my worst fears came true. June 20 would forever be marked by the death of one twenty-three-year-old protester, Neda Agha-Soltan. I was checking for news on the Internet. By then, I had seen many videos coming out of Iran with the warning: "graphic content."

The clip was short, only forty seconds long: we see a girl holding her chest and being helped to the ground by two men, one on each side. She is wearing blue jeans and a dark *roosari* (head scarf) and a tight, dark *ropoosh* (a long jacket worn by women in Iran in order to comply with the rules of *hejab* or Islamic covering). The two men are wearing blue jeans and short-sleeved shirts. One man has white pony-tailed hair, and the other is much younger with dark black hair. They help her down as we hear the voiceover of men speaking; we can hear one saying, "*Abjee* (sister) *abjee*—bring a car to take this one." We see a pool of blood gather under the girl's head. One of the men helping her keeps saying, "*Neda joon natar. Neda natars* (Neda dear don't be afraid. Neda don't be afraid)." Another man is heard saying, "Put pressure on it." The two men who helped her to the ground are trying to stop her bleeding, and a third has now approached and wants to help. We then hear the horrified screams of one of the men, "*Vay, vaaaay.*" The companion with the white pony-tailed hair, whom we later learn was her music teacher, is now saying, "Neda, stay, Neda stay, Neda don't go." Blood starts coming out of her mouth and nose, making red, almost symmetric paths crossing her beautiful face and forming a pool under her head. The camera moves forward to a shot that shows six hands on her trying to stop the bleeding and one man kneeling in front of her rather helplessly. All this time, we hear "Neda stay, Neda don't go, Neda open, Neda open." Someone else says, "Open her mouth"; she turns to one side unconscious and her eyes roll back. We then hear the man who knew her name shout in a shrill and most disturbing scream, "*Dayoos haaaa, dayoos haa!*" At that point, we know that she has taken her last breath. We hear screams. The clip ends as abruptly as it began (YouTube, Basij Shoots to Death; Girl Shot Dead).

Why did the Neda video have such an impact? On the obvious level, the answer is simple: whenever we see an innocent and peaceful protester dying on camera, it is bound to attract attention and stir emotions. Yet, there were a few other videos of protesters shot and dying, but none of them made this kind of impact (YouTube, How Many More Should Die). Something about this clip made it special; something made it iconic. It is necessary to peel away the layers of meanings and try to decode what it is that gives this clip its significance and why it instantaneously turned Neda into the Marianne or the female emblem of the uprising in Iran.

Neda was a young, beautiful, and slim woman wearing the kind of *hejab* that in Iran immediately signifies that she was liberated. This lax *hejab* became popular and prevalent after the landslide election of the reformist president, Mohammad Khatami, in 1997. Khatami advocated not only the importance of a civil society, but also advocated freedom of expression which translated into more lenient regulation of dress and behavior and gave birth to this kind of very Iranian-reformist *hejab*. Politically, the *roopoosh-roosari* combination simply signifies that the wearer is not a hardliner and that she is probably either proreformist, secular-minded, and/or just antiregime all together. This *hejab* is as sexy a version of the Islamic covering imposed by law as is possible to wear in Iran. In fact, it is safe to say that most women who wear this kind of *hejab* are those who would not wear any Islamic covering if they had the choice. It is the *hejab* of those who don't believe in wearing one. It is no coincidence that in a nation that identifies itself as Islamic, the way a person dresses is an all-important sign of not only lifestyle choice but also political leaning. In Iran, one look at how someone dresses, and the observer can tell if the wearer is proregime or not. When the way she dresses, how she spends her leisure time, what she drinks, and whom she has sex with are all regulated by a repressive state, then lifestyle choices take on the importance of ideologies. The elections and the difference between candidates was more about lifestyle choices than about any single ideology.

Many voted against the incumbent and hardliner, Mahmoud Ahmadinejad, because they were tired of being told what to wear and how to behave. Indeed, the majority of the women who voted for reformist candidates Mir Hossein Mousavi or Mehdi Karroubi wore this *ropoosh-roosari* combination. Zahra Rahnavard's (Mir Hossein Mousavi's wife) decision to wear a colorful and floral patterned *roosari* and blue jean shirt under her black *chador* was deemed scandalous by hardliners and did much to endear her to her husband's young and female constituents. In Iran, *hezbollahi* or hardliner women and men are almost never seen in blue jeans. The hardliner men wear long-sleeved shirts usually of beige or white color with black or army-colored pants, while the women dress in black *maghnaaeh* (a head covering that attaches with a elastic band and ensures that no hair is seen) and in *chador* (traditional head-to-toe covering, usually black).

From the very opening of the clip, we know that the young woman was a *roopoosh-roosari* kind of woman. Her blue jeans and Adidas-style striped red and white sneakers also signify the type of woman Neda was. The blue jeans that she wore, and the appearance of her music teacher and Arash Hejazi, the doctor who helped her, all convey the fact that these people are certainly secular Iranians. Her thin figure, perfectly plucked eyebrows, and signature Iranian nose job also suggest the kind of woman she was: one of the thousands of young, beautiful women who try to look as Western as possible despite or in outright defiance of the imposed *hejab* and thirty years of Islamist indoctrination. They turn to *Vogue* and *Elle* for inspiration and copy Western fashions with amazing exactitude. They, more than anything, are the living, walking, and laughing symbols of how the Islamic Revolution has failed. That Saturday, Neda, who symbolized the failure of coercive Islam in Iran, died. Her death gave the struggle for civil rights and freedom a face. It is befitting that the struggle should have a female face: women, whose civil rights have been the most damaged by the Islamic Revolution of 1979, gave the reformist campaign its soul, its zeal, and feminized the uprising.

What is most disturbing in the video is that we see people trying desperately to keep Neda alive but failing to stop the rapid pace of blood flowing out of her. The blood makes traces down her statuesque profile, yet she looks clean to the end; there is not much blood in this video because the one gunshot wound was not visible to the camera. The clean, quick nature of her death made it more shocking than other deaths captured on video. She died quietly, gently, without much gore; we saw clearly her beautiful features until her very last gasps. The horror of the act is amplified through the loud pleading of her companion asking her to stay, which escalates into shouts of disbelief ending with an expletive meant most certainly for the government and the *Basij* (the plainclothes militia) who had been sent out on that day to put fear into the protesters with arrests, beatings, and killings. *Dayoos*, an expletive of Azeri origin, means a man whose wife dishonors him, the worse kind of insult in a patriarchal society.

The fact that it was a young, beautiful woman who was unlucky enough to be the only one shot that day on that side street made this crime even more horrendous. It was almost as if the Islamist hardliners had deliberately picked out this young woman to kill, as if with Neda they could wipe out the new, secular, and youthful Iran that had put fear into the ruling government, shaking the foundation of the Islamic regime. Neda's person, her innocence, her Westernized well-kept look, and her random senseless death mirrored and came to personify the postelection uprising in Iran. This movement that began as an electoral campaign, that was more about the right to individual expression and opportunity than anything else, and the uprising that sprang from the desperate anger engendered by this election were fittingly embodied by the random and poetic death of a young *roopoosh-roosari* woman that the world got to witness thanks to YouTube and the Internet.

## REFERENCES

Sabety, S. Today! Iranian.com. http://www.iranian.com/main/blog/setareh-sabety/today.
YouTube. Basij shoots to death a young woman June 20th. http://www.youtube.com/verify_age?next_url=http%3A//www.youtube.com/watch%3Fv%3DOjQxq5N--Kc.
———. Girl shot dead in Tehran June 20, 2009. http://www.youtube.com/verify_age?next_url=http%3A//www.youtube.com/watch%3Fv%3DQZZGJ3aOyRQ.
———. How many more should die? Tehran demonstration. http://www.youtube.com/watch?v=dvMnqvdSnc0.
———. A Persian girl got shot in Tehran, Iran, on June 20th, 2009. http://www.youtube.com/verify_age?next_url=http%3A//www.youtube.com/watch%3Fv%3DIQn4CluQhRw.

*Chapter Twelve*

# The Role and Impact of New Information Technology (NIT) Applications in Disseminating News about the Recent Iran Presidential Election and Uprisings

Mahboub Hashem and Abeer Najjar

The latest Iran presidential election seems to have sharply split the Iranian society between two antagonistic camps. The conservatives gather under the leadership of Iran's Supreme Ayatollah Ruhollah Sayyid Ali Hoseini Khamenei and the Guardian Council, who wholeheartedly supported the current Iranian president, Mahmoud Ahmadinejad. The reformists or moderates are under the leadership of former presidents Akbar Hashemi Rafsanjani, Seyed Mohammad Khatami, and former prime minister Mir Hossein Mousavi, as well as Cleric Mehdi Karrubi, former Speaker of the Iranian Majlis and chairman of the National Trust Party, all of whom claimed irregularities and fraud at the polls. The latter also maintained that Mir Hossein Mousavi won the election on June 12, 2009, rather than the current president Amadinejad. Yet, their claims were not investigated and were dismissed by the Supreme Ayatollah Khamenei, who only ordered a partial recount of the votes, which gave the sitting president Ahmadinejad a landslide victory. Then, Ahmadinejad was declared the winner, according to government election results. This ultimate decision sparked large demonstrations and popular uprisings, which turned bloody between riot police and opposition supporters. Once again, demonstrations by tens of thousands of reformists as well as hundreds from the opposite side (conservatives) took to the streets simultaneously. Reformists were demonstrating against the alleged fraudulent results of the presidential election, and conservatives were protesting against the role played by former president Akbar Hashemi Rafsanjani toward the pro-Mousavi protests. Many experts in the media—news reporters, journalists, editors, and bloggers—discussed the influence of online social networks and how they changed the fabric of the Internet. In addition, most of them spoke about how Iranian authorities cracked down on foreign media reporting in the country, disrupted cell phone use and text messaging, and also restricted Internet access, making it hard to get information out of Iran. Indeed, this election was a significant event in the history of the Islamic Republic of Iran since its establishment in 1979, especially due to the wave of public protest which revealed the citizens' lack of confidence in the regime. Even though the regime tried to use local media to spread false reports depicting the country's alleged calm, news of chaos in the streets spread across the world through social media networks such as Facebook, MySpace, Wikipedia, YouTube, Flicker, Twitter, and other websites, most of which were made inaccessible for Iranians by their government (Arouzi 2009; Bernal 2009; Boyle and Choney 2009; Bunt 2009; Carafano 2009; Christensen 2009; Coleman 2009; Dubner 2008; Engdahl 2007; Folkenflik 2009; Gross 2009; Hare 2009; Iran and Ruhollah 2009; Iran's Presidential 2009; Mackey 2009; Maina 2009; Mercier 2009; Rumford 2009; Solis 2009; Tehran Blocks 2009; Wandel 2008; Wood and Smith 2001).

## THE ISLAMIC REPUBLIC OF IRAN

Ayatollah Ruhollah Musavi Khomeini was an Iranian religious leader and politician. Through tapes from the French capital, Paris, and, in 1979, his coming to Tehran, the Iranian capital, he led the Iranian Revolution that overthrew the latest shah of Iran, Mohammad Reza Pahlavi, and established the Islamic Republic of Iran. Subsequently, Khomeini became Iran's Supreme Leader (a position created in the Constitution as the highest-ranking religious and political authority in the country). After he passed away, this authority transferred to the current Ayatollah Khamenei.

Iran is a Persian country situated in Western Asia; therefore, the two terms, *Persia* and *Iran*, are used interchangeably in cultural contexts. It ranks among the top twenty countries in terms of area, with a population of over 70 million. Geographically, its central location between Europe and Asia makes it a very important country to the rest of the world. Economically, Iran has large reserves of petroleum and natural gas, which renders it even more important on the international scene (Iran and Ruhollah 2009).

Additionally, Iran is a well-wired and networked nation, with more than twenty million people who use the Internet on a regular basis. About 66 percent of Iranians are age thirty and younger. They mostly own computers and mobile phones and know how to use them for a variety of purposes. As a result, Iranian youths experienced what is called citizen journalism during and after the election, which is a huge shift from traditional journalism, especially in a presidential election. Since New Information Technology (NIT) devices provide new means to reach others quickly, particularly other young audiences, Iranian youths proved to be fascinated with those devices, and they used them effectively. As such, they relied heavily on them to inform their compatriots and the outside world about the delicate situation in Iran. Furthermore, Iranian youths, along with the leading opposition candidate, Mir Hossein Mousavi, used NIT applications successfully and advertised for his presidential election campaign on Facebook and other social networks in order to gain global acceptance and participation. This action was mainly targeting all youths everywhere, since they are the major users of social networks, are generally outspoken in their views, and feel more comfortable expressing themselves on Facebook. However, despite of all the benefits of social networking and the huge role that Facebook played in the Iranian presidential election, Coleman (2009) reported that, on May 23 and prior to the election date on June 12, 2009, Iran blocked Facebook in order to stop supporters of the leading opposition candidate from using the site for his campaign.

## THE IRANIAN CRISIS AND SOCIAL NETWORKS

Social networks' influence, when misused, can create misunderstanding of an issue. Rumors, deceit, and wrong information can spread fast and complicate the situation instead of rectifying it. In addition, news media and social networks try to exaggerate the reality sometimes in order to manipulate or influence audience opinions into taking sides. Social networks are so influential that many observers said that online networks like Twitter and Facebook have reached a peak. They became so powerful to the extent that millions of people have figured out how they can get to Mousavi's Facebook site. They also believe that social networks, as tools, have an ability to create a metaphorical world that gathers thousands of different perspectives, geographical, cultural, and philosophical (Gross 2009). In the case of the events that took place in the Iranian presidential election, it was clear that the availability of firsthand information sources were rare and almost incapable of obtaining or conveying their news to global viewers had it not been for social networking sites. It was perhaps the first time that a political issue of this magnitude had been dealt with by people after the spread and use of these networking tools. Their effectiveness and impact were proven by the number of people reached either to offer a window on what was happening or to form groups to take active action in the Green Revolution. This is clearly a social development on a global level since people could express themselves and reach a large audience to either inform or to spread awareness. Due to heavy censorship of media, citizen journalists sprung to the forefront and relied greatly on NIT applications to take upon themselves the responsibility to communicate what was happening to both Iranians and to the outside world. Therefore, under tight control of media, the burden of reporting on Iran's election crisis and the ensuing uprising was falling gradually on Iranian youths, who knew how to use social media networks to their advantage. As a deterrent, the Iranian government issued a threat to online users that they could face trial and even capital punishment for incitement. As a result, the online confrontation paralleled the political face-off playing out offline between opposition supporters and the forces of the government (Boyle and Choney 2009).

Filtering social networks and censoring mainstream media did not sway opposition supporters from using antifilters and proxies to access the web world in order to continue telling their stories of what was happening on the ground. They did so by reporting on rallies and casualties secretly using alternate web servers set up abroad. Twitter and mobile phone services took center stage in the election's aftermath as people found several ways to unblock websites and sent out many reports about the crisis from Tehran. Those Iranians with the will found more than one way to say what they wanted and to avert the government from stopping them. Furthermore, a web-based service called Social Networking focuses on building online communities consisting of people who share similar activities and interests. People interact by e-mail or instant messaging. Therefore, Social Networking was a useful technique for presidential campaigns to promote positive images of candidates for the presidential election, as its global exposure to all groups of people makes it easier for them to exchange opinions about those candidates. The decision to block those social networks was announced by the Ministry of Communications and Information Technology without any comments on this action from the Iranian authorities. It was also proven from BBC sources that CNN employees working in Tehran could not access Facebook either. This blockage affected the Iranian election as locking down websites such as Facebook limited the potential for open discussion between candidates or people of different communities and groups (Bunt 2009; Carafano 2009; Coleman 2009).

This was not the end of the story. Iranians tuned into these social networks to provide not only reports but also to arrange protests all around the globe and to organize activities that supported street journalists who played an important role in keeping the people outside Iran informed. Others took photos and made videos of the turmoil in Iran and posted them on news websites, bypassing government restrictions, until the global news networks picked up these images and telecast the situation in Iran. Even though accuracy and reliability of social networks' information may be questionable, the reality was that these media were the only available tools for people in Iran who witnessed firsthand what was happening on the ground.

Facebook is a major Internet application that has helped disseminate news, videos, and images during the postpresidential election in Iran. Facebook, Twitter, SMS messages, and other social networks enabled us to learn more and gain a deeper understanding of the crisis that was based on people's opinions as opposed to information from news channels. The postelection riots in Tehran caused major restrictions on the news media, especially televised scenes of the protests. However, social networks, most notably Facebook and Twitter, were flooded with people's opinions about the outcome of the elections and suppression of protesters. It is believed that in such dire circumstances, people should avail themselves of the opportunity to use social networks to expand discussions and deliver the news to the world which, in the case of the Iranian protests, remained disconnected to traditional media. Such networks are not subject to similar laws that apply to traditional media and, consequently, the censorship of information or photographs are hard to apply. NIT applications played a very important role in the Iranian protests because without the availability of such technologies, Iranians worldwide would not be able to communicate their feelings and emotions with one another and the rest of the world.

## SOCIAL MEDIA'S ROLE IN THE IRANIAN CRISIS

Extensive media coverage highlighted the role of social media networks, both in helping organize activities and sharing the progress of events. Hence, social media played very important roles in the Iran presidential election and ensuing uprising. First, they helped Iranian reformists communicate with each other and with the outside world. Second, they helped the rest of the world interact with both Iranians and sympathizers of the protesters. For instance, it has been said that YouTube and Flicker brought multimedia out of the troubled Islamic Republic. Twitter and Facebook reports spread videos instantly. Blogs, Wikipedia, and citizen journalists helped propagate and filter this information. More importantly, these networks assisted people who were interested in taking action in the absence of mainstream media. While it is hard to visualize what exactly happened on the streets of Tehran during those days of the Iran election crisis, social media were there and opened a nonstop line of available information to the public at a time when Iranian authority was trying to ban all individuals who did not please that authority (Carafano 2009). Furthermore, Gross (2009) noticed the massive Iranian movement aimed at reversing the election results and possibly even toppling the Iranian regime through the use of social media networks' instantly shared protesters' actions, and the whole world was watching.

Social media reached their highest points during the weekend of June 19 to 21, 2009. It was the bloodiest Iranian weekend after the presidential election, especially when Neda Soltani, a young Iranian woman, was mortally shot by the *Basij* and died on camera. Then, these media spread dozens of pictures, videos, web tools, multimedia short films, and talks from within Iran. These pictures or videos brought people together worldwide to detest the harsh violence inflicted upon protesters by the Iranian government. Among the myriad tweets, Facebook messages, and YouTube videos, that sole incident was a galvanizing moment in Iran's troubled election and ensuing uprising, and it shook the entire world and showed how powerful social media can be in such circumstances. In addition, government-run television informed the public that at least ten people were killed and one hundred injured on Saturday, June 20, 2009, as thousands of protesters swept into the streets of Tehran in disobedience to warnings issued on Friday, June 19, 2009, by Iran's Supreme Leader and Security Council (Bernal 2009).

In summary, the significance of various NIT applications as tools for mobilizing discourse and activism had been brought into sharp focus in the events surrounding the June 12, 2009, Iran presidential election. Tweets linked to other social media and established a major part of the public politics and protest following the disputed election results. The use of various social media applications to facilitate discussion, debate, and the exchange of ideas or current information among interested people on a worldwide scale was a well-established occurrence in the history of Iran politics and NIT. Yet, the cyberactivism surrounding the Iranian protests was unprecedented, driving the global debate, while governments and established media struggled to keep pace with what was going on. There is no doubt that NIT applications proved themselves as outstanding elements of main-street communications, for citizen reporters found that they could share and exchange stories with people around the world in a matter of minutes (Bunt 2009; Carafano 2009). The influence of social media on traditional media was very evident in the international news coverage of events which followed the Iranian presidential election. For instance, CNN was blamed by many Western reporters for being reluctant or late to cover the Iranian election. This influence spilled over into the Arab media concerning their coverage of the Iranian crisis. The following section sheds more light on this type of coverage.

## THE GULF MEDIA COVERAGE OF THE IRANIAN CRISIS (AL-ARABIYA NET AND *AL-QUDS AL-ARABI*)

Arab-Iranian relations have both strengths and setbacks. Currently, major issues affecting these relations include Iran's nuclear program, its alleged support of Hamas and Hezbollah, the republic's involvement in the Iraqi issue, and its occupation of the three Emirati islands since 1971, among others. Saudi Arabia is at the forefront of the Arab bloc against Iran, particularly in the Gulf Cooperation Council (GCC) region. However, almost all of the GCC countries have security concerns distressing their relation with Iran; however, Qatar is believed to enjoy a better relation with the Islamic Republic (Ramazani 1992) as part of the frequently referenced alliance among Syria, Iran, Qatar, Hezbollah, and Hamas (Badran 2009).

This section examines how two pan-Arab news sources, namely, Al-Arabiya news website and *Al-Quds Al-Arabi* newspaper covered news about the post-Iranian presidential election crisis. The news sources are chosen for their connections to Saudi Arabia on the one hand and Qatar on the other for the possible influence of the agenda of the two respective countries on the news content of these news outlets. Hence, it is important to look at how these two Arab news sources frame the crisis in Iran following the presidential election of 2009. This is in addition to examining whether Al-Arabiya and *Al-Quds Al-Arabi* have a common frame of the events or if their coverage presented multiple frames in tune with their ideological orientations.

Al-Arabiya is one of the Middle East Broadcasting Corporation (MBC) Group channels, which is owned and managed by a Saudi businessman, Sheikh Walid Al-Ibrahim, who is close to the Saudi royal family and the brother-in-law of the late King Fahd. The channel comes as the second source of news to the Arab public next to Al-Jazeera (Etling, Kelly, Faris, and Palfrey 2009). Millions of Arabs depend on the Al-Arabiya website for their daily news (Lynch 2007). The site ranks as number seven in the Arab websites referred to by Arab bloggers (Etling et al. 2009). Al-Arabiya, like Al-Jazeera, is believed to be balanced and objective in its news reports, though, as Najm Jarrah (2008) notes:

> Distortions and omissions come mainly when their sponsor-governments' agendas come into play. This is more of a problem with *Al-Arabiya* than *Al-Jazeera*, but both have demonstrated some degree of susceptibility to it over the years. *Al-Arabiya* is often accused of putting a Saudi spin on its coverage of regional developments.

Al-Arabiya bureau in Tehran was shut down starting June 14, 2009 (Sambidge 2009).

*Al Quds Al-Arabi* is a pan-Arab newspaper based in London. The newspaper is sponsored by the Qatari government. Haidar al Rabie of Pan Arab Media (2008) asserts that the paper receives financial support that could support two newspapers from Qatar. In addition to *Al-Sharq Al-Awsat* and *Al-Hayat* newspapers, *Al-Quds Al-Arabi* participates in setting the "terms and rhythm of pan-Arab public discourse" (Kraidy 2005). The newspaper's editor-in-chief,

Abd Al-Bari Atwan, is a pan-Arab commentator frequently interviewed by Al-Jazeera. He has established himself as an important political commentator side by side with the Egyptian veteran journalist Mohamed Hassanein Heikal (Iskandar 2007). Furthermore, one of the newspaper's founders, the Lebanese journalist Sana al-Alool, is known for her connections to the Qatari government (Rabie 2008).

## CAUSES OF THE CRISIS:
## REPRESSIVE REGIME VERSUS WESTERN CONSPIRACY

Maamoun Fandy argues that Al-Arabiya takes part in the "uncivil war of words" between Riyad and Doha (Fandy 2007). One can assume that the two news outlets represent the major trends in Arab media coverage and portrayal of the Iranian crisis. The coverage and analysis provided by the Arab news media on the Iranian postelection crisis was colored by the conservative-reformist dichotomy. This coverage is consistent with the split in the Iranian political scene. As in the coverage of any other conflict, the news coverage of this political crisis was highly influenced by the mutual accusations made by the news sources from the two camps to vilify members and leaders of the other bloc. Accusations of conspiracy, spying, and treachery were made public by the religious leaders in Iran against those involved in the demonstrations following the elections. Many of the news stories in Al-Arabiya and *Al-Quds Al-Arabi* were focused on these accusations. Remarkably, in this crisis there was very little room to verify accusations of treachery or of the cruelty of the *Basij* militia in dealing with protesters.

Largely, *Al-Quds Al-Arabi* newspaper framed the post-Iranian crisis as an external matter, a Western invention or creation, and a result of a Western intervention. In the newspaper, modest investigation, acknowledgment, or emphasis was exercised on the internal side of the story: the concerns of the protesters, their composition, or demands (Abu Jajah 2009, June 26). Unlike *Al-Quds Al-Arabi*, the Al-Arabiya site showed more interest in the Iranian side of the crisis. Various news stories and commentaries were made on the women's movement, student movements, labor, and other social movements (Student 2009, June 25; Iranian Women 2009, June 28). The Iranian saga was, to a great extent, framed as a revolution against repression. Al-Arabiya coverage was focused, on some level, on the security forces and their violent responses to demonstrations. This emphasis was clear in images and headlines that all together made the event appear more dramatic. Terms like *arrest, violence, confrontations, great threat, repression, terrorizing, killing, Intifada,* and *revolution* were repeatedly mentioned in the headlines of Al-Arabiya news stories and analyses on this issue (Malik 2009, June 21; Nemri 2009, June 18; Obama 2009, June 23; Zein 2009, June 25); whereas, terms like *unrest, isolation, tension,* and *pressure* appeared more in *Al-Quds Al-Arabi* stories and commentary (Iran Accuses 2009, June 17; Mousavi Says 2009, June 26). More references were made in the newspaper to the external dimension of the story.

In Al-Arabiya, the Green Revolution was framed as a protest by the reformists who were depicted as liberal, pro-Western, and demonstrating against the extreme religious authority. The Green Revolution was compared to the Islamic Revolution of 1979 (Zahed and Al-Fayez 2009). The protests were presented as very widespread and powerful to the extent of questioning the ability of the Iranian authorities to regain control over the protesters, especially in the very first days of protest and demonstrations (Saraf 2009, June 20). Al-Arabiya started off reporting the crisis as more dramatic in scale and influence, as a point of no return, then turned to describe it, a few days later, as a "hole in the shirt" and a "crack in the wall" (Cherbel 2009, June 20; Zein 2009, June 17). Loaded terms appeared in the headlines of Al-Arabiya, portraying the actions as a "tear in the Iranian shirt" or "*amama*" (head cover used by clerics), or a "hole in the Iranian castle," and a "fraction in the Iranian glass" (Cherbel 2009, June 20; Nemri 2009, June 18; Zein 2009, June 17). Notably, the news site uses stronger language to describe the actions of the Iranian authorities against the demonstrators. The Iranian government is described in the headlines as "illegitimate" (Ali 2009, June 24); and in another item there was a reference to the Iranian president Ahmadinejad as a "dictator" (Saraf 2009, June 20).

Repression was the major cause of the unrest in Iran according to Al-Arabiya. The term *al-qameah* (repression) was commonly used in Al-Arabiya news stories and commentaries. Ali Hmadeh, of the Lebanese newspaper *al Nahar*, wrote in Al-Arabiya that this "revolution is subject to a vast scale of repression" and went on to state that the Iranian revolution is going through the phase of "the thick stick." For him, journalists were too repressed and imprisoned by the regime itself (Hmadeh 2009, June 25). Additionally, Raghda Dirgham wrote in Al-Arabiya that the Iranian regime will try to create trouble and unrest in the neighboring countries of Iraq, Lebanon, and Palestine in order to distract the world's attention from the *Intifada* in Iran and to justify further repressive measures against protestors (Dirgham 2009, June 26a).

In contrast, there was little use of the term *qameah* (repression) as one of the major grounds for the demonstrations in *Al-Quds Al-Arabi*. News in this paper focused on the Iranian government's accusations of the United States, Britain, and Israel inflaming the political situation in Iran (Iran Accused 2009, June 25). Allegations of Central Intelligence Agency (CIA) financial support for the protesters in Iran were reported in the newspaper (Iranian Demonstrators 2009). It provided more news on the relations between the West and Tehran (Iran Accused 2009, June 25). One headline read, "Iran Accused the United States and Britain of Inflaming Demonstrations" (Iran Accused 2009, June 22). The headline of the newspaper's article, written by Atwan, reads, "The West Hijacks the Iranian Protests" (2009, June 24). More news was reported on Hezbollah and the Venezuelan president Chavez making similar accusations to the West (Chavez 2009, June 26). Iranian politicians' statements on this issue would make it to the news headlines of *Al Quds Al-Arabi*, as follows: "Muttaki Is Speaking about Britain's Nasty Plans"; "Nijad Calls upon Obama and Brown to Stop Interfering in Iran's Affairs"; "Larijani Threatens the West" (Iranian Revolutionary 2009, June 22), and "The West Is Naïve to Hope That the Iranian Government Is Crumpling" (Iranian Authorities 2009, June 22).

Al-Arabiya's news and commentaries dealt with the fraud in the Iranian elections as a fact; they had no doubt there was deception, while *Al-Quds Al-Arabi* dealt with the alleged deception as a mere accusation and reported Njiad's words on the significance of the results and the process of the Iranian elections (Nijad: The Elections 2009, June 25). He was quoted describing the elections as "a chief turning point in the history of the revolution and humanity at large" (Nijad: The Elections 2009, June 25).

## GROUPING OF RELEVANT PARTIES
## BY BLAME AND GUILT ATTRIBUTION

Grouping the parties of the crisis took different levels in both Al-Arabiya and *Al-Quds Al-Arabi*. According to Al-Arabiya, the grouping was as follows: the reformists under the leadership of Akbar Hashemi Rafsanjani on the one hand and the conservatives or religious "extremist mullahs" under the leadership of Grand Ayatollah Hossein Ali Montazeri on the other. In *Al-Quds Al-Arabi*, the camps were presented as the Iranian regime against the West, including the United States, Britain, the CIA, as well as Israel and their followers or "spies," meaning the protesters in Iran and international journalists (Ahmadinejad 2009, June 26; Iran Accused 2009, June 22; Iran Continues 2009, June 23; Nijad Calls 2009, June 22). Parties, descriptions, and labels varied according to the news channel. Though Al-Arabiya, for instance, did not report the conspiracy accusations, there was an emphasis on the possible role of President Barak Obama as a party whose actions could make a difference (Dirgham 2009, June 26b; Obama Condemns 2009, June 23).

Unlike *Al-Quds Al-Arabi* newspaper, youth and women appeared as part of the political equation in Iran and as parties with concerns and demands in many of the news stories of Al-Arabiya (Iranian Women 2009, June 28; Student 2009, June 25). Furthermore, to *Al-Quds Al-Arabi*, Ahmadinejad won the elections because of his adherence and devotion to the "impoverished" who voted for him (Ash-Shaher 2009, June 22). The scale of voting in favor of Nijad was unprecedented in other countries, whereas the opposition leader, Mir Hossein Mousavi, was described as a "loser" and "defeated" presidential candidate by the same newspaper (Iranian Revolutionary 2009, June 22).

Although *Al Quds Al-Arabi* published more news stories on the crisis during the examined period, both of the news outlets used personalization in their coverage of the crisis. The stories were told through the public statements made by the officials from both camps and through their political history. Al-Arabiya and *Al-Quds Al-Arabi* equally used the external-internal kind of analysis and presented the crisis through politicians such as Mousavi, Rafsanjani, Ahmadinejad, Obama, Brown, and others.

The personalization of the protests was also practiced through public personalities as well as politicians in the Al-Arabiya site. Neda Soltan was an important character through which Al-Arabiya discussed the Iranian protests (Obeid 2009, June 22, p. 3). According to Farraj Ismail of Al-Arabiya, Neda turned out to be a symbol of the reformist movement and the revolution (Ismail 2009, June 24).

Not surprisingly, the two sources reported events with various levels of trust. Al-Arabiya shows no doubt in its reports that Neda was killed by the *Basij* militia (Ismail 2009, June 23; Obeid 2009, June 22); the *Al-Quds Al-Arabi* newspaper reported this event as an accusation made by Neda's fiancé (Ismail 2009, June 24). The same variances are found in their coverage of fraud in the elections.

Undoubtedly, the accuracy and balance of international and Arab media coverage of the post-Iranian election crisis were a concern to many observers. *Al-Quds Al-Arabi* was no exception to this. However, *Al-Quds Al-Arabi* published more articles on international and Arab media coverage of the Iranian crisis (New Media 2009, June 25; Persian 2009, June 25). Ali Fakhro found the Arab media to be very influenced by what he calls "Western propaganda" in their coverage, and Bashir Nafe claims the news coverage is a "mixture of facts and wishes" and closer to myths than to reality (Persian 2009, June 25). Moreover, news stories on the coverage by the German press (Juma 2009, June 23), the requests made by the Iranian government to the BBC correspondent to leave the country, and their accusation of CNN and BBC of attempting to divide the country (Iran Renews 2009, June 23), besides the closure of Al-Arabiya bureau in Tehran (Al-Arabiya 2009, June 22), were all published in *Al-Quds Al-Arabi* newspaper. The editor of *Al-Quds Al-Arabi* newspaper, Abd Al-Bari Atwan, was criticized by one of the Al-Arabiya writers for his position on the Iranian protests as expressed in the editorials of his newspaper. Gamal Sultan found Atwan's position on the Iranian crisis to be very contradictory to what he had expressed on the protests in Egypt (2009, June 21).

## DISCUSSION AND CONCLUSION

One of the salient aspects of the Iran election crisis has been the heavy use of social media. Iranians have relied on these media to spread information on protests and to communicate their situation to millions of concerned people worldwide. Actually, much has been recorded through social media networks which are capable of relaying information, ensuring the likelihood that the outside world comprehends the succession of events through their continuous reports. Hence, people have established a timeline of events using testimonial evidence from social media such as Facebook, Twitter, Flicker, YouTube, and other websites to portray a broad picture of the state of affairs and what was being said about it.

The Iranian presidential election and uprising events showed how NIT networks became a worldwide bonding agent. Simply put, social media networks became critical tools through which individuals could relay information about the Iranian crisis. Such networks had a great impact on the presidential election and ensuing uprising in Iran, especially in assisting protesters and those opposing the Iranian government restrictions during the crisis. Iran authority restricted Internet access because the protests grew in strength, and so they made information hard to get out of Iran. As a result, NIT users employed other means far from the restrictions to inform the world about the situation. Mir Hossein Mousavi used Facebook to contact his supporters and the outside world in order to keep them current on what was happening, demonstrating how important the functions of social media are in these situations.

By the same token, many insist on saying that what may be called the "Twitter Revolution" and high-tech social networks grant no assurance that free expression will continue to be free or that the people will also continue to pay attention to the outcome. Additionally, the end result is that these technologies can be temporary. Though they may have instant effect, for they are used for the moment and they can create strong passion, the passion tends to dissipate, whether the objective is met or not. That is the nature of social media networks.

Notably, besides the mobilizing force of the social media sites felt during the Iranian crisis, these sites have played an important, informative role that enabled the Iranians to get through restrictions imposed by the Iranian government. Major news sources relied on social media to report their news on Iran, including BBC, CNN, and other major Arab news sources. Social media sites were the major sources of news; this was evident in how the crisis was reported in Al-Arabia Net and *Al-Quds Al-Arabi* newspaper. Although, in the news reports analyzed from both Arab news outlets, the news was highly influenced by the polarization of the political scene in Iran, and the two sources frame the crisis differently based on their ideological orientation.

## REFERENCES

Abu Jahjah, D. (2009, June 26). Iran's crisis mirrors the Arab consciousness: Secularism is essential to settling it. *Al-Quds Al-Arabi*. London: The Arab Press Network, 21(6239). http://81.144.208.20:9090/pdf/2009/06/06/All.pdf.

Ahmadinejad is asking Obama not to interfere in the affairs of Iran. (2009, June 26). *Al-Quds Al-Arabi*. London: The Arab Press Network, 21(6239), p. 2. http://81.144.208.20:9090/pdf/2009/06/06-26/All.pdf.

Al-Arabiya office in Tehran will remain closed till further notice. (2009, June, 22). *Al-Quds Al-Arabi*. London: The Arab Press Network, 21(6235), p. 3. http://81.144.208.20:9090/pdf/2009/06/06-22/All.pdf.

Ali, N. M. (2009, June 24). Karroubi challenges Khamenie: Iran's next government is illegitimate. Al-Arabiya. http://www.alarabiya.net/articles/2009/06/24/76856.html.

Arouzi, A. (2009). Iran to media: No cameras allowed. NBC News: About World Blog. http://worldblog. msnbc.msn.com/archive/2009/06/16/1967136.aspx.

Ash-Shaher, S. (2009, June 22). Who voted for Nijad? *Al-Quds Al-Arabi*. London: The Arab Press Network, 21(6235), p. 19. http://81.144.208.20:9090/pdf/2009/06/06-22/All.pdf.

Atwan, A. The West hijacks the Iranian protests. (2009, June 24). *Al-Quds Al-Arabi*. London: The Arab Press Network, 21(6237), p. 1. http://81.144.208.20:9090/pdf/2009/06/06-24/All.pdf.

Badran, T. (2009). Hezbollah's agenda in Lebanon. *Current Trends in Islamist Ideology*, *9*, 6.

Bernal, D. M. (2009, June 13). Twitter users shame CNN for not covering Iran elections, riots. News Junkie Post. http://newsjunkiepost.com/2009/06/13/twitter-users-shame-cnn-for-not-covering-iran-elections-riots.

Boyle, A., and Choney, S. (2009). Iran's Internet battle hits new heights. Amid demonstrations, a high-stakes cat-and-mouse game plays out online. http://msnbc.msn .com/id/31411475/ns/ technology_and_science-tech_and_gadgets.

Bunt, G. (2009). Gary Bunt on the 2009 Iranian presidential elections. The University of North Carolina press blog (UNC press). http://uncpressblog.com/2009/06/22/gary-bunt-on-the-2009-iranian-presidential-elections.

Carafano, J. (2009). All a twitter: How social networking shaped Iran's election protests. http://www.rightsidenews.com/200907215605/editorial/all-a-twitter-how -social-networking-shaped-irans-election-protests.html.

Chavez believes that the CIA behind the unrest in Iran. (2009, June 26). *Al-Quds Al-Arabi*. London: The Arab Press Network, 21(6239), p. 2. http://81.144.208.20:9090/pdf/06/06-26/All.pdf.

Cherbel, G. (2009, June 20). A crack in the Iranian castle. Al-Arabiya. http://alarabia.net/views2009/06/20/7647.html.

Christensen, C. (2009). Iran: Networked dissent. http://mondediplo.com/blogs/iran-networked-dissent.

Coleman, D. (2009). Iran blocks Facebook prior to upcoming presidential election. http://www.readwriteweb.com/archives/iran_blocks_facebook.php.

Dirgham, R. (2009, June 26a). How the Arabs and the U.S. deal with Iran: New rules. Al-Arabiya. http://www.alarabiya.net/views/2009/06/26/77040.html.

———. (2009, June 26b). Obama's administration opportunity to build strong ties with Iran. Al-Arabiya. http://alarabiya.net/views/2009/06/26/77040.html.

Dubner, S. J. (2008, February 15). Is MySpace good for society? A freakonomics quorum. *New York Times*. http://freakonomics.blogs.nytimes.com/2008/02/15/is-myspace-good-for-society-a-freakonomics-quorum/?hp.

Engdahl, S. L. (Ed.). (2007). *Online social networking*. Farmington Hills, MI: Greenhaven Press.

Etling, B., Kelly, J., Faris, R., and Palfrey, J. (2009). Mapping the Arabic blogosphere: Politics, culture and dissent. *Internet and Democracy Project*. Berkman Center Research Publications, No. 2009-06. http://cyber.law.harvard.edu/publications/2009/Mapping_the_Arabic_Blogosphere.

Fandy, M. (2007). (*Un)civil war of words: Media and politics in the Arab world*. Westport, CT: Praeger Security International.

The finacé of the Iranian Neda accuses the *Basij* militia of killing. (2009, June 24). *Al-Quds Al-Arabi*. London: The Arab Press Network, 21(6237), p. 2. http://81.144.208.20:9090/pdf/2009/06/06-25/All.pdf.

Folkenflik, D. (2009). Social media allow reports despite Tehran's curbs. http://www.npr.org/templates/story/story.php?storyId=105490051.

Gross, D. (2009). *In Iran protest, online world is watching, acting*. http://www.cnn.com/2009/TECH/06/19/iran.internet.protests/index.html.

Hare, B. (2009). Does your social class determine your online social network? http://www.cnn.com/2009/TECH/science/10/13/social.networking.class/index.html.

Hmadeh, A. (2009, June 25). Repression in Iran: What does "Hezbullah" think of it? Al-Arabiya. http://www.alarabiya.net/views/2009/06/25/76948.html.

Iran accused the United States and Britain of inflaming demonstrations. (2009, June 22). *Al-Quds Al-Arabi*. London: The Arab Press Network, 21(6235), p. 1. http://81.144.208.20:9090/pdf/2009/06/06-22/All.pdf.

Iran accused the United States, Britain and Israel of fomenting the protests and warned to cut ties with London. (2009, June 25). *Al-Quds Al-Arabi*. London: The Arab Press Network, 21(6238), p. 1. http://81.144.208.20:9090/pdf/2009/06/06-25/All.pdf.

Iran accuses the West of mitigating demonstrations and Mousavi's supporters to continue their protests. (2009, June 17). *Al-Quds Al-Arabi*. London: The Arab Press Network, 21(6235), p. 1. http://81.144.208.20:9090/pdf/2009/06/06-25/All.pdf.

Iran and Ruhollah Khomeini. (2009). Wikipedia. http://en.wikipedia.org/wiki/iran-ruhollah-khomeini.

Iran continues its condemnation of the Western intervention in its affairs and accuses CNN and BBC of attempting to weaken and divide the country. (2009, June 23). *Al-Quds Al-Arabi*. London: The Arab Press Network, 21(6236), p. 3. http://81.144.208.20:9090/pdf/2009/06/06-23/All.pdf.

Iran renews its condemnation of the Western intervention of its issues: It accuses CNN and BBC of aiming at dividing the country. (2009, June 23). *Al-Quds Al-Arabi*. London: The Arab Press Network, 21(6239), p. 3. http://81.144.208.20:9090/pdf/2009/06/06-23/All.pdf.

Iran's presidential election and the triumph of social media. (2009). Virtue.com. http://virtue.com/blog/2009/06/18/iran%E2%80%99s-presidential-election-and-the-triumph-of-social-media.

Iranian authorities threaten to bring Mousavi to court. (2009, June 22). *Al-Quds Al-Arabi*. London: The Arab Press Network, 21(6236), p. 1. http://81.144.208.20:9090/pdf/2009/06/06-22/All.pdf.

Iranian demonstrators are sponsored by the CIA and the Iranian opposition in exile. (2009, June 25). *Al-Quds Al-Arabi*. London: The Arab Press Network, 21(6236), p. 2. http://81.144.208.20:9090/pdf/2009/06/06-25/All.pdf.

Iranian revolutionary guards threaten to stop those who take illegal actions. (2009, June 22). *Al-Quds Al-Arabi*. London: The Arab Press Network, 21(6236), p. 2. http://81.144.208.20:9090/pdf/2009/06/06-22/All.pdf.

Iranian women: An important force amongst the reformist. (2009, June 28). Al-Arabiya. http://www.alarabiya.net/articles/2009/06/28/77032.html.

Iskandar, A. (2007). Lines in the sand: Problematizing Arab media in the post-taxonomic era. *Arab Media and Society, 2* (Summer 2007). http://www.arabmedia society.com/?article=226.

Ismail, F. (2009, June 23). The finacé of the Iranian Neda accuses the *Basij* militia of killing. Al-Arabiya. http://www.alarabiya.net/articles/2009/06/23/76942.html.

———. (2009, June 24). The story of bird which flies penetrating the blockade and brings news on the Iranian revolution. Al-Arabiya, p. 2. http://www.alarabiya.net/articles/2009/06/24/76942.html.

Jarrah, N. (2008). First look: Watching BBC Arabic TV. *Arab Media and Society, 5* (Spring 2008). http://www.arabmediasociety.com/?article=674.

Juma, A. (2009, June 23). The young Iranian woman Neda becomes the revolution's icon of the German media. *Al-Quds Al-Arabi*. London: The Arab Press Network, 21(6239), p. 2. http://81.144.208.20:9090/pdf/2009/06/06-23/All.pdf.

Kraidy, M. (2005). Reality television and politics in the Arab world: Preliminary observations. *Transnational Broadcasting Studies*, Fall 2005. http://www.tbsjournal .com/Archives/Fall05/Kraidy.html.

Lynch, M. (2007). The Al-Hurra project: Radio Marti of the Middle East. *Arab Media and Society, 2* (Summer 2007). http://www.arabmediasociety.com/?article=268.

Mackey, R. (2009). Landslide or fraud? The debate online over Iran's election results. *New York Times* News Blogs. http://thelede.blogs.nytimes.com/2009/06/13/landslide-or-fraud-the-debate-online-over-irans-election-results.

Maina, P. M. (2009). Social networks are a double-edged sword. http://allafrica.com/stories/200908090007.html.

Malik, A. (2009, June 21). The Iranian Intifada and the Israeli reluctance. Al-Arabiya. http://www.alarabiya.net/views/2009/06/21/76552.html.

Mercier, G. (2009). Iran: The reformists keep the "green revolution" alive. http://newsjunkiepost.com/2009/07/30/iranthe-reformists-keep-the-green-revolution-alive.

Mousavi says he was pressured to withdraw his request to cancel the election. (2009, June 26). *Al-Quds Al-Arabi.* London: The Arab Press Network, 21(6239), p. 2. http://81.144.208.20:9090/pdf/2009/06/06-26/All.pdf.

Muttaki is speaking about Britain's nasty plans. (2009, June 22). *Al-Quds Al-Arabi.* London: The Arab Press Network, 21(6235), p. 2. http://81.144.208.20:9090/pdf/2009/06/06-22/All.pdf.

Nemri, J. (2009, June 18). Iran is tearing its tight shirt. Al-Arabiya. http://www.alarabiya.net/articles/2009/06/18/77032.html.

New media changes Iran's image in the American consciousness. (2009, June 25). *Al-Quds Al-Arabi.* London: The Arab Press Network, 21(6235), p. 3. http://81.144.208.20:9090/pdf/2009/06/06-25/All.pdf.

Nijad calls upon Obama and Brown to stop interfering in Iran's affairs and Larijani threatens the West. (2009, June 22). *Al-Quds Al-Arabi.* London: The Arab Press Network, 21(6235), p. 2. http://81.144.208.20:9090/pdf/2009/06/06-22/All.pdf.

Nijad: The elections are a turning point in the history of humanity. (2009, June 25) *Al-Quds Al-Arabi.* London: The Arab Press Network, 21(6235), p. 1. http://81.144.208.20:9090/pdf/2009/06/06-25/All.pdf.

Obama condemns the repression of the demonstrators in Iran. (2009, June 23). Al-Arabiya. http://www.alarabiya.net/articles/2009/06/23/77032.html.

Obeid, M. (2009, June 22). Neda Sultan is leading the reformists' revolution from her unknown grave in Tehran. Al-Arabiya. http://www.alarabiya.net/articles/2009/06/22/76734.html.

Persian BBC gives voice to the Iranian opposition. (2009, June 25). *Al-Quds Al-Arabi.* London: The Arab Press Network, 21(6235), p. 2. http://81.144.208.20:9090.pdf/2009/06/06-25/All.pdf.

Rabie, H. (2008). *Al-Jazeera* newspaper: Is it lost in the sea of politics? Pan Arab Media: Misk Group. http://panarabmedia.net/NewsSystem/Articles/38.

Ramazani, R. K. (1992). Iran's foreign policy: Both north and south. *Middle East Journal, 46*(3) (Summer 1992), 393–412.

Rumford, R. (2009). Facebook jumps the walled garden to Twitter. http://facereviews.com/2009/08/20/facebook-jumps-the-walled-garden-to-twitter.

Sambidge, A. (2009). Iran orders closure of *Al-Arabiya's* Tehran bureau. Arabian Business.com. http://www.arabianbusiness.com/559540-iran-orders-closure-of-al-arabiyas-tehran-bureau.

Saraf, A. (2009, June 20). When the dictator falls. Al-Arabiya. http://www.alaarabiya.net/views/2009/06/20/76505.html.

Solis, B. (2009). Is Twitter the CNN of the new media generation? http://www.techcrunch.com/2009/06/17/is-twitter-the-cnn-of-the-new-media-generation.

Student movement in Iran. (2009, June 25). Al-Arabiya. http://www.alarabiya.net/articles/2009/06/25/77032.html.

Sultan, G. (2009, June 21). Clove salt . . . and melted! Al-Arabiya. http://www.alarabiya.net/Views/2009/06/21/76590.html.

Tehran blocks access to Facebook. (2009). *BBC One-Minute World News.* http://news.bbc.co.uk/2/hi/8065578.stm.

Wandel, T. L. (2008). Colleges and universities want to be your friend: Communicating via online social networking. *Planning for Higher Education, 37*(1), 35–48. Academic Research Library database. (DOID: 1579372911).

The West is naïve to hope that the Iranian government is crumpling. (2009, June 22). *Al-Quds Al-Arabi.* London: The Arab Press Network, 21(6235), p. 2. http://81.144.208.20:9090/pdf/2009/06/06-22/All.pdf.

Wood, A. F., and Smith, M. J. (2001). *Online communication: Linking technology, identity, and culture.* Mahwah, NJ: Lawrence Erlbaum Associates.

Zahed, S., and Al-Fayez, Z. (2009, June 26). Iranian social forces join the reformists to take revenge from regime. Al-Arabiya. http://www.alarabiya.net/news/2009/06/25/77040.html.

Zein, J. (2009, June 25). Al Amama is torn. Al-Arabiya. http://www.alarabiya.net/articles/2009/06/25/77032.html.

*Chapter Thirteen*

# The Role of E-diplomacy in Iranian and Xinjiang Riots

## Li Xiguang and Wang Jing

Public diplomacy refers to "the transparent means by which a sovereign country communicates with publics in other countries aimed at informing and influencing audiences overseas for the purpose of promoting the national interest and advancing its foreign policy goals" (What Is Public Diplomacy? 2009). Web-based public diplomacy, also nicknamed as diplomacy 2.0 or e-diplomacy, refers to the said diplomatic practices through digital networked technologies such as the Internet and mobile devices, commonly termed as social media.

Ever since Hillary R. Clinton became the Secretary of State, she has avidly pursued the "e-diplomacy" strategy (Lee 2009), mobilizing the American public to "get busy on the Internet" (Scola 2009) and proactively interact with foreign audiences to carry out some of America's diplomatic strategies. *Newsweek* comments that Clinton's enthusiasm about Web 2.0 tools is justified because "they offer the promise of promoting democracy in countries that currently give the United States big geopolitical headaches—particularly Iran, China and Russia" (Morozov 2009, March 2). In addition, U.S. Secretary of Defense Robert Gates proclaimed in June 2009 that social media such as Twitter, which played a critical role in documenting and coordinating the protests in Tehran, Iran, has been a "huge strategic asset for the United States" because it makes it "extremely difficult" for governments to control information, thus representing "a huge win for freedom around the world because this monopoly of information is no longer in the hands of the government" (Levi 2009).

Web-based public diplomacy, as an important strategic asset and an effective means of strategic communication, primarily attempts to set media agendas, create news frames, switch news contexts, and fabricate speculative narratives and sensitive topics. In so doing, it imposes one country's value system and media standards on the rest of the world, resulting in increased international public opinion pressure on target countries. More importantly, e-diplomacy could lead to spiraling public opinion pressure within a foreign country and cause national unrest.

## MEANS OF WEB-BASED PUBLIC DIPLOMACY: WORD-OF-MOUTH NEWS

Digital networked word-of-mouth news communication employs one of the earliest forms of news communication, but it is based on the newly emerged social media. It serves as an alternative news outlet not only for mainstream journalists, but also for the online citizen journalists. Its most distinguishing property rests on the degree of control. That is, the user controls the news communication process, content, delivery, or forwarding frequency.

In order to generate momentum in e-diplomacy activities, a significant news event or topic must be identified or engineered. Then, depending on the nature of the news, one has to pinpoint a specific target audience, communication channels, and platforms. Since many social media already have clearly identifiable groups and networks based on demographic or psychological characteristics, the most important task becomes distributing the news to the audiences that are most likely to have a stronger response. Because they are more susceptible to the viral news, once they are infected, there is a good chance that the viral news communication will start rolling.

In recent years, both state governments and separatists or extremists groups have put social media to work for them by disseminating information to their supporters or sympathizers and by calling for sometimes illegal political actions. These social media tools can even enable them to circumvent local law enforcement systems and organize cross-border political protests and/or riots without being caught.

After the 2009 Iranian presidential election, the incumbent Mahmoud Ahmadinejad won a controversial win. Soon after, Twitter, YouTube, Facebook, and Flickr all became the predominant mediums and platforms for information disseminators and protest organizers from opposition groups and their Western supporters. In the past, Western countries utilized traditional media such as international radio to organize dissenters. However, the Iranian presidential election became a case in point where Western countries no longer depended solely on certain radio stations or news agencies to achieve their political agendas; they can do this much more effectively and efficiently through the new social media.

Although the validity of much information exchanged through networked social media cannot be substantiated, the widespread use of digital technology does indicate that social media has emerged as the most pervasive tool to achieve political agendas and shape public diplomacy. One could also argue that the information age has reached a phase where the traditional "production-communication-consumption" paradigm of information communication is being rapidly replaced by "produsage" (Produsage 2009) paradigm.

## PLATFORM OF WEB-BASED
## PUBLIC DIPLOMACY: SOCIAL MEDIA

Social media is also known as social networking media and serves as the platform of web-based public diplomacy. Despite the fact that there is much to be argued in terms of its function and impact in international communication and political mobilization, the Iran situation did demonstrate its potential for tremendous influence on e-public diplomacy. The opposition groups and their Western supporters, via the microblogging service Twitter and other social networking websites, not only built up support within and outside Iran, but also managed large-scale protests in a timely fashion.

Opposition leader Mousavi's Facebook page had only about 5,000 supporters in May, but the number soared to 110,000 (A Guide 2009) in less than a month just before the election. These followers actively updated news pieces, including demonstration information, victims lists, and related articles links. Pictures and videos of street protests, especially those of police violence, were uploaded, sometimes directly from cell phones to YouTube and Flickr, among others.

Some government-sponsored media outlets from the West established streamlined cooperation with these major social media websites during the Iranian protests. For instance, the opposition groups utilized Voice of America (VOA) and British Broadcasting Corporation (BBC) satellite TV channels and websites to mobilize Mousavi's supporters (The Role 2009). In its news reports, VOA also integrated Twitter feeds, user-generated videos, and blog posts. However, although VOA Persian News Network (PPN) received an average of three hundred citizen videos from Iran every day during the crisis, journalists themselves also questioned the authenticity of these video clips. At a panel on the new media's role in the Iranian elections hosted by the Center for International Media Assistance, VOA PPN journalist Setareh Derakhshesh stated, "The major question was 'Is it authentic?'" (Weiss 2009).

## TECHNICAL SUPPORT FOR WEB-BASED
## PUBLIC DIPLOMACY: ANONYMOUS PROXY

The technology that provides anonymous proxy became one the most important tools for the opposition groups during the Iranian protests. As many people firmly believe that the Internet technology would eventually enable citizens in nondemocratic countries to obtain more rights, Internet anonymity did play a significant role in facilitating online coordination of demonstrations. During the unrest, supporters of the opposition soon rallied technical support for the members of the opposition, especially proxy servers that could help Iranians circumvent firewalls. These services could not only allow protesters to upload stories and images, but also grant them access to websites otherwise blocked by the government.

Proxy services provided the opposition with the means to access intelligence information, up-to-the-minute accounts of the civil disobedience, and contingency plans. Since the Iranian government blocked a substantial number of Western websites in an effort to contain the disturbance, many Western countries offered proxy servers that were outside the border of Iran and therefore could not be traced by the government.

The Onion Router (Tor) is software that enables its users to communicate over the Internet without disclosing their identities and was originally developed under the sponsorship of the U.S. Naval Research Lab. Since the Iranian election, the usage of Tor in Iran increased sixfold, surging from seventy-fifth worldwide to the top fifteen (Lewman 2009). Tor facilitated the opposition group's ability to visit websites that were blocked, particularly the social media sites, and effectively helped protesters stay connected among themselves and with the outside world. Iran has 35 percent to 40 percent Internet penetration (Lewman 2009); as a last resort, blocking access to these websites would mean shutting down the whole Internet system. Furthermore, this drastic action would alienate more Iranian citizens and impose tremendous stress on the economy.

## KRISTOL'S XINJIANG PROPHECY

*New York Times* journalist Nicholas D. Kristol, after the eruption of riots in the town of Khotan in the Xinjiang region of China, predicted in April 2008 that networked social media would play an increasingly important role in future confrontations between ethnic groups. This prediction became a reality in just a matter of a year. On July 5, 2009, a group of young Uighur-Chinese men, mobilized by cell phone text messages, rushed to the street, killing other Chinese at random. During the government-organized media tour immediately after, several journalists publicized the tour's route and stops via Internet and mobile devices. Family members of these Uighur men, who were captured after the riot, quickly learned of this information and arrived at the scene. The situation soon changed into a road show, where reported "protests" only took place in front of the media.

Western press portrays the media tour as a maneuver of Control 2.0, a coinage that refers to a supposed new order of information management and control in China. The Chinese government's efforts to let the world know the truth is framed as "getting the government's official explanation and version of the facts out first" to "pre-empt other media, including international media" (Mackey 2009).

The series of journalistic descriptions of the Xinjiang riots are reminiscent of those about the so-called color revolutions taking place in Central Asia a few years back. Color revolutions are also known as media revolutions, where the media not only watched, but also played a significant role in fermenting protests, amplifying events, and forcing the ruling parties to surrender (Schipani-Adúriz 2007).

## WEB-BASED DEMOCRACY AND SMART MOB

Smart mob refers to a self-forming social organization that emerges through digital media technology. The concept was first raised by Howard Rheingold in his 2003 book *Smart Mobs: The Next Social Revolution*. Rheingold believes that, as a result of the development of PC-mediated digital media technology and the proliferation of Wi-Fi, mobile phones, and other personal digital devices, human society is gradually changing its social structure and methods of exchanging information. The difference between a smart mob and an ordinary mob hinges on their ways of sharing information—a smart mob uses networked computers to distribute information, thus achieving a synergy. As online political activities become much more convenient and inexpensive, previously disconnected political organizations and individuals can now gather together at the same online discussion board or blog, "organizing without organizations" (Shirky 2009). Web-based political actions usually start with a spontaneous and instantaneous smart mob, which would magnify a recent news event, and using network technology, coordinate online protests by petitioning, harassing, humiliating, prying, hacking, exposing scandals, and/or disseminating false information. To our society, the Internet could become a double-edged sword. Rheingold warns of the danger of the two types of extreme, but not impossible, societies: a society strictly controlled by the government through digital network, as described in *1984* by George Orwell, or a society full of troubles created by smart mobs with certain agendas. Needless to say, more often than not an entity (organization or individual) controls the smart mob system, an entity that incites its particular audience at appropriate times and invites them to target the victim(s) in mind.

The new frontier of web-based public diplomacy appears to be most beneficial to the United States while detrimental to developing countries. After the Iranian postelection uprising, a former U.S. intelligence officer commented, "The CIA suddenly realizes that it is much easier to indoctrinate the American values via the Internet than by sending agents to do the same job on site" (The Internet 2009). Through escalated online struggles, the American ideology seems to be exerting stronger influence, forcing developing countries to be on the defensive. This time, America finds an advantageous battlefield. Using the Internet to take issue is far less repulsive than directly interfering, and developing countries are cornered to a passive position even when their actions are legitimate.

Unlike during the time of the Cold War, in which governments dispatched personnel directly to other countries to help with street protests and the like, in this new age of antiterrorism, the aim of web-based public diplomacy appears more likely to be creating smart mobs in other countries. In fact, ever since the inception of the Information Age, prominent government leaders have firmly maintained that the information and Internet technologies would be the most crucial weapon in ideological struggles, believing that they would solve all global problems. For example, Ronald Reagan considered Information Technology (IT) as "the David of the microchip that will bring down the Goliath of totalitarianism"; Bill Clinton concluded that executing Internet censorship is like "trying to nail Jell-O to the wall"; and George W. Bush pictured a world where "the Internet took hold in China" and asked us to "imagine how freedom would spread" (Morozov 2009, March/April).

It is, therefore, reasonable to assume that social media will be more commonly adopted in the future with the intention of bringing about changes in the "countries that currently give the United States big geopolitical headaches" (Morozov 2009, March 2) and to garner regime change. In the past ten years, many scholars disputed the notion of cyberutopianism, believing that using the Internet to change a nation's regime is a manifestation of technological determinism and cannot withstand scrutiny. The underlying assumption of cyberoptimism is the conviction that once a state relaxes the access to the Internet, younger generations will swarm to antigovernment websites, question the legitimacy of their government, and eventually take the matter into their own hands. However, the problem with this line of reasoning is that, with an open access to the Internet, more young netizens would rather visit pornographic and gambling websites than surf political issues. Furthermore, in developing countries such as China, utopia does not reside in regime change. What people really need is a stable society with a prosperous economy, employment opportunities, health insurance programs, guarantees of education, and pensions. None of these could be realized in an unsteady and divided nation.

It is important to note that although some of the web-based political actions may be justified, once the chaos starts to spread in real life, some people will seek the opportunity to organize moblike activities by disseminating false information and inciting aggravated irrational behaviors, behaviors that often lead to a deadlier confrontation and make conflict resolution harder. Furthermore, since sources of information cannot be easily verified, it is conceivable that some individuals or groups with certain agendas, hiding behind their computers or mobile devices, would fabricate stories and Photoshop pictures to ignite technology-equipped, hot-headed supporters and create larger-scale anarchy.

The anonymity of social media, the widespread usage of networked technologies, and the difficulty of verifying accuracy of information prove to be highly convenient for plotting unrest within and outside a country's border. The anonymous nature of the Internet could allow the organizers of a political action to avoid detection, ensuring the action will move on under appropriate control. The omnipresent networked technologies facilitate real-time on-site or remote command by indicating course of action, contact information, defense strategies, and contingency plans. Moreover, the high penetration rate of these technologies enables rioters or protesters to solicit support from the international community, who may be blinded by one-sided truths and have a tendency to sympathize with the minority. Finally, unfiltered information gives rise to intentional misinformation aimed at producing shock value, hence irrationality.

## REFERENCES

A guide to new media in Iran. (2009). Center for International Media Assistance at the National Endowment for Democracy. http://www.ijnct.org/files/NewMediainIran.pdf.

The Internet becomes an infiltrating tool of the West: Politicalization of the Web more prominent. (2009, July 3). *Global Times.* http://news.xinhuanet.com/Internet/2009-07/03/content_11647152.htm. Original article in Chinese.

Lee, M. (2009, March 23). Hillary Clinton pushes e-diplomacy at State Department. Associated Press. NextGov website. http://www.nextgov.com.

Levi, M. (2009, June 18). Gates calls Twitter "a huge strategic asset." *CBSNews.* www.cbsnews.com.

Lewman, A. (2009, July 8). The role of new media in the Iranian election (online video). National Endowment for Democracy. http://www.vimeo.com/5496977.

Mackey, R. (2009, July 8). Managing dissent in China and Iran. *New York Times.* http://thelede.blogs.nytimes.com/2009/07/08/managing-dissent-in-china-and-iran.

Morozov, E. (2009, March 2). Facebook diplomacy. *Newsweek.* www.newsweek .com.

———. (2009, March/April). Texting toward utopia: Does the Internet spread democracy? *Boston Review.* http://www.bostonreview.net/BR34.2/morozov.php.

Produsage: A working definition. Produsage.org. http://produsage.org/produsage.

Rheingold, H. (2003). *Smart mobs: The next social revolution.* New York: Basic Books.

The role of new media in the Iranian election. (2009, July 8). National Endowment for Democracy. Washington, DC. http://pomed.org/wordpress/wpcontent/uploads/2009/07/pomednotesnedmedia.pdf.

Schipani-Adúriz, A. (2007, Winter). Through an orange-colored lens: Western media, constructed imagery, and color revolutions. *Demokratizatsiya.* http://findarticles .com/p/articles/mi_qa3996/is_200701/ai_n19432274.

Scola, N. (2009, July 27). The next diplomatic cable. The American Prospect. http:// www.prospect.org/cs/articles?article=the_next_diplomatic_cable.

Shirky, C. (2009, February). *Here comes everybody: The power of organizing without organizations.* Reprint edition. New York: Penguin.

Weiss, J. (2009, July 13). New media use in Iran dismays Iranian officials, challenges journalists. International Journalists' Network. www.ijnet.org.

What Is Public Diplomacy? (2009). USC Center on Public Diplomacy, University of Southern California. http://uscpublicdiplomacy.com/index.php/about/what_is_pd.

*Part Three*

# IDEOLOGICAL-POLITICAL DIMENSIONS

## Chapter Fourteen

# Khameni's Group against Khomeini Followers

## Madhav D. Nalapat

While Iran may be a regional superpower with significant influence across the region in which it is situated, this position is owed to its financial resources and its locational strengths rather than to religious ideology. Grand Aytollah Ruhollah Khomeini is justly known for the political transformation that he was the catalyst for in Iran in 1978 and 1979, replacing the monarchical regime of the Pahlavi dynasty with the rule of the Supreme Jurisprudent. However, those who see the Grand Ayatollah as being within the Shiite tradition are in error. Khomeini's theology has very little in common with the self-sacrificing, mystic ethos of the fundamentals of Shiite Islam, and much more in congruence with the teachings of Abdal Wahab, the preacher who joined with the Al Saud dynasty to further the geopolitical objectives of the British Empire in the Arabian Peninsula. The Saud-Wahab partnership inculcated the Bedouin of the desert with a conviction that the tolerant Turkish-model faith that they practiced was in fact *haram* (forbidden by Allah) and that they needed to move to the pure faith of Wahabbism. This faith, which advertised itself as genuine Islam, was in fact a creed that was the polar opposite of the faith that was discovered fifteen centuries ago in a series of revelations.

Islam is a democratic faith that sees each believer as the other's equal. Under Wahabbism, the Bedouin were encouraged to, in effect, believe that the Al Saud were given divine sanction to control much of the peninsula, including the two holiest cities in Islam: Mecca and Medina. To follow the Al Sauds (and their near relations, the Wahabs) without question was seen as tantamount to a divine commandment. Respect for the earliest founders of Islam was to be obliterated by means as drastic as the destruction of sites

and structures associated with Prophet Mohammad and his family and followers. In order to generate a fighting spirit among his flock, Abdal Wahab
airbrushed out of Islam the essential humanity, mercy, and compassion of the
faith, replacing these attributes with an insistence on intolerance and cruelty
toward those seen as apostate. Or, in other words, those who did not accept
the lordship of the Al Sauds over every aspect of their lives would become
subject to this treatment.

By giving the unlettered Bedouin the confidence of being a chosen instrument of the Almighty, assigned the task of promoting the faith under the
absolutist leadership of a single family, Wahabbism created a mind-set that—
together with the generous assistance of Britain—enabled the Al Saud family
to take control of much of the peninsula from the Turks and their supporters.
In negation of the self-abnegation of the Islamic faith, the unified state was
named after the family, to the approval of the Wahabbist clergy. Since its
origins three centuries back, Wahabbism has been harnessed to a slew of
geopolitical objectives: first, by Britain against the Turkish Caliphate, and
subsequently by the successor to the British Empire in the region, the United
States, in its battles against Arab secular nationalists (1960s–1970s), and
finally, by the Soviet Union in the 1980s. The backing given to the Wahabbi
establishment by the United States (which until 9/11 even gave that faith the
right to appoint Muslim chaplains to the U.S. armed forces) has combined
with the financial resources of the Al Sauds to ensure the displacement of
the fundamental core of Islam (inclusive and moderate) with the exclusiv-
ist, supremacist creed of Wahabbism within large swathes of the worldwide
Muslim community, or *Ummah.*

The Prophet Mohammad, in line with the core tenets of Islam, was a tolerant human being who showered his beneficence even on those who declined
to accept that the Word of God had been revealed to him. He gave women in
particular a status and honor unusual in that time. Mohammad even worked
for his first wife, Khadija, and he showed his fairness even at the point of
death, when he conscientiously shared his remaining time with each of his
wives. He did this until they themselves asked him to spend the balance of his
allotted time on earth with Aisha, who among his wives gave him the most
comfort at this terminal stage. Thus, they denied themselves of the privilege
of his company in a manner as unselfish as the Prophet himself.

In contrast, under Wahabbi theology, women play a subservient role and
are denied the right to work or even to travel on their own. In the citadel of
Wahabbism, Saudi Arabia, women are even forbidden to drive a car. The
message of Wahabbism is that women are by their nature licentious and un-
trustworthy, needing always to be in the firm control of a male. Interestingly,
this Wahabbi tenet is identical to that of the conservative Hindu lawgiver,

Manu, who wrote three millennia ago that a woman should always be in the control of men, first her father, then her husband, and finally her son. Another parallel between the system expounded by Manu and Wahabbism is caste. The Wahabbis implicitly sanction the absolutist rule of a particular family (the Al Sauds) over the rest of the population, thereby forming the ruling caste prevalent during the time of Manu. Fortunately, unlike the more recent versions of Manu's Law, which is Wahabbism-Khomeinism, the caste and gender oppression that led to the enervation of Hindu society and caused a millennium of slavery under the hands of first the Mughals and later the British, are losing their hold over Hindus in India. In contrast, Wahabbism-Khomeinism continues to spread across the globe.

In contrast to the discretion and respect shown to women under Islam, both Khomeinism and Wahabbism insist on all women donning the same attire, one which has been designed to place severe restrictions on their freedom of movement, besides being nowhere sanctioned by the Word of God as revealed to Prophet Mohammad. The unmerciful, compassionless worldview of Wahabbism is in direct contrast to the qualities of the Almighty as enumerated in the Quran: "The Beneficent, the Most Merciful, the Most Gracious." Every religious text has its war and peace segments, including the Christian Bible, the Jewish Torah, and the Hindu Gita. So does the Quran. Within other faiths, the moderate core usually gets precedence over the extreme opposite. However, the Wahabbis and the Khomeinists have sought to drain Islam of the moderation that was characteristic of the faith in its Golden Age (the first six hundred years) and create in its stead an unmerciful, compassionless monotone that stresses only hatred and conflict.

Interestingly, despite the near identity between Wahabbism and Khomeinism, several Western scholars and policy makers have been indulgent toward Wahabbism while being hostile toward Khomeinism. To an extent, such appeasement—caused by geopolitical alliances of the past—has been on the retreat since September 11, 2001, but not yet on a scale that replicates the distaste shown to Khomeinism. A consequence has been the continued spread of Wahabbism across the globe, in contrast to the theology of Khomeinism, which has remained confined to Iran and has yet to infiltrate Shiite communities elsewhere.

Grand Ayatollah Ruhollah Khomeini, although he sought to fuse alien strands into traditional Shiite theology, was nevertheless sincere in his beliefs. All his life, he has held on to them, at a substantial personal cost. Although those close to him began to enrich and empower themselves during his time as Supreme Jurisprudent of Iran, the man himself lived a frugal life. This absence of graft made him a danger to those seeking to harness theology into the cause of power and wealth, which is the way matters had developed in

Saudi Arabia. Once Khomeini passed away in 1989, this New Class (or New Caste) sought to get a successor appointed who would use theology for collateral purposes rather than consider himself bound by it, the way Khomeini had. They found such an individual in Ali Khamenei, who was swiftly—and according to Shiite practice in Iran—improperly made an Ayatollah from a Hejatollah and subsequently the Supreme Jurisprudent, Khomeini's successor. While Khomeini saw his role as protecting the supremacy of his theology, that of Khamenei was narrower: the protection of the privileges of the emergent New Caste who have taken over the resources of Iran since 1979.

Although Khomeini had made Khamenei the president of Iran in 1981 and got him reelected to the same post in 1985, the junior cleric was nevertheless kept at a distance by the Grand Ayatollah, and more consequently for themselves in the future, his family. For Khomeini, Ali Khamenei was not a confidant nor an advisor, but a human instrument to be used at his master's command. Part of the reason for this was an absence of theological sophistication in the Hejatollah, who compensated for this lack by always remaining bound to what his superiors wanted. Khamenei's *azeri* ancestry distinguished him from the Persian-dominated circle around Khomenei, a drawback that he sought to overcome by forging personal alliances with prominent Persian politicians, predominant among whom was Ali Akbar Hashemi Rafsanjani, the patron of the merchant communities of Iran. It was Rafsanjani who engineered Khamenei's 1989 defeat of the theologically more accomplished (but therefore less tractable) Grand Ayatollah Mohammad Golpaygani. It was, by the lights of the Iranian New Caste, a wise choice. Since his assumption of office as Supreme Jurisprudent, Khamenei has protected the coalition of Revolutionary Guards, loyalist clergy, and politico-business interests that has run Iran since his assumption of office in 1989. Unlike Grand Ayatollah Khomeini, who had an independent reach into the populace because of his history of opposition to the Pahlavis and his theological writings, Khamenei is wholly dependent on the New Caste for his support base.

Since he took office two decades ago, Khamenei has ensured that the present ruling elite in Iran has as large a share in the resources of the country as the supporters (domestic and foreign) of Reza Shah Pahlavi had in the past. The path to business success in Iran is not an MBA from Harvard or one of India's Institutes of Management, but kinship with a Revolutionary Guard commander or a cleric close to Khamenei. The successor to Khomeini has surrounded himself with clerics who are as theologically undistinguished as himself. In the process, he has severely degraded an institution unique to Shiite ideology, that of the Ayatollah Ozma, an individual who by his scholarship and piety is qualified to guide large numbers of followers. In the past, the selection of such *marjas* was made almost democratically, when large numbers of people congregated regularly to hear the sermons of a particular cleric. Although Grand Ayatollah Ruholla Khomeini had his differences with peers, barring a few instances such as the persecution of Grand Ayatollah Montazeri, he accepted the system that created theologians in a manner independent of the Supreme Jurisprudent.

Not so, Khamenei. From the start, he teamed up with Rafsanjani in efforts at rigging the process for selection of *marjas*, eliminating many who regarded him with contempt or who were opposed to the rush for riches that characterized Iran's New Caste. He also backed Rafsanjani in his covert efforts to reduce to a nullity the power of Ayatollah Mohammed Khatami, who was elected president in 1997. However, relations between the two cooled considerably during the period 1999 to 2001, largely because of Rafsanjani's efforts at ensuring that only his loyalists got the major positions within the system. Those who felt threatened by the Bonapartist ambitions of the Chairman of the Guardians Council succeeded in convincing Khamenei that Rafsanjani had to be brought down. This was done in 2005, when state media and security institutions gave visible support to his rival for the presidency, an unknown populist named Mahmoud Ahmadinejad, whose primary qualification was his links to key Revolutionary Guard commanders.

The managed election of Mahmoud Ahmadinejad saw the fall of the once all-powerful Rafsanjani. Thereafter, the ambitions of Khamenei grew. He would, with the help of his supporter, the newly elected president, take on the Khomeinists. These were (often not privately) contemptuous of the man who now saw himself as the master of Iran. They sneered at his imperfect knowledge of Persian culture and Shiite theology and at his servile behavior toward the New Caste. They watched as this group took on the coloration of the cohort around the hated Pahlavis and noted the sybaritic lifestyle of the families and friends of this caste, which they compared to the austere standards set by Khomeini and those close to the founder of the Islamic Republic. Interestingly, the Khomeinists began to gravitate toward former rivals, such as the reformist Mohammad Khatami and, one-time Khamenei patron, Ali Akbar Hashemi Rafsanjani. The family of the Grand Ayatollah Khomeini, who had been kept at a distance by Khamenei since 2004, also began to give them overt support, though technically this was only against Ahmadinejad and not the Supreme Jurisprudent himself.

By this time, the venality and heavy-handedness of the New Caste had led to disaffection within the once-loyal bureaucracy and even the security services, the middle rungs of which were kept largely outside the net of patronage created by the Khamenei-led cohort. Low salaries, price increases, and high unemployment within the general population led to a disaffection with the Khamenist system that could not be overcome by the numerous populist plans announced by Ahmadinejad, nor by his vituperation against the United States and Israel. Indeed, the vituperation against the Jewish state is another of the Wahabbite strands that have found their way into Khomeinism. Historically, the people of Iran have had few quarrels with the Jews and little sympathy for the Palestinian people. However, Grand Ayatollah Khomeini, eager to spread (his version of) the Shiite faith within the *Ummah*, saw a hard line on Israel as the means of winning the hearts and minds of Muslims worldwide. Since the 1980s, Iran has been generous in its funding of anti-Israeli groups in Palestine and Lebanon. However, such a policy has had little real resonance within the Iranian public, most of whom remain much more concerned about the problems at home rather than the attempt of Iran-backed militias to attack Israel through asymmetric warfare. Although actual figures are hard to come by, observers within Iran say that as much as $2 billion is spent annually by Iran on such Israel-targeted groups, a figure at least ten times more than that ever spent by Saddam Hussein in Iraq.

Since 2007, Khamenei has intensified efforts at eliminating followers of Rafsanjani or Khomeini from positions of major patronage. In the process, he has alienated both camps and has created an alliance between them. Once the Khomeinists began to see the internal enemy (Khamenei, as personified by Ahmadinejad) as being a far more deadly menace to Iran than the external enemy (the United States and Israel), they moved toward the reformist camp led by Mohammad Khatami. This clustering of forces ought to have secured an easy victory for Khomeinst Mir Hossein Mousavi against Khamenist Mahmoud Ahmadinejad in the 2009 presidential election but for the claim that the results were tampered with by the New Caste.

Had the Khameneists retained the support of the bureaucracy and the middle rungs of the security services, their ability to contain the fallout from the victory of Ahmadinejad over the much more respected Mousavi would have been greater. As matters stand, however, morale within the security services is low, as it is within much of the bureaucracy. The reason for this state of affairs is the same as the reason why the public at large are now opposed to the Khameinists: the venality and incompetence of the New Caste.

By taking on the Khomeini loyalists who protested at such venality and the government officials who registered their dismay at the incompetence at the top levels, the New Caste has put the very future of the Khomeini-created institution of the Supreme Jurisprudent in danger. Most of the people in Iran have now experienced twice in their lifetimes the risk involved in trusting a dictator with their fate: the Shah and now the Supreme Jurisprudent. By conniving at the moneymaking of the New Caste and by joining hands with them through marriage (in the style of the Al Sauds and the Wahabs), the Khameneist clerics have devalued and discredited the theology that was formulated by the founder of the Islamic Republic, the Grand Ayatollah Khomeini. What is taking place in Iran is a Second Revolution that may install within the country the nationalist democracy that got stifled by the CIA in 1953, when that agency led a successful coup against Prime Minister Mohammad Mossadeq.

Both Wahabbism and Khomeinism have their origins in policies that seek to deny the Arab and Iranian people the freedoms that are the birthright of each human being. The people of Iran did not ask for, nor get, any outside help when they carried out the 1979 revolution. Neither have they sought external assistance for the 2009 revolution, which hopefully will conclude in a democratic Iran that resembles Turkey more than it does Saudi Arabia.

*Chapter Fifteen*

# Silencing Iran's Twitterati

## *How U.S. Sanctions Muzzle Iran's Online Opposition*

Trita Parsi, David Elliott, and Patrick Disney

The popular uprising that followed the dubious outcome of Iran's June 12 presidential election peaked with nearly three million protesters taking to the streets, over 4,000 political prisoners, hundreds dead, and countless beaten, raped, tortured, or abused by security forces. Although most of the world's major news outlets had reporters on the ground for election day, the Iranian government shut down normal press activities after the announcement of Mahmoud Ahmadinejad's reelection. Journalists were barred from leaving their hotels. The security forces targeted demonstrators with cameras or recording equipment. A few days after the vote, most international reporters were forced to leave the country because their two-week visas had expired, and the government refused to renew them. Iran's state-run news coverage glossed over the massive protests, and the government closed down scores of reform-minded newspapers. Reporters who did cover the demonstrations risked arrest and imprisonment, resulting in a near total blackout of professional media coverage of postelection Iran.

The government's clampdown on press freedom was not out of the ordinary. But for the first time, when traditional media were suppressed by an authoritarian government, digital media stepped in to fill the void. Throughout the postelection crisis, the one overwhelming question being asked by observers around the world was: "What can we do?" Showing one's support for the prodemocracy movement by posting on a website may make one feel better, but it hardly improved the situation on the ground in Iran. Iranians took advantage of digital media technologies to bolster their opposition activities, yet in an ironic twist, U.S. sanctions actually raised doubts about whether such services could even be provided to Iran legally. Despite most U.S. policy makers being sympathetic toward Iran's democracy movement, the sanctions that the United States had built up over the previous two decades actually hindered the Green Movement's ability to utilize communication tools and information sharing online in their struggle against the Iranian government.

## ROLE OF DIGITAL MEDIA IN POSTELECTION IRAN

Digital media played three key roles in postelection Iran: it allowed Iranians to communicate with each other, it allowed Iranians to communicate with the outside world, and it gave people outside of Iran a way to communicate with and show their support for the Iranian people.

Iran has one of the most active populations of Internet users in the world. The country has the third highest population of bloggers, with more than 60,000 actively maintained blogs. Roughly 60 percent of the population is under the age of thirty. These youth have fueled Iran's rapid growth in Internet usage—faster than any other country in the Middle East—from under one million users in 2000 to around 23 million in 2008 (OpenNet Initiative 2009). Whereas in the past, repressive governments like Cuba or the Soviet Union were threatened by the free flow of information via newspapers and broadcasts, the growth of the Internet in Iran has developed into the newest weapon of choice for prodemocracy dissidents. Now, when the hardline government shuts down opposition newspapers, dissidents often turn to publishing online, where they are able to reach a much wider audience and where the government has a harder time shutting them down.

Soon after the official results of the vote were announced, millions of Iranians took to the streets in protest all across the country. Anger soon turned to seriousness as citizen activists banded together—united more by their opposition than by any cohesive political strategy—to form a popular opposition movement. Citizens marched under their own direction. They informed each other about upcoming demonstrations using SMS text messaging, e-mail, Facebook, and, to a lesser extent, Twitter. But these digital media tools were a double-edged sword for the opposition movement in many ways.

Social media technologies like Twitter and YouTube are imperfect tools for organizing a nationwide protest movement. They are the least private form of communication available, literally posting messages on the Internet for all to see. So, naturally the government could monitor all the same activities that the protesters themselves depended on for organization and coordination. For example, if one were to publicize an upcoming rally by listing the time and location on a Facebook page, chances are the government's security forces—having Facebook profiles of their own—would be waiting at that location to arrest anyone who showed up. Government forces also posted false information on the web, telling protesters to go to the wrong square or falsely claiming that a rally had been cancelled. But while social media are less than helpful for organizing meetings and planning protests, they are indispensable tools for gaining exposure after the fact, and this was what truly separated Iran's protest movement from any other in history.

Iranians utilized the power of Web 2.0 to communicate their message of protest to each other and to the world. Early images of large crowds of protesters sent out over Twitter emboldened others to join in. Facebook messages circulated widely detailing how protesters could protect themselves when security forces arrived on the scene with batons and tear gas. And powerful YouTube videos of "Allahu Akbar" chants ringing out through the night illustrated the spirit and passion of the opposition movement's defiance. All of these were important for sustaining the opposition during the first chaotic days and weeks, putting the lie to government propaganda efforts that portrayed protesters as elite youth from Northern Tehran only. With images and videos circulating in real time showing the opposition spread throughout the country and across all segments of society, millions of ordinary Iranians had proof that they were not alone in their discontent; for the first time in the Islamic Republic, real and substantive criticism of the entire ruling system was being aired out in the open.

Similarly, the rest of the world was able to witness the growth of the protest movement and the subsequent government crackdown as they were relayed from the participants themselves. For the average consumer of television news, the coverage from postelection Iran was extraordinary and unusual. Whereas previously viewers were told of events by a professional and dispassionate correspondent, news coming out of Iran was unfiltered and instant. News outlets had no better access to information than an ordinary viewer. The video of Neda Agha-Soltan's death was first released on Facebook. Professional journalists had to create a Facebook profile for themselves to be able to view it since Facebook material is available to account holders only. It is precisely because of the speed by which social news spread over Facebook that the image of Neda's dying moments became the symbol of Iranian resistance so quickly. Had it not been for the social networking site, the video may never have been made available for the world to see.

In much the same way, the rest of the world depended on digital media technologies for their only entrée into the Iranian crisis. The Iranian Diaspora organized demonstrations in cities around the world, spreading awareness and bringing their governments' attentions to the crisis in Iran. Even more widespread than public demonstrations, though, were private individual displays of support via digital media tools. Blogs and Facebook pages turned green; Twitter avatars changed to virtual "Where is my vote?" placards; and You-Tube brought celebrity ambassadors like Jon Bon Jovi and Joan Baez into Iranian society squarely on the side of the opposition.

## SANCTIONS STANDING IN THE WAY

Starting with the hostage taking of November 4, 1979, at the U.S. Embassy in Tehran, the United States has built up a robust sanctions regime against Iran. President Carter cut diplomatic ties with the Islamic Republic in response to the takeover, though it was not until the Clinton administration that an embargo on nearly all trade between the two countries was put in place via Executive Order. As a result of Clinton's orders, Americans are prohibited from exporting goods or services to Iran, with a few key exceptions: licensed agricultural products, medicine and medical devices, articles intended to relieve human suffering, and "information and informational materials," among others.

The exception under U.S. sanctions laws for "information and informational materials" is derived from what is known as the Berman Amendment, named after the chairman of the House Foreign Affairs Committee Howard Berman (D-CA).[1] Conspicuously absent from the list of items that constitute "informational materials" is Internet technology—really any technology developed since the mid-1990s—due to the fact that the Berman Amendment was written in 1988 and updated only a few years later to reflect the invention of CDs.[2]

Sanctions against Iran are intended to choke off support for Iran's nuclear program and military, as well as to deny Iran necessary investments in its petroleum sector that would support its economic development in general. As a U.S.-designated state sponsor of terrorism, there are also a number of other restrictions governing financial transactions with Iran, including a prohibition on monetary donations or remittances above $100. In order to provide for most other types of goods and services to Iran, an American must obtain a special license from the U.S. Treasury's Office of Foreign Assets Control (OFAC) for each product.

In practice, sanctions on Iran have had a broader reach than even their authors intended. Comprehensive export restrictions combined with Americans' fear of terrorism and terrorist financing in recent years have resulted in companies and organizations cutting off even the most innocuous of exports and services to the Iranian people. Cases like the Holy Land Foundation in Dallas, Texas, have made it nearly unthinkable for most Americans to donate to even the most respectable charities in the Middle East and Iran for fear of unintentionally violating antiterrorism laws.

Even for technology with no military applications and obvious benefits for the development of independent civil society, such as instant messenger programs or e-mail platforms, the perceived risks to American companies of violating software export regulations on Iran are great. From a strictly business perspective, the downside of violating U.S. sanctions far outweighs the relatively minor profit to be had by providing services in sanctioned countries like Iran. For this reason, it is not uncommon for businesses to withhold select products and services—or to forego the country entirely.

For example, this was the case with both Microsoft and Google's instant messenger software. Both companies cut off access to instant messenger services for users in state sponsors of terrorism (Cuba, Syria, Sudan, North Korea, and Iran), citing U.S. sanctions. The ban was upheld throughout the Iranian election crisis. Microsoft's official explanation stated that its messenger service is enabled through a download not authorized by U.S. export regulations and therefore it does not qualify for the "informational materials" exemption. Other Microsoft services not enabled through a controlled download, they pointed out, remained available for all users—services like Hotmail and Windows Live Spaces.

Similarly, and perhaps more consequentially for Iranians, there is some doubt among legal experts about whether Twitter might also be prohibited under sanctions. Twitter users are not required to download software to run the program from their desktop, as is the case with MSN Messenger and Google Talk. However, Twitter users are assigned a specific Uniform Resource Identifier (URI) to create their own unique miniblog page which, under a strict interpretation of regulations, could be considered a provision of service rather than "information." Given the interpretation of the law that OFAC has made public, which paints a very narrow view of "information and informational materials," the doubt that some have about Twitter's legal status is not completely baseless.

Of course, any anxiety that executives at Twitter might have had was immediately and extralegally put to rest by the U.S. State Department shortly after the Iranian election when the Obama administration asked Twitter to forego routine maintenance in order to continue providing uninterrupted service to Iranians. While this unusual move may have illustrated that the Obama administration has no intention of investigating Twitter for operating in sanctioned countries, it hardly reversed the prevailing legal interpretation governing those other companies not specifically recognized by the Secretary of State.

While their strict legal interpretation of the Berman Amendment was technically accurate, Microsoft and Google overlooked the potential for communication services to play a vital role in fostering a freer and more open society in places like Iran. The free flow of information encourages more transparent and democratic systems of governance, and restricting populations from accessing effective tools of communication runs counter to universal moral principles.

But, it would be wrong to blame corporations for following the law. The responsibility lies with the regulators, whose job it is to recognize when governmental policies run counter to U.S. interests. By hewing to its strict interpretation of the Berman Amendment throughout the Iranian crisis, and thus not allowing Iranians to access tools of communication online, the United States inadvertently aided the Iranian government in its crackdown on popular dissent.

More than six months after the election, U.S. policy makers took notice. Representative Jim Moran (D-VA) spearheaded an effort to correct U.S. sanctions laws to allow for Internet communications and information services to be provided to Iranians. His bill, the Iranian Digital Empowerment Act, led the way for a decision by the State Department to recommend that a general license be issued "that would authorize downloads of free mass market software by companies such as Microsoft and Google to Iran necessary for the exchange of personal communications and/or sharing of information over the internet such as instant messaging, chat and email, and social networking." Once issued, it is expected that the license will assure tech companies that their providing communication and information services to the Iranian people is in keeping with U.S. export regulations.

## CENSORSHIP VS. ANTICENSORSHIP TECHNOLOGIES

While the chilling effect of American sanctions on digital media in Iran stemmed mostly from legal ambiguity, there is one area of U.S. sanctions that is both crystal clear and counterproductive to U.S. interests: the prohibition on exports of anticensorship technology.

On June 22, 2009, the *Wall Street Journal* reported that Nokia-Siemens Network (NSN), a joint venture between the two telecom giants Nokia and Siemens, sold advanced censorship and monitoring technology to the Iranian government that allowed nearly every type of phone or Internet communication to be monitored. Since NSN is not an American company, U.S. sanctions were not applicable. Iranian security forces were able to use this advanced technology to monitor phone and e-mail communications to uncover plans for large demonstrations and arrest those involved. Some Iranians told of cases in which the government went beyond monitoring communications and actually altered the information contained in e-mail messages. In these instances, when protesters sent messages to each other to coordinate rallies, security forces monitoring them would actually change the information contained in the e-mail—such as the meeting place and time—then wait for protesters to arrive on scene and arrest those who showed up.

Other attempts by the government to stifle the population's ability to access information and communication tools included sporadically blocking specific websites like Facebook and YouTube, coordinating cyberattacks on opposition websites, and limiting the country's bandwidth to prevent users from uploading large files like photos and videos. Once the government's web-spying activities was made public, then the Islamic Revolutionary Guard Corps (IRGC) officially purchased a controlling stake in Iran's telecommunications industry, leaving little doubt that phone and Internet communications in Iran were monitored at all times by security personnel. Thus, the government was able to obtain some of the most advanced capabilities for curtailing the Iranian people's freedom to communicate, while private citizens had to struggle against both U.S. sanctions and government censorship to access even the most basic digital media tools online.

Still, all of the government's efforts at controlling Iranians' freedom of speech following the election were only effective up to a point. Despite the government's crackdown, users were still able to access news and information via Twitter, and YouTube still documented the nightly chants of "Allahu Akbar" in defiance of the regime. And yet, in the battle over information in postelection Iran, American sanctions often posed an important barrier to Iranians looking to make their voices heard.

Throughout the crisis, enterprising computer programmers and software engineers in the West were developing ways to support Iran's burgeoning online opposition movement. Proxy servers were set up all over the world for Iranians to circumvent government censors by modifying their IP addresses. Specific programs were also developed to allow users in Iran to upload software onto their computers that would enable them to mask their activities on the Internet. Congress even authorized $20 million to develop technologies that would specifically, among other things, help Iranians counter governmental efforts to block, censor, or monitor the Internet. Unfortunately, while Silicon Valley made great strides in developing the most advanced anticensorship technology available, American sanctions continued to prohibit citizens or companies from sending those technologies to Iran.

For some, even this was not enough to deter them from aiding Iran's online opposition. One young computer programmer in California developed software to encrypt an Iranian user's online activities by burying them beneath innocuous data requests. This enterprising software engineer uploaded his program onto USB thumb drives and smuggled them into Iran—without the approval of the U.S. government and in direct violation of U.S. sanctions.

Because of this type of assistance and countless other similar examples, many Iranian Internet users were able to circumvent government censorship and surveillance efforts to access social media online.

It remains to be seen whether the decision made by the Obama administration in December 2009 to waive sanctions on communication software will extend to anticensorship and encryption software as well. The State Department communicated its intention to authorize software "necessary for the exchange of personal communications and/or sharing of information over the Internet," but given OFAC's record of narrowly interpreting exceptions to sanctions laws, it is likely that the unintended effects of U.S. regulations will continue to be an obstacle to the Iranian people's ability to access news and information online.

## DISCUSSION AND CONCLUSION

What all this means for the future of Iran's online opposition is unclear. As new technologies are developed to allow people living under repressive governments to communicate freely with each other and the outside world, free of censorship and government surveillance, the capacity of the Iranian people to make their voices heard will improve. But so too will authoritarian governments continue to press ahead in clamping down on Internet activity, using the most advanced tools for censoring and curtailing speech available to them. Most likely, though, Internet users will remain one step ahead of the curve. President Clinton said authoritarian governments' efforts at controlling the spread of information on the Internet are like trying to nail Jell-O to a wall. Iran's ruling clerics are simply no match for the population of young, savvy cyberdissidents who will make sure that their message is heard.

But while the conflict over the future of Iran rages on, Western governments looking for ways to promote democratic ideals and foster a greater role for civil society in Iran should remember to first do no harm. Decades of increased pressure against Iran have created a faulty paradigm in Washington in which the effectiveness of sanctions is measured only by the amount of pain they inflict. The more crippling the sanctions, the better—or so it is believed.

In order to do everything possible to not stand in the way of those Iranians already pressing for universal principles of freedom of speech and political liberalization, the way in which Western countries deal with authoritarian regimes must be reassessed. The digital age has changed the way populations push back against their repressive governments. Rather than guns, tanks, or bombs, the strength of Iran's digital dissidents comes from their will and ingenuity to use new technologies, granted that access to those technologies is not inhibited. As the Iranian people's struggle against repression continues to evolve, those Western countries who favor their success should stand ready to change their own approach as well.

## NOTES

1. The U.S. Treasury's Office of Foreign Assets Control (OFAC) defines information and informational materials as including "publications, films, posters, phonograph records, photographs, microfilms, microfiches, tapes, compact discs, CD-ROMs, artworks, and newswire feeds."

2. The Berman Amendment amended the Trading with the Enemy Act as well as the International Emergency Economic Powers Act, both of which authorize the president to impose economic sanctions on a country, either during wartime or peacetime. The definition of "information and informational materials" was updated by the Free Trade in Ideas Amendment in 1994 to reflect new technology, specifically CD-ROMs and CDs.

## REFERENCES

OpenNet Initiative. (2009, June 16). Internet filtering in Iran. http://opennet.net/ research/profiles/iran#footnote5_oi6x5t9.

Dareini, A. (2009, September 27). Iran's rev. guard buys stake in Iran Telecom. Associated Press. http://abcnews.go.com/International/wireStory?id=8686181.

Rhoads, C., and Chao, L. (2009, July 22). Iran's web spying aided by western technology. *Wall Street Journal*, p. A1.

U.S. Treasury. Office of Foreign Assets Control. An overview of OFAC regulations involving sanctions against Iran. http://treas.gov/offices/enforcement/ofac/ programs/iran/iran.pdf.

U.S. Treasury. Office of Foreign Assets Control: Iranian Transaction Regulations. Statement of licensing policy on support of democracy and human rights in Iran and academic and cultural exchange programs. http://www.ustreas.gov/offices/ enforcement/ofac/programs/iran/license_pol.pdf.

U.S. Treasury. Sanctions Programs Summaries: Iran. http://www.treas.gov/offices/ enforcement/ofac/programs/iran/iran.pdf.

*Chapter Sixteen*

# Legal Opinion as Political Action

## *The Significance of Ayatollah Montazeri's Postelection Fatwa in Delegitimizing the Islamic Republic of Iran*

Ahmad Sadri and Mahmoud Sadri

Two models of government present themselves to the Shi'a (and by implication Sunni) Muslims. First, the differentiated democratic model practiced in Iraq under the leadership of the Grand Ayatollah Sistani. This is a liberal, inclusive model where religion remains in the civil society and functions as a critic of the democratic state. The second is the nondifferentiated Islamist model that emerged in Iran thirty years ago during the Islamic Revolution. In this model, the separation of the powers and the integrity of the democratic process are compromised by a theocratic structure that reigns supreme over executive, legislative, and judiciary mechanisms of the state. In the wake of mass protests that ensued after the Iranian government's win of the June 12, 2009 presidential election, the Islamist-Iranian model is undergoing a crisis of legitimation.

But it is important to bear in mind that the Islamic Republic of Iran is not and has never been a solid theocracy. Unlike the Vatican, it didn't have a claim to represent the Apostle Peter with his biblical power to loose and to bind. Nor was it able (like the Vatican) to refer to a story about a secular leader (Constantine) donating the power to rule to the chief cleric of the church (Pope Sylvester.) The Islamic Republic of Iran was not based on a strong theological basis because Shiite Islam has been (with minor footnotes during the Buyed and Safavid dynasties) an apolitical, millenarian faith passively awaiting the coming of its Messiah, the Mahdi.

When Shiite theology came out of its quietist period at the turn of the previous century, it first adopted a liberal posture. The rumblings of an Islamist state were heard in the Middle East only in the wake of the collapse of Arab nationalism. It was in this atmosphere that Ayatollah Khomeini pieced together a theory called the "Mandate of the Islamic Jurist" as the basis of a Shiite theocracy. The majority of the Shiite scholars shunned this move as heretical while secular forces considered it a step toward religious dictatorship. This situation is analogous to the rejection of the Zionist ideology that advocated a state in Israel prior to the coming of the Messiah. Religious Jews rejected it for its heretical nationalism, and the liberal Jews dismissed it as a reactionary reghettoization of Judaism.

So, it is not surprising that at the outset of the Iranian Revolution Ayatollah Khomeini gave up on the idea of an Islamic government and settled for a compromise that was called the Islamic Republic of Iran. In this permutation of the original idea, Iran was called Islamic only because the majority of people in Iran happened to be Muslims. The first constitution of the Islamic Republic therefore forecast a rather democratic polity. But something odd happened in the process of the ratification of this constitution: a band of Islamists led by the Ayatollah Montazeri managed to take over and insert the original blueprint of an Islamist state back into the constitution of Iran. This allowed the office of the Supreme Leader, and such clerical institutions as the Guardian Council of the Constitution and the Council of Experts of the leadership, to remain above and beyond the reach of democratically elected parliament and president. In this manner, the unelected theocrats took two-thirds of the state power, dwarfing the parliament and president.

Montazeri was thus influential in grafting an Islamic theocracy to the modern democratic constitution. In time, an uneasy if fascinating symbiosis developed between democracy and theocracy in Iran. Given its theological and ideological weaknesses, the Iranian theocracy, its grand claims to represent God on earth notwithstanding, was addicted to the legitimizing ambrosia of yearly democratic boosts. This explains why there has been nearly a general election per year in the last three decades in Iran.

Iran was not a People's Democratic Republic of the kind that littered the world before 1989. For all its severe limitations, the Iranian democracy was real. Of course, there were lots of limitations. A theocratic Supreme Court called the Guardian Council vetted candidates before an election and selectively adjudicated voting irregularities after each election. During elections, the state militias of *Basij* stood ready to campaign for the personal choice of the Supreme Leader. The question is why Iranians participated in this type of election. The answer is simple. Participation in elections prevented total domination by the theocrats, introduced competition, increased transparency, and ensured a modicum of circulation of elites at the lower rungs of the system. Besides, there was always an outside (but real) chance of a sudden, pleasant surprise. A bit of luck and a huge landslide could overwhelm the theocratic stopgaps and lead to historical victories such as that enjoyed by Mohammad Khatami in 1997 and 2001.

It was the fear of these kinds of upsets that led the theocratic structure to end the unstable equilibrium of democracy and theocracy at the June 12 election. But the cost has been enormous. The Islamist-Iranian model is undergoing a crisis of legitimation. Nothing symbolizes this change more than the religious edicts issued by the eighty-seven-year-old Grand Ayatollah Montazeri, who was one of the architects of the present regime.

The tradition of issuing politically significant edicts or legal rulings (*fatwas*) has a long history in modern Shiite history. It extends back to the dramatic "Tobacco Protests" instigated by the 1890 *fatwa* of Ayatollah Seyed Hassan Shirazi against the "Tobacco Concession" granted by Naser al-Din Shah to the British Imperial Tobacco Company. It presaged the collapse of absolutist rule and the coming of the 1905 constitutional revolution that was, in its turn, supported by the *fatwas* of the grand Ayatollahs: Khorasani, Tabataba'i, and Mazandarani. Similarly, Ayatollah Khomeini's 1962 and 1977 *fatwas* against the excesses of the Mohammad Reza Shah's government played a pivotal role in the downfall of the Pahlavi dynasty. Along the same line, and at the same rank in terms of significance, is the recent *fatwa* of the grand Ayatollah Montazeri. It spells out the conditions of voiding the social contract that is the basis of the legitimacy of any regime in general and the Islamic Republic in particular.

Ayatollah Hossein-Ali Montazeri wrote these legal rulings in response to traditionally ornate and legally well-crafted queries of the Iranian dissident cleric in exile, Mohsen Kadivar (currently a visiting professor at Duke University) who holds the degree of Ijtihad[1] as well as a doctorate in Islamic philosophy and theology. These legal responses have been consequential in the political events of the last century in Iran. Mohsen Kadivar considers Ayatollah Montazeri's recent rulings (see the Appendix) on par with the most influential of such rulings in recent Iranian history. It must be borne in mind that the Constitutional Revolution of Iran at the turn of the twentieth century and the Islamic Revolution three decades ago were also heralded by similar political-religious *fatwas*.

Ayatollah Montazeri was the closest disciple and later the heir apparent of Ayatollah Rouhollah Khomeini, the charismatic founder of the Islamic Republic of Iran. After publicly denouncing some of the harsh practices of the state in the 1980s, Montazeri was dismissed from his position by the Ayatollah Khomeini. Ever since, Montazeri has been confined to his house and a small circle of his graduate seminarians in the city of Qum. In the wake of the disputed election of June 12, 2009, and the subsequent suppression of demonstrators and imprisonment of hundreds of dissidents, Ayatollah Montazeri has issued a number of radical legal rulings. The man who helped construct the legal backbone of the constitution of the Islamic Republic has now created a legal instrument for a revolution against that system. The late Ayatollah Khomeini paved a path from the quietist Shiite jurisprudence to an Islamist political philosophy that (with the help of Montazeri) became the legal framework of the Islamic Republic of Iran. Now Montazeri has crafted a theoretical tool for deposing and dismantling that very polity.

At the heart of Ayatollah Montazeri's new rulings is the theory of automatic annulment of the political system when the leaders lose the trust of the people. The relationship between the people and their leader, according to this ruling, is analogous to that between a client and his appointed agent. Once the agent loses the trust of the client, the legal relationship is automatically dissolved. In such a situation, the clients (i.e., the people) are not obliged to produce proof for the incompetence and malfeasance of their political leaders. They do not even need to formally dismiss their leaders. Montazeri argues that a leader who loses the trust of the people has by virtue of this loss of popular faith lost his position. Once a client loses his confidence in the agent, the legal contract between them is automatically dissolved. Here the legal principles of presumption of innocence and assuming good faith unless the contrary is proven are also suspended. Without the trust of the client, the agent cannot presume to represent the person. The same concept, Montazeri maintains, applies to the relationship between the people and their political appointees. Once the leaders lose the confidence of the people, the burden of proof is on them to prove that they are worthy of popular confidence and trust. In other words, Montazeri's *fatwa* relieves the people (who are power-less in confronting the immense bureaucratic and security machine of the state) from legally proving the misconduct of the leaders. Rather, it falls upon the leaders to demonstrate their innocence.

As a legal remedy to crises of trust between people and the government, Ayatollah Montazeri rules that such disputes must be adjudicated by an im-partial body. In the context of the Islamic Republic of Iran, this means that available legal authorities (such as the Guardian Council, or the Expediency Commission, and the Elites of Leadership Assembly) are not qualified to settle the disputes concerning the legitimacy of the government because they are suborned by the Supreme Leader's office. Indeed, they are implicated in alleged governmental misconduct. Finally, Ayatollah Montazeri rules that the struggle against the usurping authorities is religiously incumbent on all believers. As such, nobody has leave to shirk the responsibility of ousting usurping political leaders. Political struggle for freedom, in other words, is not optional.

The explosive time frame of the Iranian Revolution has made for a unique event in the history of political philosophy. Montazeri, who once helped design and implement the new Islamic polity in Iran, has now formulated a theory for its dissolution. The Thomas Hobbes of this Commonwealth has now emerged as its John Locke.

## APPENDIX[2]

Legal rulings of Grand Ayatollah Montazeri on the political legitimacy of the Islamic Republic of Iran. Translated by Ahmad Sadri and Mahmoud Sadri.

## Text of the letter by Mohsen Kadivar

### IN THE NAME OF GOD THE MOST MERCIFUL

To the auspicious audience of theologian and jurist, our most erudite and coura-geous master, the Grand Ayatollah Montazeri, may his presence endure.

Peace be upon you,

I congratulate and offer my good wishes on the occasion of the birthday of Imam Ali (Peace be upon him), commander of the devout, guide of the op-pressed, and the superlative leader of those who seek justice and freedom. We celebrate this holiday at a time when dozens of your eminence's followers have perished, hundreds are wounded, and thousands more have been imprisoned for daring to peacefully protest the trampling of their rights by the Iranian govern-ment. It is cause for sorrow that this assault on people's rights has been waged in the name of Islam and Shiite beliefs. Grievously have the wicked flown the green banner of Ali[3] while treading on the black path of Muawiah.

I have been instructed by your eminence that transmitting the wisdom of the Quran and the teachings of our Prophet and his household is the surest way of fighting injustice and oppression at all times. Now, this modest student of yours is constrained by the necessities of the times to seek your guidance in keeping the dim flame of hope alive in the innocent hearts of a young generation. This generation has been treated with utmost cruelly in the name of Islam. It has been offered superstition in the name of Shiite beliefs, and it has been wounded and weakened by lies, dishonesty, and betrayal. Now this generation is at your door that is a beacon of hope for the oppressed people of Iran. This generation shall never forget your courageous defense of the plundered rights of the people in 1997 that culminated in more than five years of house arrest for your eminence. Now, I hope that your eminence honors this humble student by offering your legal rulings on the following questions and thus pierce the darkness of this dungeon. These are indeed questions that the long suffering, but proud people of Iran ask their religious leaders.

I take this opportunity to express my gratitude that you will spend your pre-cious time to prevent the "justice-oriented" Shiite jurisprudence (*fegh'h*) from sliding into the depths of the "security-oriented," apologetics of oppression that has been the hallmark of the "Ash'ari"[4] school. This is a favor you extend to the pious believers who thirst for truth. I thank you from the bottom of my heart and hope that you will remember this humble and cast away student in your prayers.

May your exulted honor be everlasting.

Mohsen Kadivar,
July 6th 2009

## Text of Ayatollah Montazeri's Response

### IN THE NAME OF GOD, THE MOST MERCIFUL

"And soon will the unjust assailants know what vicissitudes their affairs will take!"[5]

Prominent Sir, *Hujjat ul-Islam wal-Muslimin*,[6] Dr. Mohsen Kadivar, may his effusions be everlasting,

I greet you and reciprocate your good wishes. Noting that a detailed answer to your questions requires a more expansive occasion, I nevertheless briefly touch upon some answers.

*First Question*

Since, according to binding law, namely, conditions implicit in the contract of employment of public servants occupying certain positions are contingent upon such necessary qualities as justice, honesty, competence, and popular electoral support, what is the ruling on those who continue to occupy such public offices after they have repeatedly failed to uphold the conditions of their employment and obtained qualities contrary (to those necessary for their office) leading to conviction approaching certainty (that they have forfeited the right to occupy those public offices)?

*Response to the First Question*

Voiding any of the said conditions (for the occupation of public office) mentioned in the above question, (conditions that) according to both reason and religious law are of the essence of the aptness and legitimacy of the principle of management and administration of public affairs, shall necessarily constitute the automatic dismissal (of the occupying individual) without the need to take further action (by the people) for such dismissal. Under such conditions, the directives of such (holders of public office) will not be authoritative.

But voiding conditions that according to reason and religious law are not of the essence of discharging managerial and administrative duties, but which nevertheless have been agreed upon by the parties, will give the choice to the people to dismiss their managers and administrators. In this case, people can, if they so wish, dismiss the occupant from public office as a result of his violations of agreed-upon conditions.

However, voiding conditions of justice, honesty, or obtaining and maintaining the popular electoral support are among the (former) conditions that are of the essence of management and administration of public affairs. Voiding of these (essential) conditions therefore will lead to the suspension of the principles of "Assuming the Best" (*al-haml-u 'ala al-sehhah*) and "Innocent until Proven Guilty" (*asalat-ol bara'ah*) in cases related to the discharging of public duties.

The burden of presenting reliable and reasonable proof that religious or civil law have not been violated in discharging public duties, that rights of people have not been violated, and that the occupier still deserves the public trust rests on the occupier. (People need not prove his misdeeds, rather) it is his duty to persuade the people (that he has not violated the conditions of his employment). If there is a disagreement in such a case, the occupier ought to defend himself in front of a free, fair, and impartial judge. According to reason and religious law, the judgment of an organization that is dependent on him will not be authoritative.

## Second Question

What is the religious obligation of people vis-à-vis such occupiers (of public office) who despite repeated "enjoining to righteousness and dissuading from evil"[7] administered to them by people of good faith, nevertheless persist on their actions in violation of religious law?

## Response to the Second Question

As stated above the occupiers (of public office) who have, based on reason and religious law, forfeited their managerial and administrative positions are automatically released of their duties. Their continued occupation of their jobs has no legitimacy whatsoever. If they persist on remaining at their positions by force or by deception, people must ascertain their lack of legitimacy and demand their dismissal in the least costly and most expedient way while observing the axiom of "the easiest and most beneficial path." It is self-evident that this is a general duty that applies to everyone regardless of social position. No excuses may be adduced to shirk this responsibility.

Of course, elites who are more familiar with civil and religious law are capable and possess an authoritative voice bear more responsibility. They must unite and cooperate to spread the information and devise solutions by founding parties, organizations, and private as well as public gatherings. Imam Ali, our leader, stated in his last will and testament: "Do not abandon the principle of 'enjoining to righteousness and dissuading from evil' for then the worst among you will dominate you and your prayers will not be heard." The domination and control of the wicked is the natural result of abandoning the principle of "enjoining to righteousness and dissuading from evil" because the wicked abuse all opportunities (to consolidate their dominion).

*Third Question*

Do perpetrating and persisting on cardinal sins, detailed below, void the principle of "disposition to justice" (necessary for those in positions of political authority) and engender the (opposite) principle of "disposition to injustice"?

- Ordering and causing the murder of innocent individuals.
- Causing (with greater liability than the perpetrating) armed intimidation and harassment, as well as striking and injuring of innocent people in public venues.
- Forceful prevention of the exercise of the religious obligation of "enjoining to righteousness and dissuading from evil" and the duty to "exhort the leaders of the Muslim community" through blocking of all the rational and legitimate channels of peaceful protest.
- Abolition of liberty, incarceration of the "enjoiners to righteousness and dissuaders from evil"; and exertion of pressure on those individuals in order to extract false confessions from them.
- Prevention of the circulation of information and censorship of the news that is the required prerequisite of the exercise of the two religious obligations of "enjoining to righteousness and dissuading from evil" and "exhorting the leaders of the Muslim community."
- Defamation of dissidents and justice-seekers on the grounds that "he whoever disagrees with the government is a mercenary of the foreigners and a spy of the alien powers."
- Fraudulence, bearing of false witness, and untruthful reporting in matters related to the public's rights.
- Betraying the nation's trust.
- Tyranny of opinion and ignoring of exhortations of the exhorters and admonitions of the knowledgeable.
- Prevention of the exercise of the religiously sanctioned right of the right holders in their collective right for determining of the national destiny.
- Demeaning Islam and debasing the (Shiite) religion through presentation of a violent, unreasonable, aggressive, superstitious, and tyrannical portrait of Islam and the Shiite religion to the world.

*Response to the Third Question*

Perpetrating all the above-mentioned sins or persisting on some of them constitute the most telling and salient evidence of the lack of "the disposition to justice." (Such actions) are the embodiment of open inequality and injustice. Truly, if such sins would not constitute the corruption and clear violation of justice in the public eye, then what sins would constitute such a violation?

It is evident that if any kind of sin, particularly any of those listed above, is perpetrated within the framework and in the name of religion, justice, and law, it will have ramifications beyond the sin itself as it involves the additional sins of deception and tainting the countenance of religion, justice, and law.

In cases where certain affairs seem to be just and legitimate from the point of view of the rulers, yet illegitimate, corrupt, and tantamount to the injustice and loss of rights from the point of view of the people, then an appeal to the judgment of just, neutral, and mutually agreeable arbiters must be the operative principle.

## Fourth Question

Can the appeal to phrases such as "protection of the regime is among the most incumbent of the necessities" justify the violation of people's legitimate rights and trampling of numerous moral and religious standards such as sincerity and honesty? Can one, under the pretext of "the expedient interest of the regime" lay aside the authentic principle of "justice" that has been the distinguishing attribute of the political jurisprudence of Shiite Islam throughout history? What is the religious duty of the faithful if some government officials would have mistakenly replaced their own personal interests for those of the regime and continue to persist in their error?

## Response to the Fourth Question

Protection of the regime, in itself, is neither essential nor, per se, obligatory; particularly when the regime is equated with a person. When one speaks of a regime whose protection is among "the most incumbent of the necessities," only a regime that is preparatory and instrumental to the upholding of justice and discharging of religious obligations and rational premises can be intended. The necessity of the protection of such a regime is of the "contingent" variety (that is the necessity is contingent on its discharging of its proper functions). With this in mind, resorting to the phrase: "protection of the regime is among the most incumbent of the necessities" when it is made with the intention to justify and conceal the operations of the administrators and their functionaries who pretend to render justice on behalf of others is fallacious because it emphasizes the general principle while what is in doubt is its instantiation (*al-tamassok bel-'amm fe-shobhat el-mesdaghiyah*); it prejudges the case and reaches a self-serving conclusion without exposing the premises to examination. If offering such an argument is the result of ignorance, then it should be corrected by "enjoining to righteousness and dissuading from evil."

But it must be self-evident that one cannot protect or fortify the Islamic Regime with unjust and un-Islamic acts, as the very need for an (Islamic) regime is based on the necessity of rendering justice and protecting rights, or, to put it more succinctly, the implementation of Islamic commandments. How is it imaginable that through injustice and un-Islamic acts, a just and Islamic regime would be secured and strengthened?

A regime that is based on club wielding, injustice, violation of rights, usurpation and adulteration of votes, murder, subjugation, incarceration, medieval and Stalinist tortures, repression, censorship of newspapers and means of communication, imprisonment of the thinkers and elites of the society on trumped-up charges, and extraction of untrue confessions, especially when these are extracted under duress, is condemned and unworthy before (the tribunal of) religion, reason, and the world's wise observers.

Based on the authentic traditions that have reached us from the infallible household of the Prophet (peace be upon them), admission and confession in prison do not have one iota of legal or religious value and cannot become a basis for a verdict. (Wasa'el al-Shiieh, the chapter on admissions, section 4; also, the sections on the punishment for theft, section 7.)

The discriminating people of Iran, too, are fully aware of the nature of such confessions, whose earlier examples are recorded in the histories of the Fascist and Communist regimes. The nation of Iran realizes that such confessions and false show trial interviews are extracted from their captive sons through force, torture, and threats in order to conceal the regime's own wrongdoings and with the intention of besmirching and degrading the people's peaceful and legal protests.

Those involved in such plots must realize that the managers, operators, and agents of the extraction and broadcasting of such false confessions and interviews are religiously errant and legally liable. The country belongs to the people, not to you and me. The decision belongs to the people. (Political) administrators and managers are people's servants. People must be free to assemble to defend their rights through oral and written means.

The Shah of Iran heard the voice of the revolution when it was too late. It is hoped that those in charge of Iran's affairs will not wait that long, that they will show flexibility in the face of the demands of the nation. It is advisable to stop the loss as soon as possible.

## Fifth Question

What are the religious clues for ascertaining that the condition for "tyrannical mandate" has been obtained; and what is the duty of the learned *Ulema* (may God exult their word), and (what are) the obligations of the public upon its (tyrannical mandate's) advent?

## Response to the Fifth Question

Tyranny means deliberate opposition to the commandments of religion, the principles of reason, and the covenants of the people, as embodied in laws. He who is in charge of the affairs of the people and opposes these principles would be a tyrant and his mandate would be, likewise, tyrannical.

The obligation to determine such a condition lies, in the first place, with the educated elites of the society, those who are knowledgeable in religion and independent from the rulers. Similarly, it is incumbent upon the society's thinkers, legal scholars, and experts who are familiar both with the principles of reason and law and the procedures of establishing the deliberate opposition (of the above-mentioned government officials to the will of the people) to adduce solid and ascertainable evidence (of such misdeeds). The said elites will be able to perform this duty only if they are free and independent of all government influence and political and factional considerations.

Secondarily, it is incumbent upon the public within the radius of their own awareness of the commandments and laws and with the help of their religious and rational resources to remain in direct contact with the religious, cultural, economic, and political realities and be aware of the deliberate opposition of the rulers to religion and law.

Finally, to summarize, justice or injustice of the rulers is a palpable reality in the society, and its ramifications are evident. This face is not covered behind a mask. Everyone, within his or her capacity to understand and act, has a responsibility to resist instances of injustice and corrosion of people's rights and must alert others as well. (The spreading of awareness shall be done) so they too can engage in "enjoining to righteousness and dissuading from evil" and strive toward offering a solution.

Indeed it is not conceivable that a justice-seeking person would be unwilling to walk on the path of justice, or that he would be fearful, or occupy him/herself or others with delusions and procrastinations under the pretext that a person is powerless to effect change. Fearing those created by God is tantamount to taking partners with God, and engaging in self-delusions and procrastination is embracing darkness and casting others unto it.

It has been the tradition of the infallible Imams (peace be upon them) to struggle on the path of social justice. If they only occupied themselves with private religious matters, then why would they be subject to so much oppression, violations, incarceration, surveillance, and, ultimately, martyrdom?

God has taken a solid oath from the knowledgeable, particularly the knowledgeable in religion, not to remain silent in the face of injustice: "Allah has taken a pledge with the learned that they should not acquiesce in the gluttony of the oppressor and the hunger of the oppressed" (Nahjul Balagha, third sermon).

Obviously, upholding this covenant has great rewards just as it has great costs: "Do people reckon that they will be left to say 'We believe,' and (that they) will not be tried? We certainly tried those that were before them, and assuredly God knows those who speak truly, and assuredly He knows the liars" (the Quran, chapter of Spider [29], verses 2, 3).

"It won't straighten by a whim; it won't materialize by a wish,
This is a path of long and grave suffering"
May God grant you success.
17th of the month of Rajab, 1430, 19th of the month of Tir, 1388 [July 10th 2009]
The holy city of Qum
Hossein-Ali Montazeri

## NOTES

1. This is the highest degree in Islamic jurisprudence offered in Shiite seminaries. It takes the legalistic form of permission by a grand Ayatollah to an adept student who has achieved the ability to research, discover, and interpret Islamic law.

2. This text has been translated by the authors, in close consultation with Mohsen Kadivar.

3. The First Imam of the Shiites. The Sunni Muslims know him as the fourth Rightly Guided Caliph.

4. Followers of the early tenth-century antirationalist jurist Abu al-Hasan al-Ash'ari.

5. Quran: Chapter 26, Verse 227. The Yusufali translation.

6. This is an honorific title reserved for a high-ranking cleric. Its literal meaning is "the witness for Islam and Muslims."

7. One of the principle religious obligations of every Muslim.

*Chapter Seventeen*

# Televising the "Velvet Revolution"

## *Show Trials in the Aftermath of Iran's Tenth Presidential Election*

### Ibrahim Al-Marashi

In the fallout of Iran's tenth presidential election, Iranian reformists, scholars, and activists were put on trials that were broadcast on Iran's state television. The show trials consisted of a campaign of "fabri-indictments" that were designed for domestic audiences in order to discredit the reformist movement and to silence critics. Furthermore, the trials served as a venue to convince the Iranian public that foreign players, ranging from the United States to the Soros Foundation, were scheming to foment a "velvet revolution."

The higher echelons of the state found themselves in a continual fight for the control of information after the contested June 2009 election. The leadership sought to convince the Iranian public and the world that Mahmoud Ahmadinejad was in control and had consolidated power and that the conservatives in Iran had won out over the reformists. The challenge to the state was that "small media," ranging from individuals who used Twitter to Facebook, disputed the Iranian state's version of events. Furthermore, the Iranian conservative political networks felt besieged by transnational broadcasting communications, such as BBC Persian and U.S. channels beamed into Iran, whether it was from the expatriate community in Los Angeles or those sponsored by the U.S. government. The show trials were staged to deliver the state's narrative in response to these inimical media platforms. The Iranian state thus sought to use the show trials in its salvo in a war of the airwaves and to defeat a reformist cyberrevolution.

## THE ROLE OF MEDIA PRIOR TO IRAN'S ELECTION

Even prior to the June election in Iran, there had been the rise of a new generation of web journalism, with Iranian citizens contributing to an ever-growing Blogistan where even Mahmoud Ahmadinejad had his own blog. He has even published criticisms on it, with Jack from the U.S. writing, "I hope someone puts a bullet in your head very soon."

The 2009 presidential campaign in Iran was one of the first that witnessed televised, divisive debates between the candidates, including personal attacks on the candidates' characters, where even spouses of the candidates were criticized. During one televised debate, Ahmadinejad accused Mir Hossein Mousavi's wife, Professor Zahra Rahnavard, also dubbed as "Iran's Michelle Obama," of not having a PhD, and Rahnavard retaliated by convening a news conference criticizing Ahmadinejad for slander.

During the campaign, the candidates produced sophisticated election ads prior to the polls. Mousavi's election video, imbued with Iranian nationalist themes, featured Iranian pop music (technically banned in the Islamic Republic) and clips of young Iranian scientists (a symbol of the progress achieved in the Iranian nuclear program). All the Iranian presidential candidates were active on Facebook and Twitter, and Facebook groups emerged, such as, "I bet I can find 1,000,000 people who dislike Ahmadinejad," and the parody, "Googoosh for President," a reference to an Iranian 1970s-era pop diva. This mobilization of the media during the presidential campaign would later prove crucial in terms of contesting its results.

## THE ROLE OF MEDIA IN THE
## IMMEDIATE AFTERMATH OF THE ELECTION

The election results pitted elements of the state, including the Supreme Leader Ali Khamenei and the Revolutionary Guards, against vocal and emboldened elements of Iranian society challenging Ahmadinejad's reelection. This event was not the first time media played a role in contesting a suspect election. Clandestine radio in Serbia, like the station B92, played a role in mobilizing protests against the reelection of Slobodan Milosevic in 2000, and those mass demonstrations ended his rule, thus perhaps explaining why the Iranian conservative establishment felt threatened by the mobilization of various underground media networks against it.

The crisis in Iran was not merely a domestic conflict between reformists and a conservative establishment but represented another, greater battle for information. According to Annabelle Srebreny, the Iranian Revolution of

1979 was a revolution of "small media." The audiocassette was one of the greatest tools at Ayatollah Khomeini's disposal, which recorded the cleric's sermons against the Shah. These small tapes were smuggled from his exile in Iraq into Iran by a network of sympathizers. Once Khomeini was exiled in Paris, he had the international media at his disposal, launching his own international war of the airwaves against the Shah.

Exactly thirty years after the Iranian Revolution, Twitter, Facebook, CNN I-Reports, YouTube, and the pictures and videos Iranians take with their cell phones have become the twenty-first-century version of the cassette tape. Indeed, YouTube gave life after death to the young victim Neda Agha-Soltan, just as the televised death of the young boy Muhammad al-Durrah during a clash with Israeli soldiers became the symbol of the Palestinian Al-Aqsa Intifada of 2000.

The video of Neda has raised questions about how can one verify the events captured on the cell phones of Iranians. Critics of her video have asked, "How can we know that the event we watched is real?" A similar tragedy took place prior to the fall of the Shah in the city of Abadan, where a fire killed three hundred Iranians in a movie theater. While the Shah sought to blame the tragedy on fundamentalists who wanted to destroy a cinema, a symbol of the decadent West, the Iranian public believed that the Shah's secret police were behind the fire. It was an event that signaled the final downfall of the Shah. Thus, if the Iranian public believed that the Ahmadinejad-allied militia, the *Basij*, was responsible for Neda's death, then the narrative surrounding Neda's death took on a life of its own. It did not matter to the Iranian opposition if her death could not be verified. Conversely, even if the show trials were received by skepticism by parts of the Iranian public, they probably served as the truth for the conservative elements of society supportive of Ahmadinejad.

Empowered citizenships communicating with new media formats in Iran were also met with new technologies of censorship. While the Revolutionary Guards (*Pasdaran*) controlled tanks and ballistic missiles, they were also tasked with cyberweapons to cripple rival websites. The reformists retaliated by attacking websites allied with the conservatives behind Ahmadinejad. The Iranian state did not shut down the Internet entirely in Iran because the state needed it too, as when the Revolutionary Guard warned Mousavi supporters about gatherings in the streets by posting their warning on the website. The traditionally secular Turkish military had done the same in 2007 when posting a warning note on its website to curtail the actions of the religious AK Party, in what has become known as the "e-coup."

While an innovative array of media were used prior to the election and the subsequent events following the referendum, the Iranian state chose not to use new media to communicate its view but rather a tried media format, the show trial, which had been in use since the early years of the revolution.

## THE ARREST OF KIAN TAJBAKHSH

Iranian agents arrested Kian Tajbakhsh, an Iranian American and scholar of sociology and urban studies, in front of his wife and small daughter at their home in Tehran on July 9, 2009. It was the second time he had been arrested in Iran since 2007, when he was forced to deliver a statement alleging his involvement with foreign powers subverting the Iranian state.

The second arrest of Tajbakhsh was first announced on the Iranian state-sponsored, English-language Press TV on July 13, alleging that he was cooperating with Hossein Rassam, the head of the security and political division of the British Embassy in Tehran, in fomenting the postelection turmoil. The Iranian authorities detained him to obtain a forced statement from him to use in a televised show trial to falsely accuse foreign powers of interfering in Iran's postelection crisis.

The show trials were designed to convince Iranian audiences that the alleged had conspired to launch a "velvet coup" in Iran. The accusations centered around an argument that a velvet coup model had been planned for Iran, orchestrated from abroad. Kian Tajbakhsh, who had been in Iran since 1998, according to the semiofficial Fars New Agency, was accused of implementing a velvet coup on behalf of the Soros Foundation and other NGOs. The article stated:

> Kian Tajbakhsh has also compared these measures with the velvet coups of several countries. The events seen in the elections period, such as the creation of symbols, human chains, claims of fraud, declaration of victory before the votes were counted and large gatherings outside government centers intended to take them over, show that in Iran too there was to be a velvet coup. (Accused 2009)

The subsequent trials of Tajbakhsh which began on August 1, along with others accused of fomenting sedition, were broadcast on Iran's state television. During these trials, Tajbakhsh stated that in 2006 he introduced the former Iranian president Khatami to George Soros in order to plan a Velvet Revolution. However, when Tajbakhsh was arrested in 2007 and made a public confession on July 17 of that year, he made no mention of the alleged Khatami-Soros meeting. The alleged link between Soros and Khatami reveals how the threat perceptions of the Iranian conservative elites had changed. In 2007, Tajbakhsh was accused of serving as an agent of the United States and the Soros Foundation to foment a revolution in Iran, without indicting reformists such as the former president. Two years later, the conservative power brokers chose to use Tajbakhsh as a means of subverting the reputation of the reformist movement.

In an editorial by Abdollah Ganji (2009) in the paper *Javan*, he criticizes Khatami for holding this alleged meeting with Soros, indicating how the accusation against Tajbakhsh had become ingrained in the Iranian conservative narrative. The author argued that Tajbakhsh, who was arrested with Haleh Esfandiari and Ramin Jahanbeglu in 2007 on charges of planning a "colored" revolution in Iran, was guilty of using civil society organizations to weaken the Islamic Republic. *Javan* is a conservative Tehran-ideological paper affiliated with the Revolutionary Guards and illustrates how the discourse of the show trials proliferated in the Ahmadinejad loyalist media. The article continued by giving details of this meeting occurring in the United States and a speech where Soros praised Khatami. The aforementioned editorial and Tajbakhsh's forced statements serve as an example of the government's strategy to use "fabri-indictments" to legitimize their domestic standing and to discredit the reformist opposition. The accusation led to a war of words within the Iranian media establishment, with reformist papers attacking the conservative papers for spreading this rumor and using Tajbakhsh as a pawn in this effort.

The show trial served as an attempt by the state to rally public opinion to its side. According to an article in *Aftab-e Yazd*, a reformist paper (Anonymous 2009), however, "It is very difficult to believe that the confessions of a few prisoners, made after about two months in solitary confinement, could widely convince people about any 'velvet revolution.'" Another author (Anonymous 2009) wrote, "And to judge by copious anecdotal evidence and the blogs of people living in Iran, a very large number of Iranians do not believe the confessions they have heard from prisoners; they see the trial primarily as evidence for the Islamic Republic's descent into tyranny." This author argues that while show trials in the 1980s of Iranian Communists did not lead to an outcry, the wretched conditions of the defendants caused more revulsion that the fabricated indictments which they delivered. The Iranian public of today is more skeptical of the state in light of the election results of 2009 and thus unlikely to believe that the accused, paraded around on Iranian state TV, had any connections to fomenting a Velvet Revolution. This skepticism is in part due to the media revolution that has occurred in Iran, where Iranians can access information outside of the conservative media establishment from reformist websites and transnational satellite channels.

While the show trials may not have convinced the entire Iranian public of the state's argument, the shows served the purpose of reinforcing the belief of the core constituencies that buttress the conservative alliance in power after the June 2009 election. While the accusations of Tajbakhsh working with Khatami and the Soros Foundation to foment a Velvet Revolution sounds like a conspiracy theory, it may agree with the thinking of the urban and rural poor, as well as *Basijis* (members of the mass mobilization militia) and *Pasdars* (the Revolutionary Guards) that serve as the core of Ahmadinejad's support network.

The show trials not only sought to rally the loyalists around the Ahmadinejad government, they served as an indictment of the Iranian educational establishment. The Supreme Leader Khamenei had labeled professors of secular disciplines as "commanders" waging "soft warfare" against the Iranian youth (Kurzman 2009). The terms *soft warfare* and *velvet revolution* reinforced each other during the show trials where those on the stand were accused of spreading the corrupting ideas of social scientists ranging from Weber to Habermas. Linking the accused to the secular social sciences during the show trial reinforced a narrative against what the conservatives deem as the deviant currents within the education system. According to Kurzman (2009), Ayatollah Mohammad Emami-Kashani, a member of the Assembly of Experts, declared in a televised sermon in September 2009, "The human sciences should not be taught in the Western style in the country's universities." The same Ayatollah in the 1990s argued that the satellite dish was a tool of the West's cultural war to undermine Iranian society.

Social scientists like Kian Tajbakhsh were paraded on Iranian TV and served as a surrogate, a sort of punching bag for the regime to lash out against the social sciences, civil society, and U.S. foreign policy. Unfortunately, in addition to being forced to participate in the show trials, he was subjected to months of solitary confinement, long interrogation sessions, an initial twelve-to-fifteen-year prison sentence, and the lodging of further charges that threatened a possible death penalty, before his sentence was reduced to five years on appeal. He was released on a "temporary furlough" during the March 2010 Iranian New Year (*Nowruz*) celebration—eight months after his arrest.

## DISCUSSION AND CONCLUSION

Mass media and new communication technologies played a pivotal role in the lead-up to Iran's presidential election and proved to be crucial to the movement that contested the outcome of those elections, demonstrating that even Iran is not immune from the media saturation of politics. Thus, the Iranian state adopted its own mediatic strategy to counter the flow of seditious information circulating within Iran and from without. The five-part show trials served as a tool in this regard.

The accused during the show trial were accused of fomenting a Velvet Revolution. A Velvet Revolution did not occur in Iran, with the concept serving as more of a rhetorical tool used by the conservatives to discredit the reformists. While the Velvet Revolution may be a mere threat perceived by the state, nonetheless a mediated revolution in virtual and cyber communications did succeed after June 2009. The Iranian Revolution of 1979 was considered the last great revolution of the twentieth century. Iran in 2009 proved to be the stage of the first great virtual revolution of the twenty-first century.

## REFERENCES

A most questionable trial. (2009, August 27). Aftab-e Yazd Online. Open Source Center (OSC) Document IAP20090827950067.

Accused say fraud in elections was a lie. (2009, August 1). Fars News Agency. OSC-Document IAP20090803950116.

Anonymous. (2009). Iran: The revenge. *New York Review of Books*, *56*(7). http://www.nybooks.com/articles/23293.

Ganji, A. (2009, September 22). Soros's greens. *Javan*, p. 2.

Kurzman, C. (2009). Reading Weber in Tehran. *Chronicle of Higher Education.* http://chronicle.com/article/Social-Science-on-Trial-in/48949.

*Chapter Eighteen*

# The Ramadan Controversy

*Dilemmas in Mediating between Cultures through the Study of Dutch and Iranian Media Discourses in the Post-Iranian Uprising*

Payal Arora and Ashok Panikkar

Playing the role of mediator between Islam and the West is one that is particularly fraught with danger. Mediators often find themselves in a critical dilemma of placement of the self within larger contesting discourses. Tariq Ramadan, a Swiss-born Islamic scholar, is one such appointed mediator between Dutch statehood and its multiethnic Islamic population. He was invited by the Rotterdam City Council to serve as an integration advisor for its multicultural population. However, his affiliation with an Iranian TV station sponsored by the regime caused considerable consternation, with his credibility being questioned by the Council. The post-Iranian election and uprising triggered a wave of reactions culminating in the dismissal of this prominent scholar, recently named by *Time* magazine as one of the world's top one hundred scientists and thinkers. This chapter focuses on the nature of media discourses and ideological leanings among key actors to explain how these issues can escalate, often with severe consequences to those involved. The authors use this event as a springboard to analyze the role of public mediators in complex political and cultural environments, using the lens of mediation and dialogue. By attending to issues of language and the framing of perspectives in the media, this chapter proposes a nuanced and novel approach to mediation and discourse construction in arenas of chronic dispute.

## THE CONTROVERSIAL CELEBRITY
## MEDIATOR BETWEEN ISLAM AND THE WEST

Tariq Ramadan is a Swiss-born Arab Muslim scholar and activist renowned for his expansive contributions to the understanding of Muslims in European society. He has been placed by the *British Prospect* and the *American Foreign Policy* magazines as eighth in a list of the world's top one hundred contemporary intellectuals in 2008 (*The Guardian* 2008). While Swiss in nationality, he comes with a notable ancestral background of political power, as the son of Said Ramadan and the grandson of Hassan al Banna, who in 1928 founded the Muslim Brotherhood in Egypt (Laurence 2007). Given his unique cross-cultural positioning, he has been sought after to serve as a key advisor and mediator between the West and the Islamic domains. After all, his view appears reconciliatory, emphasizing the distinction between religion and culture, where Islamic values and European citizenship are not necessarily in conflict. Yet, controversy seems to follow him no matter where he goes (Buruma 2007). In 2004, his visa to the United States was revoked using the ideological exclusion provision of the USA PATRIOT Act due to his visible vocal and financial support to the Palestinian cause, interpreted as supporting and financing terrorism. He has been blacklisted by Saudi Arabia, Tunisia, and Egypt. Adding to the list of tensions, he has been caught in several battles in France, including being accused of being an anti-Semitic for attacking French-Jewish intellectuals in their defense of Israel. That said, he is tremendously popular, particularly among young, educated European Muslims for negotiating Islamic and Western identity and culture and serving as a dignified role model to follow (Ramdani 2009).

## CLASH OF THE TITANS:
## ROTTERDAM CITY COUNCIL VERSUS TARIQ RAMADAN

Tensions among the Dutch regarding the Muslim community are at an all-time high. Moroccan and Turkish immigrants came in large numbers in the 1970s to labor and stayed on, balkanizing into low-income neighborhoods with poor housing quality, chronic unemployment, and high levels of crime. Distrust among the non-Muslim Dutch has not just circulated, but also exponentially grown particularly due to incidents such as the murder of Theo van Gogh by Mohammed Bouyeri, a Moroccan-Dutch Islamic extremist in November 2004, as well as the arrest of the Hofstad Group on charges of terrorism. In the meantime, Muslims have witnessed increasing suspicion and fear of them that seem to gain strength as time goes on. In 2006, a poll was taken on perceptions in Dutch society of Islam. It was found that 63 percent of Dutch citizens felt that Islam is incompatible with modern European life, and many expressed being threatened by immigrant or Muslim young people (*Angus Reid Global Monitor* 2006). Such sentiments feed into further social segregation of the Muslim community from the rest of the society. This is reflected partly in contemporary Dutch politics where Geert Wilder, the hard-right, anti-Muslim and anti-immigrant politician, is now ahead in the EU polls, particularly gaining momentum on issues of immigration, beliefs of Islam, banning of the *burqa*, and control of Moroccan youth in the cities.

While about 5 percent of the total Dutch population is Muslim, Muslims currently dominate the media debates on culture and politics (Ministry of Foreign Affairs 2002). As these feelings resonate in the media and seep into general discourse, many Muslims claim to experience alienation and disconnect from both their first-generation immigrant parents and from Dutch society. Instead, Islam is seen as the pervasive glue, creating an affiliation that transcends national boundaries, creating a global Muslim community feeling. Therefore, the Dutch government, in order to prevent further alienation, hired Ramadan in 2007 to serve as a key advisor on civic integration and multicultural policies. In particular, he was invited by the Rotterdam City Council, since about half of the population in Rotterdam are not of Dutch origin, and the city has currently enormous socioeconomic-cultural problems. His duties were to provide participatory dialogues on religious identity and citizenship with a special emphasis on Islam as well as to shape social policies on Islamic-Dutch cultural integration.

This relationship had already started to fray by early 2009 as Ramadan was accused by the *Gay Krant*, a newspaper for the homosexual community, for making homophobic and misogynistic statements. This prompted a demand by the right-wing political party to dismiss Ramadan as city adviser. However, having investigated these accusations further, the case was dropped. Furthermore, his hosting of the *Islam and Life* show on an Iranian Press TV station, which is financed by the Iranian regime, seemed to stir sentiments again. This show is intended to be primarily an educational platform on Islam as a way of life for a multiethnic and global audience, Muslim and non-Muslim alike. Yet, with the Iranian election and uprising, a renewed impetus to dismiss Ramadan came about, and this time succeeded. The rationale by the Rotterdam City Council was as follows:

> The council finds that in deciding to work with Press TV, Professor Ramadan has failed to take sufficient account of the sentiments that this might evoke in Rotterdam and beyond. This is made worse by the fact that he continued to work there after the elections in Iran when the authorities very seriously clamped down on freedom of speech. (Van Eerten 2009)

In response, Ramadan released a statement defending his choices. In essence, he attributes this dismissal as deeply politically driven, serving the upcoming Dutch elections. More importantly, he argues that any mediation takes place at the internal level and that it is dangerous to view the Iranian regime, however tempting, as a homogenous entity:

> In Iran, the relationship between religion and politics is extremely complex. The simplistic view that posits two opposing camps—the fundamentalist conservatives versus the democratic reformists—displays a profound ignorance of Iranian reality. Moreover, no evolution toward democratic transparency can take place under pressure from the West: the process will be internal, lengthy and painful. (2009)

## DIALOGUES ACROSS CROSS-NATIONAL MEDIASCAPES

The furor in the media mirrors the public's confused expectations of Ramadan. In the next few paragraphs, we will explore why it is necessary to be realistic about his role as a mediator in the discourse between cultures.

## DEAD-ENDS IN THE ISLAM-WEST DEBATE

Islam and Christianity have a tremendous history in the competition for converts. Much literature has been written about how these two great religions and their respective cultures interact, respond, and react to one another (Blankenhorn, Filali-Ansary, and Mneimneh 2005; Paden 2005). While this is not the place to go deeply into the reasons for such long-standing disputes and tensions between these two religions, it is important to keep in mind that the forces of globalization have compelled these two cultures to encounter one another more frequently, more intimately, and more visibly. These encounters have seeped into all realms of public life, pressurizing state involvement. It would be naïve to see these two forces as sharing equal platforms in power and politics with the state, particularly in the West. That said, it would be equally naïve to perceive Islamic forces as primarily victims and marginalized forces, given their larger global affiliation, community, and distinct and diverse cultures.

Therefore, for the purposes of conciliation, the debate has taken on multiple tangents, sometimes simultaneously, of suppression, of outlawing, of embracing, and of understanding. One such strand in the debate is the faith versus freedom paradox: one party free to maintain the authenticity of their religion while the other party equally free to reject this very authenticity and even claim infringement on their public sphere. State versus religion is another age-old binary, where citizenship and belief struggle to reconcile.

Multiple efforts at resolving these tensions are being undertaken; one such effort is to emphasize universal human values over religion-specific values, with the idea of ironing out all differences. This, however, has been a weak resolve as it is too abstract and too broad to be applied to specific social policy. Another effort is that of multiculturalism, of live and let live; yet, this fosters a compartmentalization of cultures with little resemblance to social realities of cross-cultural interaction. A third approach has been to clearly state what constitutes public versus private practice since "public expression of religious conviction, is inherently problematic" (Blankenhorn et al. 2005). This erasing of difference publicly while giving free rein to it privately rests on the rationale that visibility of belief is prime provocation. In minimizing the presence of difference, social harmony can prevail.

However, as we have seen in multiple recent public controversies, whether it was the proposition to ban the headscarf in France (Graff 2004) or the Swiss vote on banning the building of minarets in their country (Switzerland Votes 2009), this is hardly an easy idea to implement. These public controversies call attention to the fact that religious and cultural practices are hardly something that can be easily contained in the private realm without deeply alienating, offending, and in general, creating tremendous conflict. Yet another strategy of resolution is to create bifurcations within the contentious religious group, which in this case, would be the Islamic population. Therefore, media discourses of radical or fundamentalist Islam versus normal or moderate Islam are intended to appease both parties, acknowledging the plethora of violence in the name of Islam at the same time acknowledging that the majority of the Islamic practicing population are "decent, faithful and peaceful" (Blankenhorn et al. 2005). This is yet another dead end, however, in conflict resolution, as this framing of schizophrenia within this community is seen as condescending and, at worst, deeply offensive. This implies that membership within such a faith comes with a need to prove in public one's qualification of moderation. Underlining these multiple dead ends is found in the following:

> The presumption of incompatibility has provided the dominant motif for story-telling about Islamic and Western cultures. Both Western observers and Muslims paint with broad brushstrokes when they engage in generalization about macro-cultural units of analysis, and fail to account for the diverse strands of cultural legacies. As protagonists of the story of incompatibility, they often resort to a language of exclusivity. This language is preoccupied with defining boundaries, and manifests a retreat from intercultural experiences to psychological and cultural segregation. Implicitly or explicitly, the "other" is depicted as

a threatening monolith. The result is that Muslim and Western analysts have placed such strong emphasis on extremist tendencies among their purported adversaries that a "clash of symbols" has begun to emerge, in which the most superficial and eye-catching aspects of the "other" are highlighted at the expense of shared and convergent values. (Said and Funk 2002)

In essence, the differences between Islam and the West are portrayed as the "clash of civilizations," a wasted effort at reconciliation where the twain shall never meet; counteracting this is the euphoric effort to build and demonstrate common grounds between these cultures, often portrayed as aligning closely with the Western framework of ideals and values.

## WHAT IS THE ROLE OF A MEDIATOR IN POLITICAL AND SOCIOCULTURAL CONFLICT?

In order to understand the role of mediators in political or sociocultural situations, we need to differentiate between facilitators and mediators. At best a TV show host is a neutral facilitator who brings panelists with conflicting points of view to engage in a conversation with each other. She does not share her own perspectives, seek to persuade, or resolve disputes. Through skillful facilitation, she seeks clarification and greater understanding. At worst the TV host is a partisan moderator with strong views who through debate challenges and tries to persuade people to come around to his point of view. From what we understand, Tariq Ramadan was a moderator who brought a very specific point of view to the show *Islam and Life*. This does not perforce mean that he could not have been neutral, just that his strong opinions within and outside of the show compromised his neutrality.

Mediation is a dispute resolution methodology with a well-defined process. The mediator brings parties in conflict together, helps them develop better understanding, and moves them toward resolution. According to Moore,

Mediation is generally defined as the intervention in a negotiation or a conflict of an acceptable third party who has limited or no authoritative power, who assists the involved parties to voluntarily reach a mutually acceptable settlement of the issues in dispute. In addition to addressing substantive issues, mediation may also establish or strengthen relationships of trust and respect between parties or terminate relationships in a manner that minimizes emotional costs and psychological harm. (Moore 2003)

While there are many schools of mediation and types of mediators (Karpov and Haywood 1998; Saikal 2003), the two commonly used in political and sociocultural situations are third-party neutral mediators, whom we will call professional mediators, and credible figures from the disputing groups, whom we will call interested mediators. The first group has specialized training and a type of neutrality called omnipartiality; that is, they try to empathize with both sides and to help all parties meet their genuine interests. The second group uses its influence to bring people to the table for dialogue and to resolve conflict.

## WHY DID THE IRANIAN UPRISING SERVE AS A KEY TRIGGER TO DISMISS RAMADAN?

Unlike professional mediators or genuine third-party facilitators, Ramadan, being from and functioning within two worlds, finds himself in the all-too-predictable quandary of being an advisor to the two communities as well as trying to maintain enough distance to be credible as an intermediary. This is an unenviable situation for him. In a crisis situation (if it were not the Iranian election, it might well have been another issue some months down the line), his audiences would, naturally enough, force him to choose sides. It is harder for a nonprofessional or interested mediator (one who has substantive interests in the case or an investment in the outcome) to maintain distance from the content of the issues at stake, as opposed to the professional mediator whose primary interest, other than helping polarized groups engage with each other, is in maintaining the integrity of the process. The Iranian election was merely the immediate provocation; the multiple roles inhabited by Ramadan were eventually unsustainable.

Tariq Ramadan's role in the discourse between Islam and the West is shaped by his being in the awkward situation of someone who straddles both cultures. However, those who wanted him to be a bridge builder, one who could help integrate a recalcitrant Muslim minority with a restive and suspicious majority, overestimated his value as a true mediator. Neutrality is critical to be trusted as a mediator between polarized groups. "I want to be an activist professor," Dr. Ramadan once told Ian Buruma. Being an activist requires that you choose sides. According to Scott Appleby,

> He [Ramadan] is accused of being Janus-faced. Well, of course he presents different faces to different audiences . . . he considers the opening he finds in his audience. Ramadan is in that sense a politician. He cultivates various publics in the Muslim world on a variety of issues . . . he's got his ear to the ground of the Muslim world. (Buruma 2007)

While this strategy may help him retain the ear of the Muslims, it also leaves his Western audiences bemused by his contradictory statements.

Hence, even as he is banned in some Islamic countries for not being Muslim enough, he is accused of doublespeak by his Western critics.

## SHOULD MEDIATORS BE FROM EITHER SIDE OF A DIVIDE TO BE GENUINE FACILITATORS?

Because "the identity of the mediator affects the mediator's influence, trust, and legitimacy" (Bercovitch 2007), the case is often made that authority figures such as religious leaders and prominent personalities from one or the other religion have an advantage over professional omnipartial mediators. Theorists who claim this do so because they suggest that these authority figures are usually trusted persons, have influence and leverage, and can, where necessary, bring resources and pressure to bear on the parties to settle. While this type of mediation has historically been used often, we need to recognize some of its limitations:

1. Authority figures, when they are trusted, can both bring people to the table and keep them there. However, when they bring extrinsic pressure on their people to create agreement, they can run the risk of alienating the very people who trust them.
2. Similarly, authority figures are often dependent upon the community for their own credibility. When their views cease to reflect the bias and prejudices of the larger group, they risk losing their authority.
3. Religious leaders are constrained by their own strong belief systems and allegiances to their community. When mediating disputes involving their own and competing groups, they are likely to be viewed as partisan and distrusted by the other party.
4. While persons rooted in a culture or religion are far more knowledgeable and able to bring the symbols and signs of their religion into the discussion, this intimacy itself can make it harder for them to step outside of the boundaries, vocabulary, and biases of their group. Where the fundamentals of their faith are at odds with those of the other group, it can be difficult for them to mediate. Sometimes in order to keep the mediation going, they are forced to seek particular interpretations or passages that either water down the problem tenets and passages or dilute them sufficiently to make them seem less threatening and more acceptable. This prevents them from getting to the volatile core issues that need to be addressed. Without being able to honestly address core divisive issues, mediation cannot create genuine understanding, empathy, or resolution.

The professional mediator's trust and credibility do not inherently come from the person being from and belonging to a certain ethnicity, religion, or nationality, while it is true that all these do play a part in building trust, at least in the beginning. Credibility comes from a track record; from the skill and ability to demonstrate a willingness to listen and be empathic to the party's needs and vulnerabilities; from the ability to create and sustain a safe space where difficult conversations can be had; and from the trust that no coercion or pressure will be put on the parties to get them to sign off on agreements that harm them. A professional mediator, not having to speak for a constituency, also has the ability to raise and facilitate discussions, however painful, in a safe environment.

The professional mediator's agreements are, at the point of creating, nonbinding, but can be entered into court records or written up as a contract with the help of lawyers. Once having done so, the agreements become binding and also have the advantage of having been crafted by the parties themselves and hence are more likely to be followed through. In order to be effective, it is necessary for a mediator to have a working knowledge of the domain areas, whether they are religion, culture, or economic issues; it is not necessary for the mediator to be from within or of the culture.

## MEDIA AND THE CONDUCT OF
## MEDIATION IN THE PUBLIC GLARE

Television is arguably the major institution that mediates contemporary public discourse (Dahlgren 1995). It is well accepted that this technological forum allows for multiple voices to circulate and negotiate, shaping public perception on issues and events. Television is an active participant and key instrument in the cultivation of citizenship and culture (Livingstone and Lunt 1994). Yet, the nature of mass media discourse is often reduced to the level of spectacle, given its inherent need to appeal to and to entertain a large and varied audience demographic. Furthermore, ongoing sociocultural dialogue, the essence of genuine mediation, is constrained by the structural allowances of the television medium.

This is not to say that media figures have little influence in public debate. On the contrary, they can be deeply influential and pivotal in public debates, providing certain framing of sensitive issues and events that can dominate audience perceptions. Media personalities also often have the capacity to bring differing perspectives to the table. While this is necessary, the ability to present multiple perspectives does not per se lend itself to helping parties move toward the resolution of their disputes.

Ramadan was trying to play too many contradictory roles—an Islamic expert, TV show host, a bridge builder who had strong opinions of his own, an advisor on intercultural integration, and a neutral mediator. He was bound to alienate some of his audience as well as his employers. For good reasons, most mediation happens outside of the public glare. It is one thing to raise awareness and educate the people about various standpoints and perspectives through public discussions in the media. It is quite another to expect well-entrenched parties to engage in sensitive discussions in public. It is an axiom that for mediation to work, the parties require a safe space where they can talk freely and evince curiosity about the other side's perspectives even when these perspectives are at first glance deeply offensive, problematic, and may entail dredging up historic grievances. In doing so, parties are likely to make themselves vulnerable to having their cherished ideas questioned and even proven. There is also the risk of upsetting the more orthodox members of their own constituencies who may accuse them of selling out or betrayal.

Hence, we need to recognize the role media can play in this kind of discourse and its limitations. The discourse that takes place in the media can help inform and educate. We also need to bear in mind that deep-rooted political and cultural ideologies and social beliefs are rarely changed because of articles and TV shows. More often than not, people tune out media that they disagree with and switch to channels that validate their biases. Issues related to religion, culture, and identity can rarely be discussed at the rational and empirical level because there are historic and emotional issues at stake. People need safe spaces and, most of the time, private conversations and dialogues for airing, let alone challenging, deep-seated beliefs. The problem with the public conduct of mediation is that it encourages public posturing, oversimplification of very complex issues, and a further polarizing of the groups. Leaders and critics of both sides find themselves constrained by the need to protect, defend, and justify their opinions. There is little learning and almost no reflection that can take place in such public moments and spaces.

## DISCUSSION AND CONCLUSION

Mediation is a complex and messy process, and dialogue is hard to condense into sound bites. After all, "conflict resolution does more than address material clashes of interest; it speaks to social reintegration, restoration and redemption, existential security, personal transcendence and transformation" (Said and Funk 2002). Mediators must eschew the glare of publicity if they want to do real work. Activists can communicate in order to influence. Journalists and academics who are acceptable to both sides must choose whether they will use their expertise to influence public opinion through the media or whether they want to engage in helping parties understand each other and negotiate differences. If the latter, they would be better off to keep their opinions to themselves and do the hard work of helping polarized groups engage behind the scenes. The authors, while recognizing the importance of the role that public intellectuals such as Tariq Ramadan play in the discourse between Islam and the West, cannot but feel that in being party to and subject of the discussion themselves, they cannot play the role of a neutral mediator. Therefore, this essay is by no means a case in support of the dismissal of Ramadan from his mediation post at Rotterdam. Instead, we bring to the surface what we consider the more relevant issue of what constitutes a suitable mediator for such chronic and sensitive cross-cultural realities, highlighting the trade-offs that occur in appointing a highly public figure such as Ramadan to address the growing "Islamophobia" in the Netherlands.

## REFERENCES

Bercovitch, J. (2007). Religion and mediation: The role of faith-based actors in international conflict resolution. *International Negotiation, 14*, 175–204.

Blankenhorn, D., Filali-Ansary, A., and Mneimneh, H. I. (2005). *The Islam/West debate: Documents from a global debate on terrorism, U.S. policy, and the Middle East.* Lanham, MD: Rowman & Littlefield.

Buruma, I. (2007, February). Tariq Ramadan has an identity issue. *New York Times.* http://www.nytimes.com/2007/02/04/magazine/04ramadan.t.html.

Dahlgren, P. (1995). *Television and the public sphere: Citizenship, democracy and the media.* London, UK: Sage.

Graff, J. (2004, February). Should France ban head scarves? *Time.* http://www.time.com/time/magazine/article/0,9171,586181,00.html.

Islam incompatible with Europe, says Dutch. (2006, June). *Angus Reid Global Monitor.* http://www.angus-reid.com/polls/view/12143.

Karpov, Y. V., and Haywood, H. C. (1998). Two ways to elaborate Vygotsky's concept of mediation. *American Psychologist, 53*(1), 27–36.

Laurence, J. (2007, May/June). The prophet of moderation: Tariq Ramadan's quest to reclaim Islam. http://www.foreignaffairs.com/articles/62630/jonathan-laurence/the-prophet-of-moderation-tariq-ramadan-s-quest-to-reclaim-islam#.

List: The 100 leading intellectuals. (2008, June). *The Guardian.* http://www.guardian.co.uk/uk/2008/jun/23/2.

Livingstone, S. M., and Lunt, P. K. (1994). *Talk on television: Audience participation and public debate.* New York: Routledge.

Ministry of Foreign Affairs. (2002, November). Islam in the Netherlands: Factsheet. http://home.deds.nl/~quip/archief/culture/Islam%20in%20Nederland.html.

Moore, C. W. (2003). *The mediation process, practical strategies for resolving conflict.* San Francisco, CA: Jossey Bass.

Paden, J. N. (2005). *Muslim civic cultures and conflict resolution: The challenge of democratic federalism.* Washington, DC: Brookings Institute Press.

Ramadan, T. (2009). Choosing the path of critical debate on Iran. http://www.monthlyreview.org/rzine/ramadan190809.html.

Ramdani, N. (2009, December). Escaping the "minority reflex." *The Guardian.* http://www.guardian.co.uk./commentisfree/belief/2009/dec/03/tariq-ramadan-muslims-europe.

Said, A. A., and Funk, N. C. (2002). The role of faith in cross-cultural conflict resolution. *Journal of the Network of Peace and Conflict Studies, 22*(1), 37–51.

Saikal, A. (2003). *Islam and the West: Conflict or cooperation?* New York: Palgrave Macmillan.

Switzerland votes on Muslim minaret ban. (2009, November). http://news.bbc.co.uk/2/hi/8384835.stm.

Van Eerten, T. W. (2009, August). Tariq Ramadan to take legal action against Rotterdam council. http://www.rnw.nl/english/article/tariq-ramadan-take-legal-action-against-rotterdam-council.

*Part Four*

# CULTURAL AND
# COMMUNICATION DIMENSIONS

*Chapter Nineteen*

# Faster Than a Speeding Bullet, More Powerful Than a Locomotive

*Mutual Instrumentalization of Culture, Cinema, and Media by Iran and the United States*

Hamid Naficy

The 2009 postelection protests in Iran were a struggle over the soul of the Islamic Republic and its future structure and direction. They also marked the forceful reemergence of culture and media as ideological apparatuses into the Iranian public sphere, mediascape, cyberspace, and blogosphere, wielded by Iranian state and foreign governments, Iranian reformists, and protesters both inside Iran and in the Diaspora. The U.S. government engaged in such instrumentalization of culture and media for political purposes most recently when in its 2000 "war on terror" it embedded news reporters with its military forces in Iraq and Afghanistan and employed psychiatrists and psychologists as consultants in interrogating detainees in Abu Ghraib and Guantanamo prisons (Summers 2007). It also embedded anthropologists with brigade- and division-level forces to use their cultural knowledge to prevent "misreading local action" (Beeman 2008), used Iranian fiction films and documentaries as viable sources of information about mind-set and feelings of the society (reminiscent of the project that anthropologists Margaret Mead and Gregory Bateson undertook during World War II to obtain information about the enemy countries by studying their movies), and underwrote Iranian oppositional media and political groups with the aim of democratizing and even dismantling the Islamic regime. These practices came under vociferous criticism by the respective professional societies in the United States because of their potential to compromise both the truth and the professional ethics of their disciplines.

The Islamic Republic's instrumentalization of culture and media began early on with attacks on and the banning of Western and Iranian exile cultural products and technologies, including Western movies, exile TV programs, videocassettes, and satellite TV (Naficy 2002). Its most organized effort came later, in the early 1990s, when it began a campaign against Western cultural assault and media imperialism, in what it perceived as the West's effort to counter and dismantle the regime by "soft power." The proponents of this cultural assault thesis claimed that the West, particularly the United States, having been disappointed in toppling the Islamic Republic by force in the 1980s through its proxy, Saddam Hussein, had now turned to implementing a soft revolution or a Velvet Revolution, of the type that had transformed authoritarian Communist regimes into nominal liberal democracies. They argued that the agents for these revolutions were not military forces but civil society institutions and intellectuals financed, supported, and guided by American government and allied sources. One proponent in 2009 colorfully, but ominously, termed this line-up of cultural forces against the regime as a "cultural NATO." In the past two decades, this debate has resurfaced time and again in different forms to undermine and destroy government opposition and reform movements both in Iran and the United States. Its most recent resurfacing was in the aftermath of the June 12, 2009, disputed presidential election, restoring Mahmoud Ahmadinejad to a second term in office, which led to the suppression of cultural producers and media, and the arrests, interrogations, exile, torture, rapes, and execution of dissidents. In classic Gramscian manner, the cultural instrumentalization has continued to change shape in order to remain relevant, ensuring the hardliners both in the United States and Iran ascendant. This article historicizes this most recent resurfacing of the cultural assault in the context of the mutual debate about political instrumentalization of culture and media in order to show its roots, variety of forms, and continual evolution.

## CLASH OF CIVILIZATION AND WESTERN CULTURAL ASSAULT

Inside Iran, the debate over instrumentalization of culture by foreigners fully emerged in the summer 1991 over what the governing right-wing faction called an organized, multifaceted *tahajom-e farhangi* (cultural assault) of the country by Western imperialism. The proponents believed that the enemy—the West and its domestic collaborators, the intellectuals—was targeting Iran and its Islamicate values not directly by political and military means but by the more potent hidden weapon of cultural transmogrification (Khorrami 1997). This was the reverse side of the clash of civilization thesis, first promulgated by Bernard Lewis around the same time in his article "The Roots of Muslim Rage" in *The Atlantic Monthly* (September 1990) and later developed further by Samuel Huntington, who argued that fundamental sources of conflict in the post–Cold War world would not be primarily ideological or economic but cultural and civilizational, with Islamic resurgence forming a major foe. While clash of civilization discourse fed the fear in the West of Islam, the cultural assault debate nurtured in Iran the fear of the West. Islamist filmmaker Morteza Avini identified this debate as dating to the end of the war with Iraq in 1988 and to the realization that the end of the hot war was not the end of attack on the Islamic Republic (1992). Many high-ranking political figures, including Supreme Leader Ayatollah Ali Khamenehi, then president Ali Akbar Hashemi Rafsanjani, and then minister of culture and Islamic guidance Mohammad Khatami, as well as most of the press, participated in this debate. The language was strident and alarmist. Khamenehi, for example, analogized this cultural assault to a new weapon, a chemical bomb, launched by the West to undermine the Islamic regime and its values, a weapon that, as he noted, works silently, invisibly, and imperceptibly (Khamenehi 1994). He elaborated: "What the enemy is doing is not only a cultural assault (*tahajom*) but also a cultural surprise attack (*Shabikhun*), a cultural plunder (*gharat*), a cultural massacre (*qatl-e am*)" (1994). The upstart literary journal *Gardun*, whose cover (nos. 15–16, 1 Mordad 1370) about Iranian exiles had sparked the cultural assault debate, was shut down and its editor forced into exile.

## GOVERNMENT CULTURAL ASSAULT

Soon, in what amounted to a governmental cultural assault, attacks on writers, publishers, and the press increased; many authors and editors were jailed, and publishing and printing houses were shut down (Siavoshi 1997). The newly reconstituted Writers' Association of Iran in an open letter in 1994, entitled "We Are Writers" and signed by 134 intellectuals, protested the mistreatments of writers and insisted on the civil rights of writers of all kinds, including screenplay writers, and their right to be recognized as professionals. This proved ineffective.

## *IDENTITY* TV SHOW

Instead, the category "intellectual" was dragged through the mud. A notorious weekly television program, *Identity* (Khorrami 1997), apparently produced under the Ministry of Intelligence supervision, inflamed the cultural invasion debate by charging that Iranian intellectuals—inside and outside the country—were wittingly or unwittingly instruments of a foreign cultural assault on Islamic Iran. It depicted prominent secular thinkers as anti-Islamic, morally corrupt traitors, Freemasons, Zionists, Baha'is, and foreign spies. It employed interviews, documents, innuendos, accusatory narration, clips from Iranian exile television in Los Angeles, which it routinely identified as "anti-revolution television," and clips of prison "confessions." More sophisticated than the televisual *Savak Shows* of the Pahlavi period, *Identity*, in its many programs, not only attacked individual authors but also cultural foundations outside the country which promoted and celebrated Iranian history, culture, and society, such as Foundation for Iranian Studies, Mahvi Foundation, Kian Foundation, and Par Foundation. Certain fields of study, such as Iranian studies, historiography, and narrative literature; topics such as secular nationalism; associations of Iranian scholars such as the Center for Iranian Research and Analysis (CIRA); and respected intellectual and academic publications such as *Iran Nameh* and *Encyclopaedia Iranica* also came under fire. Long before the administration of President George W. Bush launched its program in the 2000s to destabilize the Islamic government using public diplomacy channels and funding of disaffected Iranians at home and abroad to foment a Velvet Revolution, *Identity* repeatedly charged that world imperialism and Zionism, headed by the United States and Israel, were secretly financing and otherwise assisting a hidden network of individuals and organizations in the fields of social sciences, humanities, and the arts in order to undermine and distort Iranian history and culture, particularly the contributions of Shii Islam both historically and in the recent Islamic Revolution.

This mobilization of public sentiment over cultural imperialism took its toll not only on those directly accused, but also on the high-ranking officials who were regarded as too liberal. Mohammad Khatami, who as Minister of Culture and Islamic Guidance had been an enduring, liberal leader, presiding over the flourishing of the arts and cinema since the revolution, resigned in mid-1992. In February 1994, President Rafsanjani's brother Mohammad, who had headed the broadcasting networks for many years, was ousted. Soon after, Mohammad Beheshti, who as director of Farabi Cinema Foundation had built it up into a formidable film institution, was also removed. These changes followed the earlier dismissal of Prime Minister Mir Hossein Mousavi, during whose reign these and other liberal officials had created the nucleus of a dynamic Islamicate cinema, culture, and broadcasting. With their removals, a new post-Khomeini, postwar cultural era began, one that would eventually return Mohammad Khatami to power as president.

## IMPEACHMENT, ARRESTS, BANNING, MURDERS

The cultural imperialism debate raised its destructive head once more in the waning years of the twentieth century. The lightning rod was Seyyed Ataollah Mohajerani, Minister of Culture and Islamic Guidance in the cabinet of President Mohammad Khatami. The first sign of cultural thaw under the new leadership was the granting of exhibition permits to films that had been banned from two to sixteen years, among them Ali Hatami's *Haji Washington* (1982), Dariush Mehrjui's *Lady* (1992), Mohammad Reza Honarmand's *The Visit (Didar)* (1995), Davud Mirbaqeri's *Snowman* (1995), and Mohsen Makhmalbaf's *A Moment of Innocence* (1996). Almost immediately, however, a rumble of discontent about the new minister's liberal tendencies and insufficient Islamic credentials spread throughout the hardline members of the Majles and the right-wing press, which culminated two years later in a contentious, public, protracted parliamentary impeachment against him (Etemadi et al. 1999). This was an internecine debate between two camps: one favored a traditional, autocratic, monologic approach to culture; the other supported a modernist, pluralistic, and multivocal approach—both within the framework of an Islamic state.

The impeachment failed, quelling for a time the cultural assault debate. Khatami followed this victory with his proposal for a "Dialogue among Civilizations" at the UN in September 2000 to counter the forces of xenophobia and intolerance both at home and abroad. However, cultural imperialism and clash of civilization, hydra-headed monsters, resurfaced in Iran and in the West whenever the going got tough for the hardliners on both sides.

In the long run, Khatami was unable to deliver on the promises of his new concepts and reforms against formidable entrenched Islamist opposition and a conservative structure, consisting of unelected bodies and a Supreme Leader who controlled the judiciary, the armed forces, the security apparatuses, and the broadcast media. Everywhere there were signs of deadly power struggles over culture, such as the assassination in 1998 of democratic and secular activists Dariush and Parvaneh Forouhar and three writers and opposition figures, Mohammad Mokhtari, Mohammad Jafar Pouyandeh, and Majid Sharif, apparently by rogue elements within the state security apparatus. Incredibly enough, these elements were arrested, thanks to Khatami's transparency doctrine. Muslim reformist intellectuals spearheading the reformist press took these murders as ominous warnings, as Payam-e Emruz noted, "Some writers refused to walk out of their homes alone. Many writers would not sleep in the same place at night. Every intellectual in the country felt that a noose was hanging around his neck" (quoted in Sciolino 2000). Investigative Muslim journalist Said Hajjarian, editor of *Sobh-e Emruz*, who had revealed the behind-the-scenes security service's involvement in the extrajudicial executions of dissident intellectuals, was badly injured in an attempted assassination. These developments heightened the sense of fear and outrage, as did the security forces' attack on a Tehran University dorm in summer 1999. As Human Rights Watch reported, by December 2000, more than fifty reformist daily and weekly newspapers had been shut down, and more than twenty "reform-minded journalists, editors, and publishers" were jailed, including Akbar Ganji, another investigative journalist at *Fath* newspaper (Iran 2002). Despite the atmosphere of fear, public intellectuals, including reformist clerics such as Hasan Yusefi Eshkevari, remained creative in their improvised oppositional tactics. In a cat-and-mouse game with the hardline courts, for example, some reformist newspapers resurfaced as differently named clones as soon as they were shut down. It was thus that publisher Hamid Reza Jalaeipour and editor Mashallah Shamsolvaezin put out in rapid succession *Tous, Jame'eh, Neshat,* and *Asr-e Azadegan,* bearing similar layouts and editorial policies.

A three-day conference in April 2000 in Berlin, Germany, which hosted over a dozen reformist and independent intellectuals from Iran and the Diaspora, became an object of tumultuous protest by the exiles, particularly by members of the Communist Workers Party of Iran and the Peoples' Mojahedin Organization of Iran, reviving the cultural imperialism campaign inside Iran. The video of the protest, showing two exile protesters taking some of their clothes off to offend the speakers and to protest the Islamic government's practice of torture, was spun by the conservative press and particularly by the government-run *Voice and Vision of Islamic Republic* (*VVIR*) into a weapon to discredit the reform movement. Several participants were arrested, interrogated, imprisoned, and mistreated. Shahla Lahiji, one of the arrested conference participants, correctly characterized the *VVIR* exposé on the Berlin conference as another version of the *Identity* program (Zakariai 2000). The cultural imperialism campaign continued to change shape in order to remain relevant, ensuring that the hardliners stayed in power.

## IRANIAN EXILE AND DIASPORA MEDIA

Iranians were highly attracted to foreign films, music, pop culture, and satellite television, hemmed in as they were by the government monopoly on broadcast media and news. Bahman Ghobadi's touching film *The Turtles Can Fly* (*Lakposhtha Parvaz Mikonand*) (2003) dramatized this need of Kurdish Iranians for news during the American-led war on Saddam Hussein's Iraq. Some Iranians considered these Western media necessary, while others condemned them as being deleterious to national identity and part of the West's cultural assault against the Islamic Republic. These media and products, part of the American global industrial, financial, and cultural power, had in recent years surpassed tangible goods such as grain and automobiles as the United States' "most important and valuable" global products (Lancaster 1998). The massive Persian-language pop culture in Diaspora, particularly that emanating from Southern California which was transmitted globally, added to the sense of cultural assault at home. Among these were music and television programs aired on cable TV, broadcast TV, public access channels (nearly eighty different weekly programs between 1981 and 2000), and satellite TV channels (twenty-five by the mid-2000s [Naficy 1993; Setoodeh 2003]). The hundreds of films that Iranians made abroad, a variegated "accented cinema," added to the sense of cultural assault but also offered a rich window onto their tumultuous lives in exile and Diaspora (Naficy 2008; 2001).

Islamic Republic leaders were aware of the efficacy of such a transnational cultural power, far exceeding that of military power in its impact on hearts and minds. Ali Khamenehi said as much: "Audio and video waves that are worse than warships and warplanes are being used to disseminate a rogue culture aimed at the imposition of unethical values and Westernized ideas in order to captivate and humiliate Muslims" (quoted in Khosravi 2003). But this culture was not imposed on, but embraced by, its subjects, despite, or perhaps because of, the regime's various efforts to ban or curtail Western movies, pop culture, videocassettes, and satellite television transmissions.

In the aftermath of the vociferous protests against the disputed 2009 presidential election, these exile media assumed, or were assigned, a more powerful political role inside Iran. Perhaps for the first time, exile televisions channels were directly implicated in fomenting antiregime activities, resulting in the execution of dissidents inside Iran. Mohammad Reza Ali Zamani and Arash Rahmanipour, both of whom had been arrested before the election, were condemned to death and executed in late January 2010. Zamani was charged with *moharebeh* (taking up arms against God) by working with the "terrorist group" Iranian Association for Monarchy (Anjoman-e Padeshahi-e Iran), insulting the sacred beliefs, propaganda against the sacred system of the Islamic Republic, conspiracy and assembly with the aim of acting against national security, and illegal exit from the country. According to the indictment, "the defendant had become 'familiar with the Iranian Association for Monarchy through its satellite channel, Your TV (Televizion-e Shoma), broadcasting from London'" (Three 2009).

Zamani and Rahmanipour were both put on television show trials, aired by Islamic Republic's English-language satellite TV channel, Press TV, during which they "confessed" to their wrongdoings. On that show, Zamani explains that "after watching the channel for a considerable amount of time, I decided to contact the society in their London office," offering to join it abroad to overthrow the regime. However, his contact, Dordaneh Fouladvand (pseudonym), told him that, before leaving the country, he should "carry out a mission for the society." She "ordered" him to distribute in the capital Tehran a large number of CDs containing antireligious material in addition to Salman Rushdie's illegal book, *Satanic Verses*, after which he and his cohorts had headed toward the north of Iraq and illegally exited Iran (CIA Agent 2009). In addition to this agitprop action, Zamani had collaborated with Radio Tondar, the radio voice of the Iranian Association for Monarchy, passing on news and making broadcast packages for it (Tait 2009). That the defendants were associated with this monarchist group was to discredit the reformist movement by showing that it was directed from outside and by reactionary forces; that they had been arrested before the presidential election and were nevertheless executed was apparently aimed at frightening the opposition, particularly those working with foreign and exile media.

## AMERICAN AND IRANIAN PUBLIC DIPLOMACY—WAR BY OTHER MEANS

Since the September 2001 Al-Qaeda attacks on the United States and U.S. declaration of a "global war on terror," the global distribution of American pop culture products has become an integral component of an emerging multilateral postmodern Cold War, this time mobilized not so much against Communists but against Islamic and other militants, Jihadists, and terrorists, including the Ayatollahs' regime in Iran—an elaboration of the clash of civilization doctrine. To thwart the rising tide of global anti-American sentiments and terrorism, stoked partly by the U.S. failures to bring the promised peace, prosperity, and democracy to Afghanistan and Iraq in the aftermath of toppling the dictatorial regimes of Taliban and Saddam Hussein, the U.S. government beefed up its public diplomacy efforts and its collection of intelligence from foreign sources. This included the traditional methods of creating and strengthening radio and television stations to explain American ideology, way of life, and policies to outsiders, such as Voice of America (VOA) Persian service radio and television channels and Radio Free Europe/ Radio Liberty's Farda Radio aimed at Iran and Iranians.

It also included a novel method, which involved the creation in 2005 of the Open Source Center, a new intelligence unit that keeps an eye on the global flow of nonsecret information. The center's officers, stationed within the CIA, scan not only scholarly publications of target countries, but also government-run and commercially produced broadcast media, newspapers, Internet blogs, geospatial data, and other informal and open sources (such as T-shirts) to get at the pulse of public sentiments and opinions regarding the United States. It also screens Iranian movies, widely available in the American marketplace, for what insight they reveal about Iranian society, people's ways of life, their grievances against the Islamist regime, and their opinions about a range of topics. Scanning the Internet, the officers found that Persian was among the top five languages that bloggers used and that these blogs were highly informative not only because of their texts but also because of their accompanying images (Shane 2005).

The shift from gathering secret information from enemy countries through espionage to collecting information from public sources in those countries—engaged in by both American and Iranian governments—is highly significant in terms of its implications for the politics of global cultural exchanges and mediawork. The Iranian government arrested an increasing number of bloggers, sentencing them to jail terms ranging from a few months to several years. In 2004 alone, it arrested some twenty bloggers and Internet journalists. The Committee to Protect Journalists reported that by February 2010 there were fifty-two journalists in Iranian jails, a record high which accounted for a third of all the journalists imprisoned in the world (With 52 2010). A month later, Reporters without Borders reported that, "With some sixty journalists and bloggers behind bars and another fifty forced to seek asylum elsewhere, the Islamic Republic of Iran has become the largest prison in the Middle East—and one of the world's largest prisons—for journalists and netizens" (Countries 2010).

In the meantime, American secret funding of opposition groups increased in response to the belligerent politics and poetics of President Ahmadinejad. The U.S. administration allocated $75 million for public diplomacy, on top of the already designated $10 million, to fund U.S. and Iranian exile media to destabilize the Islamist regime and to encourage democratic efforts within the country. Over $36 million were to go to Voice of America and Radio Farda and $20 million to Iranian legal, human rights, and media NGOs (Azimi 2007). This sudden infusion of funding for media campaigns bolstered oppositional efforts outside and inside Iran, but it was also interpreted by the clerical regime as another American-sponsored cultural assault—a slow-burn discursive coup to topple the regime—a Velvet Revolution. This, in turn, intensified the Iran government's external funding of pro-Islamic Republic NGOs in North America, its harassment of the opposition in Diaspora, and its internal suppression of the opposition, particularly in the social science and humanities fields.

## TARGETING SOCIAL SCIENCES AND HUMANITIES

Khamenehi considered the popularity of social science and humanities theories and theorists, who advocated an autonomous public sphere as a site for democratic struggle, a worrisome trend, resulting in the condemnation of leading Western thinkers, among them Jürgen Habermas, John Kean, Talcott Parsons, Richard Rorty, and Max Weber. He also called university professors "commanders" on the front lines of "soft warfare" (Kurzman 2009). Such remarks may have expedited the deprivation of five social science professors from Tehran's Allameh Tabatabai University from teaching in 2009 and the jailing, solitary confinement, interrogation, and charges of espionage against others. Many university sociology students were deprived of education for one or more terms. The serious espionage charge was lodged particularly against Iranian dual national social science/humanities professors traveling to Iran such as Ramin Jahanbegloo, Kian Tajbakhsh, Haleh Esfandiari, and dual national reporters and filmmakers such as Roxana Saberi and Maziar Bahari.

At least a dozen intellectuals in these fields were forced to appear in show trials, making televisual or other media confessions and interviews, about their involvement with the U.S. government and civil society organizations, such as National Endowment for Democracy, Woodrow Wilson International Center for Scholars, Open Society Institute, Smith Richardson Foundation, Soros Foundation, and the Dutch NGO, *Hivos*, the revolving door between the U.S. government personnel and such organizations, and their projects to promote reform and destabilization of the regime in Iran through soft power (Esfandiari 2009). Significantly, some of their interrogators were themselves university professors. If the reformist Green Movement persists, such an attack on academic fields of study is likely to be transformed into another wider cultural revolution, reminiscent of the one instituted immediately after the 1978–1979 revolution, which resulted in the wholesale revision and Islamization of university curricula nationwide.

Since the disputed election, more protesting intellectuals, academics, journalists, artists, filmmakers, political activists, even former officials have been arrested and charged, whether they were beneficiaries of U.S. public diplomacy funding or not, while others were released (all those named above except Tajbakhsh). Iranian intelligence officials claimed that "a group of expatriates function as liasons between foreign governments and the opposition inside Iran." These included the former minister of culture, Atollah Mohajerani, and prominent cleric, Mohsen Kadivar, both of whom now live in the United States (Slackman and Kulish 2010). Several political activists were executed.

In addition to these repressive measures, the Islamic Republic engaged in its own version of public diplomacy. To combat the Western government's campaign against it, to counter the Western monopoly of global news flow, and to promote an Iran-centric perspective on the world, it launched in the late 2000s two television news networks, Shabakeh Khabar (IRINN) in Persian and Press TV in English. The vision statement of Press TV, the channel that addresses a worldwide audience, hides such political motives under humanitarian rubrics. It places its emphasis on giving voice to the "often neglected voices and perspectives of a great portion of the world" and on "building bridges of cultural understanding" (Press TV 2010).

However, IRINN is openly a government mouthpiece. In 2008–2009, it aired the series *Secret of Armageddon: The Army of Shadows* (*Raz-e Armagedon: Artesh-e Sayehha*), directed by Said Mostaghasi, an updated and, as the title and the accompanying ominous music underscored, a more menacing version of the *Identity* program. Featuring interviews with progovernment social science scholars, journalists, and various "experts" and showing stills, films, and news clips from around the world of anti-Muslim incidents, the program attempted to establish the existence of a new "Crusade" against Islam and the Islamic Republic, waged with weapons of culture and media. Referring frequently to this as "cultural NATO," various speakers claimed that this Crusade was organized by Zionists, Jews, Baha'is, and evangelical Christians who, inspired by the Protocols of the elders of Zion, Freemasonry, and other ideologies, were conspiring to destroy Islam and take over Iran and the world.

In a further attempt to instrumentalize, even militarize, culture and media, the Islamic Revolutionary Guard Corps moved in the postelection period to take over a majority share in the nation's telecommunication monopoly (to the tune of U.S. $8 billion). This was perhaps partially driven by the desire to prevent another massive postelection campaign by protesters who had inventively used the country's telecommunication and Internet infrastructures to transmit their oppositional videos, pictures, blogs, slogans, text messages, phone calls, and news clips to the world. These media outlets had proved highly influential globally, for they were in turn picked up, echoed, and retransmitted widely by the mainstream foreign press, American-funded anti-Islamic Republic media, and democratic forces in Diaspora whose own access to Iran was denied by the regime.

To further impede the transnational circulation and coordination of criticism among Iranians, the Islamic Republic's campaign went global: it began a wide-ranging "campaign of harassing and intimidating members of its Diaspora world-wide—not just prominent dissidents—who criticize the regime" (Fassihi 2009). This unprecedented action consisted of slowing down the Internet speed, blocking social networking sites (Facebook, Twitter), video sharing sites (YouTube), and cutting e-mail service inside Iran. It also involved tracking the activities of Iranians on networking sites worldwide, creating fake sites for the protesters to rope in more victims, monitoring Iranian protesters in Diaspora (nine hundred were tracked in Germany), videotaping their public demonstrations in order to harass them and their families at home, and sending them anonymous threatening e-mails to cease and desist from "spreading lies and insults" (Fassihi 2009). Iranians, however, found ever more ingenuous alternatives to stay in touch, reconnect, and coordinate.

## FILMMAKERS STRIKE BACK

Many filmmakers came out in support of the Green Movement and its presidential candidates, producing lively campaign TV spots and films, such as Dariush Mehrjui, and many boldly supported the postelection protests, such as Rakhshan Banietemad. Some filmmakers were arrested, while others, such as Majid Majidi and Mojtaba Mirtahmasb and actress/filmmaker Fatemeh Motamed Aria, were banned from leaving the country as they were about to board planes. These and other forms of internal exile did not deter the filmmakers and their supporters, however. Many launched discursive campaigns of their own, using the media.

In 2009, as a jury member at the Montreal Film Festival, Jafar Panahi, wore green to signal his support for the protest movement and held up a photograph of Neda Agha-Soltan, a protester whose on-camera shooting death in Tehran's streets had made her an icon of the protesters. Soon after the election, Panahi was said to be preparing a pro-protest film, which led to his arrest in his home, perhaps as a preemptive measure. All his films were banned. Another director, Mohammad Rassoulof, was also arrested at Panahi's home, along with fourteen others (these latter were released). These arrests caused fifty prominent filmmakers, actors, and artists to write a public letter to the Ministry of Culture and Islamic Guidance and the Judiciary in which they asked for the release of Panahi and Rassoulof, correctly reminding the authorities that "in the past 30 years it was the filmmakers who as cultural ambassadors brought worldwide prestige to the name of Iran" (Cinema 2009). The prestigious Cannes Film Festival retaliated in 2010 by nominating Panahi as a jury member, perhaps the first instance in the festival's history in which a sitting jury member is held in prison.

Another novel protest approach emerged when prominent Iranian filmmakers refused to sit on the jury of the premier Iranian film festival, Fajr International Film Festival, which occurs every February. Actress Fatermeh Gudarzi, veteran actor Ezzatollah Entezami, screenwriters Minu Farshchi and Farhad Tohidi, director Asghar Farhadia, and renowned filmmaker Abbas Kiarostami sent various excuses such as foreign travel and illness for not accepting jury duty for 2010. Prominent directors Rakhshan Banietemad and Rasul Sadrameli, supporters of the oppositional presidential candidate, Mir Hossein Mousavi, refused to enter their films in the festival. And some directors, whose films were screened at the festival, refused to appear in postscreening press conferences and interviews. Many prominent foreign filmmakers in sympathy with their Iranian counterparts refused to attend or to enter their works in the festival. Among these were Ken Loach (Britain), Philippe Lioret (France), Theo Angelopoulos (Greece), and Elia Suleiman (Palestine). Festival organizers countered by slating for screening some previously banned films, hoping this action would neutralize the protesters' boycott (Fajr Festival 2010; Fajr Film 2010).

The action on Fajr followed an earlier important move in October 2009 by 142 Iranian filmmakers to shun the Cinéma Vérité in Tehran, the premier national festival of documentary films organized annually by the Documentary and Experimental Film Center of the Ministry of Culture and Islamic Guidance. In a statement the protesters said:

> Extreme restrictions that have recently been placed on documentary filmmakers, in capturing what is occurring in our turbulent society, are unprecedented. We can see so many films that potentially could have been made these days, but we are not allowed to make them. Therefore, due to our commitment and respect for the truth and the reality, we have come to the decision to not take part in the forthcoming festival. (142, 2009)

Many veteran and rising documentarians signed the letter, including Rakhshan Banietemad, Reza Haeri, Pirooz Kalantari, Bahman Kiarostami, Parviz Kimiavi, Ramtin Lavafipour, Mojtaba Mirtahmasb, Ebrahim Mokhtari, Mehrdad Oskoui, Maani Petgar, Shadmehr Rastin, Mahvash Sheiykholeslami, Kamran Shirdel, Mohammad Shirvani, and Farhad Varahram.

Given these domestic difficulties, increasingly the dreaded and simultaneously alluring external exile became an option for some filmmakers. Bahman Ghobadi (Roxana Saberi's fiancé), whose 2009 *No One Knows about Persian Cats* (*Kasi as Gorbehha-ye Irani Khabar Nadareh*) about the explosive underground music scene, presciently depicted Tehran as a powder keg ready to go off. He was arrested and his film banned. He was eventually allowed to leave the country; he now lives in different places, Iraqi Kurdistan and Germany, among them. To counter the government ban on his film, he decided on a novel distribution method: making it available free of charge, copied and passed from hand to hand or shared on the World Wide Web. Mohsen Makhmalbaf, currently in exile in Europe with other members of his filmmaking family, became a spokesman for the movement, issuing Internet videos critical of the restoration of Ahmadinejad and urging foreign governments not to recognize his presidency. He later dedicated his lifetime achievement award from the Nuremberg Human Rights Film Festival to the cleric Mehdi Karroubi, a presidential candidate in the 2009 election, who had boldly charged the Tehran prison authorities with sodomizing young girls and boys who had been arrested during postelection protests. Actress Golshifteh Farahani, blacklisted by the Iranian government for acting without permission in Ridley Scott's film *Body of Lies* (2008), chose exile and from there recorded a protest music video with fellow exiled musician Mohsen Namjoo.

After screening her film, *The Rake* (*Darkhish*), based on Franz Kafka's short story about torture in prison, "In the Penal Colony," at the German Film Festival, Perspective, devoted to documentaries and features dealing with human rights issues, filmmaker Narges Kalhor applied for political asylum in Germany. Made without permission, and in part inspired by the protest movement, she felt her return would land her in jail. Her case is newsworthy, because her father, Mahdi Kalhor, himself a former filmmaker, is President Mahmoud Ahmadinejad's close advisor on cultural affairs and a media spokesperson for the regime (Schaer 2009).

If this historical and contextual account is any indication, the clash of soft power between Islamic Republic and Western powers and between the Islamist regime and its opponents at home and in Diaspora is likely to continue to evolve, shape-shift, multiply, and intensify in the future. At the same time, if the regime loses legitimacy not only among its opponents, but also its supporters, as is indicated by the continued protests, more than its soul will be at stake.

## REFERENCES

Avini, S. M. (1992/1371). Chera Rowshafekran Mowred-e Ettehman Hastand? *Sureh*, *4*(4), pp. 4–9.

Azimi, N. (2007, June 24). Hard realities of soft power. *New York Times*, pp. 50–55.

Beeman, W. O. (2008, March 4). Iraq's lethal fieldwork. *Le Monde Diplomatique*. http://mondediplo.com/2008/03/04anthropology.

"CIA agent" Ali-Zamani's confessions in court. (2009, August 9). http://www.presstv.ir/detail.aspx?id=102974&sectionid=3510302.

Cinema artists demand Jafar Panahi's freedom. (2009). *Workers News Agency of Iran*. http://www.ilna.ir/printable.aspx?ID=113819. In Persian.

Countries under surveillance: Iran. (2010, March 12). Reporters without Borders. http://en.rsf.org/iran-iran-12-03-2010,36684.html.

Esfandiari, H. (2009). *My prison, my home: One woman's story of captivity in Iran*. New York: HarperCollins.

Etemadi, F. et al. (Eds.). (1999/1378). *Doktor Mohajerani: Az ra'i-ye E'temad ta Estizah*. Tehran: Elm.

Fajr Festival and the challenge of boycott from filmmakers. (2010). Mardomak. http://www.Mardomak.me/news/challenge_for_Fajr_Festival/#.

Fajr Film Festival jury announced—many boycott the event. (2010, January 27). *Payvand Iran News*. http://www.payvand.com/news/10/jan/1271.html.

Fassihi, F. (2009, December 4). Iranian crackdown goes global. *Wall Street Journal.* http://online.wsj.com/article/SB125978649644673331.html.

Iran: Human Rights Watch. (2002). *World report.* http://www.hrw.org/wr2K2/mena3.html.

Khamenehi, S. A. (1994/1373). *Farhang va Tahajom-e Farhangi.* Tehran: Sazmane Farhangi ye Enqelab-e Eslami.

Khorrami, M. (Ed.). (1997/1376). *Hoviyat.* Tehran: Hayyan.

Khosravi, S. (2003). *The third generation: The Islamic order of things and cultural defiance among the young of Tehran.* Stockholm: Stockholm University.

Kurzman, C. (2009, November 1). Reading Weber in Iran. *The Chronicle of Higher Education.* http://chronicle.com/article/Social-Science-on-Trial in-/48949/.

Lancaster, J. (1998, October 27). Barbie, *Titanic* show good side of "Great Satan." *Washington Post* Foreign Service, p. A1. http://www.john-lancaster.com/Site/Iran.html.

Lewis, B. (1990, September). The roots of Muslim rage. *Atlantic Monthly.* http://www.theatlantic.com/doc/199009/muslim-rage.

Naficy, H. (2008). Iranian émigré cinema as a component of Iranian national cinema. In M. Semati (Ed.), *Media, culture and society in Iran: Living with globalization and the Islamic state* (pp. 167–192). New York: Routledge.

———. (2002). Islamizing film culture in Iran: A post-Khatami update. In R. Tapper (Ed.), *The new Iranian cinema: Politics, representation and identity* (pp. 26–65). London: I. B. Tauris.

———. (2001). *An accented cinema: Exilic and diasporic filmmaking.* Princeton, NJ: Princeton University Press.

———. (1993). *The making of exile cultures: Iranian television in Los Angeles.* Minneapolis, MN: University of Minnesota Press.

142 Iranian filmmakers boycott the Cinéma Vérité Festival in Tehran. (2009, August 20). *Still in Motion.* http://stillinmotion.typepad.com/still_in_motion/2009/08/142-iranian-filmmakers-boycott-cin%C3%A9ma-v%C3%A9rit%C3%A9-festival-in-tehran.html.

Pfau, M. et al. (2005). Embedded reporting during the invasion and occupation of Iraq: How the embedding of journalists affects television news reports. *Journal of Broadcasting and Electronic Media, 49*(4), 468–487.

Press TV. About us. (2010). http://www.presstv.com/aboutus.aspx.

Schaer, C. (2009, October 15). Daughter of Ahmadinejad's adviser seeks asylum in Germany. *ABC News International.* http://abcnews.go.com/International/ahmadinejad-advisers-daughter-seeks-aslyum/story?id=8833070.

Sciolino, E. (2000). *Persian mirror: The elusive face of Iran.* New York: The Free Press.

Setoodeh, S. (2003, September 15). It's prime time for Persians. *U.S. News & World Report,* 48.

Shane, S. (2005, November 15). A t-shirt-and-dagger operation. *New York Times,* p. WK5.

Siavoshi, S. (1997). Cultural policies and the Islamic Republic: Cinema and book publication. *International Journal of Middle East Studies, 29*(4), 509–530.

Slackman, Michael, and Nicholas Kulish. (2010, January 27). Iran continues focus on outside provocateurs, now blaming Germany. *New York Times*. http://www .nytimes.com/2010/01/28/world/middleeast/28iran.html?ref=world.

Summers, F. (2007). Psychoanalysis, the American Psychological Association, and the involvement of psychologists at Guantanamo Bay. *Psychoanalysis, Culture, and Society, 12*(1), 53–62.

Tait, R. (2009). Iran activist sentenced to death for election protests. *Guardian*. http:// www.guardian.co.uk/world/2009/oct/08/mohammad-reza-ali-amani-death.

Three sentenced to death in post-election "show trials." (2009, October). International Campaign for Human Rights. http://www.iranhumanrights.org/2009/10/sentences.

With 52 journalists in jail Iran hits new shameful record. (2010, March). *The Committee to Protect Journalists*. http://cpj.org/2010/03/with-52-journalists-in-jail-iran -hits-new-shamefu.php.

Zakariai, M. A. (2000/1379). *Konferans-e Berlin: Khedmat ya Khianat*. Tehran: Tarh-e No.

*Chapter Twenty*

# Social Networking Media and the Revolution That Wasn't

## *A Realistic Assessment of the Revolutionary Situation in Iran*

### Jonathan M. Acuff

The controversial reelection of Iranian President Mahmoud Ahmadinejad resulted in demonstrations that captivated the world. Yet many U.S. media commentators and members of the think tank community fundamentally misinterpreted what happened, or more precisely, what did not happen in the Islamic Republic. During the remarkable events in Iran during the summer of 2009, many commentators in the U.S. media suggested that the massive street demonstrations were attributable to the new social networking media, particularly Twitter and Facebook. Such observers asserted that the ability of Twitter to distribute messages to every cell phone user who so chose to subscribe his or her device and the use of Facebook as a resource for posting up-to-date video footage and photos of the protests produced a snowball effect. According to this logic, the initial, largely spontaneous gatherings by supporters of the defeated presidential candidates Mir Hossein Mousavi and Mehdi Karroubi mushroomed with the broader reach of these media, putting tens of thousands of Iranians in the streets and, in the view of these commentators, placing the Iranian regime in jeopardy.

Yet this account demonstrates the striking amnesia of the U.S. press, particularly among the cable news providers who most commonly offered this interpretation. Almost exactly twenty years before, similar opinions were voiced during the seven-week occupation of Tiananmen Square by prodemocracy protesters. The Chinese students interacted with each other and the international reporters via fax machine, which caused many in the Western media to marvel at the putative ability of modern telecommunications and the twenty-four-hour news cycle to drive events. Yet, fax machines proved no protection against the harsh crackdown by the People's Liberation Army that resulted in over 2,000 dead. In contrast, the successful, relatively bloodless revolutions in Eastern Europe in 1989 were in no small part influenced by the mass distribution of the writings of dissidents via photocopiers. The *samizdat*, as they were known, made the work of Vaclav Havel and others easily accessible, even when such subversive writings were officially proscribed. While they certainly make social mobilization easier, fax machines, photocopiers, cell phones, Facebook, and Twitter do not make revolutions. Given that in one form or another "new media" were present at the birth of all three above instances of mobilization and yet the results were dramatically different in each case, variation in the types of mass media cannot explain why some protests turn into revolutions, and others do not.

In contrast to the generally positive assessment of the role of new media in fomenting revolution offered by most contributors to this volume, I shall argue herein that these media play no independent role in the transformation of regime vulnerability into actual revolution. The ability to transmit information to the masses seems to be a necessary condition for revolutions—one is reminded of the pamphleteering of Thomas Paine in the American Revolution or even the cassette tapes of the Ayatollah Khomeini smuggled from Paris to Tehran in the 1979 Iranian Revolution. However, be they old or new, mass media are not in and of themselves sufficient to create revolutions.

The chapter proceeds thus. I begin with a brief survey of the academic literature on social movements and media. I then summarize some of the most commonly voiced perspectives emanating from American media outlets concerning the impact of mediated communication and the prospects for large-scale social change in Iran. I conclude with an application of theories of revolutions from comparative politics and historical sociology. Insights from these theories should lead us to be far more skeptical than the postindustrial utopianism so commonly voiced regarding the impact of contemporary mediated communication in effecting social change.

## MEDIA, SOCIETY, AND INTERPRETATIONS OF THE IRANIAN PRESIDENTIAL ELECTION PROTESTS

The claim that variation in media forms has a decisive effect in large-scale social change has a rich academic lineage. One of the most important figures in the study of mass communication in the United States, Marshall McLuhan, argued that "the electric puts the mythic or collective dimension of human experience fully into the conscious wake-a-day world" (1966). While McLuhan emphasized a kind of media from determinism, subsequent scholars utilized different frameworks to reach a broadly similar conclusion—that the form of mass communication has a profound effect on daily praxis, how collectivities organize, and even consciousness. For example, while James Carey's work (1992) adopted a more social constructionist bent than McLuhan's, he nonetheless emphasized the enormous effect modern media forms have in creating culture. From very different intellectual origins than either McLuhan or Carey, Raymond Williams (Higgins 2001) nonetheless argued that late modern media systems were particularly constitutive of capitalism.

More recent scholarship has tended to emphasize the effects of the Internet and other contemporary mediated communication on political and economic institutions, social mobilization, and culture and identity (see for example Albarran and Goff 2000; Bennett and Entman 2001; Dizard 2000). While this highly varied scholarship by no means converges on a consensus as to the social effects of new media, a prominent strain in this literature suggested that modern mediated communication has a destabilizing effect on oppressive political hierarchies, even when such power structures were oftentimes replaced by nearly as oppressive corporate entities. With the media forms came a much diminished state, with limited capacity to regulate media systems, much less obstruct discrete communications. While some saw the coming changes generated by postmodern mass communication as heralding a "global village" (McLuhan and Powers 1992), and others viewed such a convergence as an attack on culturally distinct communication systems, as Hamid Mowlana (1996), now an adviser to Ahmadinejad, would have it, many communications scholars saw in the rise of new media a fundamentally transformative effect for societies that would be very hard for hidebound organizations like the state to control.

The position of the literature on the transformative relationship between new media forms, media systems, and social mobilization was echoed loudly by the American media during the Iranian presidential election of 2009. Moreover, as this technological emancipation theme had a corollary in the U.S. think tank community, an echo chamber quickly developed between putative experts and television news depictions of the events in Iran. U.S. media, particularly cable news, tended to accept a certain line of reasoning emanating from both media experts themselves and neoconservative think tanks because it coincided with the conventional wisdom in these organizations—new media matter. As Noah Shachtman of the *New York Times* has succinctly stated this view, "Communication itself erodes despots' authority" (2009).

CNN, MSNBC, and Fox quickly heralded the emergence of the "Twitter Revolution" and fed their viewers a diet of near continuous feeds of cell phone and Facebook video paired with running commentary from the news-room and consultants as to the impact of new media in causing the protests. Indeed, even during a rare self-evaluative moment during this coverage, CNN's June 18 interview of *Wired* magazine senior editor Nicholas Thompson resulted in the confident verdict that though it was hardly proving to be a "Twitter Revolution," new media were nonetheless decisive in putting tens of thousands of Iranians in the streets (YouTube 2009, June 18). The big three networks fared little better, with ABC's *This Week* proclaiming "It is a political protest wrapped in a technological revolution," with the featured interview with one correspondent in Tehran resulting in the statement, "This is a country that lives on text messaging" (YouTube 2009, June 16).

Yet despite the size and frequency of the protests that began in June and have flared up intermittently since then, the insurrection against the Iranian government's version of the election results does not necessarily represent the deeper conditions of social unrest and discontent that would signal the onset of a revolution. This assessment flies in the face of the claims of many self-anointed experts from such conservative strongholds as the American Enterprise Institute, the Heritage Foundation, and the Hudson Institute, the views of which dovetailed with the media utopianism. Confident that a regime such commentators viewed as morally bankrupt had finally met its match in (conveniently) American social networking media, during the crisis several members of these think tanks sallied forth to the op-ed pages of major U.S. newspapers claiming with an abundance of confidence that this was, at long last, the revolt of the Iranian youth and urban middle class so often predicted over the past eight years by former Vice President Cheney and his disciples in the Pentagon. Other analysts of a similar bent suggested the election represented a "theo-fascist coup" (Wurmser 2009) against the ruling clerics and that, in keeping with the worldview of Mr. Cheney and others, the United States and its allies should thus assume a much more confrontational posture.

Yet a far more nuanced picture soon emerged from scholars whose primary focus was not on the causal role of new media. No revolution was in the offing, nor would one be in the near to medium term. These scholars tend to stress not just the considerable scale of the opposition to the regime, but also the paradoxically weak position of its opponents, particularly when compared with the scale and organization of the protests that precipitated the Iranian Revolution of 1979. For example, University of South Florida professor Mohsen M. Milani argued that Iran's regime is far more rational than is often portrayed by both the U.S. media and neoconservative analysts. The nuclear aspirations of the regime and its suppression of dissent are part of a larger strategy that they see in terms of a struggle for survival against the existential threat posed by the

United States. Thus, the crackdown should be seen in the context of the view of many Iranians—and not just religious clerics—that the United States poses a fundamental threat to Iran (Milani 2009). Even the view that Ahmadinejad may have won the election, though clearly not by the margin endorsed by the Guardian Council, was forwarded in an op-ed in the *Washington Post* (Ballen and Doherty 2009). However, Mansoor Moaddel (2009) of the University of Michigan subsequently argued very persuasively that much of the poll data prior to the election were faulty and that Iran has been subject to rapid shifts in public opinion in the past, sharply reducing our confidence in the extant polls. Taken together, it is difficult to discern precisely where the Iranian public's preferences lie. Thus, we should avoid overconfidence in inferring how the protests will affect Iran's future, particularly when such conclusions conform to our own preconceptions.

Of particular importance to many less optimistic observers was the relatively low level of organization of the protests, as well as how the opposition will come to terms with the religious core to political legitimacy since 1979, despite the problems of the regime. Misagh Parsa (2009), professor of sociology at Dartmouth College and an expert on revolutions, has noted in the online journal *Gozaar* that the Iranian opposition:

> would require a strong, secure leadership that can break away from the existing system and present a democratic alternative acceptable to the majority of the protesters who are risking their lives. The leadership must forge a broad coalition of students, women, and the rest of the population to be able to challenge the regime. The coalition must include the major social classes and collectivities in order to disrupt social and economic structures.

Although it is intrinsically appealing to believe that the United States is such a beacon of hope and democracy that we inspire freedom-loving people everywhere to throw off their chains, given the long-term stability of totalitarian regimes like North Korea, which many think tank analysts similarly claimed was ripe to fall in 1994, or even one of our so-called allies in the region, Saudi Arabia, we should be more skeptical concerning the claims of those who interpret every mass protest as "freedom on the march" or that every country will experience a Velvet (Czechoslovakia) or Orange (Ukraine) Revolution. In this context, it is also worth noting that the Orange Revolution has proven far from "revolutionary." Although it overrode the attempted pilfering of the 2004 presidential election led by Prime Minister Viktor Yanukovych, Ukraine's politics since have become considerably more ambiguous, with the ostensibly liberal victors of this struggle proving far less amenable to democratic governance than initially appeared. Street protests oftentimes do not a movement make, technologically inspired or not. So it was for the motley group of Communists, neo-Fascists, Orthodox nationalists, and the otherwise disgruntled in the 1993 Constitutional Crisis in Russia, during which the Russian legislature's White House was seized by the protesters and then gutted by tank fire from Boris Yeltsin's forces.

The tragic failure of the summer protests to override the results of the Iranian election, let alone spark a revolution, should remind us that utopian interpretations of technology and social movements often "run into a hard reality" (Bob 2005). Using the criteria of existing theories of revolution, it is clear that Iran was—and remains—far from reaching the requisite threshold of a political or social revolution. It is not that such a revolution is impossible. Rather, there are specific political, economic, and social conditions that increase the probability of revolution. Contemporary Iran reflects some, though not all, of these indicators.

## THE IRANIAN REVOLUTION TO COME? THE ELECTION PROTESTS, SOCIAL SCIENCE, AND THE POSSIBILITY OF FUNDAMENTAL CHANGE IN IRAN

Social scientists know a lot about revolutions, and the tools they have accumulated by grinding the grist of academic debates are quite useful in explaining what happened in Iran recently, as well as the probable political future of Iran. Will Iran experience a revolution? Alternatively, will the repressive policies of President Ahmadinejad and Supreme Leader Khamenei succeed in crushing dissent? One of the most commonly employed explanations of social revolutions is found in the classic treatment of the subject by sociology professor Theda Skocpol, who is currently Dean of the Graduate School of Harvard University. In one of the most cited works of social science during the last half century, Skocpol (1979) argued that social revolutions—events that fundamentally transform the political, economic, and social institutions of a society—are the result of a sharp reduction in the coercive capacity of the state, particularly with regard to its position in international politics, paired with large-scale mobilization of the rural masses against the state's elites. Unlike the Iranian Revolution of 1979, Iran's population is now concentrated in urban areas and the rural masses that remain are by and large in Ahmadinejad's camp. It is clear that the protests in Iran garnered relatively little support outside Tehran, Shiraz, Isfahan, Tabriz, and Mashad and that at no time did it seem as though the enormous police and military forces available to the Iranian state were faltering. Riot police and the *Basij* militia were more than adequate to clear the streets and arrest some senior leaders of the nascent political opposition. The regular military forces and the Revolutionary Guard were barely deployed. Indeed, the last round of demonstrations were suppressed using remarkably little force, demonstrating no evidence of a reduction in the state's coercive capabilities. Although Iran remains a pariah state for the international community, this has had little impact on the material capabilities of the regime to suppress opposition in June or going forward.

From the perspective of Skocpol's structural theory of revolution, conditions in the country make it unlikely that Iran will face a social revolution in the near future. For this to change, we should look to circumstances that sharply curtail the coercive capacity of the state. For example, a sharp, sustained fall in oil prices would reduce the ability of the Iranian state to adequately fund and equip its police and military. Paired with a much more robust set of enforceable international sanctions—a highly dubious proposition, both in terms of their adoption and deleterious effect on the regime itself—the relative position of the Iranian state in international politics would be altered, possibly rendering Iran vulnerable to a mass revolt against the state and clerical elites that govern.

Another prominent tool in the academic study of revolutions has been rational choice theory (Smith 2003; Taylor 1988). From the perspective of rational choice scholars, revolutions occur when there is a dramatic shift in the costs of continued allegiance to the status quo versus the calculated benefits for individuals of political change. Such costs have typically been expressed in economic terms. For example, in the run-up to the 1979 Iranian Revolution, the annual inflation rate was more than 40 percent. Dissatisfaction with the economic performance of the Pahlavi Shah was widespread among all segments of Iranian society. Of particular importance were the *bazaaris*, urban small-business owners who were being ruined by the Shah's economic policies and taxes. Thus the 1979 revolution occurred because it was far costlier for the vast majority of the Iranian population, particularly those with economic influence, to continue to support the Shah. Such social action was also predicated upon the perceived low probability that the Shah's security apparatus, particularly his secret police, the SAVAK, would succeed in defeating the opposition. After a harsh crackdown that resulted in thousands of deaths in 1978, the Shah's regime had not only failed to drive protesters from the streets and quell strikes, the frequency and scale of both had dramatically increased.

While the contemporary Iranian economy is far from sound, it is nowhere near the disastrous conditions of 1979. Unemployment is very high among the urban youth. But Ahmadinejad's social programs have tended to reduce the shortcomings of heavy-handed and inefficient state control over the economy and served to secure the rural poor as a stable political base. Moreover, GDP growth has fluctuated between 5 and 7 percent per year during Ahmadinejad's term in office, an improvement over the anemic Iranian economy of the 1980s and early 1990s. Inflation is high at 28 percent, but its effects are somewhat mitigated by the aforementioned state programs, something the Shah failed to do. On the other hand, rational choice theorists would note that the economic growth of the late 1990s has raised expectations, particularly among the aspiring urban middle class, who now constitute a much larger segment of Iranian society than they did in 1979. If these expectations are frustrated by a prolonged global economic slump—as was the case in the 1970s—that retards Iran's ability to leverage its oil profits and produce growth, rational choice theory predicts the calculus of the urban middle class will change. With regard to the probability that the coercive institutions of the state will fail to protect the regime, despite enormous bloodshed at the hands of the Shah's security forces, that revolution succeeded. However, it did so with much less violence, something hard to countenance given the disturbing imagery of the crackdown on the contemporary protests as the Iranian state cleared the streets during the summer protests. Nightly chants of "God is Great" and "Death to the Dictator" continued to emanate from Tehran's rooftops long after the suppression of the larger street protests and were heard again in early December. However, there is little doubt that the security forces successfully suppressed the mass protests that characterized the summer of 2009. Of particular import for the media as causal driver perspective is the surprising effectiveness of the Islamic regime's ability of late to suppress the opposition's use of contemporary media communication to organize (Worth 2009, November 24). From the rational choice perspective, the economy has to get much worse for most Iranians to calculate that the risks of defying the *Basij* militia, the police, and the military are worth the payoffs.

A third method of analyzing revolutions is referred to by the broad term of *institutionalism*. Representing a wide variety of contemporary scholars, it is also somewhat consistent with the early nineteenth-century observations of Alexis de Tocqueville. In his mammoth *Democracy in America*, Tocqueville noted the dense latticework of American civic associations and the propensity of Americans to readily participate in civil society. More recent work by institutionalists maintains this focus on the organizational structure of political, social, and economic institutions, as well as the ability of said organizations to motivate or deter citizen participation in politics and society (Goodwin 2001; Migdal 1988; Parsa 2000). From this perspective, rapid shifts in the preference of some state and social institutions in favor of political change or longer-term organizational problems, often manifest in the form of historically poor institutional design and/or dysfunctional ideological positions by the governing elite, render states vulnerable to revolution.

With regard to contemporary Iran, institutionalists would note that historically, secular Iranian civil society has been somewhat thin. While the Shah went to great lengths to rapidly modernize Iran in the 1960s and 1970s, he encouraged the development of a modern civil society only to the extent that these new institutions would remain personally loyal to him. This effort ultimately failed, and new institutions became a source of organized opposition to his regime. Trade unions proved an organizational source of mass resistance, as did the newly established secular universities. But more importantly, the ancient organizational resource of Shia Islam proved much harder to co-opt in the long run. The ability of trade unions to foster massive strikes, combined with mass protests organized and led by university students and a considerable proportion of the Shia clerics (*ulema*), paralyzed the Iranian state in 1979.

However, in contemporary Iran these institutions are no longer so independent. The state is part and parcel an Islamic institution, with the Supreme Leader Khamenei a senior Shiite cleric as well as a political figure. The doctrine of *velayat-e faqih*, the "Guardianship of Islamic Jurists," makes legal institutions Islamic in a fundamental sense. The Iranian parliament, the *Majlis*, is rendered largely powerless when confronted by several other institutions that are dominated by the *ulema*. The composition of the *Majlis* is restricted by the Council of Guardians, clerics appointed by the Supreme Leader who determine which candidates are eligible to run for office and certify election results, as they notoriously—and implausibly—did in Ahmadinejad's favor only hours after polls closed on June 12, 2009. The Supreme Leader also appoints the leadership of the judiciary, the state-run media, and the Revolutionary Guard Corps, the paramilitary organization responsible for protecting the Islamic Revolution. All of the organs of the Iranian state are linked directly or indirectly to the Shia clerical elite. There is little independent basis of organized opposition that can emanate from within the state, while the former revolutionary role of Shi'ism has been largely eliminated, as it is now largely synonymous with the state itself. While the universities emerged as a source of opposition to the Islamic regime's policies in the 1990s and figured prominently in the June protests, they are also heavily infiltrated by the secret police and monitored closely by the *Basij* militia. A series of protests in 1999 by university students were brutally repressed, and the presence of the *Basij* and police on campus has been increasing.

From the perspective of institutionalists, there are nonetheless some cracks appearing in the seemingly impermeable armor of the Iranian state and its viselike grip over all of Iranian society. In the late summer, a group of clerics known as the Assembly of Seminary Scholars and Researchers in the holy city of Qum declared that the Guardian Council was wrong to insert itself so directly into the political process by certifying what is clearly a fraudulent election. This suggests that despite the union of mosque and state, there are some fractures within the ruling clerical elite. In some quarters of the *ulema*, these fractures have deep roots that date to the period of the consolidation of the revolutionary regime. Such was the dissent of recently deceased senior cleric Grand Ayatollah Hoseyn Ali Montazeri, who broke with Khomenei in 1989 and was a critic of the ruling clique for twenty years. Montazeri sided with the protesters in June. In addition, presidential candidate Mousavi called for a general strike on June 30, 2009. While this strike largely failed to materialize, it points to the potential of the mobilization of the working class and their reincorporation as an organized force for resistance to the regime. However, institutionalists would also be quick to note the disparate nature of the opposition. With few civic institutions through which to organize, it is difficult for the various sectors of Iranian society to mount a concerted effort to seize control over the governing institutions of the state.

Moreover, institutionalists would highlight the very different objectives that most likely characterize the few organized sources of resistance. On the one hand, it is clear that the university students seek fundamental political change. During the renewed protests of December 2009, many of them dispensed entirely with donning the opposition color green of Mousavi and instead chanted more radical slogans that directly challenged the Islamic character of the state (Worth 2009, December 11). Conversely, it is unlikely that the clerics in Qum want more than reform to the existing system. It is even more difficult to divine the preferences of the protesters in the streets in June. Up to this point, political parties in the *Majlis* have proven an inadequate basis through which to organize a broad-based opposition. Absent concrete institutions to organize and channel these groups toward a common political program, institutionalists would argue that revolution is a low-likelihood event. While the Iranian variant of the union of mosque and state has several enduring pathologies that make governance in Iran inefficient and at times even awkward, the institutional architecture of Iran's state and society also makes it difficult for organized opposition capable of toppling or transforming state institutions to emerge.

The last and perhaps most eclectic approach to the academic study of revolutions has a forbear who is perhaps the most influential scholar in the history of social science, Max Weber. Writing in the late nineteenth and early twentieth centuries, Weber noted the enormous transformative potential of leaders who were viewed as legitimate via their personal charisma and the charismatic appeal of the ideas they embodied. For Weber, charisma had little to do with its colloquial usage today, "popularity" or "charm." Rather, it referred to the ability of a few leaders to convince their followers of transcendent qualities of their beliefs and actions, ideas that acquired a character adherents believed was essentially unlimited in its ability to change the world (Acuff 2003; Hanson 1997; Jowitt 1993; Weber 1978).

In contrast to the calculating behavior assumed by rational choice theorists or the organizational limits to social mobilization noted by institutionalists, Weberians argue that revolutions are the result of charisma's singular ability to compel one to risk all—even life and limb—in the pursuit of a revolutionary belief system. Historical examples of charismatic leaders would include such figures as Martin Luther, Lenin, Gandhi, and Martin Luther King, all of whom led revolutionary movements that fundamentally changed both the societies in which they occurred and the world at large.

With regard to Iran, Weberians would note the charismatic nature of political Islam and its Shia progenitor in 1979, the Ayatollah Khomeini. The specific content of Shia Islam applied to politics became the objective of the bulk of the 1979 revolutionaries and the leadership of Khomeini a force with its own logic that inspired enormous sacrifices. In this context, it is worth remembering that the coercive apparatus of the Shah's state was considerable—Iran possessed the world's fourth largest air force, a powerful army, and the SAVAK was perhaps the most effective organization of repression in the Middle East. Yet at the height of the revolution, approximately 1,000 soldiers were deserting each day. Moreover, many of Khomeini's followers willingly martyred themselves in clashes with the army and police, resulting in demonstrations at their funerals and the sacrilization of the revolutionary movement as an extension of the Shia faith itself. Due to the charismatic influence of Khomeini and the ideas he advocated, revolutionary activity against the Shah became a duty of the faith, a profound transformation from dissent into a religious obligation for the majority of the population.

In contrast, contemporary Iran's Islamic institutions retain little of the charismatic character they possessed when they were instituted. Even the ritualized shout of "Death to America" that begins each political gathering of the faithful seems noticeably less inspiring than it was three decades ago. Yet the reverse is equally true of the opposition. As one protester remarked to *New York Times* columnist Roger Cohen (2009), "We need a Gandhi. We need Mousavi to risk his life and stand there." While one should not understate the enormous personal risks he has taken by openly criticizing the regime and Khameini and Ahmadinejad personally, Mousavi is still just about the last person to qualify as a charismatic leader. Weberians would note that he is a product of the Iranian bureaucracy, an important political figure as prime minister during the Iran-Iraq war, but nonetheless a person whose background makes him more of a functionary than a revolutionary. While he has clearly emerged as the primary leader of the opposition, both as a candidate and in his numerous appearances in the demonstrations, from the Weberian perspective this role sits uneasily with him. His public pronouncements have not employed a transformational, radical discourse that is meant to inspire people to transcend the law and risk all in the name of a revolution. Rather, his speeches demonstrate a willingness to use the existing structure of Islamic law and institutions to effect change, not to establish a new revolutionary regime. Moreover, when he was prime minister from 1981 to 1989, Mousavi was more than willing to use the organs of the Islamic state to crack down on dissent. He is thus a rather unlikely revolutionary, and is hardly a liberal democrat as the concept is understood in the West. Until a charismatic leader emerges and becomes a carrier for a similarly transformational ideology, Weberians would be profoundly skeptical of the prospects for revolutionary change in Iran.

## DISCUSSION AND CONCLUSION

When, if ever, can we expect fundamental change in Iran? A synthesis of each of the above approaches is nigh impossible, as their claims are mostly competing. However, several common strands are evident, none of which have much to do with how the subject has been treated in the U.S. press to date or in new media utopianism. Absent a reduction in its coercive capabilities, such as with a prolonged collapse in oil prices and a global economic slump, the Iranian state will not be very vulnerable to revolution from the street. In addition, the Iranian opposition must focus on institution building— that is, it must transform itself from a large crowd of urban protesters who spontaneously gather into a sustainable, organized set of institutions with a clear political platform and a strategy to accomplish a shared set of goals. The inherent difficulties in such a process are exacerbated by the specific state-society relations that structure Iran. Without a more formalized organization of the opposition, people will have difficulty believing the risks they take as individuals will be worth it or are likely to succeed. In this scenario, Iranian state's coercive capabilities will thus continue to be deployed at isolated individuals, not at groups that are more capable of resisting. Finally, it will be difficult to stir the Iranian people to make the enormous personal sacrifices necessary to create a successful revolution without both a coherent, unifying belief system and leaders capable of inspiring them in the face of extreme violence.

At the tail end of the summer skirmishes, one protester was heard to remark that "we do not want war, just democracy." That may be so. But this demonstrator and the other people risking their lives in the streets should not expect such an outcome absent a violent struggle. Advances in media systems do not make regimes cave. As outside observers looking in, we should not fool ourselves by believing the Iranian regime will give up as easily as the USSR or its proxy states in Eastern Europe. Despite the regime in Tehran's appalling human rights record and the overwhelming superiority of Western militaries, nor should we in the West believe that we have either the moral authority or even the material capabilities to affect the outcome much. We may influence the possibility of success for the opposition on the margins. But to transform a state via revolution is the provenance of the Iranian people, just as it was for the American colonists in 1776.

## REFERENCES

Acuff, J. M. (2003). Islam and the charismatic revolutionary transformation of Iran. *Totalitarian Movements and Political Religions*, 4(2), 133–157.

Albarran, A. B., and Goff, D. H. (Eds.). (2000). *Understanding the web: Social, political, and economic dimensions of the Internet.* Ames, IA: Iowa State University Press.

Ballen, K., and Doherty P. (2009, June 15). The Iranian people speak. *Washington Post.* http://www.washingtonpost.com/wp-dyn/content/article/2009/06/14/AR2009061401757.html.

Bennett, W. L., and Entman, R. M. (Eds.). (2001). *Mediated politics: Communication and the future of democracy.* Cambridge, MA: Cambridge University Press.

Bob, C. (2005). *The marketing of rebellion: Insurgents, media, and international activism.* Cambridge, UK: Cambridge University Press.

Carey, J. W. (1992). *Communication as culture: Essays on media and society.* London: Routledge.

Cohen, R. (2009, June 15). Iran on a razor's edge. *New York Times.* http://www.nytimes.com/2009/06/16/opinion/16iht-edcohen.html.

Dizard, W. (2000). *Old media, new media: Mass communication in the information age.* New York: Longman.

Goodwin, J. (2001). *No other way out: States and revolutionary movements, 1945–91.* Cambridge, UK: Cambridge University Press.

Hanson, S. E. (1997). *Time and revolution: Marxism and the design of Soviet institutions.* Chapel Hill, NC: University of North Carolina Press.

Higgins, J. (Ed.). (2001). *The Raymond Williams reader.* Oxford, UK: Blackwell.

Jowitt, K. (1993). *New world disorder: The Leninist extinction.* Berkeley, CA: University of California Press.

McLuhan, M. (1966). *The Gutenberg galaxy: The making of topographic man.* Toronto, BC: University of Toronto Press.

McLuhan, M., and Powers, B. R. (1992). *The global village: Transformation in world life and media in the 21st century.* New York: Oxford University Press.

Migdal, J. S. (1988). *Strong societies and weak states: State-society relations and state capabilities in the Third World.* Princeton, NJ: Princeton University Press.

Milani, M. (2009, June 16). The Supreme Leader is supreme. http://roomfordebate.blogs.nytimes.com/2009/06/16/where-will-the-power-lie-in-iran.

Moaddel, M. (2009, June 15). A response to Ballen and Doherty. http://www.juan cole.com/2009/06/iran-election-fraud-moaddel-on-ballen.html.

Mowlana, H. (1996). *Global communication in transition: The end of diversity?* Thousand Oaks, CA: Sage.

Parsa, M. (2009, June 16). Iran's election and potential for change. http://www .gozaar.org/english/articles-en/Iran-s-Election-and-Potential-for-Change.html.

———. (2000). *States, ideologies, and social revolutions.* Cambridge, UK: Cambridge University Press.

Shachtman, N. (2009, December 13). Social networks as foreign policy. *New York Times Magazine*, p. 62.

Skocpol, T. (1979). *States and social revolutions.* Cambridge, UK: Cambridge University Press.

Smith, B. (2003). Collective action with and without Islam. In Quintan Wiktorowicz (Ed.), *Islamic activism: A social movement theory approach* (pp. 85–104). Indianapolis, IN: Indiana University Press.

Taylor, M. (Ed.). (1988). *Rationality and revolution.* Cambridge, UK: Cambridge University Press.

Weber, M. (1978). *Economy and society.* Roth, G., and Wittich, C. (Trans. and Eds.). Berkeley, CA: University of California Press.

Worth, R. F. (2009, November 24). Iran expanding effort to stifle the opposition. *New York Times*, p. A1.

———. (2009, December 11). Iranian protests turn more radical. *New York Times*, p. A6.

Wurmser, M. (2009, June 16). Why engagement failed. http://roomfordebate.blogs .nytimes.com/2009/06/16/where-will-the-power-lie-in-iran.

YouTube. (2009, June 18). Twitter revolution in Iran. http://www.youtube.com/ watch?v=OpQC-DJL_Ho.

———. (2009, June 16). Tweeting a revolution in Iran. http://www.youtube.com/ watch?v=jerEgzueiVo&feature=related.

*Chapter Twenty-One*

# Are We Neda?

## *The Iranian Women, the Election, and International Media*

### Sareh Afshar

The word *Iran* brings to mind carpets, oil fields, exquisite cuisine, and more recently, nuclear weapons. Iran's people, however, are recognized in two very different lights; the dominant image born out of the 1979 revolution was that of bearded men and veiled women who by the very nature of their physical appearance embody Islamic extremism and intense anti-Western sentiments. But following the presidential election of 1997, which for the first time witnessed an actual reformist's rise to power, international media engaged in systematically framing Iran's population as one which was entangled in a dichotomy: the modern Persians versus their traditional counterparts.

While both men and women could be targeted in portraying the former, the stark contrast between a properly veiled woman and a mal-*hejab* or bad-*hejab* could be much more readily conveyed through imagery, and therefore women have become the subject of many photos coming out of Iran as of late. However, this fascination with Iran's women has been only skin-deep, very much similar to media coverage of Persians in general.

There is no question that Iranian women, who have officially been politically active for over seven decades—and much longer before that without the actual guidance and support of any formal organizations—merit international attention. Yet in its incapability to correctly understand a people, their cultural and religious background, and also in order to preserve the social constructs media organizations strive to both obtain and maintain worldwide, the media has done these women many injustices—more so perhaps than they have their countrymen.

Iranian women's rights movements are today considered one of the nation's most active arenas in the fight for social freedoms and an end to the many discriminative practices still existent in the state. These movements are by no means emergent—though media outlets paint them as such.

In order to provide a more lucid understanding of the long-standing efforts undertaken by Persian women, this chapter attempts to illustrate the historical grounding of women's movements in Iran. It also presents readers with the complex intersection at which these women find themselves—gender and race. This worldly crossroad is rather unfriendly to Iranian women, as is the case of any woman from a racial minority, rendered more confusing for those who are "almost white" at times than those who are blatantly not. Having found its theoretical grounding, the chapter then focuses on international media coverage of the death of Neda Agha-Soltan and the intriguing complexity posed by the story of one woman. Neda was portrayed as one thing outside of Iran, while she is worshipped inside its borders for another. This again brings us back to the media's failure in capturing the true spirit of a nation, their wants and desires, all at the price of maintaining the dominant hegemonic norms sweeping the globe.

## THE IRANIAN WOMAN, THE "OTHER" WOMAN

> In my various journeys across the world and in the many interviews I have had, I have realized that Iran is still unknown to the people of many countries. That is to say, inaccurate propaganda has portrayed Iran as worse or better than it actually is. Many people judge my country merely by the twenty-eight years of the Islamic Republic government and have forgotten its prior history, as if Iran were created in a single night. (Ebadi 2007)

The presence of Iranian women in their country's social, political, and economic arenas comes as no surprise to the many professional women who have fought hard and long to achieve such status, be it domestically or outside of Iran. However, the portrayal of such efforts in foreign media outlets is relatively new. Perhaps ironically, these outlets seem to covertly hinder recognition of previous work undertaken by these women in order for them to arrive where they are today; this is both due to the perceived novelty of their news reports in the minds of their audience and also by what may be identified as the alienation brought on to Iran by its government and the policies implemented by the United States after the revolution of 1979. Whatever the cause, the end result is the mysterious cloak of unfamiliarity which shrouds Iran's image today, as Shirin Ebadi, the 2003 Nobel Peace Prize Laureate, best describes above.

Sidestepping the complex issue of why Iran has sparked recent interest at the international level (Kamrava and Dorraj 2008), there is no doubt as to the increased coverage it has received, both through traditional media forms and new, interactive ones. The presidential election held in June 2009 led to the climax of this exposure, with discussions revolving around Iran's nuclear program, its role in the Israel-Palestine dilemma, its failing economy, an ever-growing population of dissatisfied youth, and of course, the question of women. The latter two matters were of particular importance domestically as well, but this was no marvel.

The baby boom Iran experienced during the early 1980s, as a result of the population growth campaigns which the newly formed revolutionary government had embarked on, has led to its current status as a young nation, with roughly 60 percent of its population of slightly more than 70 million under the age of thirty (International 2009). Given the circumstances, the youth theme has been a pivotal factor in every political candidate's agenda for well over a decade (Roudi 2009). Gender-related topics have also been key to such candidates' positions: in 1997, reformist Mohammad Khatami won the presidential vote with statistics pointing to his success in capturing the interest of the country's youth, and its women (Ghazi 2000).

However, unlike the youth's unmistakable influence over the outcome of the electoral process, the significance of the women's vote is not as easy to grasp. The exotic frame, through which Iran's women are portrayed in international—and more specifically Western—media can be attributed to their biological nature and their culture. As Wilkins (1995) notes, while American women are trivialized due to the gendered format of newscasting in the United States, the intensity of such disparaging practices in U.S. media is seen more vividly when dealing with foreign-born women because of "the mystery that seems to shroud Western understanding of different cultural groups" (Wilkins 1995).

The unfamiliarity of most U.S. civilians with Iran is indisputable (Ebadi 2007), which goes hand in hand with the first problem posed in media representation of Iranian women: the lack of recognition for historic feminist movements in Iran which have allowed women to enjoy the relative freedom and rights they currently possess. This in turn has led to a false labeling in Western-produced news programs, which refer to contemporary activities presumed in this area as emerging feminist movements. Such misconceived notions can be better understood when one traces the similarities between what has been identified as black feminism (Hamlet 2000) and that which can be identified as Iranian-Islamic feminism. According to Hamlet (2000), "the black feminist . . . challenges the public discourse about African American women by presenting themselves as they know themselves to be" and not framed in the fashion that others wish them. African American women felt a "need to define their own realities, shape their own identities, hear their own voices, and find inner peace" (Hamlet 2000)—the same can be said for all women whose ideals aren't reflected in the Eurocentric feminist discourse dominating the field. This resemblance is noteworthy, because Iranian-Islamic feminism is also cornered in the intersection of race and gender—and intriguingly so.

While the Iranian woman can find herself walking hesitantly along the fringes of society, she is also highly susceptible to a misconception of her own race, because she is "erroneously perceived as having white privilege rather than as occupying a marginalized ethnic status" (Campbell 1995). In fact, most Iranians don't face the dilemma of being deemed what Kray (1995) dubs "almost white," which she uses in describing the racial status of Jewish Americans. Such realization may never come, unless they cross the boundaries of their native homeland.

History courses in Iranian middle schools teach children that they are of the Aryan race, and Iranians are taught to hold their race, culture, and ancient civilization in high regard. These ideals are internalized by many Iranians, even notable ones; this can be witnessed vividly in the opening of Satrapi's highly successful satirical graphic novel, *Persepolis: The Story of a Childhood*:

> In the second millennium B.C., while the Elam nation was developing a civilization alongside Babylon, Indo-European invaders gave their name to the immense Iranian plateau where they settled. The word "Iran" was derived from "Aryana Vaeja" which means "the origin of the Aryans". . . . [Cyrus the Great] established what became one of the largest empires of the ancient world, the Persian Empire, in the sixth century B.C. . . . Iran was often subject to foreign domination . . . yet the Persian language and culture withstood these invasions. The invaders assimilated into this strong culture, and in some ways they became Iranians themselves. (Satrapi 2004)

While this may seem like an ethnocentric view which can be found among many cultural circles, arguments abound that what some refer to as "Persian pride" has actually rendered Iranians as borderline racist. Khalili (1998) even imagines that the covert ethnocentrism harbored by Iranians goes as far as their conceiving themselves as "the most superior of all the people of the Third World." Under such pretexts, the intricate weave of gender and race and its effects on the global understanding of the position of the Iranian woman and the complexity of the issues she is faced with are seen in a more realistic fashion; this in turn highlights the need for historical grounding of the twenty-first-century Iranian woman.

## IRANIAN/ISLAMIC FEMINISM

Many distant observers fail to see the deep roots of today's women's movements in Iran. Unlike many of its neighboring countries, Iran's women gained suffrage rights in 1963 as one of the modernization programs introduced in the Shah's White Revolution package (Keddie 2003; Sanasarian 1982). The so-called emerging women's rights movement—which interestingly, in its current format, has been in existence since 1979—finds its actual origins in the Iranian Women's Movement which was born after the Constitutional Revolution of 1906. This era saw a growth in women's newspapers and periodicals, opening to women an arena previously thought to be only suitable for men: the world of literary writing (Milani 1992). However, the role played by certain remarkable men, who helped women in their struggle to pave the way for the flourishing of such movements, should not be overlooked.

The "woman question" was actually first raised by Akhundzadeh, who Amin (2002) refers to as a "renewalist"; he tried to articulate the need for societal reform in his famous piece, *The Three Letters*. This event took place in 1865. Other nineteenth-century thinkers, such as Mirza Malkam Khan, pursued this question through various print media forms (Amin 2002). Famous poet Parvin E'tesami was said to have achieved her status because of her father's enlightened approach to the necessity of women's education. E'tesamol Molk, who was highly devoted to the plight of women, translated a book in 1900, retitled *Women's Education*, in which he addressed the issues surrounding the circumstances of the life of Iranian women, calling for an end to their disenfranchised state and advocating their entry into the public arena (Milani 1992).

While historic instances of women rising up against patriarchal laws and power imbalances are abundant in Iran's history, as in any other part of the world, Iran is said to owe the differences in its approach to women's issues with that of its neighboring states to two factors: the first is the side effects of the Woman's Awakening project, which was launched in 1936 but ended in 1941 when Reza Shah was abdicated and his son Mohammad Reza took his place as the monarch (Amin 2002; Keddie 2003). This project was unique in its kind, since it aimed mostly at educating women in rural areas, who were traditionally deprived of such opportunities. While it was met by resistance from some of the indigenous women, the project was generally perceived as an effective one, one of the immediate results of which was viewed in women's participation in the protests leading up to the Islamic Revolution (Sullivan 2000).

Secondly, and rather astoundingly for many unfamiliar with the cultural values of traditional Persian families, was the Islamic Revolution itself.

Contrary to widely accepted mistruths, the Islamic Revolution opened up a new door for many Iranian girls and women living in such families. Fathers and brothers, the familial patriarchal figures of authority, no longer had any justifiable excuse to forbid their daughters', wives', and sisters' presence in a society which was founded on so-called Islamic values and mores. Colleges were therefore witness to an ever-increasing female student body, while offices acknowledged the work done by women. Women's employment was on the rise, especially in cases where women were thought necessary by the new government to see to jobs which would be immoral for men and could provide grounds for societal corruption (such as selling women's clothing and undergarments). Therefore, while women did lose some of their rights, and while they were forced to veil after the revolution, which they had not foreseen, they were not complete losers by it (Ebadi 2007; Kamrava and Dorraj 2008; Sullivan 2000).

The issue of veiling is probably the most complex for the outside viewer to understand. The veil is not considered an Islamic invention; it was used in Iran and many parts of the ancient world, long before any of the Abrahamic religions were born. Interestingly, in ancient Persia, veiling was a custom limited to elite women (Keddie 2003); if a woman of lesser importance was seen wearing this item, she could be taken before a judge and even imprisoned (Kamrava and Dorraj 2008). It only started to be seen as a religious symbol after the spread of Islam in the country, and even then mainly among those living in more populated areas. Nomads in Iran have still kept much of their traditional garb, simply because it best meets the needs of their lifestyle of constant mobility (Keddie 2003).

In truth, the veil has served a variety of purposes in different historic moments of Iranian women's collective past. At times, the veil has been donned as a symbol of protest: during the prerevolutionary street protests, women covered their hair to signify their defiance of the values implemented by the monarch (also, for the role of iconic Islamic figures presented by orators such as Dr. Ali Shariati, see Sullivan 2000). Recently, the pushing back of the veil and the increased showing of hair, seemingly an embodiment of converse nature denoting women's wants as complete opposites of the generations before them, has been in fact another representation of a call for decreased patriarchal rule over a woman's body (Amin 2002; Nguyen 2009).

It is this unifying stance against the dominance of male values and control over women's bodies which has been the precursor to the contemporary Iranian/Islamic feminist movement, which some activists have asked be called "indigenous feminism" so as to include the secular feminists, adding valuable context to the movement. In recent years, women with secular viewpoints, or better expressed as those who opt for the separation of religion from govern-

ment, have joined forces with women who have had official Islamic training
to provide reinterpretations of Islamic law based on a woman's point of view.
Among these women are Shirin Ebadi, Mehrangiz Kar, Simin Behbahani,
Shadi Sadr, Laleh Eskandari, Tahmine Milani, Elahe Koulaei, Farah Karimi,
Fatemeh Haghighatjou, and Jamileh Kadivar. Currently, some of these activists are running a campaign to collect one million signatures to call for much
needed reform in a push for gender equality in Iran. This mission, dubbed
the 1 Million Signatures Change for Equality Campaign (Change n.d.), was
awarded one of two Reporters without Borders awards by the Deutsche Welle
International Weblog Awards (The BOBs) in 2008 (Generación 2008). Nevertheless, women have a long way to go before they obtain all they desire in
today's Iran. To say that the presidential election of 2009 and its outcome
bore great significance for most Iranian women is by no means an exaggera-
tion (Ebadi 2008).

## THE PEOPLE'S VOTE, THE PEOPLE'S VOICE

The Islamic Republic was witness to its tenth presidential election during
June of 2009. In the frenzy leading up to voting day, reporters, both domestic
and foreign, provided extensive coverage of the events unfolding rapidly on
the streets, especially those taking place in the capital, Tehran. The coverage,
however, did not end once the ballots were cast and the results announced;
rather, especially that of international media outlets, increased in frequency
and depth. Even with the passing of five months since the vote, the outcome
of the election was still unclear for many objective observers. What can
be inferred from the happenings which followed the announcement of the
reelection of Mahmoud Ahmadinejad for a second term as president is that
a significant number of Iranians took to the streets in protest, claiming that
the election was predetermined and that their votes did not count. Civilians,
who believed an Ahmadinejad reelection as highly unlikely and the tally as
fraudulent, rallied at massive peaceful demonstrations, aiming to get at least a
recount of the vote or to have a new election carried out under the supervision
of impartial international officials.

However, in the Friday prayer ceremony immediately after the vote, which
was performed by Iran's Supreme Leader, Ayatollah Khamenei, protestors
were warned to end their dissent and to accept the official results provided by
the Interior Ministry, a division whose minister was chosen directly by Ahmadinejad himself. The following Saturday, protesters, who identified themselves as members of the Green Wave or Green Movement, had spread word
about yet another peaceful gathering in defiance of Khamenei's demands,

which was scheduled to take place in the late afternoon at Tehran's Revolutionary Square. As early as noon, members of the paramilitary *Basij* organization were stationed in the square and around the campus of the University of Tehran, which is historically considered a strategic meeting point for college students who support left-wing opposition groups. Soon afterwards, the Revolutionary Guards joined these forces, and as people spilled out onto the streets in rebellion, violent clashes occurred, resulting in the detainment, injury, and death of many of those who rejected Ahmadinejad as the country's legitimate president. Among these protestors was a young woman who became known as the symbol of the Green Movement: Neda Agha-Soltan.

Neda became a household name almost overnight; media coverage of her last moments was disturbingly excessive. Due to the ban placed upon foreign reporters at the time and the system of prior restraint instilled upon domestic print media in Iran, the only relatively free form of speech existing in Iran, journalists were leaning heavily upon amateur digital videos caught on cell phones and cameras and then uploaded to the Internet and disseminated mostly via social network sites, namely Facebook and YouTube. Neda was shot by a man identified as a *Basij* member on June 20. Almost instantaneously, her death, which was captured on two different cell phones, was being replayed not only in high numbers on the Internet, but on most respected television channels devoted to round-the-clock news casting. Her bloody image was splattered across the cover of numerous newspapers internationally, although it failed to make it to the heavily censored pages of domestic newspapers.

The truth remains that Neda was not the only person killed that day. International fascination with her death, however, was unequal with that of any other. Images, of course, have been thought to bear more power than words in transferring meaning, and the gut-wrenching pictures and videos of her last moments are hard to wipe from the mind. Yet the real question remains unanswered: why were these images disseminated in the fashion that they were?

The first playbacks of Neda's death on satellite television channels such as BBC Persian, BBC World, CNNi, Al-Jazeera, France24, and Euronews were all very vague: not only could they not verify the veracity of the story, but they failed to do so even in regard to her name. It seemed that international news channels were eager to capitalize on the very graphic death of a woman, whether or not this death had actually occurred was of lower priority. Even more alarming though was the mere fact that images like the ones released of Neda would normally be deemed as improper and disrespectful of a person's life, death, and privacy—more so in Western cultures than those found in Iran. Yet all of this happened, and not so surprisingly as an earlier study by Wilkins (1995) provides support for such social constructs in news programming in the West.

In her study of photographs of Middle Eastern women released in the U.S. press, Wilkins (1995) found that women, unlike their male counterparts, were identified more readily through their "relationship to a larger social grouping" than through their professional affiliations. By analyzing 84 and 469 images of women and men, respectively, found in the *New York Times* during a two-year time period (between July 1991 and June 1993), she concluded that beyond the obvious result of the plethora of photographs dedicated to men outnumbering those of women by a ridiculously vast margin, that women were framed either "as victims, as passive, and more often than not, as veiled" (Wilkins 1995). The Neda packaged together by the media conformed to all these models, as is discussed below.

## NEDA AGHA-SOLTAN PROJECTED
## THROUGH THE INTERNATIONAL MEDIA LENS

### Neda: The Victim

Perhaps the most discernible frame used to depict Neda was that of the victim. In this instance, one can temporarily overlook her race and focus on her gender. Scholarship on the representation of gendered violence in mass media can be traced back to Tuchman (1978) and her seminal piece on the symbolic annihilation of women, with a focus on its presence in television programming. According to Tuchman (1978), television is more likely to depict women as victims of violence rather than its perpetrators; this especially holds true if the woman is single. Evidence of such treatment was found by Gerbner and Gross (Gerbner 1978) in their research on television programming through which they calculated a violence-victim ratio, its significance lying in its prediction of social power. Gerbner's (1978) analysis of the dominant imagery of female victimization bears uncanny resemblance to Neda's death's video footage: "lying prostrate in the hands of males who range from noble rescuers to rapists." During her last moments, Neda lay on the ground, aided by two men; one was physician Arash Hejazi, the other her music teacher, who later changed his story of the events of that day, reportedly under pressure from Iranian authorities.

Violence against women is a transnational trend which is today seen across the continuum of media products, ranging from news to Hollywood-produced entertainment to products of the music and video game industries (Cuklanz 2006). In terms of news discourse, Cuklanz (2006) identified the traditional coverage of instances of rape, sexual assault, and battering by their focus on sensationalist and voyeuristic appeal. Also notable in her analysis of media framing of victims is her referral to the work of Benedict (Cuklanz 2006) on how such outlets either exploit the assaulted women as virginal and chaste, falling prey because of their innocence, or castigate them as vamps, therefore questioning the victim instead of the predator. The initial depiction of Neda, be it due to the confusion surrounding her unfortunate death in a time of crisis or in a more cynical mind-set, as a result of what Tuchman (1978) would have deemed symbolic annihilation, was an almost picture-perfect cut of the sweet and virginal woman; martyred by being subjected to the violence of men; helped along in her last desperate moments by men; and finally, mourned for by men. Nowhere in Neda's video are there any other women present. We only hear the distant screams of a woman in the video after blood starts gushing from her nose and mouth. The pictures of Neda and Caspian Makan, which were displayed across different international news channels, were said to have been of her and her "fiancé"; only recently was it revealed that he was in fact her boyfriend (A Death 2009) and that the innocence of their relationship had been built up by the media in efforts to make Neda seem like the iconic, traditional, young Iranian woman. Neda went to school, studied philosophy (her major was actually Islamic Theology), had a fiancé, and, as will be discussed in the next frame, a simple passerby, who happened to be present in the wrong place at the wrong time.

### Neda: The Passive Observer

Wilkins (1995) defines passivity in mediated images as that which depicts "persons who are not in some work-related capacity . . . or actively seeking media attention . . . and composes a cultural landscape by a photographer in order to illustrate a story." In her study of photographs of Middle Eastern citizens, she found that while men were shown assuming active roles "either upholding or breaking the rules" (Wilkins 1995), women were portrayed as powerless and restrained by their circumstances, forced to passively suffer the hardships that have tragically fallen upon them; as passive bystanders, the media constructs the social role of women as "observers rather than as active participants in their community" (Wilkins 1995).

Ironically, on a day when everyone present in Iran and those who followed the country's current events from outside of its borders feared the worst government clampdown on protesters (many of those who had been present in prior protests sought the safety of the confines of their homes), one woman's bold venture onto the streets was identified by the media, both domestic and foreign, as a stroll for fresh air. Neda had knowingly parked her car in one of the side streets leading to North Kargar Avenue, one of Tehran's key avenues which commences at Revolutionary Square. Anyone familiar with Tehran would have a hard time believing the story fabricated by the media about her automobile's malfunctioning air conditioning system as the sole reason for her presence in the lethal downtown area that day.

Once again though, one shouldn't restrict this story to Neda. It is imperative to consider the roles played by her male counterparts in this petrifying scenario. Arash Hejazi, who was also on the same side streets Neda was browsing, was never referred to as a passerby; he was the doctor who was there to protest the election's outcome, fight for his rights, and the one who after failing to save Neda's life, shared the digital video footage of her chilling final moments. Her music teacher was referred to as her mentor and friend, someone who had served as her protector and finally convinced her to return to her car and leave the scene from which she died just a few feet away. And of course, not to be forgotten, the villain in this story, the *Basiji* member who was fighting to please the will of more men, namely Ahmadinejad and Kamenei; he was never referred to as someone void of intention either. Neda was garishly dangled on television news worldwide, portrayed as the disinterested bystander who suffered the consequences of a power struggle between men, walking a side street in order to avoid media exposure, and who was caught randomly and unknowingly on film, thanks to the new technological capabilities of phones.

Even the last portion of Wilkins' (1995) definition of passivity holds true: as soon as the blood starts streaming down her face, screams and shouts can be heard in the background, bringing to mind a similar culturally set background Campbell (1995) recognized and criticized in the images of the 1990 movie *Not without My Daughter*. Director Gilbert was said to have used manipulative techniques to create an overwhelming feeling within the Western viewer of "loud, illogical people with no conversation rules" (Campbell 1995) instead of "positioning the expressive communication style as a cultural difference" (Campbell 1995). Neda's veil, however, is perhaps the most important and most debatable cultural artifact in this ninety-second clip.

## Neda: The Veiled/Unveiled, Almost White, Modern Iranian Woman

As stated earlier, veiling is not a practice born out of Islam, or even its predecessors, Christianity and Judaism. The veil, however, is oftentimes seen as a means to relegate a woman's multidimensional characteristics to a single layer, one which is more often than not deemed as symbolic of her "national backwardness, as well as female illiteracy and subjugation" (Moghadam 1993). On the surface, one can look at Neda's video and in noticing the black scarf lying on the ground under her head regard it as an apparent mark of her oppression. But in order to scratch the surface and go beyond the ostensible meanings her image carried, one can look further than that and notice the fact that her headscarf is in fact loose, in the fashion of that which Western media have attempted to expose "as cultivated political acts that manifest a defiant desire for Western-style democracy" (Nguyen 2009). Nevertheless, as previously stated, the veil in Iran has carried many different meanings throughout the nation's history, which outdates Islam by more than a millennium.

The tendency of foreign media has been to show the new trends of how the Islamic headscarf is donned, along with modern Persian dress codes, to signify a modern Iranian woman—one who is ready and willing to leave behind her backward religious beliefs and become a modern woman, making efforts to resemble her European and American sisters. Neda had all these qualities attributed to her without any actual confirmation of her belief system, religious or political (Fakhraie 2009; Inakumar 2009; Nguyen 2009; Peterson 2009).

Inakumar (2009) notes that Neda's "phenotypic whiteness, beauty, youth, and gender gave her a claim to the 'white woman in trouble' status." This argument helps shed light both on the reason for the extensive coverage offered her through various media outlets and on the lack of coverage given to others who died during the civil unrest immediately before and after her death, particularly men. Inakumar (2009) goes further by stating that it is the veil's absence, coupled with Neda's "approximate whiteness," which allowed for her recognition by Americans as a legible female subject. Inakumar's view seems to fall in line with the media's constant referral to her as an underground musician and a philosophy major, in efforts to portray her as a woman who was flowing against the tide of tradition engulfing her fellow countrywomen and men. They somehow all fail to tell us that Neda was in reality a theology major, that she was a divorcée who was having difficulty finding a job, that she came from a normal, middle-class family situated in Tehran. They fail to mention that she too was there on Saturday the 20th, not as a passive observer, but as someone who was vexed by the results of the elections in which some forty million Iranians took part, a sizeable percentage of whom felt disenfranchised and were demonstrating in order to make their voices heard, both inside and outside the country. Neda (which translates roughly to "a sound or voice bearing a message or calling") was aware of what she was fighting for, and even in her death the international media failed to see the pleading look in her eyes as she lay on the pavement. Neda was supposed to be a symbol of remembrance, not only for Iranians, but also for the international community. Unfortunately, media portrayals managed to downgrade that image of the ordinary civilian-turned-activist which Neda stood for, instead instilling in people a sense of yet another innocent victim of a barbaric regime in some distant part of the exotic Orient, who despite her modern Western garb and attitude, was forced to suffer the consequences of the power structure in her country—a country ruled not by women, but men.

## ARE WE NEDA?

Iranians comprehend how their fellow countrymen and women who considered themselves a part of the Green Wave can compare themselves to Neda, feverishly chanting slogans such as "We are all Neda!"; "Our Neda (voice) has not died: it's the government which has died!"; and "Oh martyred sister, I will take back your vote!" Posters depicting Neda smiling into a camera, headed "We Are Neda," were seen carried by international protesters who stood in solidarity with the silenced Iranians. But within Iran's borders, Neda Agha-Soltan was not the only household name: Sohrab A'rabi, Taraneh Mousavi, and Mohsen Rouh ol'Amini, a student in the Engineering Department at the University of Tehran, had their deaths publicized through domestic non-government-controlled channels just as widely as Neda's.

To Iranians, this loss of the nation's youth who had stood up to fight for their rights and freedom of expression, pulling from a rich repertoire presented to them by their parents and grandparents, empowering them with many tactics which had proved successful in the social movements leading up to the Islamic Revolution of 1979, has not gone unnoticed. They now have new symbols, the Nedas and Sohrabs and Taranehs and Mohsens, which all families can relate to: Iran's youth are considered a highly educated population, and the struggling economic situation, which has only deepened over Ahmadinejad's first term as president, has kept many Iranians in school longer in hope of finding a better job in a very unfriendly market where unemployment rates keep rising (Moaveni 2009). This level of awareness, coupled with political, economic, and social hardships, has led most families to deal with the same issues these martyrs fought and ultimately died for. Therefore, Iranians do feel a special bond with victims such as Neda.

To them, Neda is not an overblown, distorted figure representing Western values of unveiling, beauty, and whiteness; she is an average, urban young woman living in Tehran. To them, she is not a passive witness to the turmoil and unrest which swallowed up the city almost overnight; she is one of the courageous few who braved out into the world's most dangerous streets, intentionally choosing the time and place. To them, she is not an innocent victim, unaware of the injustice crowding the cities of the world, nor is she the woman in need of male guardianship; she is every bit as independent as every one of Iran's youth who protested in the aftermath of the disputed elections and ever aware of the danger she faced, her bold move even more worthy of praise in light of her knowledge.

She was and remains one of them, as even today, months after her passing, people hear echoes of "It could have been me"; "It could have been my daughter"; "It could have been my sister"; "It could have been my friend." Ultimately, Neda *is* all those people: she is every Iranian, woman or man.

## REFERENCES

Amin, C. M. (2002). *The making of the modern Iranian woman: Gender, state policy, and popular culture, 1865–1946.* Gainesville, FL: University Press of Florida.

Campbell, J. (1995). Portrayal of Iranians in U.S. motion pictures. In Y. R. Kamalipour (Ed.), *The U.S. media and the Middle East* (pp. 177–186). Westport, CT: Greenwood Press.

Change for Equality. (n.d.). http://www.campaignforequality.info/english/.

Cuklanz, L. M. (2006). Gendered violence and mass media representation. In B. J. Dow and J. T. Wood (Eds.), *The SAGE handbook of gender and communication* (pp. 335–353). Thousand Oaks, CA: Sage.

A Death in Tehran. (2009, November 17). PBS|*Frontline.* http://pbs.org/wgbh/pages/frontline/tehranbureau/deathintehran/view/?utm_campaign=viewpage&utm_medium=toparea&utm_source=toparea.

Ebadi, S. (2008, March 2). Suffering and suffrage in Iran: Women are still denied their freedom. Times Online. http://timesonline.co.uk/tol/comment/columnists/guest_contributors/article3471226.ece.

———. (2007). *Iran awakening: One woman's journey to reclaim her life and country.* New York: Random House.

Fakhraie, F. (2009, June 22). *Neda Agha-Soltan 1982–2009.* Fatemeh Fakhraie. http://fatemehfakhraie.com/2009/06/22/neda-agha-soltan-1982-2009/.

Generación Y Wins Best Blog of 2008. (2008, November 28). *The BOBs-Deutsche Welle.* http://www.thebobs.com.

Gerbner, G. (1978). The dynamics of cultural resistance. In G. Tuchman, A. K. Daniels, and J. Benet (Eds.), *Hearth and home: Images of women in the mass media* (pp. 46–50). New York: Oxford University Press.

Ghazi, S. (2000, June). *Emancipation under the veils.* UNESCO. http://www.unesco.org/courier/2000_06/uk/doss13.htm.

Hamlet, J. D. (2000). Assessing womanist thought: The rhetoric of Susan L. Taylor. *Communication Quarterly, 48,* 420–436.

Inakumar. (2009, June 27). *Neda Soltani, race, and digital labor.* Difference Engines. http://www.differenceengines.com/?p=189.

International Data Base. (2009). U.S. Census Bureau. http://www.census.gov/ipc/www/idb/country.php.

Kamrava, M., and Dorraj, M. (2008). *Iran today: An encyclopedia of life in the Islamic Republic* (Vol. II). Westport, CT: Greenwood Press.

Keddie, N. R. (2003). *Modern Iran: Roots and results of revolution* (2nd ed.). New Haven, CT: Yale University Press.

Khalili, L. (1998, September 29). *Forgiving Salm and Tur: A polemic on race. The Iranian.* http://www.iranian.com/LalehKhalili/Sept98/Race/index.html.

Kray, S. (1995). Orientalization of an "almost white woman—a multidisciplinary approach to the interlocking effects of race, class, gender, and ethnicity in American mass media: The case of the missing Jewish woman. In A. N. Valdivia (Ed.), *Feminism, multiculturalism, and the media: Global diversities* (pp. 221–244). Thousand Oaks, CA: Sage.

Milani, F. (1992). *Veils and words: The emerging voices of Iranian women writers.* Syracuse, NY: Syracuse University Press.

Moaveni, A. (2009, June 9). Will Iran's "marriage crisis" bring down Ahmadinejad? *Time.* http://www.time.com/time/world/article/0,8599,1903420,00.html.

Moghadam, V. M. (1993). *Modernizing women: Gender and social change in the Middle East.* Boulder, CO: Lynne Rienner.

Nguyen, M. T. (13, June 2009). You say you want a revolution (in a loose headscarf). Threadbared. http://threadbared.blogspot.com/2009/06/you-say-you-want-revolution-in-loose.html.

Peterson, L. (2009, June 26). Global politics of "pretty" women bends coverage of Iran's election protesters? Women's News Network-WNN. http://womennews network.net/2009/06/26/global-politics-of-%E2%80%98pretty%E2%80%99 -bends-coverage-of-irans-election-protesters/.

Roudi, F. (2009, June). Youth, women's rights, and political change in Iran. Population Reference Bureau. http://www.prb.org/Articles/2009/iranyouth.aspx.

Sanasarian, E. (1982). *The women's rights movement in Iran: Mutiny, appeasement, and repression from 1900 to Khomeini.* New York: Praeger.

Satrapi, M. (2004). *Persepolis: The story of a childhood* (Vol. 1). New York: Pantheon.

Sullivan, Z. T. (2000). Eluding the feminist, overthrowing the modern? Transformation in twentieth-century Iran. In B. G. Smith (Ed.), *Global feminisms since 1945* (pp. 235–64). London, UK: Routledge.

Tuchman, G. (1978). The symbolic annihilation of women in the mass media. In G. Tuchman, A. K. Daniels, and J. Benet (Eds.), *Hearth and home: Images of women in the mass media* (pp. 3–38). New York: Oxford University Press.

Wilkins, K. G. (1995). Middle Eastern women in Western eyes: A study of U.S. press photographs of Middle Eastern women. In Y. R. Kamalipour (Ed.), *The U.S. media and the Middle East: Image and perception* (pp. 50–61). Westport, CT: Greenwood Press.

## Chapter Twenty-Two

# Symbols, Signs, and
# Slogans of the Demonstrations in Iran

## Elham Gheytanchi

As images of the crackdown by government militias and plainclothes police-men on the demonstrations were broadcast after the controversial results of the tenth presidential election in Iran in late June 2009, the world was re-minded of the Iranian Revolution of 1979 as masses marched in the streets of Tehran and other cities chanting slogans.[1] Even if Iran's political institutions have so far remained intact in the face of the recent agitation, the political cul-ture has forever changed, a shift reflected in the slogans chanted by people in the streets. These protests and slogans (*shoar* in Persian), chanted and simul-taneously e-mailed, Tweeted, and YouTubed, best illustrate the gradual but persistent change that has taken place in Iranian political culture. If someone has not followed the events in Iran, reading the slogans alone will give a clear picture of the uprising in June 2009 and the popular demands.

Modern Iran since the turn of the twentieth century has witnessed popular dissent and its outpouring in the streets. The 1979 revolution was the result of a continuous series of street demonstrations in Tehran and other major cit-ies. Street protests during 1978–1979 were organized by opposition forces, despite political repression by the state. As Abrahamian (2009) argues, "the crowd which played a more central role in the Iranian revolution of 1977–[19]79 than in any other major revolution behaved less like an irrational mob than as the rational entity." The public acted orderly and marched according to the tactics of nonviolent democratic struggles.

There is a historical tradition of mass protest in Iran. These protests have targeted the state and demanded an end to corruption, autocracy, foreigners' intervention in Iranian internal affairs, and recently, theocracy. Even though the protesters are suppressed with varying degrees of police brutality, neither the protests nor the ritual of slogan chanting have been eroded. Rather, anti-state demonstrations and slogans have resurfaced from time to time despite state repression. In 1891, protesters in Tehran demanded cancellation of the tobacco monopoly sold by Nasser al-Din Shah to a British businessman. During 1905–1911, protesters objected to the Anglo-Persian Agreement, and the protests led to the Constitutional Revolution. During 1951 to 1953, the mass protests supported Mossadegh and his action to nationalize the oil industry. In 1963, demonstrators protested in the streets against the Shah's White Revolution, which aimed to abolish the feudal landlord-peasant system and gave women the right to vote. As with any ritual, street demonstrations in Iran follow a pattern; slogans are chanted, the public marches orderly, and signs and symbols are held by the demonstrators to communicate their demands.

Symbols, signs, and slogans are the ways in which the demonstrators have communicated their message to the government and the world. Street protest and a historical tradition of chanting slogans continue to dominate Iranian politics to this day. The aim of this chapter is to show the resurgence of this tradition thirty years after the 1979 revolution and explore the meaning of the symbols, signs, and slogans in the demonstrations protesting the result of the controversial election in 2009.

## PRESIDENTIAL CAMPAIGNS: MAY 20 TO JUNE 11, 2009

For about one month preceding the election day on June 12, 2009, young Iranians—men and women—who constitute the majority of the country's population, poured into the streets all over Iran to campaign for the presidential candidate of their choice. Choice, however, is a relative concept in the Islamic Republic of Iran. The four presidential candidates had already been vetted by an unelected body of clerics and jurists called the Guardian Council (Schirazi 1998). The young men in the streets, accompanied by an unprecedented number of young women yearning for political freedom, improvement of economic conditions, and better relations with other countries of the world, were determined to exercise their right to vote and change the status quo. The streets of Tehran, Isfahan, Shiraz, and other cities were filled with enthusiastic campaigners for the four presidential candidates: Mir Hossein Mousavi, Mehdi Karoubi, Mohsen Rezai, and the incumbent, President Mahmoud Ahmadinejad.

Mousavi started campaigning on Facebook on May 20, 2009, and it took the government only three days to ban Facebook. His supporters reverted back to SMS messaging to organize rallies that were banned on June 11 by the Ministry of Communication. Finally, the presidential candidates' debate on state TV, IRIB (Islamic Republic of Iran Broadcasting), called *Seda va Simaye Jomhouri Eslami* [*Iran in Persian*] on June 4–5, 2009 and posted on YouTube, allowed thousands of Diaspora Iranians to follow the heated rivalry from afar.

During the presidential campaigns, a sense of euphoria dominated national politics. State TV for the first time in the life of the Islamic Republic broadcast a series of lively debates among the candidates. Harsh words were exchanged when Ahmadinejad attacked Mousavi's record as prime minister (1981–1989). Mousavi's enthusiastic campaigners compensated for the TV time denied to their candidate by chanting slogans in the streets of major cities.

Mahmoud Ahmadinejad, the Supreme Leader's favored candidate, running for his second term, had the advantage of advertisement time on the state TV and radio stations. Mohsen Rezai, a former *Sepahi* (the Islamic Revolutionary Guard Corps), received modest state support. However, it was the reformist candidates, Mehdi Karrubi, former speaker of the Parliament, and Mir Hossein Mousavi, Iran's prime minister during the Iran-Iraq war (1981–1988), who sparked the most interest among the public, and especially the youth. Karrubi and Mousavi promised gender equality, better economic policies, and an end to corruption if they were elected.

When Mousavi was seen on national television putting on a green shawl meant to highlight that he is a *Seyyed*, a descendent of the Prophet, Karrubi supporters chanted, "*Azadi Andishe, Ba shawl-e Sabz nemisheh*" [Freedom of expression, not possible with a green shawl]. The supporters of Karrubi wanted to render Mousavi's gesture ineffective with their slogan. The color green has long been sacred in Islam, signifying the line of the Prophet Mohammad. The supporters of Karrubi, former speaker of the Parliament and a clergyman himself (not a *Seyyed*), wanted to dismiss Mousavi's claim to higher religious standing and therefore reject his claim to upholding democratic values. As this slogan and others that follow show, slogans are time specific, respond to the realpolitik, and are effective because the leaders respond to the slogans chanted in the demonstrations.

## THE AFTERMATH OF THE JUNE 12 ELECTION

On the eve of election day, all SMS messaging was cut throughout the country, making it practically impossible for the voting booths to communicate with each other. On the day after the election, the state TV announced Ahmadinejad as the winner of the presidential election with 63 percent of the votes. The Ministry of Interior announced that many voting booths had shown more than 100 percent voter turnout, making it possible for Ahmadinejad to win by wide margins. These claims were quickly questioned by all other presidential candidates. Mohsen Rezai announced that in 170 of the voting booths, 95 to 140 percent of the ballots allowed were counted. Rezai's claim that the election was tampered with, along with mounting evidence gathered by those in charge of the voting booths throughout the country, rendered the official election results suspect.

As soon as the results were announced, an all-embracing and grassroots movement—with the color green as its symbol—was born, opposing what many saw as a full-fledged military coup of the electoral process by Ahmadinejad, the Supreme Leader, and the Revolutionary Guards. The Twitter tag #Iranianelection became one of the most popular trends in Twitter in the week following June 12, 2009. Videos of the street protests and demonstrations in Tehran, Shiraz, Isfahan, and other cities were uploaded and viewed by the world, especially after a week when the state had expelled all foreign reporters from the country.

For three consecutive days after the election, masses of Iranians marched peacefully in silence asking one question, written on their placards: "Where is my Vote?" The initial demonstrations were carried out in complete silence while the demonstrators held up their signs protesting the official results of the election. The peaceful demonstrations were, however, forcefully crushed by the security forces and *Basij* (paramilitary group) in favor of Ahmadinejad.

A Twitter message from Bandar Abbas, a port city in the south of Iran, protested the official results of the election. It read: "*Raye ma ra dozdidand, bahash darand poz mida!*" [They have stolen our votes and they are flaunting them!] A young man was seen in a photo taken in Shiraz, holding up a sign that said "*Raaye sabz man esme siyah to nabood,*" [My green vote was not your black name.] in reference to Ahmadinejad's proclaimed landslide victory. State TV had announced that 63 percent of votes cast had gone to Ahmadinejad; this was clearly a lie, it seemed to people on the street. Millions of Iranians marched in the main streets of Tehran, chanting "63% *koo? Doroghgoo!*" [Where are the 63%? Liar!]

During the presidential debates broadcast from the state TV (unprecedented in the thirty-year life of the Islamic Republic of Iran), Ahmadinejad had requested and received twenty minutes of extra TV time to respond to Mousavi's criticism of his government. Ahmadinejad had stated that he should be granted the extra time because "[A] liar is [a] traitor and traitors are fearful." In the days following the election day on June 12, 2009, in an unprecedented attempt to stem the growing dissent, the political establishment decided to block all SMSs, Internet connections, and mobile phones. Demonstrators in at least twenty different locations in Tehran gathered, waving placards that read *"Doroghgoo khaen ast va khaen tarsoost va tarsoo sms ghate mikonad."* [The Liar is a Traitor and the Traitor is fearful and the fearful cuts off SMS.]

## RESURGENCE OF SLOGANS FROM 1978–1979

There were some slogans that referred to 1978–1979 demonstrations. A photo taken at a rally in Isfahan shows a middle-aged man holding up a sign: *"Dictatori tamaeh, na shah na amameh!"* [Dictatorship is finished! Neither Crown nor Turban!] referring to Ahmadinejad's close ties with the Supreme Leader, Ali Khamenei.

It took a week for the Supreme Leader to publicly condemn the demonstrations. Ali Khamenei did so in the Friday prayer following the election. His sermon served as a clear indication that the armed forces under his supervision would not stand any dissent.

Whereas during and after 1979, the Islamists prided themselves on their ability to galvanize ordinary citizens who opposed the reign of the Shah into resisting and ultimately winning against his well-equipped military, thirty years after, the Islamic Republic militiamen seemed to have become the suppressing force. Ayatollah Khomeini remarked, on several occasions, that the power of the people will win over any military power, even if it is the most advanced in the region as the Iranian military was, particularly during the last years of the Shah's reign.

Other huge banners replied to Ahmadinejad's comments. One read, *"Ahmadi Goosaleh, bazam migi footballeh?"* [Ahmadi, the calf, do you still think this is a soccer game?] In Persian, *goosaleh*, meaning calf or donkey, is a derogatory term. The last time angry protesters shouted *goosaleh* was in 1978–1979. At the time, those opposing the Shah would shout *"Allah-o-Akbar"* [God is Great] every night, starting at 9:00 p.m. to be exact, from their rooftops, and many would listen to the sermons of Ayatollah Khomeini—then living in exile—on cassettes that they copied and circulated. The security services of the Shah (SAVAK) had tried to track down and collect these to no avail.

In 1978, the above-mentioned slogan was directed at Major General Gholam Reza Azhari, the prime minister from November 6, 1978, to December 31, 1978, who said in the Parliament that the *"Allah-o-Akbar"* heard in the streets of Tehran and other major cities was really from cassettes—much like Khomeini's sermons, played aloud at night by traitors. In 1979, the anti-Shah demonstrators chanted, *"Azhari Goosaleh, bazam migi navareh? Navar ke pa nadareh!"* [Azhari, the calf, you still think that it is a tape? The tape does not have feet!]

Nights turned into a nightmare for Iranian security forces after June 12, 2009, as the shouts of "*Allah-o-Akbar*" were heard from rooftops.[2] Many still remember "*Allah-o-Akbar*" chanted during 1978–1979 up to the day that Shah left Iran in February 1979. Thirty years after the revolution, Iranians responded again to state terror—this time from the Islamic state—by saying once more, "God is great." This chant has not changed since the revolutionary days of 1978–1979, but the current government cannot tolerate it. Most recently, the shouts of "*Allah-o-Akbar*" were heard around the time of Iranian National Student Day, 16 Azar, December 7. There are reports of arrests made the next day.

Ayatollah Khomeini asked Iranians in 1978–1979 to march peacefully in the streets and give flowers to military personnel. When the military responded by opening fire on them in 1979, the demonstrators chanted "*Artesh jenayat mikonad, Shah hemayat mikonad.*" [The military commits a crime, the Shah supports it.] In 2009, those who witnessed shots being fired from the rooftops of *Basij* stations in Tehran, killing unarmed and defenseless demonstrators, shouted, "*Basij Jenayat mikonad, Rahbar hemayat mikonad.*" [*Basij* commits a crime, the Supreme Leader supports it.]

The most famous slogan of the 1979 revolution was "*Na Sharghi, Na Gharbi, Jomhoori Eslami.*" [Down with the East (the Communist bloc), down with the West (the USA), long live the Islamic Republic.] In March 1979, Iranian national TV reported that the overwhelming majority of Iranians (98 percent) cast their vote in a referendum for the establishment of an Islamic Republic. The televised report showed Iranians at the polls with placards saying "*Esteghlal, Azadi, Jomhouri Eslami.*" [Independence, Freedom, Islamic Republic.] Thirty years later, Iranians shouted "*Esteghlal, Azadi, Jomhouri Irani*" [Independence, Freedom, Iranian Republic], protesting what they saw as widespread fraud in the tenth presidential election.

What started as a silent march to recover votes gradually became a movement for civil and political rights. The sound of bullets and the smell of tear gas in the streets replaced the euphoric atmosphere of the preelection days. In 1979, when the military of the Shah opened fire on people demonstrating in the streets against his regime, the demonstrators at the time shouted, "*Toop, Tank, Mosalsal digar asar nadard.*" [Canons, Tanks, Machine Guns will not be effective anymore.] In June 2009, marching through bullets and tear gas, demonstrators shouted, "*Toop, Tank, Basiji, digar asar nadard.*" [Canons, Tanks, *Basiji* will not be effective anymore.][3] *Basiji* refers to the militia, or rather the corps of teenage boys, who volunteered in the 1980s to fight Saddam's army during the Iran-Iraq war—now recruited and ordered to suppress what the authorities call "internal enemies of the state."

Ahmadinejad found himself compelled to give a response. In a televised appearance, he referred to the demonstrators as "*khas-o-khashak*," or riffraff, describing them as "soccer fans who are upset because their team has lost." The next day, demonstrators marching in green wristbands and headbands carried a huge banner that read "*Doctor kapshen pareh, khashak ke pa nadareh!*" [Doctor with the torn overcoat, riffraff don't have feet!] The doctor is Ahmadinejad, who has a PhD and is famous for his simple, worn overcoat.

## MUSIC'S RESPONSE TO STATE REPRESSION

Ahmadinejad's remark referring to the demonstrators as "riffraff" sent ripples around the world, causing musicians, Iranians and non-Iranians, to make music to rebuke his statement and support the demonstrators. The title "*khas-o-khashak*" was placed on YouTube in several versions, and in some cases the musicians were unidentified or simply referred to as "underground music group in Tehran." Perhaps the most popular of such music pieces is Hamed Nikpay's short song titled "The Owner of This Land," posted on YouTube on June 19, 2009.[4] Here is the translation of his song:

> You are a thorn, a riffraff
> You are lower than dirt
> I am the aching lover, blazing and lit. I am the light
> You're the oppression, you who is blind to the truth
> You're the black halo, without light
> I am the fearless fighter
> I am the rightful owner of this land!

Celebrities such as Madonna[5] and U2[6] showed images of the protests in Iran in their concerts. U2 turned its screen green as a sign of support for the Green Movement in Iran. The famous song, "Bella Ciao," was redone in honor of the demonstrators opposing the results of the election in Iran.[7] Inside the country, Mohamad Reza Shajarian, the most popular singer of classical Iranian music, publicly objected to the broadcast of his songs by the state TV to protest the way in which the state TV had portrayed the protests or the lack thereof. Many posted Shajarian's old songs mixed with images of the recent demonstrations to show he had joined the rank of Green protesters. Shahram Nazeri's old song, "Hafez-e jan-e vatan,"[8] ["The Keeper of the Soul of the Country"] was posted on YouTube with images of recent demonstrations and a message that read "Nazeri has become green"[9] or "see Nazeri's response to 'riffraff.'"

There were also many music videos posted on YouTube from unknown artists and singers. Some compared and contrasted images of the protests, demonstrations, and brutal suppression in 2009 with images of protests during the revolutionary period of 1977–1979.[10] Among the songs were also those dedicated to the "martyrs of the Green Revolution," such as Neda Agha-Soltan and Sohrab Arabi.[11] The diversity of video clips showed that the supporters of the Green Movement do not only come from the upper class or the secular forces. Many of the commemorative songs had obvious religious undertones.

## NEDA: AN ICON OF THE OPPOSITION MOVEMENT

One week after the election, the brutal death of Neda, a young woman and student of philosophy, on a street in Tehran posted on YouTube made headlines throughout the world. Neda became an instant icon, the symbol of innocence in the face of crude brutality of the state. To mark the fortieth day after the death of Neda Agha-Soltan, Sohrab Arabi, and other young Iranians killed by gunshots fired on the streets of Tehran, a newly formed committee of Mourning Mothers of Iran gathered at Neda's graveside, chanting "*Nirooyeh Entezami, Sohrab baradaret koo? Neda Khaharet koo? Nedaye ma namordeh, in jomhouri ast ke mordeh.*" [Security forces, Where is Sohrab, your brother? Where is Neda, your sister? Our Neda (*neda* means "voice") has not died, it is the Republic that has died.]

Neda has figured into international politics regarding Iran. President Obama referred to Neda in his speech to accept the Nobel Peace Prize on October 9, 2009, and the Yemeni government named a street in the capital after Neda to show their discontent with alleged Iranian involvement in their internal affairs (Black 2009). The Iranian state TV has responded with a theatrical show displaying their version of the killing of Neda; namely, a conspiracy plot performed by the British journalists who were trying to stage a Velvet Revolution with the help of traitors such as Arash Hejazi, the Iranian doctor who tried, in vain, to save Neda's life. In addition, the hardliners staged a demonstration in front of the British embassy demanding the extradition of Dr. Hejazi to Iran.

## NEW SLOGANS

There is one other slogan aimed directly at President Mahmoud Ahmadinejad, who once prided himself on his rhetoric and ability to unify Iranians in their nationalistic goal of achieving nuclear energy. His stated goal no longer seems to be unification; rather, he has proved to be the most divisive leader in what remains of an Islamic Republic in Iran, as he declares war on his opponents—fellow Iranians—some of whom were directly involved in the 1979 revolution. In a recent demonstration in Tehran, a solo voice soon grew in volume as the crowd joined in, chanting, *"Ahmadi Hasteyie, boro bekhab khasteheyie!"* [Nuclear Ahmadi, go to sleep, you are tired!]

For the Qods Day sermon of Friday, September 18, 2009, the Green Movement announced a new slogan: *"tofanghet ra zamin bogzar ke man bizaram az didar in khoonbar, che dar Gaza—che dar Lobnan, che dar Qods che dar Iran."* [Put down your gun, for I am sickened of seeing this blood-soaked thing, in Gaza or in Lebanon, in Jerusalem or in Iran.]

The demonstrators showed their outrage at China and Russia's full support and acknowledgment of Ahmadinejad's presidency. On July 17, protesters shouted slogans against the governments of these two countries for recognizing the spurious government of Ahmadinejad. Whereas the government-backed *Basij* shouted the usual slogans against the USA and Israel, the Green protesters shouted "Death to Russia" and "Death to China." Once more the Iranian public demanded an end to foreign intervention in their affairs, but contrary to 1978–1979 when the memory of the U.S.-backed coup against nationalist prime minister, Mohammad Mossadegh, was still fresh, in 2009 the demonstrators wanted an end to Russian and Chinese support of the alleged illegitimate president of their country.

On December 7, 2009, Iranian National Student Day, university students led the demonstrations despite the militarized atmosphere. In Tehran University, the students chanted slogans against the *Basijis* who violently and systematically crushed the demonstrators. Some of their slogans directly targeted at the *Basij* were: *"Basiji Fascist-e, Pool migire miyisteh."* (Basijis are Fascists, they get money and fight.) *"Pool naft chishodeh? Kharj-e Basiji shodeh."* (Where is the oil profit? It was spent on the *Basij*.)

In an attempt to turn the public against the Green Movement, shortly after the student-led demonstrations ended, the state TV showed a clip allegedly of demonstrators burning the picture of Imam Khomeini. A new wave of condemnation by hardliners surfaced, while many reformers questioned the validity of the clip and condemned the state TV's inflammatory action. There were many demonstrations organized by the state in which pro-establishment slogans were chanted. Some of these slogans were *"Yad-e Imam payandeh baad, Rahbar ma Khamenei zende baad"* [Long live the memory of Imam (Khomeini), Long live our leader, Khamenei], and *"Rahbari-e Mellat-e Ma Elahist"* [The leadership of our nation is divine.][12] The clash of slogans reflects the high level of tension between the Green Movement, the reformists, and the opposition camp, the hardliners consisting of Sepah, the Supreme Leader, and the supporters of Ahmadinejad.

## DISSEMINATION OF PROTESTERS' SLOGANS IN
## CYBERSPACE AND THE GOVERNMENT'S RESPONSE

The slogans chanted in the streets of Iran, heard through YouTube clips and over the Internet, tell a story of political dissent and popular agitation against the status quo. These slogans, chanted by the masses during major political upheavals in Iran, are a stirring indication of a popular social movement on the rise, agitating against the political apparatus in Iran. Iran is a country where poetry and symbolic language are critical elements of the culture. Political figures pride themselves on their activation of the poor masses through *shoar enghelabi* [revolutionary slogans] in their fight against the Shah in 1977–1979; the power of these slogans cannot be denied. Chanting slogans is a political act, and the consequences vary from arrest, imprisonment, torture, even death.

A blogger once wrote that if YouTube were a country, it would be the third most populated in the world.[13] At the time of this writing, there are 64,500 videos posted for the Iran postelection crisis. A Google search for the term *Iran election* returned one million results on June 29, 2009, and more recently it returns thirty-one million results. The rapid dissemination of news and videos of the demonstrations over the Internet have taken place despite the expelling of all foreign reporters from the country one week after the election results were announced. In the absence of foreign journalists and correspondents, the role of the citizen journalist is ever more important to reflect the existing public dissent.

Whereas during 1977–1979 the disenchanted public was led by a leader whose sermons were distributed, the angry public created an influx and malleable social movement with no central leadership in 2009. As Mahasti Afshar eloquently says in reflecting back on her own activism during 1978–1979: "In 1978, a pre-mediated fixed message was created by one charismatic leader on a physical object and disseminated secretly in mosques and the bazaar. In 2009, a message evolved in real time through a mix of accidental leaders and masses of ordinary people and disseminated openly in cyberspace" (2009). In 2009, the rapid dissemination of video clips of the demonstrations forced Mousavi and Karrubi to radicalize their stand as they incidentally—since it was not planned and not controllable from outside—found themselves in a precarious position to respond to popular discontent.[14] Karrubi and Mousavi became the de facto leaders of the Green Movement. As revolutionaries themselves, they grew increasingly disenchanted by the degree of the political violence exerted by the state and *Basij* forces who received their orders directly from the Supreme Leader.[15] The dissemination of video clips showing the violence against the demonstrators and the lack of fair reporting by the state TV has resulted in a deep hatred of the public toward the state TV, as reflected in their slogans such as *"Seda va sima nang ma!"* [State TV, shame!] As a result, BBC Persian, Voice of America (VOA), and other satellite TVs have attracted more viewers.

Cyberspace has also been the meeting point for the Iranian Diaspora, activists in Iran, and those who are observing Iran after the controversial election. Many Iranian Americans, for instance, became involved in the protest through Facebook and Twitter. The government of Iran first responded by blocking sites inside Iran. In the months that followed, however, the government took harsher measures, and it has recently established a twelve-member unit inside the armed forces called the Internet Crime Unit to track bloggers or anyone active in cyberspace who is "spreading lies and insults about the regime." Some who have placed the V sign for victory to show their support for the Green Movement in Iran have been harassed and threatened by the Iranian intelligence forces. Iranians living abroad who visit their homeland have reported that upon arrival in the airport, they are asked to give their Facebook passwords (Fassihi 2009). Sepah has opened its own unit for cybercrimes, and its website called *Gerdab*[16] [whirlpool] posts the pictures of demonstrators and asks the public to aid them in identifying those "who threaten national security."

Another way the Iranian government has responded to cyberspace activism of Iranians inside and outside of the country is by making parallel sites to distract visitors. For instance, the intelligence unit in Sepah made a site called *Sabz Alavi* [green *Alavi*] and declared that they have always been green, the true followers of the Prophet Mohammad.[17] The launch of a new site[18] was intended to compete with the Green Movement that first opposed the results of the election and gradually evolved into a civil rights movement.

## DISCUSSION AND CONCLUSION

On the whole, the demonstrations in 2009 in Iran created a revolutionary atmosphere through the use of signs, symbols, and the tradition of slogan chanting (*shoars*) in the streets. The slogans were comparable with those chanted during the 1979 revolution, some were repeated (e.g., *"Allah-o-Akbar"* [God is Great]), some were modified to reflect the unfulfilled promises of the revolution (e.g., *"Azadi, esteghlal, Jomohouri Irani"* [Freedom, Independence, Iranian Republic]), and some were created anew (e.g., Where is my vote?). The demonstrations that followed the controversial 2009 election[19] were a continuation of the historical tradition of mass demonstrations to demand change in contemporary Iranian history. Iranian civil society has witnessed many social movements, but rarely have they been institutionalized. In the absence of institutionalized forms of debate, the protests and slogans are attempts to fill in that void and insert a public will. But the government cannot tolerate public dissent and perhaps even inadvertently unifies and radicalizes the opposition. The words/slogans became threatening to the state, and repression followed. Under these circumstances (after demonstrators chant the slogans and are then suppressed), the movement radicalizes, and the slogans unify otherwise neutral people. Since there exists no institutionalized effort to organize and lead the protest, the degree of political violence waged against the demonstrators rises.

Protests, demonstrations, and social movements are not unique to Iran. But social movements in Iran rarely, if ever, get institutionalized. In the United States, the civil rights movement and women's movement were institutionalized, and formal organizations developed out of these movements, making them inseparable from daily life of the citizens. No such thing ever happened in Iran. Demonstrations on behalf of the opposition are never organized solely because there is no institution or leadership that can formally organize them. This also raises the level of political violence inflicted on the demonstrators.

In 2009, the cyberspace media of Twitter, Facebook, e-mails, YouTube, and SMS messages contributed to wide dissemination, amplification, and at times radicalization of the new social movement called the Green Movement. The slogans were amplified in cyberspace, and the latter shaped the content, form, and meaning of the slogans. Juxtaposing the propaganda-driven state TV in Iran is a multilayered Internet in which the messages of the Green Movement were formed and continuously commented on by active Iranian as well as non-Iranian participants who were closely following the events inside the country.

Understanding slogans, signs, and symbols of the demonstrations in the streets of Iran is crucial to a thorough analysis of the Iranian political culture. The Islamic Republic of Iran itself came about after a series of demonstrations during the years of 1977–1979. Since its inception, state-organized demonstrations and slogans have been central to the legitimacy of the political system. Any attempt to challenge the authority of the state over the demonstrations and slogans chanted by the people in the street is a threat to the values of the Islamic state and its main ideological tenets. Therefore any analysis of Iranian politics is bound to include the effects of slogans.

## NOTES

1. For a list of *shoars* (slogans) during the 1979 revolution, see this website: http://pachal.wordpress.com/2008/06/25/104.

2. Retrieved from http://www.youtube.com/watch?v=JAXW-73qy1o&feature= related.

3. This slogan was also chanted in the Student Day demonstrations in Tehran University on December 7, 2009: http://www.youtube.com/watch?v=RhZYqi8C5uw &NR=1.

4. Retrieved from http://www.youtube.com/watch?v=HqONCJoADtQ.

5. Retrieved from http://www.keepyoutube.com/watch/?v=ZecgiAd4urQ.

6. Rapper Jay-Z and U2 brightened Berlin's Brandenburg Gate in Germany with green lighting during a performance of "Sunday, Bloody Sunday," a U2 song inspired by a 1972 altercation between British troops and protesters in Northern Ireland. During the performance, Jay-Z rapped in support of the Iranian protesters. Their green screen can be viewed in this YouTube clip: http://www.youtube.com/ watch?v=ucOFQD8kVGU.

7. Retrieved from http://www.youtube.com/watch?v=SNocyz1NRjA&NR=1.

8. Shajarian, Nazeri, Lotfi, and other Iranian musicians created an underground music group during 1978–1979 called Chavosh. The group made many revolution- ary songs that were interestingly banned after the revolution because their lyrics contained left-leaning elements. For more information about Chavosh, see http:// mvakilian.blogfa.com/post-11.aspx.

9. Retrieved from http://www.youtube.com/watch?v=MytTVYYOQm0.

10. Retrieved from http://www.youtube.com/watch?v=rGx-XMR7Yow&feature= player_embedded#.

11. Here is one example from Hassan Shamaizadeh, a pop singer residing in Los Angeles, California, USA: http://www.youtube.com/watch?v=1vI0fEphak4.

12. Retrieved from http://www.youtube.com/watch?v=uYdI6Mzot-0.

13. Retrieved from http://bluemediaboutique.wordpress.com/2009/09/23/if -youtube-were-a-country-fun-social-network-statistics/.

14. For instance, read Mousavi's first public announcement which is in direct response to the escalating tension in the society reflected in the Green Movement's website: http://www. mowjcamp.com/article/id/57.

15. In this Dutch TV interview, Karrubi compares the level of violence inflicted against the demonstrators during the Shah's reign and in 2009. He states that the previous regime would try to terrorize the people; whereas, the current political es- tablishment prefers its security forces to engage in direct force against the protesters: http://www.youtube.com/watch?v=9EqDudLe8ro.

16. Retrieved from http://www.gerdab.ir/.

17. Reported in Fars News Agency: http://www.farsnews.net/newstext.php?nn= 8808100183.

18. Retrieved from http://www.jsanews.com.

19. "Iran Protesters," as *Time* magazine calls them, as a group are a candidate for *Time*'s 2009 Person of the Year. At the time of writing this essay, the winner has not yet been determined. http://205.188.238.181/time/specials/packages/article/ 0,28804,1939691_1939704_1939715,00.html.

*Elham Gheytanchi*

## REFERENCES

Abrahamian, E. (2009, Fall). The crowd in the Iranian revolution. *Radical History Review, 105*, 14.

Afshar, M. (2009, September 8). Remarks at an Annenberg School of Journalism roundtable. http://uscpublicdiplomacy.org/index.php/events/events_detail/7285.

Black, I. (2009, November 27). Iran and Yemen in tit-for-tat battle for street cred: Governments rename streets in honor of rebel fighters and protesters. *The Guardian.* http://www.guardian.co.uk/world/2009/nov/27/iran-yemen-street-cred-rename.

Fassihi, F. (2009, December 4). Iranian crackdown goes global. *Wall Street Journal.* http://online.wsj.com/article/SB125978649644673331.html.

Gheytanchi, E., and Rahimi, B. (2009, June 1). The politics of Facebook in Iran. Opendemocracy Forum. http://www.opendemocracy.net/article/email/the-politics-of-facebook-in-iran.

How Iran's opposition inverts the old slogans. (2009, December 7). BBC. http://news.bbc.co.uk/2/hi/middle_east/8386335.stm?utm_source=feedburner&utm_medium=feed&utm_campaign=Feed%253A+PalestineNews+%28Palestine+News%29.

Schirazi, A. (1998). *The constitution of Iran: Politics and state in Islamic Republic.* London: I. B. Tauris Publishers.

## Chapter Twenty-Three

# Friend or Foe?

## *The Challenges and Tribulations of Iranian Reporters Working for Western Media*

### Siavush Randjbar-Daemi

The recent political upheaval in Iran has cast a spotlight on the operations of the mainstream media and their function with regard to the Middle Eastern country. In the days following the heady presidential election of June 12, hundreds of foreign reporters were told to leave the country as violence flared between the supporters of the reformist candidates Mir Hossein Mousavi and Mehdi Karroubi, who considered the election to have been flawed, and the government authorities. A small but influential contingent made of journalists of Iranian origins—and holders of Iranian passports—working for prominent Western news outlets chose, however, to stay behind. One of them, Maziar Bahari, paid the high cost of four months in jail in Tehran's notorious Evin prison. Most of the others eventually left the country and are currently filing their reports from abroad. Those working for newswire services are largely confined to their respective bureau in Tehran.

This chapter will focus upon the modus operandi of journalists of Iranian descent working for Western media within Iran. It will contend that they face multiple challenges, namely the loose "red lines" set upon their work by the Iranian authorities—from whom these journalists must request and obtain formal accreditation—and the imperative of their editors to give the full picture and present a description of events in Iran that would, in the words of Iranian journalists, be "never publishable" in domestic Iranian newspapers and magazines. They also have to deal with the perpetual suspicion within Iranian popular culture directed toward those working for Western entities, most notably British or American ones. This feeling sometimes borders on a distortion of reality. As Bahari (2009, November 21) highlighted in his *Newsweek* description of the prison ordeal, his interrogator adamantly included his magazine alongside such espionage organizations as Mossad, CIA, or MI5. The attitude of the interrogator highlights the extreme end of the ill-defined and vague behavior of Iranian state authorities with respect to Iranian reporters working for Western media.

This chapter shall mainly focus both upon the activities of Iranian journalists not ordinarily resident in Iran who travel there occasionally and of those who have worked in Iran for long stretches of time. It is mainly documented from personal observations during several trips, between 2005 and 2009, to Iran as an accredited journalist for two Italian national newspapers and informal discussions carried out both in Iran and abroad with several reporters. For reasons of security, several of the interviewees wished to be quoted anonymously.

## THE JOURNALIST AND THE STATE: WORKING AS A REPORTER FOR FOREIGN MEDIA IN IRAN

Except for the small number of journalists who have travelled to Iran incognito on a tourist visa hoping to be able to make a major scoop undeterred by the local authorities, all non-Iranian journalists intending to report from Iran for the foreign media need to pass through a stringent vetting process. The journalist has to present a formal request, which usually has to include a sizeable sample of published work, to the embassy of the country where the news organization that employs the reporter is based. Upon clearance from authorities in Tehran, which can take anything from a week to more than a month, the embassy is authorized to issue a ten-day press visa to the reporter. Prior to the recent upheavals in Iran, the Foreign Press section of the Culture Ministry would grant a ten-day extension to the visa as a gesture of courtesy, provided the reporter had not run into trouble during the initial part of the stay. Most of the foreign journalists who had arrived in Iran immediately prior to the June 12 election were, however, not afforded this privilege and had to leave the country upon the expiration of their initial visa. The press visa is also, in essence, a permit to operate within the city of Tehran. Travel to any other city needs explicit permission from the Culture Ministry. One of the reasons behind Greek-British reporter Iason Athanasiadis's detention in late June was, according to a European diplomat who was briefed on the issue, the fact that he had initially requested to travel to the city of Mashad but went instead to Qum on the day of the election.

Once registered with the Culture Ministry and in possession of the mandatory press identification card, the foreign journalist has to also sign a contract with one of a handful of press agencies that offer translation services to foreign journalists under license from the Culture Ministry. A translator is hence attached to the journalist for the duration of his stay. While not working as an official "minder," such as one who would accompany the reporter everywhere during the 1980s in Iran, or presently in countries such as North Korea, the translator is requested to present a report, ostensibly for a variety of state security apparatus, on the journalist's activities and his contacts with local sources of information at the end of their work.

Given the brevity of their stay and the existence of language and official barriers, foreign reporters on assignment in Iran would be usually constrained to engage with a well-oiled circuit of Iranian analysts who would be forthcoming in their contacts with the foreign press. At times, the tendency to rely upon the well-known sound bite could be surprising. I was surprised by the flurry of journalists visiting the personal residence of Ebrahim Yazdi, the former foreign minister, on the eve of the thirtieth anniversary of the revolution of 1979. The ailing and old Yazdi was effectively put through a tour de force, consisting of several concatenated interviews that occurred within the space of a few hours.

As explained by Nazila Fathi (personal communication, December 22, 2009), the longtime *New York Times* Tehran correspondent who is currently based in Toronto, Canada, Western news organizations also have to face the quixotic attitude of the Iranian authorities with regard to the issuance of visas to foreign journalists who have repeatedly visited Iran. The prevailing attitude among the Iranian officials was, according to Fathi, to block reporters from visiting Iran constantly by placing the reporters on its blacklist after the second or third visit. The amazement at the relatively open atmosphere of internal debate within the Islamic Republic's political class has changed into open criticism of the regime. In the words of one Western reporter for a European newspaper who was successful in repeatedly obtaining one ten-day stint per year in Iran, a journalist was rarely able to go beyond barely scratching the surface during such a brief residence inside Iran.

## IRANIAN STRINGER–WESTERN MEDIA: THE SOLUTION TO MANY QUANDARIES?

Reporters of Iranian origin working for foreign media are subject to a different treatment by the authorities. As opposed to their foreign colleagues, these journalists do not require visas to work in Iran, as they are mandated to travel or reside in Iran through their Iranian passports. This particular condition has proven valuable in the past few years, as nearly all the foreign correspondents based in Tehran were either compelled to leave the country or were expelled, as was the case of the *Guardian*, *Financial Times*, and *Independent* London reporters. All of these three leading UK newspapers found it expedient to hand over their Iran-based operations to Iranian staff or stringers, who would be occasionally augmented by visiting London-based senior staff.

The lack of visa requirements at times created a loophole for Iranian journalists working for foreign media who suddenly found themselves at loggerheads with the authorities. As the cases of French-Iranian Armin Arefi and U.S.-Iranian Roxana Saberi suggest, both reporters continued to file reports from Tehran after the expiration or cancellation of their press permits due to the fact that they could legitimately remain in Iran as holders of Iranian passports. In due course, however, the activity of both was curtailed and they had to either leave the country or face a period of imprisonment (Video 2009).

Possession of an Iranian passport and a minimal knowledge of the Persian language also enabled reporters working for foreign media to avoid registering with the translation agencies, thus effectively allowing them to work without any immediate or direct supervision. These provisions do not, however, exempt the Iranian journalist from requesting and obtaining the necessary press card from the Foreign Press division of the Culture Ministry. This much-coveted press card constitutes in essence, according to a Tehran-based correspondent for a major Western newspaper, clearance from the security services for the given journalist and has often, but not always, operated as a safe conduct for journalists who have been stopped and questioned on the field by the various security forces. A new revision of the press card, issued to reporters from the beginning of 2008, carries a mobile phone number that is operated by the Culture Ministry, which security forces should ostensibly dial in case of the arrest of the cardholder. The inclusion of the emergency number highlights the implicit concern of the Culture Ministry for the security of the reporters under its supervision. It also indicates that Iran's treatment of foreign reporters is markedly different from other Middle Eastern countries such as, for example, Syria, where the registration and monitoring of journalists is carried out by a single state entity, the Ministry for Information.

As accurately summed up by a European diplomat resident in Tehran, the Islamic Republic is never fully anti-Western, but rather chooses to be so if and when it deems this position expedient to its own interests. The Islamic Republic also channels its displeasure toward Western media when the same can be lampooned as the harbinger of a negative or distorted view of the Iranian political landscape, thus becoming a convenient scapegoat to present to domestic audiences. At other times, leading state figures attempt to exploit the visibility that it may gain from granting interviews to leading Western publications or holding theatrical press conferences for the benefit of foreign media, as has often been the case with President Ahmadinejad. A universal categorization of the attitude of Iranian state officials vis-à-vis foreign media operators is therefore unattainable. Over the years, it has become apparent that the Culture Ministry and security services prefer to deal with reporters on a one-on-one basis. At times, the fall from grace of single individuals is swift and unexplained. After ten years as an esteemed and officially sanctioned photographer for the Associated Press news agency in Tehran, Hassan Sarbakhshian has seen his press card revoked without apparent reason shortly before June 12 and has been compelled to leave the country on short notice (Sarbakhshian 2009). Exactly a week after attending President Ahmadinejad's postelectoral press conference at the presidential palace, where he gained access to the conference room after careful vetting and strict security, Maziar Bahari was collected from his mother's home at 7 a.m. by security officials and taken to Evin prison (Bahari 2009, November 21).

During the Ahmadinejad administration, the government has shown, however, added regard for the journalists of countries with which it maintains frosty diplomatic relations. Since his controversial reelection, Ahmadinejad has granted exclusive interviews to American and British news channels within Iran, while high-level newspapers such as the *Washington Post* or the *New York Times* are occasionally used as a diplomatic backchannel to deliver messages to the U.S. administration (Erdbrink 2009).

## ABUSED CHILDREN:
## IRANIAN JOURNALISTS ON THE FIELD IN IRAN

Working for foreign media became feasible for local Iranian reporters only at the end of the 1990s, when reformist president Mohammad Khatami's administration brought about a more lenient attitude toward international media and technology advanced to the level of enabling reporters to move away from relying upon news agency bureaus in order to gather the latest official news. According to Fathi, a working arrangement with a major news agency in Tehran was necessary, in the first part of the 1990s, in order to have access to the official state agency IRNA's newswire reports, the starting point for day-to-day reporting. During the latter years of Hashemi Rafsanjani's presidency, the local stringers of foreign media were reluctant to contact the Culture Ministry and were therefore working in a limbolike legal situation, with press cards having validity of days, or weeks. Matters did not immediately become better for all reporters with the advent of the reform-minded Khatami administration. According to Fathi, the first official in charge of foreign media at the Culture Ministry after May 1997 was a "chauvinist . . . who was

against female correspondents for foreign media." Gradually the officials re-
lented, and long-term press cards were handed out to local Iranian journalists
who represented foreign media by the year 2001, when Mohammad Hossein
Khoshvaqt, a liberal-minded relative of Ayatollah Ali Khamenei, was placed
in charge of the Foreign Press division of the Culture Ministry and started a
policy to support local reporters working for overseas media.

The situation changed vastly with the gradual connection of Iran to the
Internet. IRNA was among the very first Iranian state organizations to have
an active presence on the Internet, establishing as it did its first website at
the end of 1996, thus enabling foreign and domestic reporters to access its
news without needing to rely upon special telex machinery or a desk at a
newswire service. Iranian domestic newspapers were also at the forefront
of the transition from traditional paper media to the new electronic distribution, at times preceding their Western counterparts in making available
their full text online. During the course of the last decade, at least a dozen
full-fledged semiofficial news agencies and websites with full license to
operate inside the country were set up to provide up-to-the-minute news,
mostly in Persian. Lastly, the widespread availability of e-mail services in
Iran meant that the dispatch of written material from Iran, which previously
had notoriously poor international telecommunications, enticed foreign media organizations to establish a more permanent presence within the country
rather than relying upon newswire services and occasional trips by senior
correspondents.

Despite heralding new opportunities for Iranian reporters who had a working relationship with foreign media, the new era also indirectly ushered in the
vague and arbitrary "red lines" that the domestic media had to come to terms
with. While not being formally subject to direct censorship or limitations
prior to producing their copy, journalists working for foreign organizations
had to be, according to Fathi, self-conscious of content and terminology that
could cause the wrath of the authorities. At times, this meant that certain
topics or stories had to be discarded altogether or reported on with a note of
caution. Occasionally, the authorities themselves would summon the reporters and ask them to refrain from reporting negatively on certain topics, as was
the case, during the midterm of Ahmadinejad's first presidential mandate,
concerning themes related to the economy. By far the authorities' biggest
concern was for articles they deemed insulting or demeaning toward leading
state figures. According to Fathi, during the student riots of 1999–2003, the
authorities imposed on Iranian journalists working for foreign media a ban
on reporting offensive slogans against the Supreme Leader, such as "Death to
Khamenei." Fathi and others would resort to describing such chants as "criticism expressed toward top state authorities."

The desire to preserve the integrity of state officials would spread to lower rungs as well. The only article among the hundreds on Iran that I had published which caused a direct reprimand from Iranian officials was one which described a story—widely reported on in Iranian domestic newspapers—of a child appearing in a live show on Iranian television and likening President Ahmadinejad to his toy monkey. Stories critical of the *badhijab* drive or the muzzling of the reformist press were not the subject of complaints.

Another point of concern for Iranian journalists working for foreign media was potentially damaging content, such as an interview with a leading anti-regime exile, that their parent organization could publish alongside their own reports, or failure by the news organization to accurately cover misinformation campaigns against the Islamic Republic launched by exiles abroad. According to the opinion of several reporters, the authorities would appreciate the lack of influence of a Tehran-based stringer on the editorial content of the overseas newspaper, thus effectively exoncrating the specific reporter from a possible antiregime slant chosen by the parent organization. The Culture Ministry officials and diplomats stationed in embassies abroad went as far as to accept my explanation that, while I remained fully responsible for the text content of my stories, the titles of the same were beyond my control.

A protracted professional presence in Iran was therefore conditional, for an Iranian reporter, upon effectively avoiding ending up on the losing side of a continuous cat-and-mouse game with the authorities. According to Fathi, both long-term residents in Iran and occasional travelers of Iranian origins came to resemble "abused children: We knew the red lines, we tried to respect those red lines so that we could keep on working in Iran. That was our priority. We were like children who were abused but learned to live with it." The moment of rupture between the authorities and an individual journalist remained an arbitrary one that was impossible to gauge a priori. While a certain level of tolerance emerged on the authorities' side for foreign media workers, the intelligence agencies' supervision over their activities remained constant. In a rare public account of this surveillance, Maziar Bahari described, in an article for *Index on Censorship* and the *New Statesman* in 2007, the scrutiny he would be subject to by the Intelligence Ministry, who at times summoned him for "tea and cakes" after he attempted to interview people who would fall outside the accepted bounds for foreign media (Bahari 2007, November 8).

The individual journalists' professional scope was dependent upon the aims of the news organization that employed them. The major newswire services were the first ones to rely extensively on permanent local staff. Careful as they are to avoid foregoing a presence in Tehran, the major news agencies usually instructed their local staff to avoid irritating the authorities and therefore stick to a pattern of reporting that would ensure no interruption of local operations. This logic was enforced when violence erupted between demonstrators and police in the days following the June 12 election. Reporters working for mainstream media were, on the other hand, eager to provide as direct a rendition of the story as possible to their readers. They would, therefore, exhibit less caution and at times go beyond what was considered to be prudent journalistic practice.

## ALL FALL DOWN:
## IRANIAN REPORTERS AND THE JUNE 12 ELECTION

The pattern described above held sway, according to Fathi, Bahari, and other reporters, until the June 12 election. In the words of Fathi, "it was possible to live in Iran and cover the news there efficiently between 2001 and 2009," despite occasional accusations, during Ahmadinejad's first presidential term, of portraying the government in an excessively "bad light." For the entire duration of the electoral campaign, reporters for Western media were left mostly unhindered by the Iranian authorities and were able to perform their usual duties without major impediment. TV, photo, and print operators descended upon Tehran in droves to cover the election in quantities reminiscent of the large media presence of the Khatami years. Both the opposition and the government campaign staff were eager to provide special press passes and stands to any foreign journalist who would attend their events. Election day also passed off as yet another regular media day, despite petty pressure forced upon foreign journalists who tried to perform interviews within the long queues which had formed outside every polling station. As usual, foreign media journalists, both Iranian and foreign, descended upon the Hosseiniyeh Ershad, a live transmission point for TV crews and a convergence point for journalists trawling through the upper-class Northern areas of the Iranian capital or the humble South.

The outbreak of violence on June 13 and the rapid spread of the resentment that led to reformist supporters spilling out into the streets of Tehran and other major cities across Iran brought about abrupt changes to the media landscape. On the day following the massive rally of the reformist supporters on June 15, which attracted three million people in the streets of central Tehran, according to the conservative mayor Mohammad Baqer Qalibaf, the Culture Ministry imposed a ban on all journalistic activity which was not previously authorized by the ministry itself. No reporter could formally leave their premises to report from public places without the formal *a priori* consent of the Culture Ministry. For the first time ever, the ministry also warned reporters working for foreign media that they would not be assisted in case of arrest while attending protests. This decision was met with dismay by a longtime local staff member of a major non-Iranian news agency, who remarked that even at the height of the latest serious disturbance, the student riots of 2003 and 1999, the authorities had allowed foreign media on the scene, albeit in a controlled way. The biggest news story of mid-2009 was therefore to be largely reported without primary observations and sources.

The ban on direct reporting on the top news headline across the world was confronted differently by the various news actors. The newswire services tapped into the expertise gained through their continuous presence in Iran and their excellent contacts on the ground and succeeded on relying upon local freelance contacts, often shielded by a cloak of anonymity, in order to obtain professional-quality photographs of the disturbances and eyewitness accounts to feed into their text services. Many of the pictures which graphically described, on the newspapers and TV channels the world over, the heady events of postelection Iran were therefore obtained by the international newswire services through the skilled intermediation of their local Iranian staff. The procurement operations, which continue to this day, have been taking place under a heightened security atmosphere after the arrest of a group of high-profile photographers, led by Majid Saeedi of Getty Images, who were accused of running an illicit photo-agency operation to cover the violence of late June. One major newswire service, the Associated Press, has resorted to exonerating its Tehran staff from any transaction with local photographers, who are instructed to submit their work to AP desks abroad for consideration and purchase.

Faced with the most significant official impediment to their work routines, the Iranian reporters were faced with a difficult decision. Despite being hit with the stern warning and ban from the authorities, several high-profile journalists decided to head to the streets and keep reporting from the ground. Maziar Bahari of *Newsweek*, Nazila Fathi of the *New York Times*, and Borzou Daragahi of the *Los Angeles Times* were among the journalists who defied the ban and melted into the crowds in the heady days in the run-up to June 20, when street violence reached the peak that resulted in the death of Neda Agha-Soltan. The lack of the distinguishing foreigner markers, a local translator or fixer, visible audiovisual equipment, and considerable experience in dealing with Iranian crowds proved to be decisive in this regard. In a revealing description of those days, produced much later, Daragahi noted that he made use of the acting skills acquired during college to play the role of a middle-aged bank clerk in order to be able to drift in and detach himself with swiftness from the crowds. The *LA Times* Beirut bureau chief goes on to state that "it was not in a spirit of defiance that the journalists felt compelled to circumvent such restrictions, but of professional duty" (Daragahi 2009).

The confidence and the capacity to perform this professional duty of this small but resolute team of media workers was, however, suddenly sapped by the arrest of Bahari. The *Newsweek* journalist became the first Iranian reporter working for foreign media to be arrested while in possession of a valid press card since 2003, when Zahra Kazemi was arrested at the heightened protests and subsequently died in Evin prison. As opposed to Roxana Saberi, who was eventually tried because of charges related to a nonjournalistic position she held with a strategic research think tank, Bahari's ill-conceived charges and the gruff handling by what he considers to have been members of an intelligence unit of the Revolutionary Guard were entirely related to his activities for *Newsweek* (Bahari 2007, November 8; Roxana 2009, May 12).

The arrest of Bahari on June 21 was followed by intimidation toward other reporters. Fathi states that a group of sixteen plainclothes agents were suddenly stationed outside her residence from morning to midnight on June 27. Placed under virtual house arrest, she took the decision, on July 1, to fly out of the country with the rest of her family for a short period, taking "nothing but a few items of summer clothing." As of January 2010, she is still based in her temporary location of Toronto, Canada, feeling too insecure to venture back to her Tehran base. Bahari left the country a day after being freed from a four-month captivity and has effectively aggravated his court proceedings by refusing to abide by the request to keep details of his jail term private. His repeated interviews and articles on his captivity have turned him into a virtual exile and have shed considerable light on the extremes of the authorities' resentment of his work (Snow 2010, January 4). Daragahi faced limitations during a short trip to Iran in December 2009 and was unable to report freely from there. He returned to his Beirut base prior to the topical Ashura protests, which featured prominently in world headlines for over a week. The *LA Times* stringer Ramin Mostaghim, who was briefly imprisoned in Evin in 2003, is one of the very few remaining Iranian reporters still attempting to work at preelectoral levels in Tehran. The news agency reporters still based in Tehran are, to cite the words of one of them, "lying low while waiting for something big to happen." They are hopeful to be the first ones to benefit from an improved situation or a sudden change of the situation, if and when it will occur. It seems unlikely that the authorities will allow foreign reporters to roam the streets of Tehran and other cities unhindered for the foreseeable future, as highlighted by the extremely short trips to Iran of prominent reporters such as the UK Channel 4 anchor Jon Snow, who was only allowed into the country for an exclusive interview with Mahmoud Ahmadinejad at the Hafez Shrine in Shiraz without being able to walk about on the streets of Shiraz itself or Tehran (Snow 2009, December 23).

The authorities are unwilling to wind down the operations of Western media in Tehran entirely. However, they often resort to granting press accreditation to inexperienced young stringers and prevent veterans of the trade—who might have visited Iran dozens of times in previous decades and hence built an independent source network—from freely accessing the country. Invitations to government-organized international events and conferences is currently one of the few avenues through which journalists for the Western media may aspire to obtain a press card.

## DISCUSSION AND CONCLUSION

### The Current State of Play

The events of the postelectoral months in Iran have left their mark on the work of Iranian journalists working for foreign media. The reporters working for international news agencies have been confined to their offices for the past six months and have been largely unable to offer their subscribers the advantages previously associated to their activities and location, namely the capacity to tap into the vast reservoir of opinion and comment that is at the disposal of active and authorized media operators within the country. Newswire services such as Reuters, Associated Press, or France Presse now feature almost exclusively as monitoring services for the news reports carried by Iranian sources. In the past, such an activity was complemented with a healthy and at times essential dose of additional commentary obtained through direct contact with leading Iranian political figures. Ironically, the gap between the reporters who have remained in Tehran and their counterparts filing from abroad is weighing in favor of the latter, who have fewer restrictions and at times better access to the main sources, which are now primarily available through the Internet.

Despite their physical distance from Iran, many Iranian reporters have been retained by their parent organizations and in many cases have increased their usual reporting workload. The abundance of Internet-published news sources and the necessity to distinguish fact from rumor means that a balanced and accurate coverage of the fast-paced political developments which are taking place after the June 12 election require thorough knowledge of the Persian language that does not suffice for the journalistic profession. The experience accrued through years of working on the field in Iran is now being borne to fruition.

The fragile edifice which enabled reporters of Iranian lineage who have been reporting from the Middle Eastern country for the Western media has been severely shaken by the traumatic events of the last few months. At the time of writing, the Iranian Culture Ministry has barred all but a handful of news agency reporters and occasional visitors to the country to perform media work inside Iran. The reporters active inside the country are, moreover, barred from going beyond the piecemeal reporting from official or trusted Internet sources. This attitude is being slowly altered in favor of occasional special analysis that cautiously treads over key issues such as economic malaise or political in-fighting. The dispatches of the news agencies of specialized publications such as the *Financial Times*, which still strives to offer high-quality in-depth coverage of the Iranian economy, show, however, signs of visible restraint. Articles that include direct criticism of the top Iranian authorities are usually coauthored with a staff member posted outside Iran, in order to provide the Tehran-based reporters with the chance of relieving themselves of any responsibility over possibly "troublesome" passages of the article in question. It is unclear how long the present situation will last. If the past is any indicator, changes in the present status quo will occur swiftly and unpredictably. The small community of Iranian reporters working for foreign media is, as usual, waiting in the wings to see what destiny, both professional and personal, their country of origin will bestow upon them.

## REFERENCES

Bahari, M. (2009, November 21). 118 days, 12 hours, 54 minutes. *Newsweek*. http://www.newsweek.com/id/223862.
———. (2007, November 8). We know where you live. *New Statesman*. http://www.newstatesman.com/middle-east/2007/11/mohammadi-iran-government.
Daragahi, B. Chronicling the choreography of Tehran's political theater of the streets. *Los Angeles Times Online*. http://latimesblogs.latimes.com/babylonbeyond/2009/12/iran-chronicling-the-choreography-of-tehrans-political-theater-of-the-streets.html.
Erdbrink, T. (2009, September 11). Iran proposes control system aimed at eliminating nuclear weapons. *Washington Post*. http://www.washingtonpost.com/wp-dyn/content/article/2009/09/10/AR2009091002177.html.
Roxana Saberi very happy to be freed from Iranian jail. (2009, May 12). Associated Press. http://www.guardian.co.uk/world/2009/may/12/roxana-saberi-free.
Sarbakhshian, H. (2009). Resume. http://www.hasanpix.com/resume.php.
Snow, J. (2009, December 23). Interviewing Ahmadinejad in Shiraz. http://blogs.channel4.com/snowblog/2009/12/23/interviewing-ahmadinejad-in-shiraz/.
———. (2010, January 4). Maziar Bahari: An ordeal of terror and absurdity. Channel 4 (UK). http://www.channel4.com/news/articles/uk/maziar+bahari+an+ordeal+of+terror+and+absurdity/3488307.
Video interview with Armin Arefi. France 24. http://www.france24.com/en/taxonomy/emission/18004.

*Chapter Twenty-Four*

# Cyber Disobedience
## *Weapons of Mass Media Destruction?*
### Michele Bach Malek

*Democracy is not in the voting, it's in the counting.*

—Tom Stoppard (From *Jumpers*, Act I, 1972)

The Iranian presidential election in June 2009 and its resulting protestations not only reflected schisms in Iran and among Iranians worldwide, but also created an alarm among traditional news sources, such as the *New York Times*, CNN, and their consumers. For the first time, the reliability and competency of traditional media outlets were seriously questioned in America and worldwide. When traditional news sources were accused of failing to cover promptly the unfolding of what was perceived as the robbing of the presidential office by incumbent president Ahmadinejad and the resulting protests, the relevancy of old and traditional media practices and sources were questioned. The dawning new media, such as Twitter, YouTube, Facebook, and other social networking sites, suddenly were universally celebrated. "Iran went to hell, media went to bed" was the global call echoing the uselessness of traditional media in an age of real-time media. Are social networking sites and citizen journalists supplanting professional journalists, CNN, and the *New York Times*? Even while some media experts are eulogizing traditional media, it seems unlikely that any real damage has occurred. Like every new media outlet that emerges on the scene, such as radio after newspapers and TV after radio, questions of relevancy of preexisting media sources are expected. Despite the fanfare accompanying the new role the Internet will play, social networking sites and citizen journalism will not and should not supplant traditional news organizations—now or in the future. Like all media sources that

277

emerged before, sites such as YouTube and Twitter will transition into their role of auxiliary supports, where they will aptly be utilized for their strengths, but rejected for their shortcomings. No one is entirely dismissing the online melee that occurred following the election results in Iran. Twitter, especially, exposed weaknesses within traditional media outlets and even demanded that well-established traditional media sources like CNN step up and adroitly cover fast-changing events in a responsible and timely manner.

Paradoxically, Iran, a historically media-closed society, plays a consistently vital role in America's media growing pains; the 2009 election is no exception. Thirty years ago, in 1979, the Islamic Revolution and hostage crisis in Iran led to extended late-night news coverage, *America Held Hostage*, now simply called *Nightline*, and to cable news channels, like CNN. In June 2009, Iran again acted as the catalyst catapulting traditional media into a new age of information. However, as can be seen shortly following the elections and protests, social networking sites and citizen journalism are becoming an additional component, but not a replacement, for traditional media. Until Internet sites attain accountability, reliability, and substantiation—which by its very nature is improbable—media consumers must rely on valid and reliable news sources already in existence. In spite of increasing financial and practical difficulties, news sources such as the *New York Times*, the *Washington Post*, CNN, their European counterparts, and emerging reputable networks, such as *Al-Jazeera*, clearly reveal where reliable news exists. Assessing coverage of the June 2009 election in Iran and the protests that followed in these sources displays a clear, complete, and reliable picture of events compared to the plethora of random, disorganized, and unreliable tweets from Internet social sites, or what *The Atlantic*'s political editor, Marc Ambinder, calls "noise," not "signal intelligence" (cited in Razer 2009). Reliable and accurate news gathering takes "time, energy, courage, people, humility, creativity, and layers of editorial oversight to guarantee the authenticity of the final product" argues Ambinder. Professional and practiced journalists and journalisms must continue to weed out deluges of online chatter and ensure truth and accountability are not sacrificed on the unstable altar of emerging media.

A brief synopsis and commentary of events, as they unfolded in Iran as reported by traditional media sources such as the *New York Times*, confirms that traditional media did not "go to bed" while Iran "went to hell." Calls for killing the beast of traditional media seem unjustified. A small sampling of U.S. news sources demonstrates sufficient coverage and reliability compared to its haphazard Internet counterpart.

"Tehran's Eternal Youth" (Entekhabifard 2009) in the *New York Times* portrays, two days following the Iranian presidential election, a passionate portrait of a young Iranian woman reflecting on her childhood memories in

Iran of presidential elections. She makes the vital connection between past elections in Iran when young Iranians "abandon[ed] their country and left [to] seek asylum abroad" instead of taking up the more noble attitude of Iranian youths today who are "more likely to fight for their rights and die trying" (Entekhabifard 2009). Entekhabifard and other young Iranians were elated with the near implausible election of Mohammad Khatemi as president in 1997. She, as others, believed the new president would bring freedom of speech, democracy, equality, and justice to Iran. They were disappointed, of course. About a year after Khatami's election, reform-minded journalists and newspapers were "persecuted by hard-liners" resulting in arrests, university or job expulsion, and fear for their very lives. Today, however, more than 66 percent of Iranians are under thirty, according to World Health Statistics (2009), and they operate differently than their forebearers. According to Reuters, Mousavi would have at least one-half of this young vote (Hosseinian 2009). With Ahmadinejad controlling the election commission, a part of the Interior Ministry, the outcome appeared inevitable—Ahmadinejad would win the election. Many women, young people, intellectuals, and members of the moderate clerical establishment backed Mousavi. Ahmadinejad, nevertheless, drew passionate support from poor rural Iranians, Entekhabifard argues, as well as most conservatives. Poor, rural Iranians and Islamic conservatives are not likely to whip out photo/video-capable cell phones and upload onto various social networking sites on the Web—whether due to economics, logistics, or ideology.

Entekhabifard's article, along with her rationale, portrays the first weakness in a supposed Twitter Revolution. It is exactly Mousavi's support group that would have access to video-capable cell phones, computers with Internet capability, and enough technical savvy to use this source as a mode of civil discontent. A *New York Times* article, "Stark Images of the Turmoil in Iran," uploaded to the world on the Internet (Stelter and Stone 2009), depicts a macabre picture of a man bleeding to death on the streets of Tehran with the caption: "As one bystander tenderly held the man's head, five others held out their cameras." This is certainly a new twist to news gathering. What is the news here: The man bleeding to death supported by one sympathetic man, or the five bystanders reacting like paparazzi? Can it be rationally argued, therefore, that uploads created and posted in the frenzy of the moment are reliable news?

On June 15, 2009, three days preceding the article outlined above, the *New York Times* article, "A World of Risk for a New Brand of Journalist" by Brian Stelter, relates the writer's astonishment at what becomes another significant problem relating to citizen journalism via the Internet. Stelter delineates the plight of nonprofessional, untrained, quasi-journalists travelling to dangerous areas to collect news for fledgling nontraditional news outlets like *Current*

*TV* (a virtually unknown YouTube-style news channel) in hot spot areas such as North Korea and Iran. These nascent news intermediaries, in an effort to place a "spotlight on news stories in new ways," highlight consequences of a fragmented media landscape and a perceived, though false, decline in traditional coverage. These unconventional assignments, Stelter argues, like their YouTube and Twitter counterparts, are expressions of generational, but dangerous, changes in news coverage, where any individual on or near the field can act as camera operator, sound technician, and producer in a do-it-all-yourself position.

While acting as unencumbered reporters, free from traditional field reporters' guidelines, citizen journalists undeniably see advantages over their more restricted counterparts. Virtual reporters, however, possess little to no real experience, for the most part, and are taking considerably more risks as a result. Moreover, a total lack of backing from established news organizations, with experience and leverage to deal with foreign governments, is a monumental problem when things go wrong in citizen journalism, as they often do.

Stelter (2009) portrays this very real risk in his article as he discusses how two citizen journalists, Laura Ling and Euna Lee, were sentenced to twelve years in a North Korean labor prison while attempting to cover an event involving Korean refugees. Unfortunately, continues Stelter, they were caught by border guards. Even with interventions by their employer, *Current TV*, in conjunction with support from Al Gore, they remain apprehended. There is just not enough influence and backing with little-known Internet sites, such as *Current TV*. In apparent defeat, *Current TV* chose instead to keep quiet about Ling and Lee's imprisonment and declined commenting on their status. Stelter concludes that all the reports about the young women's detainments were "swiftly removed" from the channel's website (Stelter 2009). What else is a small startup company to do when faced with formidable powers like North Korea?

Like Ling and Lee, Iranian freelance journalist Roxana Saberi was charged with espionage during her journalistic endeavors in Iran in January of 2009. Fortunately, more than four months later, on May 11, 2009, she was released. Another journalist, Masair Bahari, a *Newsweek* reporter, was arrested in Iran and eventually released as well. The difference between these two success stories and the Ling and Lee predicament is that Saberi and Bahari benefited from arbitrations by giant media forces such as BBC, the *Washington Post*, and ABC. If a significant part of journalism moves onto the Web, foreign news models and sources will merge; what can we expect from such sources, however? What becomes of the inexperienced men and women ensnared in difficulties beyond their expertise like Laura Ling and Euna Lee? For the most part, the only support is from their insubstantial employers, who have little to no influence. Without prominent traditional megamedia institutions to intervene, success at acquiring releases in these delicate situations becomes unlikely.

An article in *Business World* (Filomeno 2009) directly relates Stelter's findings to a recent Rand Corporation study conducted earlier. This study, which addresses the perils of acting with misinformation, concludes that most people outside of Iran, including the entire foreign policy establishment in the United States, acts "predominately in the dark" concerning the Islamic Republic of Iran. Moreover, Filomeno argues, the Rand Corporation warns of a "collective ignorance" of this exceedingly complex country. With current hostilities between America and Iran, it is impossible for a country, even a large, powerful, and seemingly well-informed country such as the United States, to have any real insight into any of Iran's delicate sociopolitical systems. Ahmadinejad may be the president of Iran, as a result of a seemingly democratic election process. However, anyone with a modicum of Iranian foreign policy intelligence knows that the actual decision maker is the Supreme Leader, Ayatollah Ali Khameini. What may not be so evident, however, is that Iran, like America, includes a system of checks and balances preventing Khameini from becoming an omnipotent despot (Filomeno 2009). Ironically, Khameini's façade as a moderating force against an unpopular, hardline, dubiously elected president gains strength by appearing to be the more moderate and stable of the two. Moreover, Ahmadinejad is not as foolish as the West may think him. He wisely withdrew his statements referring to protesters as "dust" and "sore" losers: "I only addressed those who made riots, set fires, and attacked people. Every single Iranian is valuable. The government is at everyone's service. We like everyone" (cited in Filomeno). Meanwhile, if Mousavi had been elected, warns Filomeno, he could not bring relations any closer with the West because he would have been dubbed as "selling out." Therefore, Iranians today face a lose-lose decision—should they accept disastrous domestic policies, with improved foreign policies under Ahmadinejad, or improved domestic leadership, with near impossible relations with the United States under Mousavi? As described, this is an exceedingly complex international issue that is not easily perceived and, certainly, not easily rectified.

How can complex international issues, relating to a schism among Iranian elites, virtually closed off from Western society, be successfully covered by anyone who takes on the role of journalist, peacemaker, and moderator during violent and complicated protests in Iran? They cannot.

Another serious limitation of Internet social networking sources concerns reliability and accountability. Many U.S. traditional news sources ran stories outlining the supposed newfound freedom available through the Web. Even as Ahmadinejad limited and, eventually, closed Internet access and communications, new media sites and their supporters continued to challenge the traditional levers of media control. Iranians, discovering loopholes and backdoors through these restrictions, continued to blog, tweet, and post to coordinate protests and express outrage. Brad Stone and Noam Cohen (2009, June 16) wrote just one article among hundreds within established media sources that brings this supposedly newfound freedom, via the Internet, into the limelight.

Stone and Cohen, like many of their colleagues, accurately report of photo and video clips that display both "peaceful mass march[es] through Tehran" and "street fighting and casualties around the country." One Twitter feed, continues Stone and Cohen, is filled with news of "protests and exhortations to keep up the fight" in Farsi, English, and other languages. Moreover, Stone and Cohen argue, Mousavi supporters were initially able to swell to their highest numbers, most likely from connections made online. The seemingly logical, but faulty, conclusion was that social networks, by spreading Iranian defiance online, created the first ever Twitter Revolution. This term *Twitter Revolution* was applied not only to the voices of dissenting Iranians via social networking sites, but also to a revolution between traditional and online media, where the latter would be the victor.

"Twitter 1, CNN 0" published in *The Economist* on June 20, 2009, at first glance seems to mirror this expression of an online revolution, for both protesting Iranians and new media outlets. While cable news channels were occupied in extensively covering the disappearance of John F. Kennedy Jr., ten years ago, new media was covering the big story. The headline "Twitter 1, CNN 0" became the battle call, repeated throughout the world, to pull down the old and replace with the new. Old media, however, quickly recovered. In the very same edition, *The Economist* reports that by June 16, Americans were receiving accurate and extensive reports by CNN and other traditional outlets. Meanwhile, the previously much ballyhooed Twitter quickly degraded into pointlessness. By flooding threads with cries of support for protesters, Twitter users rendered the site useless as a valid source of information—ironically achieving the very task that the Iranian government was attempting, but never fully able to do. The article continues by noting that "even at its best the site gave a partial, one-sided view of events" and that "both Twitter and YouTube are hobbled as sources of news by their clumsy search engines."

Therefore, the term *Twitter Revolution*, whether used in conjunction with media events relating to Iran or references to the demise of traditional media, is superfluous. It was also a "Twitter Revolution" several months earlier when protests broke out in Moldova in April 2009. Then, as now, established journalists and media giants acknowledged the potential of burgeoning networking sites, but at the same time, warned of their precarious limitations. In the Iranian context, major media outlets, along with the U.S. Department of State, encouraged Twitter's cofounder, Jack Dorsey, to delay a planned shutdown for routine maintenance, citing the role Twitter played as a communications tool for Iranians (Landler and Stelter 2009). The key reference in this request, however, is the word *tool*. No one from reputable state institutions or established media sources expected Twitter to start and win revolutions, whether political or professional.

The role Twitter and other networking sites did play during this critical time was to allow dissenting Iranians to freely express views; however, no individual-centered Internet source, including Twitter, can replace a full and reputable accounting of events as were picked up by major news distributors. It was up to traditional news media to filter through the mishmash of video and textual clips by connecting cyberdots into a cohesive and accountable whole. Credit must be given to the many deskbound journalists who carefully sifted through masses of clips, footage, posts, and chattering to make up any cohesive footage. Nico Pitney of the Huffington Post, Andrew Sullivan of *The Atlantic*, and Robert Mackey of the *New York Times*, among many others, "waded into a morass of information and pulled out the most useful bits" (Twitter 2009). This front briefing of *The Economist* eventually concludes that "the winner of the Iranian protests was neither old media nor new media, but a hybrid of the two" (Front Briefing 2009, June 20). Yet, it was the briefing's title only, two words and two numbers—"Twitter 1, CNN 0"—that resonated around the world.

It appeared that most protesting Iranians quickly became aware of the pitfalls and shortcomings of Internet sites outlined above. When channels became blocked and/or jammed, most protestors utilized any remaining available means to access giant media outlets like CNN, BBC, and ABC. This was especially the case when established traditional media journalists, such as Lara Setrakian of ABC, left posts on Twitter to "Send footage we can't reach" (cited in Stone and Cohen 2009). Setrakian and other media professionals posted requests like these days before *The Economist*'s headline, which taken out of context, insinuated the demise of traditional media.

Obviously, journalists, such as Lara Setrakian, recognize the value of social media tools in facilitating accuracy, comprehensiveness, and detail in their own traditionally based work. It is highly doubtful, however, that these journalists worry about displacement by Twitter, Facebook, and YouTube among others. A new source of media can be both utilized for its value and rejected in its limitations; these attributes are not mutually exclusive. An example of this weeding-out process was broadcast on BBC and printed in the *Washington Post* (Musgrove 2009, June 17) which acknowledges the significance of keeping Twitter available to Iranians as long as possible, but also warns of its many weaknesses—it is not Farsi-friendly, it is off-and-on at the whim and ability of government, it is restrictive with its 140-character limit, and, as mentioned previously, it is biased in that it is used primarily by Iran's

tech-savvy young, urban population, who are, for the most part, Mousavi supporters. So Twitter's value is not in its validity, accountability, and reliability,
but simply in its accessibility to those who know how to utilize it.

Even the value of accessibility can be conflicting and problematic, however. Because networking sites are not limited to those caught in the throes
of conflict, but to anyone in the world with a computer and Internet access,
determining relevant from irrelevant posts can be nearly impossible. Mehdi
Yahyanejad, an Iranian manager of a Los Angeles-based Farsi-language news
site, notes that "here there is lots of buzz, but once you look closely . . . you
see most of it are [Iranian] Americans tweeting among themselves" (cited
in Musgrove 2009). How can anyone accurately and efficiently sift through
enumerable amounts of information and confidently claim to have identified
only the reliable posts? Remarkably, a precious few tweets, photos, and video
footage coming out of Iran were sifted from the Internet, confirmed, and, occasionally, picked up by mainstream media thanks to deskbound journalists
like those mentioned above. The majority of the footage, however, was useless because it were either discredited outright or lacked reliable verification.
As seen from this Iranian example, anyone from anywhere can and will say
or post anything via Internet; unfortunately, at present there's just no recourse
for accountability, which is the standard that established journalists must face
when authenticating their sources and material or owning up to mistakes.

Coverage was, most definitely, comprehensive in every major news network around the world during and following the election and protests in Iran;
there is no validity to claims that the world's news consumers floundered in
ignorance during these prominent events without the networking sites to keep
them informed. A number of traditional news articles and broadcasts could be
presented here to confirm this conviction. Even elite traditional sources, such
as *New Republic* and NPR, provided extensive coverage of events as they unfolded in Iran. One example is the *Christian Science Monitor*. On June 17, 2009,
C. C. Bryant outlines in "Day 5 of Iran Protests: Where Do We Stand?" a clear,
day-by-day, in-depth synopsis of events as they unfolded in Iran. Accounts are
documented from every perspective available (Islamic clerics, Mousavi's protesters, Westerners, Americans, expatriates, etc.). The article outlines the initial
election process, the proposed win by Ahmadinejad, the challenge by Mousavi,
and Ayatollah Khameini's statement of Ahmadinejad's reelection as "divine"
under the header "Day 1." The outbreak of confusion, resistance, and general
disenchantment immediately following the announcement of the Ahmadinejad
win are all presented. Moreover, crackdowns on dissenters and interviews with
human rights officials are also carefully outlined and clarified. *Christian Science Monitor* continues with a "Day 10 and Counting" summary, retroactive
from Day 5. Clear, unbiased, and comprehensive coverage, including excerpts

from diverse media outlets such as the *Los Angeles Times*, Israel's *Haaretz*, and the *Agence France-Presse* are included in a logical and wide-ranging fashion. Bryant includes a very informative, yet simply stated, list of grievances as outlined by protesters—refusal of a legitimate recount of the vote, bullying of peaceful protesters by Revolutionary Guards, shutting down of Internet and cell phone connections, and pleas for Western help.

Nazila Fathi, in her *New York Times* article (A Recount Offer Fails to Silence Protests in Iran 2009, June 17), poses another significant problem relating to placing too much credence on Internet confusion during complicated, potentially dangerous, fast-changing events. Fathi faithfully portrays the actions of supporters of the defeated Mousavi marching in a mile-long, peaceful, silent protest carrying signs in English, "Where is my vote?" Most protesters, Fathi argues, simply desired a fair and unbiased recount of existing votes before a neutral body. Many of these protesters, desiring only a peaceful and orderly voice during the schism, received a triple-edged resounding refusal—first from established, pro-Ahmadinejad, government officials, which was to be expected; then from extremists or reformist politicians who, perhaps, unrealistically demanded an entirely new election; and then, eventually, from fellow protesters "on the streets of the capital" who were whipped up into a frenzy (Fathi 2009). At this integral point, peaceful protesters, who made up the majority, had a choice to make—radicalize their views and join the potentially dangerous tumult or resign and go home. Initially, most braved it out, despite the seven killed during previous demonstrations, but when clubs crashed down upon backs, legs, and heads, many protesters made the retreat home.

Material on social networking sites, because it is available not only to the world at large, but also the protesters themselves, who are enmeshed in the melee, created another consequential effect. Naturally, throughout this period, Iranian protest participants viewed the same "gritty and uncensored images" of beatings and deaths beamed around the world (Fathi 2009). Equal access to these images may be partially attributed to what Fathi describes as a "significant lessening of dissenters" in correlation to the rise of more detailed posts via the Internet. Most likely, those identical gritty and uncensored images, celebrated as creating the path to revolution and freedom, stunted the revolutionary grassroots movements and activities they reflected.

Coincidentally, on the same day as Fathi's article, Wednesday, June 17, 2009, CNN broadcast several uploaded videos that were described by Fathi above. One was a YouTube video of an obviously malicious raid at Tehran University with images of burned-out rooms, caved-in desks, and turned-over chairs. Another showed acts of undeniably brutal acts, complete with bludgeoning, bloodshed, and blunt force upon relatively peaceful demonstrators. These clips, even with "unverifiable" labels scrolling at the bottom and viewed from the safety of our living rooms in the United States, were immensely disturbing. One can only imagine the effects these and other clips had on protesting Iranians in Tehran, who must have realized, once surfing through the vast web, what lay in store for them if they continued in protest.

The *Washington Post*'s John Palfrey, Bruce Ethling, and Robert Faris portray a different angle of Fathi's argument. It may not be only the "gritty and uncensored" images that are movement suppressors. Palfrey, Ethling, and Faris (2009, June 21) in "Reading Twitter in Tehran? What the Real Revolution Is on the Streets—and Offline," argue that the "freedom to scream" online is a paradox in that it actually assists authoritarian regimes by serving as a "political release valve." If dissidence is channeled into cyberspace, it can keep protesters off the streets. Moreover, "cyber screaming" helps security forces track political activism and troublesome "online voices." A similar venting method seems to be effectively working in Egypt where universities play the role of cyberspace by allowing political grievances to be channeled there, and even thrive there, as long as it remains there. This relief as a result of venting may explain an additional cause for the increasingly lower numbers participating in the more volatile protests in the streets of Iran.

Unedited, unlimited, unverified Internet material can not only squash a potential revolutionary movement by discouraging its participants in one way or another, it can also act in reverse by artificially escalating rebellion. What if instead of portraying events as they occur, citizen journalism, along with its networking sidekick, manipulated and created news according to a desired outcome? If the process of getting the word out is to be totally democratized, but not necessarily accurate or valid, what are the consequences? This combination of uncensored, instantaneous, democratized coverage, available to a world audience, with agenda-based manipulation is, potentially, a recipe for disaster. An account of the protest movement's dying martyr, Neda, intimates this possible consequence of democratized, cybergenerated news.

Neda Agha-Soltan—young, beautiful, and Westernized—stood as a protester, in the streets of Tehran, among a throng of protesters. As the world knows, she was shot down, in cold blood, by a sniper. As a result of an ever-ready citizen journalist, she quickly became a unifying symbol of the protesting opposition. Video footage of her lying on the street, bleeding from her nose and mouth, and staring blankly into some unknown distance was, instantaneously, uploaded and circulated throughout YouTube and other social networking sites. Within hours, Neda's innocent, dying image became the "undisputed symbol of reform-minded Iranians" (Parker 2009). Neda was an ideal unifying symbol, a young woman who virtually—literally and figuratively—personified the crux of the movement. The fact that Neda was a young, educated, "liberated beauty" in blue jeans and sneakers, who was "brutally cut down in the prime of her youth" by radical and bearded clerics or their lynch men, seems a tragic, yet uncannily idyllic, occurrence for her comrades in opposition (Parker 2009). The most chilling aspect of this scenario, however, is that no one can positively claim who, exactly, shot Neda. Immediately following the shooting, when images were first uploaded, bystanders implicated an armed government official. Doubts arose, however, shortly following the fatal shooting, as to the authenticity of this claim. Parker, in a *Washington Post* article, argues that continuing investigations may conclude that the shooter was not a regime-supported *Basij* official at all, as originally reported. It may have been, almost beyond imagination, one of Neda's fellow protesters who fired the fatal shot (Voice of Neda). Naturally, Iranian officials were the first to make this claim.

This tragic incident, most likely, can never be conclusively resolved. It can, however, portray a much darker potential to citizen journalism, where news may not be reported objectively but staged according to a desired outcome.

New media played a role during the Iranian presidential election and protests; whether it was a helpful, hurtful, or simply an alerting role has yet to be fully determined. The primary controversy with this burgeoning media phenomena is not with its subsistence, accessibility, or prospects but with its disorganized, random, and unverifiable nature. Social networking sites, as they exist today, will not and cannot replace or critically challenge the overall efficacy of professional traditional news media. Opponents may argue that print media, in particular, is suffering in increasingly difficult economic times. Many newspapers are collapsing altogether or succumbing to more lucrative counterparts. Perhaps in the distant future, newspapers, as we know them, will even cease to exist. What takes their place, however, must be an accountable and reliable medium that can be depended upon for consistently dependable news coverage and, when they blunder, as they often do, are held accountable, and forced to make reparations. If traditional media, such as the *New York Times* and CNN, didn't respond to growing unrests as quickly as some would have liked, it may be as a result of a self-imposed professional restraint in the aftermath of recent "jumping the gun" episodes. Who in America, or in the world for that matter, can ever easily forget the defectively mismanaged running and selling by the media of the Bush/Cheney invasion of Iraq on false grounds of weapons of mass destruction? This WMD media frenzy allowed speculative comments to run as truths, dissenters to speak as experts, and the overreaching desire to get the news out first and ask questions later. Traditional media blundered wildly during the period leading up to now six years and running war with Iraq. The media, however, paid a heavy price for this recklessness and rightly so. This time, during the frenzy of the Iranian election and protests, traditional media wisely reverted to its traditional role of constraint and verification, especially since they again faced an estranged Middle Eastern country, with no constructive relations with the United States for thirty years. If *The Economist* declares in its headline—Twitter 1, CNN 0—to imply some kind of media contest, in the end, it is traditional media that will win the challenge.

## REFERENCES

Bryant, C. C. (2009, June 17). Day 5 of Iran protests: Where do we stand? *Christian Science Monitor,* p. W6. http://www.csmonitor.com/World/Middle-East/2009/0617/p06s13-wome.html.

Entekhabifard, C. (2009, June 12). Tehran's eternal youth. [Op Ed.]. *New York Times,* p. A27.

Fathi, N. (2009, June 17). A recount offer fails to silence protests in Iran. *New York Times,* p. A1.

Filomeno, S. (2009, June 23). Understanding Iran. Yellow Pad. *Business World,* p. S1/5.

Hosseinian, Z. (2009, June 11). Youth challenge Ahmadinejad in poll. *Reuters.* Retrieved Fall 2009 from http://www.reuters.com/article/idUSTRE55A51020090611.

Landler, M., and Stelter, B. (2009, June 17). With a hint to Twitter, Washington taps into a potent new force in diplomacy. *New York Times,* p. A12.

Musgrove, M. (2009, June 17). Twitter is a player in Iran's drama; State Dept. asked site to keep running. *Washington Post,* p. A10.

Palfrey, J., Ethling, B., and Faris, R. (2009, June 21). Reading Twitter in Tehran? What the real revolution is on the streets—and offline. *Washington Post,* Outlook, p. B1.

Parker, K. (2009, June 24). The voice of Neda; a sniper's bullet gives a movement its symbol. *Washington Post,* p. A27.

Razer, H. (2009, June 27). A lot of noise for not much noise. *The Age* (Melbourne, Australia). Insight, p. 11.

Stelter, B. (2009, June 15). A world of risk for a new brand of journalist. *New York Times,* p. B1.

Stelter, B., and Stone, B. (2009, June 18). Stark images of the turmoil in Iran, uploaded to the world on the Internet. *New York Times,* p. A14.

Stone, B., and Cohen, N. (2009, June 16). Social networks spread Iranian defiance online. *New York Times,* p. A11.

Twitter 1, CNN 0: Coverage of the protests. (2009, June 20). *The Economist.* Front Briefing.

World Health Organization. (n.d.) Demographic and socioeconomic statistics. In *World Health Statistics 2009* (part iii, table 9). Retrieved Fall 2009 from http://www.who.int/whosis/whostat/EN_WHS09_Full.pdf.

# Recommended Sources

Abrahamian, Ervand. (2008). *A History of Modern Iran*. Cambridge, UK: Cambridge University Press.

Afary, Janet. (2009). *Sexual Politics in Modern Iran*. Cambridge, UK: Cambridge University Press.

Alavi, Nasrin. (2005). *We Are Iran: The Persian Blogs*. New York: Soft Skull Press.

Ansari, Ali M. (2007). *Confronting Iran: The Failure of American Foreign Policy and the Next Great Conflict in the Middle East*. New York: Basic Books.

Ansari, Ali M. (2007). *Modern Iran* (2nd Edition). New York: Longman.

Arjomand, Said Amir. (2009). *After Khomeini: Iran under His Successors*. New York: Oxford University Press.

Aslan, Reza. (2006). *No god but God: The Origins, Evolution, and Future of Islam*. New York: Random House.

Axworthy, Michael. (2010). *A History of Iran: Empire of the Mind*. New York: Basic Books.

Azimi, Fakhreddin. (2008). *The Quest for Democracy in Iran: A Century of Struggle against Authoritarian Rule*. Cambridge, MA: Harvard University Press.

Baer, Robert. (2008). *The Devil We Know: Dealing with the New Iranian Superpower*. New York: Three Rivers Press.

Beeman, William. (2005). *The "Great Satan" vs. the "Mad Mullahs": How the United States and Iran Demonize Each Other*. Westport, CT: Praeger.

Bergman, Ronen. (2008). *The Secret War with Iran: The 30-Year Clandestine Struggle against the World's Most Dangerous Terrorist Power*. Free Press.

Bill, James, A. (1988). *The Eagle and the Lion: The Tragedy of American-Iranian Relations*. New Haven, CT: Yale University Press.

Dabashi, Hamid. (2008). *Iran: A People Interrupted*. New York: New Press.

290     *Recommended Sources*

Daniel, Elton L. (2008). *The History of Iran (The Greenwood Histories of the Modern Nations)*. Santa Barbara, CA: Greenwood Press.

Ebadi, Shirin, and Azadeh Moaveni. (2007). *Iran Awakening: One Woman's Journey to Reclaim Her Life and Country*. New York: Random House.

Elm, Mostafa. (1992). *Oil, Power and Principle: Iran's Oil Nationalization and Its Aftermath*. Syracuse, NY: Syracuse University Press.

Erlich, Reese W. (2007). *The Iran Agenda: The Real Story of U.S. Policy and the Middle East Crisis*. Sausalito, CA: Polipoint Press.

Garthwaite, Gene. (2005). *The Persians*. Malden, MA: Blackwell Publishing.

Gheissari, Ali. (2009). *Contemporary Iran: Economy, Society, Politics*. New York: Oxford University Press.

Gheissari, Ali, and Vali Nasr. (2066). *Democracy in Iran: History and the Quest for Liberty*. Oxford: Oxford University Press.

Gold, Dore. (2009). *The Rise of Nuclear Iran: How Tehran Defies the West*. Washington, DC: Regnery Press.

Holland, Tom. (2005). *Persian Fire: The First World Empire and the Battle for the West*. New York: Random House.

Jafarzadeh, Alireza. (2008). *The Iran Threat: President Ahmadinejad and the Coming Nuclear Crisis*. New York: Palgrave Macmillan.

Karsh, Efraim. (2002). *The Iran-Iraq War 1980–1988 (Essential Histories)*. New York: Osprey Publishing.

Katouzian, Homa. (2009). *The Persians: Ancient, Mediaeval and Modern Iran*. New Haven, CT: Yale University Press.

Keddie, Nikki R. (2006). *Modern Iran: Roots and Results of Revolution, Updated Edition*. New Haven, CT: Yale University Press.

Kinzer, Stephen. (2008). *All the Shah's Men: An American Coup and the Roots of Middle East Terror*. New Jersey: John Wiley & Sons.

Kurzman, Charles. (2005). *The Unthinkable Revolution in Iran*. Cambridge, MA: Harvard University Press.

Limbert, John W. (2009). *Negotiating with Iran: Wrestling the Ghosts of History* (Cross-Cultural Negotiation Books). Washington, DC: United States Institute of Peace Press.

Mackey, Sandra, and Scott Harrop. (1998). *The Iranians: Persia, Islam and the Soul of a Nation*. New York: Plume.

Majd, Hooman. (2009). *The Ayatollah Begs to Differ: The Paradox of Modern Iran*.

Milani, Mohsen M. (1994). *The Making of Iran's Islamic Revolution: From Monarchy to Islamic Republic*. Boulder, CO: Westview.

Moaveni, Azadeh. (2006). *Lipstick Jihad: A Memoir of Growing Up Iranian in America and American in Iran*. New York: Public Affairs.

Molavi, Afshin. (2005). *The Soul of Iran: A Nation's Journey to Freedom*. New York: W. W. Norton.

Mottahedeh, Roy. (1985). *The Mantle of the Prophet: Religion and Politics in Iran*. New York: Pantheon.

Nafisi, Azar. (2008). *Reading Lolita in Tehran: A Memoir in Books*. New York: Random House.

Parsi, Trita. (2008). *Treacherous Alliance: The Secret Dealings of Israel, Iran, and the United States*. New Haven, CT: Yale University Press.

Polk, William Roe. (2009). *Understanding Iran: Everything You Need to Know, from Persia to the Islamic Republic, from Cyrus to Ahmadinejad*. New York: Palgrave Macmillan.

Pollack, Kenneth M. (2005). *The Persian Puzzle: The Conflict between Iran and America*. New York: Random House.

Saikal, Amin. (1980). *The Rise and Fall of the Shah*. Princeton, NJ: Princeton University Press.

Satrapi, Marjane. (2004). *Persepolis: The Story of a Childhood*. New York: Pantheon.

Sciolino, Elaine. (2000). *Persian Mirrors: The Elusive Face of Iran*. New York: Simon & Schuster.

Sick, Gary. (1985). *All Fall Down: America's Tragic Encounter with Iran*. New York: Random House.

Taheri, Amir. (2009). *The Persian Night: Iran under the Khomeinist Revolution*. New York: Encounter Books.

Takeyh, Ray. (2007). *Hidden Iran: Paradox and Power in the Islamic Republic*. New York: Times Books/Henry Holt Company.

Takeyh, Ray. (2009). *Guardians of the Revolution: Iran and the World in the Age of the Ayatollahs*. New York: Oxford University Press.

Ward, Steven R. (2009). *Immortal: A Military History of Iran and Its Armed Forces*. Washington, DC: Georgetown University Press.

# Index

# About the Contributors

**Jonathan M. Acuff** is assistant professor of politics at Saint Anselm College, New Hampshire. He received his PhD in Political Science from the University of Washington in 2008 and was previously a research analyst for the National Bureau of Asian Research. Acuff has served as an officer in the U.S. Army and has published on the Iranian Revolution and the connection between nationalism and religion. His essay "Modernity and Nationalism" is forthcoming in Robert Denemark (ed.), *International Studies Association Compendium* (London: Blackwell, 2010). His research interests include international security, state formation, ethnic conflict, and revolutions.

**Sareh Afshar** is an Iranian graduate student at the Tisch School of the Arts, New York University, New York. She holds a Master of Arts degree in Communication Studies, Purdue University Calumet, Indiana, where she received the Outstanding Graduate Research Award in 2010. Her areas of interest include media, culture, and performance studies.

**Banu Akdenizli**, born in Turkey, is an assistant professor of Public Relations and Publicity at Yeditepe University in Istanbul. She earned her PhD in Mass Media and Communication from Temple University, Philadelphia. Prior to joining Yeditepe, Banu Akdenizli worked as a methodologist and analyst for the Project for Excellence in Journalism at the Pew Research Center in Washington, D.C. Her first book, *Toward a Healthier Understanding of Internet Policy Development: The Case of Turkey*, was published in 2007. She holds a

BA in Sociology and an MA in Translation Studies from Boğaziçi University, Istanbul, Turkey.

**Rasha Allam** is a lecturer at the Journalism and Mass Communication Department, the American University in Cairo, Egypt, and a specialist in media management. She works as an international media consultant and serves on the editorial advisory boards of the Journal of Social Studies and the Journal of Telecommunication and Information Technology.

**Ibrahim Al-Marashi** is the associate dean of international relations and an assistant professor of communication history and policy at the School of Communication at IE University Madrid, where he teaches courses on media and the Middle East. His ongoing research examines the role of media and politics in Iran, particularly relating to Iran's nuclear debate and hydrocarbons' revenue management.

**Payal Arora** is an assistant professor in International Communication and Media at Erasmus University in the Netherlands. Her expertise lies in social computing, informatics, new media, ethnography, and international development. She has extensive consulting experience in the ICT sector, having worked on a range of projects, including the HP i-community project in Kuppam, India, to the Kellogg-sponsored speech recognition software project in NYC. Her recent work has been published in several peer-reviewed scholarly journals, including *The Information Society, Information Communication and Ethics in Society* (ICES), *International Journal of Cultural Studies* (IJCS), *Education Philosophy and Theory Journal* (EPTJ), *Association for Academic Computing and Education Journal* (AACE), *International Journal of Education & Development using ICT*, and the like. Her upcoming book by Ashgate Publishing, *Dot Com Mantra: Social Computing in the Central Himalayas*, entails an exploration of social practice with computers and the Internet in Almora, India, including the analysis of key ICT initiatives at the ground level. She earned her doctorate in Language, Literacy and Technology from Columbia University, Teachers College in New York, a masters degree in International Policy from Harvard University, and a teaching certificate from the University of Cambridge. For more details, visit her website: www.payalarora.com.

**Aliaa Dakroury** is a lecturer at the Departments of Communication, Sociology, and Law at Carleton University, Canada. Dr. Dakroury is the author of *Communication and Human Rights* (2009), editor of *The Right to Communicate: Historical Hopes, Global Debates, and Future Premises* (2009), editor of the Fall 2008 special issue on the "Right to Communicate" in the *Global*

*Media Journal*, American Edition, and coeditor of *Introduction to Communication and Media Studies* (2008). She is the winner of the Canadian Communication Association's 2005 Van Horne Award. Her work concentrates on the examination of communication and human rights, and her research interests include the right to communicate, media policy, international communication, Diaspora, globalization, ICTs, media representations, and Islam.

**Patrick Disney** joined National Iranian American Council's legislative team in May 2008. Before that, he taught high school government to seniors at Nolan Catholic High School in Fort Worth, Texas. Patrick graduated from Trinity University in San Antonio, Texas, where he majored in political science, economics, and international studies. During his studies, he focused on U.S.-Iran relations and U.S. foreign policy in the Middle East/Iran and wrote his undergraduate thesis on the conflict over Iran's nuclear program. He served as an intern in the Political/Economic section of the U.S. Embassy in Muscat, Oman, during the summer of 2006. In addition, Patrick was a contributor to the online journal *Foreign Policy in Focus*, covering the Iranian Majles elections and Iran-Iraq.

**Mahmoud Eid** is an associate professor at the Department of Communication, University of Ottawa, Canada. Dr. Eid is the editor of the *Global Media Journal*, Canadian Edition. He is the author of *Interweavement: International Media Ethics and Rational Decision-Making* (2008), series editor of *Communication Research Methods: Quantitative and Qualitative Approaches* (2007) and *Introduction to Communication and Media Studies* (2008), editor of *Cybercultures* (2005), and coeditor of *The Right to Communicate* (2009) and *Introduction to Media Studies: A Reader* (2007). His teaching experience, research interests, and publications concentrate on international communication, media studies, communication research methods, crisis management and conflict resolution, modernity, and the political economy of communication.

**David Elliott** joined the National Iranian American Council in January 2009 to serve as Legislative Associate. Before joining NIAC, David interned at the Center for Strategic and International Studies Middle East Program. He also served as an intern in the U.S. Embassy in New Delhi, India, where he was praised for "outstanding reporting" by the Assistant Secretary of State for Oceans and International Environmental and Scientific Affairs. David graduated summa cum laude from the University of Tennessee at Chattanooga. He majored in political science with a concentration in international relations. As a student, he wrote an analysis and critique of U.S.-Iranian relations, which was published by the Center for the Study of the Presidency. David was also president of the UT Chattanooga College Democrats.

**Mohammed el-Nawawy** is a Knight-Crane endowed chair in the School of Communication at Queens University of Charlotte. He teaches international communication, mass communication, media globalization, and Middle Eastern media courses. His research interests are focused on the new media in the Middle East, particularly satellite channels and the Internet and their impact on the Arab public sphere. He is also interested in issues of public diplomacy and ways of initiating effective dialogue between the Middle East and the West. He is the author and coauthor of four books: *Islam Dot Com: Contemporary Islamic Discourses in Cyberspace*, published by Palgrave Macmillan (2009); *Al-Jazeera: The Story of the Network That Is Rattling Governments and Redefining Modern Journalism*, published by Westview Press (2003); *Al-Jazeera: How the Free Arab News Network Scooped the World and Changed the Middle East*, published by Westview Press (2002); and *The Israeli-Egyptian Peace Process in the Reporting of Western Journalists*, published by Greenwood Publishers (2002). He has also published in several national and foreign journals in the international communication field. His work on Arab media in general, and *Al-Jazeera* in particular, has attracted the attention of the popular press inside and outside the United States. He is the founding editor of the *Journal of Middle East Media* and serves on the editorial board of *Media, War and Conflict* journal. He is also a board member on the Arab-U.S. Association for Communication Educators.

**Ali Fisher** is director of Mappa Mundi Consulting focusing on public diplomacy and communication strategies for governments, NGOs, and companies with international interests. These strategies are based on network analysis, including the mapping of both the networks with which an organization seeks to engage and the resources which an organization has at their disposal. The combination can provide greater efficiency, reduced financial outlay, and programs which deliver greater impact. Alongside his commercial work Ali regularly publishes academic articles, including "Music for the Jilted Generation: Open-Source Public Diplomacy," *Hague Journal of Diplomacy* (2008), and is currently editing *The Playbook: Case Studies of Engagement* with Professor Nicholas Cull and *The Trials of Engagement: The Future of Public Diplomacy* with Professor Scott Lucas. He was previously director of Counterpoint, the British Council's think tank, and lecturer in International Relations at the University of Exeter. Ali received his PhD from the University of Birmingham (UK) studying early Cold War influence operations.

**Elham Gheytanchi** teaches sociology at Santa Monica College, Santa Monica, California. She writes about Iranian culture, politics, and media. Her research focuses primarily on women's rights in Iran.

**Cees J. Hamelink** is professor of international communication at the University of Amsterdam and professor of media, religion, and culture at the Free University in Amsterdam. Hamelink has also worked as a journalist as well as a consultant on media and communication policy for several international organizations and national governments. He is currently the editor-in-chief of the *International Journal for Communication Studies* and *Gazette*, past president of the International Association for Media and Communication Research, president of the Dutch Federation for Human Rights, founder of the People's Communication Charter, and board member of the International Communication Association and the international news agency Inter Press Service. Hamelink has guest lectured in over forty countries and is currently special adviser to the United Nations for the World Summit on the Information Society. Among the sixteen books he has authored are *Cultural Autonomy in Global Communications* (1983), *Finance and Information* (1983), *The Technology Gamble* (1988), *The Politics of World Communication* (1994), *World Communication* (1995), *The Ethics of Cyberspace* (2000), and *Human Rights for Communicators* (2003). Hamelink is also a regular commentator on radio and television in the Netherlands.

**Mahboub Hashem** is former chair of the Department of Mass Communicaton, The American University, Sharjah, and has taught at several American universities. He has served as consultant, professor, director of graduate studies, founder and chair of several academic departments, and vice president and president of American Communication Associations. Hashem has delivered invited and keynote speeches at American and Arab Television Satellite stations as well as national and international conferences around the world. His areas of research interest include Information Technology (IT) or New Information Technology (NIT) effects on youth and societies; old and new mass media effects on society; leadership; cultural diversity; public speaking; effective communication skills; and verbal and nonverbal communication. Hashem has authored books, book chapters, encyclopedia entries, and numerous periodical articles. He received his MA and PhD degrees in Communication from Florida State University in 1981.

**Christine Horz** is a doctoral student at the University of Erfurt, Department of International Communication Studies, Erfurt, Germany. She is a representative of ECREA (Youth network YECREA) in the Diaspora, Media and Migration section. She has received a research grant from the Hans-Boekler-Foundation; conducted research in Germany, Central America, and Iran; and is fluent in English, Italian, French, and Farsi.

**Negin Hosseini** is a visiting research scholar at the Center for Global Studies, Purdue University Calumet. She has authored two published books in the Persian language and, since 1994, has been employed as a professional journalist by a major daily newspaper, *Ettelaat*, in Iran. She is a doctoral student in communications/journalism at the Science and Research Branch of Islamic Azad University, Tehran.

**Wang Jing** is a senior researcher at Tsinghua International Center for Communication. Present research areas include public diplomacy, media literacy, health communication, crisis management, and comparative religions. She is also interested in linguistic psychology and nonverbal communication. Currently, she is working on two books, one on media communication and branding and another on Chinese ethnic groups' religions.

**Yahya R. Kamalipour** is professor of mass and international communication and head of the Department of Communication and Creative Arts and Director of the Center for Global Studies, Purdue University Calumet, Hammond, Indiana. His areas of interest and research include globalization, media impact, international communication, advertising, cultural diversity, stereotyping, Middle East media, and new communication technologies. Among his fourteen published books are *The Right to Communicate: Historical Hopes, Global Debates, and Future Premises* (with M. Eid and A. Darkoury 2009); *The Media Globe: Trends in International Mass Media* (with L. Artz 2007); *Global Communication*, 2nd edition (2006), *Bring 'Em On: Media and Politics in the Iraq War* (with L. Artz 2005); *War, Media, and Propaganda: A Global Perspective* (with N. Snow 2004); *Globalization and Corporate Media Hegemony* (with L. Artz 2003), and other volumes. In addition to serving on the advisory and editorial boards of several prominent communication journals and professional organizations, Kamalipour is the founder and managing editor of a groundbreaking digital online publication, *Global Media Journal* (www.globalmediajournal.com), with fifteen confirmed and established independent editions around the world. He is also founder and director of the Global Communication Association (www.globalcomassociation.com), cofounder and coeditor of the *Journal of Globalization for the Common Good* (www.commongoodjournal.com), and coeditor of the Global Media Studies book series for State University of New York Press. Kamalipour earned his PhD degree in Communication (Radio-TV-Film) at the University of Missouri-Columbia; MA degree in Mass Media at the University of Wisconsin-Superior; and BA degree in Mass Communication (Public Relations) at Minnesota State University. He has been at Purdue University Calumet since 1986. For additional information, visit his personal website at www.kamalipour.com.

**Michele Bach Malek** is a faculty member of the Communications and Human Studies Division at Northern Virginia Community College (NVCC) at the Loudoun campus, Virginia. She teaches English and English as a Second Language and has over ten years of teaching experience in the area of social sciences. Living in the Middle East—Iran and Egypt—and studying Arabic and Farsi during her undergraduate and graduate degree programs, Malek has acquired a deep interest in sociocultural/political affairs relating to the Middle East, Iran in particular.

**Hamid Naficy** is the John Evans Professor of Communication in the Department of Radio, Television, and Film at Northwestern University, where he also has a courtesy appointment in the department of Art History and an affiliated appointment with the Interdisciplinary PhD program in theatre and drama. He has published extensively on these and allied topics. His English-language books are *An Accented Cinema: Exilic and Diasporic Filmmaking* (Princeton University Press), *Home, Exile, Homeland: Film, Media, and the Politics of Place* (edited, Routledge), *The Making of Exile Cultures: Iranian Television in Los Angeles* (University of Minnesota Press), *Otherness and the Media: The Ethnography of the Imagined and the Imaged* (coedited, Harwood Academic), and *Iran Media Index* (Greenwood Press). His forthcoming work, a multivolume book *Cinema, Modernity, and National Identity: A Social History of a Century of Iranian Cinema*, is due out in 2010–2011 (Duke University Press). He has also published extensively in Persian, including a two-volume book on the documentary cinema theory and history, *Film-e Mostanad* (Entesharate-e Daneshgah-e Azad-e Iran). He has lectured widely internationally and his works have been cited and reprinted extensively and translated into many languages, including French, German, Turkish, Italian, and Persian.

**Abeer Najjar** is assistant professor at the department of Mass Communication, American University of Sharjah, the United Arab Emirates. She has a PhD in International Journalism from Edinburgh University. She is a member of International Relations Associations. Abeer taught at many Arab universities and worked for ten years as a journalist in both print and broadcast media. She is frequently quoted in the press. Her main research interests include social media, popular culture, and political conflict.

**Madhav D. Nalapat** is a Gold Medalist in Economics from Bombay University. He became India's first-ever professor of geopolitics in 1999. Previous to that, he was editor of the *Times of India*. He is the originator of several geopolitical concepts, including (a) Asian NATO, (b) Constraining China rather than Containing China, (c) Concept of the Proxy Nuclear State, (d) Indutva,

(e) Playing the Business Card with Pakistan, (f) Tackling the "Mental Infrastructure" of Terror, (g) Sociocultural Factors behind Decision Making in China, and (h) A Horizontal View of Society. Nalapat has lectured on secularism and democracy in the Shahid Behesti University, Tehran, and is the India host of the regular India-Iran UNESCO Chair dialogue. He is professor of geopolitics and UNESCO Peace Chair, Manipal University, India.

**Ashok Panikkar** is the founder and executive director of Meta-Culture, a Center for Dispute Transformation and Dialogue based in Bangalore, India. He is a conflict resolution professional who has worked extensively in the United States and India. As a lead mediator and facilitator, he has successfully mediated hundreds of disputes and facilitated dialogues between extremely polarized groups, including inter-religious and inter-racial groups. Panikkar has a master's degree in Critical and Creative Thinking from the University of Massachusetts, Boston, and advanced training in Conflict Resolution, Negotiation and Dialogue Facilitation from leading institutes in the United States. He was elected to the board of the New England-Association of Conflict Resolution (NE-ACR) for the year 2004–2005. He is presently working on a book about the challenges and opportunities inherent in creating conscious individual and group transformation in the face of unprecedented and sometimes chaotic economic, social, cultural, and environmental changes in the twenty-first century.

**Trita Parsi** is founder and president of the National Iranian American Council and an expert on U.S.-Iranian relations, Iranian politics, and the balance of power in the Middle East. He is the author of *Treacherous Alliance: The Secret Dealings of Iran, Israel and the United States* (Yale University Press 2007), for which he conducted more than 130 interviews with senior Israeli, Iranian, and American decision makers. *Treacherous Alliance* is the silver medal winner of the 2008 Arthur Ross Book Award from the Council on Foreign Relations. He holds a doctoral degree from the Johns Hopkins School for Advanced International Studies, Washington, D.C.

**Tomasz Płudowski** is editor-in-chief of the *Global Media Journal-Polish Edition*, published online by the Collegium Civitas, Warsaw, Poland. He is on the faculty of the Collegium Civitas of Warsaw and Jan Kochanowski University and also teaches in the Institute of Journalism of the Jagiellonian University. He has been a Fulbright Senior Visiting Scholar in the Department of Communication at Stanford University, a Kościuszko Foundation visiting scholar at New York University, a visiting professor at the Maastricht Center for Transatlantic Studies, and assistant professor at several Polish universities. Płudowski's research interests focus on political campaigns, American politics, and international media. His publications include seven edited books, including, most recently, *How the World's News Media Reacted to 9/11*, Marquette Books (2007), and a three-volume textbook *Ameryka. Spolecze stwo. Kultura. Polityka* (WAM, 2008), a monograph on Komunikacja polityczna w ameryka skich kampaniach wyborczych (PWN 2008), and over two dozen articles published in the United States, Germany, UK and Poland. He serves as a U.S. politics commentator for local, national, and international media and Polish news agencies.

**Siavush Randjbar-Daemi** is currently a doctoral candidate at the Department of History, Royal Holloway, University of London. His core research interest is the evolution of state institutions in postrevolutionary Iran. Since 2005, he has been a freelance Iran correspondent for the Italian national newspapers *Il Messaggero* and *Europa*. In this capacity, he has covered the 2005 and 2009 presidential elections in Tehran and has reported extensively on topics ranging from the nuclear crisis to football fever and rap music from Iran in 2006 and 2008, after having obtained formal accreditation from the foreign press division of the Iranian Culture Ministry. Over the years, he has conducted one-on-one exclusive interviews with leading Iranian personalities including Mohammad Khatami, Shirin Ebadi, Zahra Rahnavard, Faezeh Hashemi, and Ebrahim Yazdi. He has also regularly filed reports on Iran from Rome, Vienna, and London, where he is currently based.

**Setareh Sabety**, born and raised in Iran and educated in the United States, is an Iranian American essayist who teaches history at Ceram University, Sophia Antipolis, France. She was runner-up in the editorial category of 2002 NAM awards (New America Media), dubbed as the "Ethnic Pulitzers," for an article published on and about 9/11. Her many poems, essays, and critical articles have appeared widely in the print and cybermedia and in collections and textbooks published by the likes of Houghton Mifflin and Doubleday Press. She is a regular contributor at Tehran Bureau and Iranian.com.

**Ahmad Sadri** is professor of sociology and the James P. Gorter Chair of Islamic World Studies at Lake Forest College. He is the author of Max Weber's *Sociology of Intellectuals* (Oxford University Press 1992, 1994) and three books in Persian. He has translated books from Persian and Arabic into English and functioned as a columnist for the *Daily Star* of Lebanon and *Etemad-e Melli* in Iran.

**Mahmoud Sadri** is professor of sociology at Texas Woman's University and the Federation of North Texas Area Universities. He is an editor of two volumes: *Reason, Freedom and Democracy* (Oxford University Press 2000), and *Migration, Globalization, and Ethnic Relations* (Pearson 2004) and numerous articles and book chapters on sociological theory, reform Islam, and Iran. He has written for Iran's reform publications such as *Shargh* and *Etemad Melli* and continues to speak on politics of Islam and the Middle East in venues such as National Public Radio, Radio Australia, BBC, and Radio France.

**Nancy Snow** is an associate professor at Syracuse University where she teaches in the dual degree masters program in public diplomacy sponsored by the S. I. Newhouse School of Communications and the Maxwell School of Citizenship and Public Affairs. Snow is on leave as tenured associate professor of communications at California State University, Fullerton, and adjunct professor of communications in the Annenberg School at the University of Southern California. Snow is the author or coeditor of six books, including the *Routledge Handbook of Public Diplomacy* (with Philip Taylor), *Propaganda, Inc.*, and *Information War*. Snow's latest book is *Persuader-in-Chief: Global Opinion and Persuasion in the Age of Obama*, whose second edition includes contributions from participants in her spring 2009 Obama Think Tank course at Syracuse University. She is senior fellow in the USC Center on Public Diplomacy and lifetime member of the Public Diplomacy Council at Georgetown University and Fulbright Association. She regularly blogs about American popular culture and politics for the Huffington Post. For details, see www.nancysnow.com.

**Li Xiguang** is the university councilor of Tsinghua University; president of Tsinghua University International Center for Communication; founder of the School of Journalism at Tsinghua University; dean of the School of Global Journalism and Communication of Southwestern University of Political Science and Law (SUPSL); president of the Academy of China and World Agendas (SUPSL); deputy director of Tsinghua University Comprehensive AIDS Research Center; and director of Tsinghua Institute for Health Communication. He is also the vice-chairman of the Journalism Education Committee of Chinese Ministry of Education.

**Kourosh Ziabari** was born in April 1990 and is a prominent Iranian freelance journalist and student of English literature at the University of Guilan, northern Iran. He is a member of World Student Community for Sustainable Development (WSC-SD) and a member of Canada's International Student Energy Summit (ISES). He is also a member of Spain's Tlaxcala network of translators for linguistic diversity. He works with the *Foreign Policy Journal* and *Middle East Online* publications.

Breinigsville, PA USA
16 February 2011
255654BV00002B/10/P